Exile and Revolution

UNIVERSITY PRESS OF FLORIDA

Florida A&M University, Tallahassee
Florida Atlantic University, Boca Raton
Florida Gulf Coast University, Ft. Myers
Florida International University, Miami
Florida State University, Tallahassee
New College of Florida, Sarasota
University of Central Florida, Orlando
University of Florida, Gainesville
University of North Florida, Jacksonville
University of South Florida, Tampa
University of West Florida, Pensacola

BIRD'S EYE VIEW OF
KEY WEST, FLA.
KEY WEST ISLAND.
C.S. MONROE CO.
1884.

EXILE AND REVOLUTION

José D. Poyo, Key West, and Cuban Independence

GERALD E. POYO

University Press of Florida
Gainesville · Tallahassee · Tampa · Boca Raton
Pensacola · Orlando · Miami · Jacksonville · Ft. Myers · Sarasota

Copyright 2014 by Gerald E. Poyo
All rights reserved
Printed in the United States of America on acid-free paper

Frontispiece: "Birds Eye View of Key West, Monroe County, Fla. 1884." J. J. Stoner, 1884. Lithograph printed in Milwaukee by Beck and Pauli. *Source:* Library of Congress, Geography and Map Division.

This book may be available in an electronic edition.

First cloth printing, 2014
First paperback printing, 2019

24 23 22 21 20 19   6 5 4 3 2 1

Library of Congress Cataloging-in-Publication Data
Poyo, Gerald Eugene, 1950– author.
Exile and revolution : José D. Poyo, Key West, and Cuban independence / Gerald E. Poyo.
pages cm
Includes bibliographical references and index.
ISBN 978-0-8130-4918-2 (cloth)
ISBN 978-0-8130-6426-0 (pbk.)
1. Poyo, José D. (José Dolores), 1837–1911. 2. Cuba—History—1878–1895. 3. Cubans—Florida—Key West—History. 4. Key West (Fla.)—History. I. Title.
F1783.P77P69 2014
972.91'05—dc23
2013034531

University Press of Florida
2046 NE Waldo Road
Suite 2100
Gainesville, FL 32609
http://upress.ufl.edu

To Noel and Jeremy

CONTENTS

List of Figures / ix

Preface / xi

Introduction / 1

1. Community / 9

2. Nationalism / 37

3. Revolution / 65

4. Preservation / 95

5. Persistence / 118

6. Martí / 137

7. Crisis / 167

8. War / 192

9. Legacy / 226

Notes / 251

Bibliography / 281

Index / 291

FIGURES

Frontispiece. "Birds Eye View of Key West, Monroe County, Fla. 1884"

1. Cuban student martyrs   30
2. José Dolores Poyo, ca. 1880   38
3. Exile newspapers, 1890s   67
4. Convención Cubana de Cayo Hueso   130
5. José Martí and José D. Poyo with tobacco workers, 1892   157
6. José Martí and José D. Poyo in a cigar factory in Key West   187
7. Cuban expeditionary force, ca. 1897   205

PREFACE

When I was a teenager living in Buenos Aires, my father, who rarely spoke of Cuba, told me that his great-grandfather, José Dolores Poyo, collaborated with José Martí in promoting Cuba's independence war against Spain. Not having grown up in a Cuban community, I knew little about Martí, only that he was a well-known journalist across the Americas, a great modernist poet, and an unceasing political activist who worked for Cuban independence. In 1975, while perusing a volume of José Martí's *Obras Completas* (Complete Works) at the Latin American Collection of the University of Florida Library, a letter reminded me of what my father had said. This letter from Martí to Poyo and the many that followed as I turned the pages revealed a close relationship between the two men. Numerous historical references to Poyo pointed to a role that was much more substantive than the published record suggested. This put me on a trail of research that I pursued over the next thirty-five years.

Unfortunately, the vast majority of Poyo's personal papers never reached the safety of an institutional archive. No complete—or even near-complete—collection of his newspaper *El Yara*, which he published in Key West for twenty years, survived. He left a modest "Donativo José Dolores Poyo" in the Cuban National Archive, but the bulk of his papers were in the possession of his son Francisco, and they disappeared after he passed away in March 1961. His daughter, who was in a rush to leave the revolutionary situation in Cuba soon after her father's death, left the collection with a friend. In 1982, during an extended research trip to Havana, I set out to find the papers. A visit to Francisco's former home led me to the neighborhood church, where the priest, after some investigation, learned that the person who received the papers had died a decade earlier. The trail ended, but perhaps the documents will reappear one day.

Another unfortunate event was the loss of Poyo's correspondence with José Martí, which disappeared along with most letters from Martí's correspondents. Martí's one-way correspondence with Poyo is certainly a treasure, but Poyo himself is silent. On a brighter front, an important collection of letters from Martí to Poyo that Poyo presumably gave to his daughter América, who passed them to her grandson Luís Alpízar Leal, surfaced in 1991 and was published by the Centro de Estudios Martianos in Havana. Even without a major collection of Poyo's papers on which to rely, I uncovered enough material to tell his story. My sources include issues of his newspaper *El Yara*, scattered correspondence with other revolutionary personalities, the memoirs of various historical actors, significant collections of other newspapers published by exiles, Spanish consular records, and some written and oral family sources.

Much of the research for this book was conducted in Cuba in 1982 with funds from a Fulbright-Hays grant and the encouragement and cooperation of scholars at the Centro de Estudios Martianos, Archivo Nacional de Cuba, Biblioteca Nacional José Martí, and the Instituto de Literatura y Lingüística, but recent research in Spain provided critical sources that allowed me to complete the project. I am grateful to Consuelo Stebbins, who in 2007 alerted me to a rich collection of consular documents in the archive of the Spanish Ministry of Foreign Relations. Research in Madrid and work in an even richer collection at the Archivo General de Administración in Alcalá de Henares finally made this book possible.

As I prepared to consult archives in Spain, St. Mary's University's Spain Abroad Program, which is associated with the Franklin Institute at the University of Alcalá de Henares, selected me as a participating faculty member for spring 2010. This facilitated four months of research in Spanish archives. I am grateful to the university's Spain Program; Rev. Rudy Vela and Grace Keyes, its past and present directors; program administrator Minita Santizo; and my colleague Larry Hufford. In many different ways, Larry and his spouse Linda freed me up to spend more time in the archives than I expected, and on many evenings they listened to my descriptions of my archival finds over wine and tapas. The eleven independent and very talented students enrolled in the Spain program made the time in Alcalá de Henares easy, enjoyable, and productive for all. A faculty development grant and a sabbatical from St. Mary's University helped finance other travel and provided time to write. I thank my colleague Dan Bjork, who read parts of the manuscript and suggested ways to help the story flow.

Producing a book always requires a talented editorial team. At the University Press of Florida, senior acquisitions editor Amy Gorelick and project editor Marthe Walters efficiently moved the project from manuscript to published book. Consuelo E. Stebbins and Anne Fountain, manuscript evaluators for the press, expressed great support for the project and offered excellent recommendations. Meticulous, insightful, and judicious copyediting by Kate Babbitt has helped the book sparkle and shine. I am grateful to them all.

I am thankful for a fifteen-year relationship with Nicolás Kanellos's National Hispanic Literary Recovery Project at the University of Houston for constantly encouraging and facilitating research about Latino historical communities and highlighting the value of these kinds of studies. One of my most satisfying investments of time has been my service as a member of the Recovery Project's Board of Directors. The Recovery Project's online digital collection of U.S. Hispanic newspapers facilitated locating numerous obscure articles about my subject.

This study owes a great deal to my father, Sergio, and uncles José and Jorge, who over many years spoke to me about their grandfather Francisco. Francisco described to them the family's feelings and views about his father's legacy. Luis Alpízar Leal, great-grandson of José D. Poyo, who worked for his entire career in the Cuban National Archive, also provided information about the family's situation in Havana after their return from Key West. Particularly important has been the support of my spouse, Miryam Bujanda, whose generosity and love helped make this project possible. My son, Noel, has lived with this story since he can remember and in recent years has been my most engaged listener and critic. More important, his presence in my life has always been an indispensable comfort and strength. May this book inspire his three daughters, Isabella, Gabriela, and Alexandra to learn more about their Cuban heritage.

INTRODUCTION

Revolution and exile. This book is about a man and his exile community in Key West struggling against the odds during thirty years to achieve revolution and an independent Cuban republic dedicated to the welfare of all its citizens. "*Adelante la revolución*" (Forward the revolution) was his mantra; immediate armed action is what he meant. José de los Dolores de la Encarnación Poyo y Remírez de Estenóz (1836–1911) died a little over a century ago, but his political career as a revolutionary nationalist and the history of his insurgent community remind us during this era of global rebellion and upheaval about the power of grievance, ideology, leadership, and popular aspirations to mobilize people and communities for radical action and change.

Cuban independence required upheaval and violence and involved a leap of faith informed with ideals and convictions, particular historical circumstances, personal pain and sacrifice, and the patriotic fervor of religious intensity. Optimistic and acting with an aura of certainty, though not without distracting bouts of self-doubt and pessimism, Poyo took a leap of faith that ultimately translated into practical methods of revolutionary action. Too much intellectual pondering threatened paralysis, which he avoided at all costs. This revolutionary imperative defined Poyo's nationalist career in Key West as a newspaper editor, cigar factory reader, activist, orator, social critic, Freemason, and even as a husband and father.

Poyo lived during an era of nationalism and political and socioeconomic change in Latin America, a period when nations struggled to emerge from the remnants of the Spanish and Portuguese empires. Thousands of Hispanics were exiles during the nineteenth century, unexpectedly torn from their homelands by political disruption, violence, or civil war. Many sought refuge in the United States—especially Mexicans, Puerto Ricans, Dominicans, and Cubans. Poyo was one of those exiles.

In their new places of residence, they participated in building communities that reflected their traditions and heritage. Often they converted immigrants who arrived for economic reasons into exiles, demonstrating that the circumstance of departure was not the only factor in the creation of exile mentalities and communities. They created political organizations, newspapers, strategies for insurrection, and even clandestine armies, all the while finding ways to make a living. Although the exile community was ideologically and socioeconomically diverse, its members generally desired to influence events in their countries of origin and return home.

Estimates of the number of Cubans living in the United States during the nineteenth century vary from a low of 20,000 to perhaps a more realistic 100,000, though many more came for business trips, vacations, or short-term residence. Smaller Cuban communities also formed in Venezuela, Central America, Mexico, Peru, Colombia, Jamaica, Haiti, and the Dominican Republic. In Europe they gathered mostly in France and to a lesser extent in England, but the favorite destination remained the United States.

Cuban contacts with the Anglo-American colonies began with a brief British occupation of Havana in 1762 during the Seven Years' War. This encounter laid the foundation for trade between Cuba and the American colonies that expanded throughout the nineteenth century after Cuba replaced Haiti as the dominant sugar export economy in the Caribbean. Cuban communities in the United States included many white and upwardly mobile immigrants who were merchants, intellectuals and writers, journalists, doctors, dentists, lawyers, and entrepreneurs. Others worked in a variety of enterprises common to large cities. Thousands had come to the United States for their education, eschewing the traditional European destinations. They attended elite schools such as Harvard and Columbia; business, commercial, and technical schools; and even boarding schools where they completed secondary education. These new generations took advantage of business contacts and networks, learned English, and generally expanded the economic opportunities and ties of the Cuban community.

After the Civil War, a booming Cuban cigar industry in the United States broadened the social and racial composition of the migratory flow. Cigar workers traveled on a circular loop between Havana, New York, New

Orleans, and Florida, taking advantage of changing economic circumstances and employment possibilities. Cubans of all classes and races established vibrant communities, became citizens, practiced democracy, participated in a dynamic capitalist economy, and integrated and transformed their traditional cultural ways in new community settings. Cubans worshipped in a variety of religious traditions, produced a distinguished body of literature, supported theatre and musical arts, and even pioneered the game of baseball in Florida's communities.[1]

These communities became congenial settings for the cultivation of nationalist thinking, and many Cubans developed a distinct exile identity. The first exiles arrived during and soon after the Latin American wars of independence (1810–1824), which left only Cuba and Puerto Rico still under direct Spanish rule. Some Cubans instigated insurrection, but entrenched Spanish and Cuban elites who were prospering from a sugar boom, the growing slave trade, and a generally comfortable relationship with Spain remained loyal. However, within a few years many Cubans on the island became disillusioned and activists began seeking change. They wanted political representation in the Spanish Cortes (parliament), the abolition of the slave trade and eventually slavery itself, and a freer economic and commercial system. When these ideas did not gain traction during the 1840s through the 1860s, many activists departed for the United States. A Cuban insurrection against Spain's rule known as the Ten Years' War erupted in 1868 that the Spanish did not completely defeat until 1880. Over the next fifteen years, expatriate communities played a critical role in organizing a second rebellion in 1895, which eventually sparked the Spanish-American War in 1898, ending Spanish rule and setting the stage for U.S. occupation of Cuba.

After the Ten Years' War, exile activists spoke and wrote freely, engaged in ongoing debates, and influenced opinion in their homeland. Some hoped that Cuba would become annexed to the United States, where they thought it would thrive as a relatively self-governing state of the union, but the vast majority of Cubans wanted absolute independence. Those advocating rebellion and independence disagreed about methods for eliminating Spanish rule and about the political and social order they wanted to see in Cuba. Moderates, who generally lived in middle-class communities in New York and other northern cities, agitated for an eventual war of independence led by the island's Cuban elites. This strategy involved waiting for liberal autonomists who were seeking an accommodation with Spain to tire and join independence seekers. Their more impatient compatriots in Florida's working-class communities, particularly Key West, urged Cuba's multiracial sectors to embrace an immediate anticolonial armed struggle led by the military veterans of the Ten Years' War.²

Critics referred to Key West as a "bandit-infested cave" and its political activists as fanatics, criminals, and malcontents. Such language was a response to the revolutionary militancy of Key West's Cuban community. Manuel Deulofeu Lleonart's 1904 study instead referred to the Cubans of Key West as "persistent, consequential, self-sacrificing patriots" who had a "perfect conscience of their social and political duties." Deulofeu called on historians to ensure that those who constituted the founding group in Key West were not lost to history.³ In that spirit, this book recovers and highlights the figure of José Dolores Poyo and offers a detailed exploration of a fascinating revolutionary enterprise. Portions of this story have appeared in print over the years (see the bibliography), but this volume is a comprehensive, integrated narrative that draws upon recent archival and newspaper research. My previous book on nineteenth-century Cuban exile communities, *"With All, and for the Good of All": The Emergence of Popular Nationalism in the Cuban Communities of the United States, 1848–1898*, examined expatriate influences on nationalist thought and serves as the basis for this deeper exploration, which examines the concrete and practical aspects of the Cuban revolutionary nationalist tradition in Key West during the same era.

South Florida's importance to the career of José Martí, the gifted political and intellectual leader who offered an inspired and clearly articulated nationalist program, has been recognized, but its distinctive revolutionary character and the systematic process through which it helped prepare, launch, and maintain the independence war has not. Besides highlighting little-remembered but consequential historical actors, this study builds on the foundational work of Deulofeu and Gerardo Castellanos García and narrates the story from an intimate local point of view, transforming Key West's place in the historiography of Cuban independence from a member of the supporting cast to a lead role in sparking insurrection.⁴

The book also adds narrative depth to the popular and grassroots dimensions of Cuba's independence struggle.⁵ From the José Antonio Aponte rebellion in 1812 to the independence war that began in 1895, Cuba's racially diverse popular classes, including former slaves, free persons of color, working-class urban and rural whites, participated in challenging Spanish colonialism, each group for its own reasons. The Cuban community in Key West was composed largely of these very demographic sectors, and their militancy and predisposition to action produced a reputation for radicalism that many in the established classes on and off the island regarded with suspicion. Spanish authorities kept close tabs on most Cuban exile communities, directing their consular offices to collect intelligence and report regularly, but they paid special attention to Key West for its proximity to the island, its tobacco wealth, its experienced revolutionary leadership, the large number of undefeated and unrepentant veterans, an unpredictable bandit element, and the constant threat the community represented. Even before the end of the Ten Years' War, revolutionary leaders celebrated Key West for its constant activism, determination, and popular traditions, a reputation that stuck and became a badge of honor for its residents and leaders.

In the Cuban struggle for independence, the indispensable military leaders Máximo Gómez, Antonio Maceo, Calixto García, and of course, Martí are well known. But the local grassroots political, labor, business, religious, and cultural leaders who organized and mobilized the Cuban communities in Key West, Tampa, New York, and other cities are not yet appreciated.[6] These local leaders cultivated and incubated nationalist and revolutionary thought, provided legitimacy to and resources for the primary political leaders, and did the hard work of mobilizing constituencies, securing resources and organizing expeditions. Uncovering the contributions of local leaders forces a reconsideration of the traditional view that the primary leaders single-handedly mobilized nationalist émigré constituencies, an interpretation that posits larger-than-life figures who arrived in Key West and other centers to mold quarrelsome, disorganized, and demoralized communities into viable and effective catalysts for revolution.[7]

Poyo exemplified these important local leaders, and this account is the first comprehensive biography of a Cuban exile community leader in the United States during the period under consideration other than Martí. He was one of numerous important but unheralded exile nationalist leaders in Key West, and his revolutionary career guides this story. Although Poyo is often referred to in historical studies, his multidimensional grassroots work and the role of his newspaper *El Yara*, the longest-lived Cuban exile newspaper of the nineteenth century, which historian José Luciano Franco referred to as a *"periódico de combate,"* has never been examined in much detail. Through *El Yara* and two decades of nationalist activism, Poyo became Key West's undisputed leader and most recognized voice for the militarist faction that eventually led the war against Spanish forces that began in 1895.

Poyo, who was especially knowledgeable about Latin American and Spanish affairs and history and sufficiently familiar with political theory to write about the republican and democratic principles necessary for Cuba's future, believed that Spain would never voluntarily dismantle its colonial system on the island. He operated from an assumption that Spanish colonialism was irreparably dysfunctional and corrupt and that, after decades of failed attempts at reform, it had to be destroyed through whatever means necessary and as soon as possible and replaced with a republic free of slavery that was dedicated to workers' rights and committed to the welfare of all its citizens. He believed that only revolution could effectively challenge Spain's intransigent and inflexible three-and-a-half-century colonial grip.

Poyo was what scholars of revolution have referred to as a "task-oriented revolutionary," a revolutionary who consistently and in a practical way struggled to reach his goal. One resident of Key West characterized him as parochial. He was not uneducated or unsophisticated, but he always focused on mobilizing the local arena and rarely projected his leadership outside the community. He organized armed expeditions and revolutionary cells in Cuba, supported insurgent actions once they began, and believed that small groups of committed and focused activists could make a difference. Poyo embraced the idea of Key West as a vanguard community with a special role to play in promoting and supporting revolution. Community leaders such as Poyo influenced the thinking and actions of the primary nationalist leaders, who saw Key West's popular constituency, political structures, financial resources, and connections with insurgent groups in Cuba as indispensable for sparking and maintaining insurgency on the island. Poyo's career highlights the sources, development, and manifestations of Key West's unrelenting popular and militant commitment to revolution. These efforts ultimately convinced Martí that his path to leadership must travel through south Florida.

For thirty years, Poyo participated in organizing the institutions necessary to create, maintain, and perpetuate revolutionary activism. Clubs, labor unions, and organized cigar factory floors inspired nationalist action.

The perpetuation and celebration of Cuban cultural and ethnic identity in the community fostered nationalist enthusiasm and a revolutionary ethos. Spanish-language schools for children and adults and literary and social clubs maintained connections with and even nostalgia for the homeland. These Spanish-language institutions were reinforced by newspapers, cigar factory readers, and oratory at patriotic gatherings and commemorations. The prosperous cigar industry in Key West meant that workers and manufacturers had resources to donate, and the island was the most consistent source of financial support for the nationalist cause.

None of this would have happened without a guiding ideology. Revolutionary movements require an ideological rationale, and Cubans developed theirs throughout the nineteenth century. With the outbreak of the Cuban Ten Years' War in 1868, nationalist thought came into its own, and Key West embraced its most militant version. This ideology committed its adherents to a self-sufficient revolutionary struggle against Spanish colonialism without outside mediation or intervention and regardless of the attitudes of the island's Cuban elites.

This revolutionary work did not proceed without significant challenges and threats, and Poyo played a role in addressing both. During the 1880s and 1890s, the Key West revolutionary community struggled to preserve its character in the face of growing Spanish immigration and labor ideologies that expressed little interest in or openly rejected the Cuban nationalist cause. The community also defended its political institutions and clandestine activities from Key West Anglo-American authorities who threatened their revolutionary capabilities. This involved participating in local and state Republican and Democratic politics to pressure local leaders, but it also involved using boycotts and other controversial strategies to deflect grave threats to the community's essentially Cuban identity.

Despite setbacks, clandestine organizing continued, and the alternative strategies organizers used illustrate the persistence and resilience that are characteristic of successful revolutionary movements. Leaders such as Poyo possessed idealism and a certain authoritarian manner, stubbornness, and inflexibility that made them immune to attacks and distractions. Though sometimes overwhelmed by the scope of the challenges, Poyo always returned to the battle after a period of reflection and recuperation.

When revolution finally erupted in 1895, Key West turned its attention to sending reinforcements to the Cuban liberation army, which involved establishing fund-raising mechanisms, purchasing vessels and weapons, mobilizing enthusiasm and ensuring discipline among exiles, maintaining communication between exiles and the insurgents, providing logistical and legal support in U.S. courts for indicted expeditionary captains, and bribing and negotiating with local officials to convince them to turn a blind eye to violations of the neutrality laws. As president of the Cuban Revolutionary Party in Key West, Poyo headed these activities and did what he could to meet the demands and needs of those who were fighting in Cuba. Ultimately, the challenge of provisioning the insurgent army was a task far beyond the capabilities of the exile communities. Limited resources and the harassment of U.S. authorities who did what they could to prevent the dispatching of arms and ammunition contributed to the Cuban liberation army's inability to definitively defeat Spain before the United States intervened in the war.

As difficult as it was, provoking revolution was easier than managing its direction or imagining the unpredictable results. Revolutions rarely deliver on promises, at least as expected. Poyo and other nationalist leaders learned this when they returned home. Nationalists sought their place in a Cuba that was controlled economically and influenced socially, culturally and politically by the United States. They also contended with a nation that was hampered with political factionalism, economic inequalities, and social divisions and not easily transformed from its crippling colonial legacy. Poyo and his colleagues tried to make sense of their experience as they observed the bitter reality of U.S. intervention and then the specter of a republic struggling for viability.

In time, a Cuban independence historical narrative emerged and Key West took its place as one of the creators of the Cuban nation, but the community's full range of activities remained obscure. What follows is a first comprehensive account of the contributions of Key West's working-class community to the Cuban nationalist movement, interpreted from the local perspective and especially through the life of one of its important leaders, José Dolores Poyo.

I

COMMUNITY

> Here [in Key West] Cubans, protected by American laws, have not only found the liberty and peace lacking in our homeland, but have entered an open field in which to progress and contribute in major ways with the natives of this country in transforming a poor village of fishermen into a flourishing city.
>
> *El Yara*, 1886

In late January 1869, 32-year-old José Dolores Poyo sat aboard a small fishing vessel with his wife and three daughters (the youngest just an infant) and his younger brother as it approached Key West, the last of a long string of isles that trail southwest some 150 miles into the Straits of Florida from the southern tip of the peninsula. "Cayo Hueso," announced the fisherman manning the vessel. There on the northwest edge of the approximately two-by-four-mile piece of land sat a low-lying little town some ten blocks square. Less than ninety miles from Cuba, Key West offered refuge to those seeking safety from Spanish authorities.

Some days before, at the *Gaceta de la Habana*, where he worked as a proof reader (*corrector de pruebas*), Poyo had found a publicly posted list of contributors to a gift honoring Cuba's newly appointed captain general, Domingo Dulce, who had arrived in Havana on January 4, 1869, to occupy his new post. Surprised and angered to see his name on the list, Poyo ripped the document from the wall, openly demonstrating his anti-Spanish attitudes.[1] Poyo was involved with underground insurrectionists in Havana known as *laborantes*, and his public action at the *Gaceta de la Habana* caught the attention of pro-Spanish activists who formed into militias known as *voluntarios*. Within a few days, Poyo learned from his friend Francisco de Arazoza, the son of the owner of *La Gaceta*, of his impending arrest, and he went into hiding to consider his next move. Poyo's impolitic display of antipathy put him at risk of arrest and deportation to Fernando Poo, an island off the African coast where the Spanish government routinely imprisoned dissidents, many of whom died of hardship and disease. He had two options: join the insurrection or leave Cuba.[2] He decided to leave.

In Key West, the Poyo family joined a nascent nationalist community that quickly created a public tradition of greeting newcomers from Cuba with great ritual and enthusiasm. Whenever a vessel from Havana approached Key West, Cubans hurried to the docks and greeted the passengers, supposing most of them to be refugees like themselves. They waved their flag of insurrection, one that filibusterer Narciso López had used some twenty years before. One Cuban recalled seeing a large crowd on the dock with people shoving and straining to see as he arrived by steamer. As the vessel neared the shore, he realized they were exiles "waiting to give us a brother's embrace." He was greeted with shouts of "Long Live Free Cuba!" He was amazed to find that Cubans had created a revolutionary center with the goal of dislodging Spanish power in their homeland.[3]

The activist community soon built a network of nationalist institutions, including clubs, a newspaper, and school, that sponsored ritual patriotic celebrations with resources contributed by cigar workers and manufacturers. The enthusiasm, financial capacity, conspiratorial activism, and ideological unity of Cubans in Key West constituted an ontological threat to Spanish colonialism in Cuba. This encouraged exile activists to cultivate and maintain a revolutionary ethos that survived through the end of the century.

Grito de Yara

Poyo's flight occurred after the outbreak of Cuba's first war of independence, which later became known as the Ten Years' War, when Carlos Manuel de Céspedes and Francisco Vicente Aguilera proclaimed freedom in the Grito de Yara, on October 10, 1868. The insurgency quickly enveloped the island's eastern provinces in bloody warfare that eventually pitted Cubans of all classes and colors against the Spanish army and its colonial supporters. Jolted by the insurrection, a new government in Spain installed just a month before the Grito de Yara instructed Captain General Dulce to negotiate with the rebels. The rebels refused to negotiate. In addition, even though he was the highest civil and military colonial authority on the island, the captain general faced resistance from *voluntarios*, intransigent and conservative pro-Spanish groups in Cuba that opposed both the insurgents and the new government's policies of accommodation. *Voluntarios* mobilized their own militias to fight the rebels and undermined Dulce's efforts to negotiate. The captain general's capacity to interact with the rebels from a stance of negotiation soon disappeared and Dulce was forced to resign and return to Spain in June 1869.

In early 1869, *voluntario* vigilantes began an onslaught of violence that was encouraged by the pro-Spanish newspaper *La Voz de Cuba*. The violence culminated on January 24 in an assault at Havana's Villanueva Theatre, where well-known Cuban liberals were attending a play that included anti-Spanish allusions. Vigilantes also looted and burned down the residence of one of Havana's wealthiest and most respected families, the Aldamas.[4] In 1869 and in subsequent years, thousands who were opposed to Spanish rule found refuge outside Cuba, avoiding arrest and the wrath of the *voluntario* loyalists. Leaders of dozens of Cuban families departed Havana for Europe and the United States, especially New York, where they threw their support to the insurrection. Others who remained in Cuba were less fortunate and suffered arrest and deportation. Any possibility of a negotiated arrangement between the government and the rebels vanished, and Cuba settled into a devastating conflict that convinced the contending parties that reconciliation was not only impossible but not even desirable.

Family

Poyo probably supported the reformist efforts of the 1860s, but when this proved futile he chose rebellion and never wavered from his mission to dislodge Spanish power. Unlike many in Havana who joined the insurgent army in the *manigua* (countryside), Poyo chose exile. Not only had he already placed his family at risk, but he was their only source of economic support. The decisions he made as a political activist always took into account the potential impact on his family, and his decision to leave Cuba reflected his desire to balance his support for the insurrection with his obligations to those closest to him; he created a seamless relationship that wove together a tight-knit family life and the independence cause.

Poyo saw his role as that of a traditional patriarch. Though he was loving and attentive to the emotional needs of his wife and children, he expected the family to support his nationalist politics and share in the material sacrifices inherent in this kind of commitment. He never imagined that they would live on this tiny island so close to their home for the next thirty years, often existing hand to mouth.[5]

Little is known of Poyo's life before he arrived in Key West. He recorded nothing of his life or his family for posterity. His grandson Raoul Alpízar Poyo and his revolutionary colleague and friend Fernando Figueredo wrote brief biographies but said little about his background. Figueredo speculated that Poyo's modesty and revolutionary commitments prevented him from talking and writing about personal matters.[6] Bits of information in baptismal and marriage documents record that Poyo was born on March 24, 1836, in Havana within the jurisdiction of the Nuestra Señora de Guadalupe Parish, located just outside the city walls. Much later this became La Caridad Parish.[7] His parents, Francisco Antonio Poyo and María de los Dolores Remírez de Estenóz, were born and raised in the same parish. His great-grandfather, Antonio Poyo, immigrated to Cuba in the middle of the eighteenth century from El Puerto de Santa María, near Cádiz.[8]

Poyo married Clara Leonor Camús y de la Merced Hoz on March 25, 1861. Clara, who was born on September 13, 1837, came from a modest family.[9] Clara gave birth to three daughters, Celia (1862), América (1864), and Blanca (1869). Blanca was just weeks old when the family arrived in Key West. In 1872, Clara bore a son, Francisco Andrés. She had at least three other sons, Juan Bautista and Carlos Manuel (1874) and Juan Luis (1876), all of whom lived less than four years, which was not unusual in an era of high child mortality.[10] In 1876, Ibrahim Poyo, José Dolores's younger brother who had accompanied him to Key West, also died, and in 1885 he almost lost his daughters to a severe illness. All may have fallen victim to the frequent outbreaks of yellow fever that were ravaging Key West during this era.[11] Perhaps Clara had other children, but only four reached adulthood. All four children married, eventually giving José Dolores and Clara thirty grandchildren.

Daughters Celia and América also supported exile political activities and both married men who were committed to Cuba's independence in June 1886.[12] Celia's husband, Manuel Patricio Delgado, and América's spouse, Francisco Alpízar, worked as tobacco workers and helped Poyo publish his newspaper. Delgado became Poyo's closest collaborator and an important local political figure in his own right. He and Celia expressed their nationalist sensibilities in the names they gave their children, which included Cuba, América, Guáimaro (the name of the town where Cuba's first constitution was written), and Hatuey. The name Hatuey was particular evidence of the family's anti-Spanish sentiments: it is the name of a legendary Taíno rebel who was captured during the conquest. When the Spaniards asked Hatuey before his execution if he wanted to convert to Christianity so he could enter heaven, he replied that if Spaniards also went to heaven, he would prefer to die a heathen.

The third daughter, Blanca, who was also interested in exile politics, married Enrique Vidal in November 1889, and the youngest sibling, Francisco, married Louisa Skillin y Seguí in February 1892. Louisa was the daughter of Louis Skillin, an Irish American cooper and sailor in the merchant marine from Portland, Maine, who emigrated to Matanzas and married Carmen Seguí. The Skillins arrived in Key West in 1886, where they demonstrated their revolutionary sympathies and worked in the cigar factories.[13] One way or another, the entire Poyo family lent support to the cause of Cuban independence, an ideal that defined the family's very purpose.

Cayo Hueso

In 1869, the rectangular grid of unpaved streets in Key West offered a picturesque scene that Cubans experienced as a congenial village that was not very different from their homeland just a short distance away. Key West's vegetation in 1874 included thick chaparral and several varieties of cactus, especially very large prickly pears. Its tropical climate was familiar to Cubans, as were its palm, guava, and banana trees. The island also had almond trees and a few orange trees. Tropical shrubbery and flowers in perennial bloom completed the scene. Residents used lumber to construct low and unassuming structures fronted by boardwalks. Although the lumber was expensive, perhaps double what it cost in most places, it was still the cheapest building material. Only the federal government used brick for its buildings.[14]

Although Key West was initially a small fishing community, residents developed businesses salvaging wrecked vessels and their contents and harvesting sponges for export. The island was conveniently located in the crossroads of the Gulf Coast, Cuba, and the Atlantic Coast, and it soon became a trading and transit center for shipping lines that connected Galveston, New Orleans, Pensacola, and Tampa with Havana and East Coast cities, including Jacksonville, Savannah, Charleston, and destinations north. After the Civil War, a reliable steamship line traveled between Baltimore and Havana, touching at Key West. In 1873 a locally owned company, Mallory and Company, inaugurated service between New York, Key West, and Galveston; the company soon expanded its itinerary to other locations, including Cuba.[15]

Cubans contributed know-how and energy to Key West's growth and developed a strong attachment to the small town. "The majority of the Cuban population that today figures honorably on the front lines of industry and commerce in this country," Poyo wrote in 1886, "came without a penny, many in tattered rags despite their honesty and capacity for work." Protected by U.S. laws, he explained, Cubans found the peace and liberty that was absent at home and opportunities to progress and transform a poor village into a flourishing city.[16] Poyo frequently acknowledged his debt of gratitude to and love for Key West and considered it his adopted home.

Cubans routinely used the island's original Spanish name, showing both their appropriation and affection. One story posited that Spanish explorers found the island covered with bones, perhaps because it was the site of an Indian battle or was an Indian burial ground, and thus named it Cayo Hueso (Isle of Bones).[17] The island, which the Spanish governor of Florida, Juan Pablo Salas, granted to Don Juan de Estrada in 1815, was purchased in 1822 by John W. Simonton of Mobile, after Spain ceded Florida to the United States. Shortly after, white settlers began arriving from St. Augustine, South Carolina, Virginia, New York, Connecticut, and the Bahamas. The new arrivals received lots on the northwestern edge of the island, the highest land on the island and the most hospitable area for building a town.

Beginning in the mid-1840s, people brought slaves to Key West to work on government fortifications and as house servants, and after the Civil War and slave emancipation many black Bahamians immigrated to the island. In 1870, only about 5,600 people lived in Key West, but an emerging cigar industry quickly transformed the quiet fishing town into one of Florida's most prosperous cities. Almost 20,000 lived there in 1890. Cuban residents usually composed between one-quarter and one-half of the population throughout the last three decades of the nineteenth century.[18]

Unlike cigar production in the north, in south Florida Cuban tobacco was rolled by highly skilled artisans from the island. "Clear Havana cigars," as they became known, avoided the high U.S. tariff on manufactured cigar imports from Cuba while taking advantage of a low tariff on tobacco leaf grown in Cuba's western region of Vuelta Abajo. A relatively large cigar factory owned by the New York–based Seidenberg and Company launched the industry in early 1869 with several hundred workers. The number of jobs increased when a Spanish cigar entrepreneur in Havana, Vicente Martínez Ybor, moved to Key West later the same year. He arrived with enough resources to rent a cluster of buildings near the docks and begin production. These two enterprises laid the foundation for a cigar industry that grew quite dramatically in the next several years, spawning more factories.[19]

Most Cuban owners of cigar factories arrived in the United States as political exiles, not tobacco entrepreneurs. In the 1870s, many established small businesses in Key West, which was close to Cuba's tobacco crops and offered a large Cuban labor force. J. S. Navarro & Co. owned the largest Cuban factory in 1880, but the first Cuban manufacturer of note was Cayetano Soria, who had earned a modest living in Cuba as a mechanic. Soria established a storefront operation in Key West that struggled through the economically sluggish 1870s, when it employed about fifty workers. In the next decade, the factory grew rapidly, and in 1887 it employed 400 workers. Others followed suit, including Eduardo Hidalgo Gato, who arrived in New York from Santiago del las Vegas in 1869, intending to return quickly on an expedition and join the liberation army fighting in Cuba. After several failed efforts to get back to Cuba, he opened a small cigar shop but remained active in political matters. For example, he served as treasurer of a Cuban nationalist club in New York. In 1876, Gato relocated to Key West to pursue his cigar business, and in 1887 he owned a factory that employed 500 workers.

Francisco Marrero, Antonio Del Pino, and Manuel Barranco followed Gato south. Marrero, a merchant from San Antonio de los Baños, had been deported to Fernando Poo in 1869 for his insurrectionist sympathies, but he had escaped and made his way to New York, where he cooperated with the revolutionary community and established a cigar factory. He later opened an operation in Key West. At first he hired fifty workers, but in 1887 his company employed 200. Del Pino, who had participated in insurgent activities in New York in the 1870s, opened a factory in Key West in 1880 that employed twenty-five workers. By 1887, his company was one of the largest in Key West and was employing 335. Barranco, who also began in New York in the 1870s, established a factory in Key West that employed fifty workers in 1880; by 1887 his company had tripled in size.

More Cuban cigar entrepreneurs entered the trade in the 1880s, including veterans Teodoro Pérez, Enrique Canales, and Gerardo Castellanos. These three men arrived after the Ten Years' War and opened small factories. The factories grew and in 1887 Pérez employed 100 workers and Canales employed 200. In 1869, factories in Key West produced some 8.5 million cigars; by 1890, they produced about 100 million, the industry's zenith in the city. Even those who became wealthy never lost their political commitment to an independent Cuba and routinely collaborated with insurrectionists, donating money and encouraging their employees to help the nationalist cause.[20]

The industry produced a working class that formed the economic base of the Cuban community. About 80 percent of Cubans in Key West worked in the cigar trade in 1880. The industry provided enough income to sustain the remaining 20 percent of the Cuban population, who worked as housekeepers, laborers, service workers, businessmen, artisans, and professionals.

In the 1880s, the Cuban community in Key West included numerous health care providers. Dr. Pedro Someillan, a *medico-cirujano* (doctor-surgeon), was located on Fleming Street. Dr. Juan Molinet, also a *medico-cirujano*, worked at Máximo Díaz's Botica Central (Central Pharmacy). Dr. Casas offered services for free to the poor between ten and three in the cigar enterprise of F. Pino. C. E. Duval provided dental services on Calle Farola, as did Dr. Quintero at La Central pharmacy, on Duval Street, which was owned by Dr. Armona. La Central offered drugs, all kinds of curatives, bandages and suspensories, mineral water, and perfumes, among other things. Midwife Tomasa Avalo had an office on the corner of Esponjas and Carolina.

Cuban restaurants and cafés dotted the town. San Carlos Institute, a popular community center and school, had its own restaurant that served lunch and dinner every day. It advertised "a good selection of candies and refreshments." The El Caimito Café on Duval, just two doors from San Carlos, was run by war veteran Juan Monzón. It served dinner every night and advertised "our favorite recipes; all good, inexpensive and attractive (*buenos, barato y bonito*)." Silversmith and watchmaker Manuel M. Escassi had a shop on Greene Street just across from the telegraph office. Antonio Comas ran the Cuba-Cataluña bakery on Santa Angela. Miguel Briñas sold musical instruments of all kinds on the corner of Carolina and Farola, including teaching manuals. Manuel M. Cordero worked as a tailor in his shop on Duval Street, but he also sold shoes. R. Tapia sold a mix of Cuban and American provisions on the corner of Green and Duval Streets including china, crystal, hardware, wine, lager, fruit, and various foods. Cigar manufacturer Eduardo H. Gato became one of Florida's leading entrepreneurs. He had cigar enterprises with offices in Key West and New York, but in Key West he expanded his interests, investing in the streetcar system, real estate, and banking.[21]

Cubans adapted easily to their surroundings, creating familiarity and belonging, but they remained committed to preserving their identity and culture. Whether at home, work or in social situations, Key West Cubans spoke their native tongue, abandoning it only when necessary, usually when speaking with American friends or with officials in city and state offices. "The Stars and Stripes float over the government buildings," noted one reporter in 1891, "but ten words of Spanish are spoken for one of English."[22] The Anglo-American inhabitants, known to Cubans as Conchs, became *concos* and their neighborhoods *conco taons*. Though streets and town squares had English names, Cubans renamed them using words from their daily parlance, such as Esponjas (Sponge), Roquirod (Rocky Road), Farola (Lamppost), Callejón de los Muertos (Dead Man's Alley) and Callejón del Telégrafo (Telegraph Alley). Bahamas Street, where Poyo lived in the 1880s, became known as Callejón de Poyo.[23]

On Cuban revolutionary holidays, flags covered the city, especially the factories and homes where Cubans worked and lived. These displays always impressed the Anglo-American residents of Key West with the intensity of the community's commitment to the cause of Cuban independence. Cubans followed Cuban customs and values in their households and neighborhoods, but transnational experience also infused their identity with elements of the culture of Key West and the United States. Many Cubans learned English (though it was not generally necessary); participated in labor activism; joined the Republican and Democratic Parties; held appointed positions in federal, state, and local government; voted in U.S. elections; played baseball; and became citizens (according to U.S. federal law, adult male immigrants were eligible for citizenship after five years).

In the 1870s, when Cubans submitted their citizenship papers at the courthouse, they were generally accompanied by American witnesses, but after the number of Cuban American citizens increased, they often served as witnesses for each other. In 1888, for example, Poyo, who probably became a citizen in the 1870s, witnessed Martín Morúa Delgado's application for citizenship. Cuban community leaders applied for citizenship as a matter of course. Juan María Reyes, a leading Cuban Republican Party activist in town, petitioned for citizenship in October 1875. Others did the same: Martín Herrera in 1877; labor activists Ramón Rivero and Guillermo Sorondo in 1878 and 1881, respectively; businessmen Cayetano Soria and Carlos Recio in 1876 and 1878, respectively; Manuel Patricio Delgado in 1881; and Manuel Deolufeu in 1889.[24]

In addition to forging stronger ties to the larger community, citizenship protected nationalists from retribution from Spanish officials in Cuba. When Spanish authorities arrested activist Cirilo Pouble, editor of the New York newspaper *El Separatista*, in Havana in 1885 and charged him with conspiracy against Spain, the U.S. consul in Havana became involved. When nationalist Julio Sanguily met the same fate, he too appealed to the U.S. consul; he also hired prominent Cuban American attorney José Ignacio Rodríguez to handle his case. In both cases the men were convicted, but the publicity and legal options their U.S. citizenship provided created the possibility of eventual release.[25] In any case, embracing U.S. citizenship did not create existential guilt, since nationalists did not yet have a country or official nationality and renounced their Spanish citizenship without regret.

Cayo Hueso's Cuban population was never static. The cigar industry's economic cycles and often volatile labor relations caused people to move quite regularly. A portion of the Cuban community was always in transit. Cigar factories in Tampa, Jacksonville, New Orleans, New York, and a variety of other cities offered alternative employment possibilities to cigar workers. As if always waiting for the moment when they would be forced to relocate, most Cubans in Key West chose not to invest in real estate. Only the wealthiest Cubans purchased land and homes. Most members of the community rented homes, lived in company-owned housing or in boarding houses, and remained ready to depart in case of unemployment because of reductions in the demand for cigars, strikes, or political crises. Their obvious fondness for Cayo Hueso reflected not only nationalist spirit but also pride in contributing to the city's growth and prosperity.

Work and Politics

Poyo emerged as a local political leader in tandem with his work to help organize Cuban refugees into a coherent exile community. His first concern was employment. His arrival coincided with the rise of the cigar industry and a demand for *lectores*, or readers, which (perhaps unexpectedly) provided him with his first political opportunities. The practice of reading aloud to workers in Cuban factories (the *lectura*) was a well-established tradition. The *lectura* first appeared in Havana's cigar factories in 1865, promoted by a worker-oriented weekly newspaper, *La Aurora*. With the backing of the reformist newspaper *El Siglo*, *La Aurora* focused on literary, scientific, and pedagogical issues and advocated reading to workers while they labored. The owner of El Fígaro factory in Havana, who had been persuaded by notable members of the reformist movement to try the new practice, instituted the first *lectura*. Another followed in the Partagás factory, owned by perhaps the largest and best-known producer of cigars in Cuba. Before the end of 1866, fearing the politicization of workers, Spanish authorities prohibited the practice, but after much protest and dissatisfaction the *lectura* returned in early 1868, this time to stay. Although not all workers arrived in Key West with nationalist beliefs, thanks to the *lectura* they were often knowledgeable about current events and politicized and were thus open to being persuaded to join the nationalist movement.[26]

Poyo apparently had no experience with this profession, but he obtained work at Seidenberg's La Rosa Española factory and then moved to Martínez Ybor's Principe de Gales establishment when it opened. *Lectores* had to be relatively educated men who could project their voices well across the factory floor and perform with an animated style and a flair for the dramatic. They usually had a political and social consciousness, and had to be sufficiently well read to recommend classic as well as contemporary book titles to workers. Since workers paid *lectores* directly without interference from the owners, Poyo interviewed with a hiring committee composed of workers; the interview included an audition on the factory floor.[27]

A light-skinned man with curly light hair and a mustache, Poyo stood about five feet six and took great care in his personal appearance. He dressed impeccably, always with a coat and tie. Poyo's friend Fernando Figueredo described him as a man of considerable education with vast knowledge on many topics, especially Latin America. Before entering journalism, Poyo briefly attended university and studied medicine. People immediately recognized his erudition, yet his modest demeanor made him approachable. He took much care in his personal relations and cultivated an ability to deal well with people, though he could be intractable and stubborn when it came to matters of importance to him.[28] One Key West Anglo-American leader, Jefferson B. Browne, who on numerous occasions challenged the Cuban community for what he considered their exaggerated political activism, remembered Poyo as "a highly cultured and educated gentleman."[29] Poyo worked as a *lector* in Key West for thirty years, a job he and other readers used to advance a nationalist discourse that converted many workers to the cause.

In the early years, Poyo stood or sat among the workers and read. In 1873, a *New York Times* correspondent offered this description of Cubans and the institution of reading in Key West factories:

> Their excited discussion of home politics and affairs has led the proprietors of every considerable factory to employ a "reader" who sits in the midst of the workmen and engages their attention by reading in a loud voice all the news, rumors, and speculations of the day, as set forth in the newspapers, private correspondence, etc. This "reader" is a most valuable and well-stored [sic] personage. He reads rapidly and loudly and is so well supplied with reading matter, either in print or in manuscript that he goes on all day without exhausting his material.[30]

The journalist interpreted this practice as one that increased the efficiency of workers; he concluded that workers did not waste time in animated debates when they were listening to the *lectura*. Though the correspondent missed the literary and educational aspect of the practice of reading to workers, his article confirmed the popularity and acceptance of the institution in Key West a short time after the founding of the cigar industry there.

As the number of factories in Key West increased, the *lectura* became more formalized, as it was in Havana. In large factories with two floors, the workers manufactured the cigars on the second floor while offices, storage areas, and tobacco preparation areas occupied the first floor. The manufacturing area, known as the *galera*, included rows of tables where the cigar makers sat almost shoulder to shoulder as they rolled tobacco. Behind the rows of tables, if there was enough room, other workers performed additional steps in the cigar manufacturing process. These included the *rezagadores*, who sorted the wrapper leaf according to quality and color; the *despalilladoras*, usually women, who stripped the central stick-like veins from the leaves; the *escogedores*, who sorted the completed cigars according to quality and tied them in bundles; and the *fileteadores*, who packed the sorted cigars in the appropriate boxes.

Everyone faced the *tribuna*, a church-like pulpit, where the *lector* sat or stood and read to the workers. The large hall had high ceilings and some windows for light but not so much light that it would ruin the tobacco leaf. The environment was entirely artisanal; there were no machines. A good *lector* could be heard across the factory floor and was interrupted only by the occasional bursts of approval produced when the cigar makers rapidly and repetitively hit the tables with their *chavetas* (knives) in response to especially salient passages in the readings.[31]

Poyo's job as *lector* gave him an opportunity to influence the thinking of workers and promote revolutionary consciousness in the factories. Guided by the demands and tastes of the workers, he read literary works, portions of which were read every day in serialized fashion, but he also read newspapers and pamphlets that included reports and correspondence about the war in Cuba. *Lectores* had access to many Cuban and Spanish newspapers that were published both on the island and in exile.

In the early 1870s, Poyo probably read carefully chosen news stories from the pro-Spanish papers *Diario de la Marina* or *La Voz de Cuba*, which were published in Havana, where most of the workers came from. But he likely read more extensively from the Key West newspaper, *El Republicano*, and from New York papers such as *La Revolución*, *El Demócrata*, *Diario Cubano*, *El Correo de Nueva York*, *La Verdad*, *La Independencia*, and *La Voz de la Patria*. These newspapers offered the latest news about the war in Cuba, engaged in ideological debates, and reported on daily events.

"Reading in the factories on the surface seems insignificant," Poyo explained, "but it is actually a perennial service of instruction, as much for the readers themselves as those listening." He thought readers should entertain but should also introduce ideas that illustrated the benefits of progress, which required one to leave behind the idealized and symbolic approach of the Romantic school, which emphasized distracting "fables." Instead, readers should select texts from the Modernist school, as exemplified by the work of Émile Zola. Poyo argued that the Modernist school described believable and unvarnished everyday reality, "the truth as it unfolds, embellishing with rich ostentatious and ponderous imagination that unending source of learning called existence." Reality offered readers a photograph of humanity's "crimes" and "goodness," and when effectively presented it could motivate people to action. "It seems useful," Poyo felt, to read "what keeps the memory of the atrocities committed in Cuba by the Spanish government alive." Poyo hoped that exiles would return home as revolutionary advocates who were well instructed in the history of Cuba and were prepared as propagandists.[32] Poyo viewed the *lectura* as a revolutionary tool and undertook the job in that spirit. He and dozens of other *lectores* disseminated revolutionary ideas to tobacco workers.

Good *lectores* also represented a moral authority on the factory floor that was respected by the foremen and even the manufacturers. Trusted readers often represented the workers in ceremonial occasions and sometimes served as mediators between the foremen and workers when there was labor conflict. When President Grover Cleveland, a cigar smoker, visited Tampa in 1886, he toured Ybor City and visited the newly established Martínez Ybor factory, which had recently relocated from Key West. Poyo, who had followed the factory to Tampa, was reading to the workers when Martínez Ybor and President Cleveland entered the factory floor. Many workers recognized the president and immediately broke into applause, much to his delight. Instead of asking the foreman to welcome the president, or doing it himself, Martínez Ybor asked Poyo, the de facto representative of the workers, for the words of welcome. As one worker commented, "with well-expressed words, he welcomed the illustrious visitor," and Poyo's speech was followed by even more vigorous acclamation. The owners and other members of management then took President Cleveland to the factory offices, where they presented him with a large box of Principe de Gales cigars, the factory's best-known brand.[33]

The Exile Press

Poyo further extended his reach and influence as a nationalist leader by drawing on his background as a newspaper proofreader to create a local revolutionary press. During his first months in Key West, he befriended Juan

María "Nito" Reyes, the *lector* at the Samuel Wolff factory who in late 1869 founded the first Spanish-language newspaper in Key West, *El Republicano*. Reyes, who was older than Poyo, had worked at *El Siglo* and *La Aurora* in Cuba. Like many contributors to those newspapers, he threw in his lot with the revolutionaries in late 1868. Reyes recognized the need for a newspaper in the rapidly growing and highly politicized working-class community in Key West, and Poyo joined him. As *lectores*, emerging political leaders, and experienced newspapermen, the two forged an enterprise that helped keep the Cuban insurrection in the minds of the community.[34]

The newspaper provided community news, but primarily it engaged in political agitation. Throughout 1869, *El Republicano* kept up a constant drumbeat that called for Cuban independence from Spain, which soon led to polemic debate on the pages of *La Voz de Cuba*, the pro-Spanish *voluntario* organ in Havana that had incited the riots in January. After a series of mutually provocative and insulting articles in January 1870, the editor of the Spanish newspaper, Gonzalo Castañon, challenged Reyes to a duel. Since the exiled editor could not travel to Havana without being arrested, Castañon traveled to Key West to seek him out.

On January 29, 1870, the Spaniard checked into Russell House, a hotel on Duval Street, and sent an aide to alert Reyes of his arrival. Reyes met Castañon in the hotel lobby and after a heated conversation the Spaniard slapped the elderly Cuban, who filed assault charges with the local sheriff. As the affair grew increasingly complicated, a number of other Cubans, including Poyo, came forward to defend Reyes's honor.[35] When Castañon began to have second thoughts about engaging in a duel, one Cuban, Mateo Orozco, persisted and called him a coward. This provocation flared into violence as both men drew guns and fired shots. Castañon fell dead in the lobby of Russell House. Orozco fled to Poyo's home, and Poyo arranged his escape.[36] Instantly, Key West gained the reputation in Havana as a hotbed of criminality and revolutionary sentiment.

Later, Poyo took over editing *El Republicano*, and in late 1876 he founded another newspaper, *La Igualdad*, which lasted only briefly. Poyo's next effort, *El Patriota*, began in April 1878 but published only a few issues. His enduring journalistic enterprise, *El Yara*, appeared on October 12, 1878, a decade after the Grito de Yara. He characterized it as a radical voice dedicated to freeing Cuba from Spanish rule.

At first *El Yara* appeared irregularly until a formula for survival emerged: it became a family enterprise to which everyone contributed resources. *El Yara* soon became more regular, and years later it appeared as a daily. Sometimes it went quiet during bad economic times or when other factors beyond Poyo's control made publication impossible. In January 1892, for example, the newspaper discontinued publication when it lost its office and two typographers became ill. After two weeks *El Yara* reappeared. An editorial explained the disruption and responded to those who had predicted that a lack of resources and support had sealed its fate. "If those of us who write for El Yara," Poyo wrote, "had commitments other than our conscience as Cubans, separatists, and liberals committed to the supreme ideal of human progress, perhaps we would have been obliged to say farewell. But it is not like that." He assured his readers that if he could not publish daily, the newspaper would appear weekly or even monthly. *El Yara* would appear as long as he was mentally able to "handle an unlearned and sincere pen" in order to promote political action, despite a continual shortage of resources and the disappointments of previous years.[37]

The newspaper was a labor of love and a commitment to nationalism. Each wage earner in the Poyo family contributed resources from their income earned from work in the cigar factories. *El Yara* was initially produced from Poyo's home. Poyo gathered news content, wrote, and edited, while Clara took care of the many logistical challenges. In the early years, Clara's brother, Rafael Camus, typeset the newspaper, though he frequently lacked enough letters. Two young tobacco worker volunteers who were drawn to the newspaper's nationalist vision, Francisco Alpízar and Manuel P. Delgado, also helped, though initially they may have been attracted as much by Poyo's daughters as by his newspaper.

Delgado became Poyo's right-hand man. Born in Havana (Luyanó), he arrived in Key West at age eight with his parents in September 1869. He attended public school, after which he went to work as a cigar maker.[38] He became a citizen and learned to speak English fluently, but he always remained committed to his Cuban identity. When a *New York Herald-Tribune* reporter asked Delgado in 1891 why he did not "stand up for the United States," he replied that he recognized and fully embraced his duties as an American citizen, but his heart remained with his native land, to which he would eventually return. When asked what he thought about annexing Cuba to the United

States, Delgado remarked that Cuba was perfectly capable of self-government and that treaties and agreements would govern its relations with the United States, as is the case in any negotiation between two sovereign states.[39]

Delgado and Alpízar took charge of the layout, while Celia and América, after tracking down the ink and paper with Clara's help, printed the newspaper on a hand-cranked press. Everyone volunteered their labor and Poyo reinvested whatever profits remained in the business. He charged five cents per issue at first; later he charged ten cents, and then twenty. The family earned income from sales in Key West, New York, and other centers for exiles, but they distributed a significant portion of their editions to clandestine networks in Havana and throughout Cuba free of charge. In San Antonio de los Baños, for example, a young Cuban named Rómulo Morales distributed the newspaper among the tobacco workers until authorities discovered his activities and forced him to flee to Key West.

Producing *El Yara* required an inordinate sacrifice from the family. They lived modestly and often went without things, in part because of the insecurities of a volatile cigar industry but also because the newspaper consumed whatever money remained after paying for rent, food, and other necessities. But the family never questioned their commitment. "Like a luminous torch," *El Yara* "projected light on the conscience of Cuba and Free America," Poyo's grandson Raoul Alpízar Poyo later declared.[40]

The end of the Ten Years' War marked a low in revolutionary morale, and until 1883 *El Yara* was the only newspaper in exile that continued to promote independence and insurgency, maintaining people's sights on a goal that had not yet been achieved. As the newspaper's reputation grew, the burden of sustaining the enterprise eased. Poyo received literary contributions, including letters, essays and poetry, not only from his colleagues in Key West, but from revolutionaries in Cuba, the United States and the Caribbean. In March 1881, for example, Poyo asked Ernesto Bavastro, a nationalist leader in Kingston, Jamaica, for revolutionary news including "doctrinal" articles for *El Yara*. He welcomed any contribution that would advance the cause, especially since he had few collaborators and he published with "immense sacrifice."[41]

Poyo also communicated with Antonio Maceo, Máximo Gómez, and Calixto García, prominent generals of the Ten Years' War, who also occasionally sent correspondence for publication. In mid-1881, Poyo published a letter from Maceo in Tegucigalpa and thanked him for a timely message that supported the principles of independence and revolution.[42] The newspaper increasingly served as a kind of information hub and clearinghouse for dispersed exiles and an ideological voice for those who supported renewal of war.

Other newspapers joined *El Yara*. Manuel P. Delgado edited a short-lived paper called *La Voz de Hatuey*. In 1884, José Rafael Estrada, who had served as a lieutenant colonel in the Ten Years' War, founded *La Propaganda*, which became an important nationalist and community newspaper. Estrada, who was originally from Sancti-Spiritus, fought with the liberation army until shortly before the war ended, when he was captured after he broke his leg.[43] Union leader Ramón Rivero, who arrived in Key West in the 1870s, began editing a labor newspaper, *El Ecuador*, in 1886. Although he was a nationalist, he insisted that labor issues be considered independently of political matters, a stance that caused considerable controversy. Rivero later published *La Revista de Florida* and *Cuba* in Tampa. Pedro Pequeño and Néstor Leonelo Carbonell also advanced a nationalist line in their paper, *El Cubano*. After the outbreak of the independence war in 1895, numerous other newspapers appeared.

El Yara rarely published alone in Key West but it was the only newspaper in the communities of exiles that appeared regularly without significant gaps from 1878 through 1898. According to *Patria*, a New York paper, *El Yara's* doctrinal or ideological character, longevity, and revolutionary posture cemented its reputation as "the dean of the Cuban press abroad." The same newspaper referred to Poyo as a "fervent patriot, indefatigable and energetic writer, who for seventeen long years has sustained a valuable campaign in El Yara."[44] Máximo Gómez, commander in chief of the insurgents, added that *El Yara* was an "ardent, loyal and eternal defender of the rights of the Cuban Nation, even in the most sorrowful and painful times for the enslaved *patria* when it seemed that all hope had died in the hearts of Cubans."[45]

Revolutionary Community

Poyo's vision for advancing independence required creating a community capable of maintaining political commitments, culture, and identity over time. He disseminated ideas about Cuban independence, revolutionary conspiracies, and military expeditions through oratory, the *lectura*, and his newspaper.

In July 1869, Poyo formed the Asociación Patriótica de Cayo Hueso (Patriotic Association of Key West). As treasurer, Poyo sent $150 to $200 weekly to New York that was collected from association members and tobacco workers in the factories.[46] Workers and manufacturers alike contributed to the numerous revolutionary initiatives and often belonged to the same nationalist clubs.

Poyo also recognized the need to mobilize women and urged his wife, Clara, and his daughters, Celia, América, and Blanca, to take the lead in this regard. Although men defined the broad directions of nationalist ideology and action, women's commitment to grassroots tasks became indispensable to the community's activism. Perhaps 10 percent of the community's women worked for wages outside the household in the 1870s, a proportion that increased to about 25 percent twenty years later. But a much larger proportion regularly worked for the revolutionary cause. Women's flexible daily routines made it feasible for them to take the lead in organizing events including parades, banquets, raffles, and picnics. They also hosted visiting political leaders. They went from door to door collecting contributions for specific projects from households and businesses. Women also did the important work of instilling nationalist values in their children. Thus, the activist culture they supported was reproduced in the next generation.

On December 6, 1878, Clara, Celia, and América and forty other women formed Club Hijas de la Libertad (Daughters of Liberty), an organization that was similar to Emilia Casanova de Villaverde's La Liga de las Hijas de Cuba (The League of Cuban Daughters) in New York, which was well known to Poyo. In the early 1870s Casanova had established the league, the first women's political club whose goal was to support the revolution. Members organized concerts, bazaars, raffles, and sales of bonds issued by the government in arms. Celia and Clara became leading figures in the Key West club, which was one of the most celebrated nationalist clubs locally.[47]

Poyo worked to attract mulatto and black members of the Cuban community, who accounted for 20 to 30 percent of the group, to the nationalist cause. In the mid-1870s, Guillermo Sorondo and Carlos Borrego founded the Colegio Unificación (Unification School), the first educational, social, and political organization for Cubans of color in Key West.[48] Other mulatto and black nationalist sympathizers in Key West in the 1870s included Joaquín and Manuel Granados, Juan de Dios Barrios, Cornelio Brito, Emilio Planas,

Francisco Segura, and Ruperto Pedroso.[49] (Many of these men later moved to Tampa.) In the 1880s, they established the Sociedad el Progreso (Society Progress), which also became an important social and political center for the entire community. Sorondo worked as an influential labor leader while Segura contributed to several labor newspapers, including *El Ecuador* in Key West and *Revista de Florida* in Tampa.[50]

In the early 1880s, journalists Martín Morúa Delgado, Rafael Serra, and Rafael Estrada arrived in Key West. Morúa Delgado and Serra shortly departed for New York, where they edited *El Separatista* (1883–1884) and *La Doctrina de Martí* (1896–1897), respectively. Estrada remained in Key West and published *La Propaganda* until his untimely death in 1888. Morúa Delgado later returned to Key West, where he married into the prominent Granados family. He published *El Pueblo* before returning to Havana in 1890.[51] Another important leader, José G. Pómpez, served as a member of the Florida legislature from Monroe County in 1889. Military leaders such as Antonio Maceo and Flor Crombet established especially strong relationships in Key West, where they raised money and regularly consulted with the local nationalist leadership. People of color integrated well into the Key West Cuban community and took leadership roles in nationalist efforts.[52]

Dozens of men and women's clubs—white, black, and mixed—formed over the years, some lasting only a short time, some lingering with few members, and some transforming into different organizations. Organized to address "a grand goal," these associations generally had a vibrant life during their first months but then languished, finally succumbing from inaction. But they always reappeared in a new form and continued the work. Their very instability revealed an organic and dynamic community that featured changing demographics, shifting ideologies, rivalries among leaders, personality conflicts, and, according to one writer, the cultural peculiarities of Cubans themselves.[53]

The tradition of community oratory also played an important role in maintaining nationalist culture and values. Cubans loved inspiring oratory and eagerly attended events featuring well-known speakers who addressed their public with a formal and inclusive greeting: "Mr. President, Mr. Secretary, Mr. Treasurer, local authorities, ladies, gentlemen, girls and boys, beloved compatriots." Oratory included many forms including the speeches of labor radicals and evangelical preaching. It was by turns poetic, reasoned, prophetic, eulogistic, and humorous. Cubans especially responded to speeches about nationalism and independence. Historian Gerardo Castellanos García dubbed it *oratoria manigüera* (battlefield oratory), a form that was vulgar, enthusiastic, fluid, rapid, impetuous, and expressed with flailing gestures and pounding on the rostrum. Speakers generally improvised their speeches and had the physical stamina to continue for long periods of time. It was not uncommon for patriotic events to feature six or seven speakers.[54]

Over the years, Key West produced many talented orators with unique personalities from whom community organizers could choose. These included black leaders Granados, Dios de Barrios, and Brito; nationalist activists Martín Herrera and Francisco María González; labor leaders Sorondo and Federico Corbet; politician Pómpez; and poet Charo Jiménez, among others. Dios de Barrios was very discreto; Jiménez's speeches featured "delicious buffoonery"; Sorondo put people to sleep; Brito could not be kept from the stage; González was fiery and cultured; and Pómpez was a master.[55]

Carolina "La Patriota" Rodríguez, one of only a few women orators, also attracted large audiences. Originally from Las Villas, she arrived in Key West to work as tobacco leaf stripper. She joined Hijas de la Libertad (Daughters of Liberty) and quickly gained a reputation as an effective nationalist fundraiser. Rodríguez also worked to help the community's most needy.[56] Whatever their style, Key West's orators commanded an audience and played a critical role in disseminating nationalist ideology and solidifying community commitment to Cuban independence.

Poyo's work as a *lector* and a newspaper editor also helped establish his prominence as an insurrectionary orator outside the factory. He was among the earliest orators in Key West. According to his friend Figueredo, Poyo's speeches were scrupulous to a fault (*"concienzudo"*) and careful; his eloquent arguments and strong sense of morality won over his listeners with the powerful effect of a "hammer falling on a poor nail."[57] Poyo became one of the regular orators at the numerous gatherings and events that sought to mobilize support for a free Cuba.

An incident that took place on November 27, 1871, provided future oratory and patriotic performance in Key West with an important forum. On that day Spanish authorities executed eight of forty-two medical students arrested in Havana for chanting anti-Spanish slogans and allegedly defacing the tomb of Gonzalo Castañon, who had been killed the year before in Key

Figure 1. The eight medical students who were executed in Havana on November 27, 1871. They were accused of defacing the tomb of Gonzalo Castañon, a prominent pro-Spanish newspaper editor, who was killed in Key West in January 1870. The annual November 27 commemoration of the students' deaths was one of Key West's most important patriotic events for almost thirty years. In author's possession.

West. Pro-*voluntario* mobs demanded a show trial, forcing the government's hand. Most of those who escaped execution suffered imprisonment and exile. In time, Fermín Valdés Domíguez, one of the arrested students who was deported to Spain, wrote an account of the episode that deepened the outrage among Cubans, particularly in Key West.[58]

The November 27 commemoration became one of the community's most revered traditions, second only to October 10, the anniversary of the outbreak of the Ten Years' War. It featured processions through the streets of Key West, emotional speeches, and theater productions.[59] Celia Poyo, president of Hijas de la Libertad (Daughters of Liberty), and her sisters put everything else aside each November to organize and preside over the "mournful" activity symbolizing Spain's oppressive rule in Cuba.[60]

Annual commemorations for the dead contributed to a generalized devotion to revolutionary martyrs, who were mourned as the redeemers of the Cuban nation. Among Cubans generally, martyrdom, or "exemplary death," wrote historian Louis A. Pérez, Jr., "served to deepen the intransigence central to the purpose of liberation, to situate each generation between ancestry, to whom a debt was owed, and posterity, to whom an obligation was due."[61] Poyo spoke at the first anniversary of the outbreak of the independence war. The event began with a requiem mass at Key West's Catholic church in memory of the fallen and then continued at the cemetery at a symbolic grave for the dead. Poyo set the tone, saying that they gathered for no other reason than to "comply with our sacred duty" and recognize the martyrs of the struggle against Spain.[62] Nito Reyes also spoke and then all knelt before a Cuban flag for five minutes of silent meditation.[63]

This tradition of recognizing the martyrs endured, and years later at a similar commemoration Poyo declared that immolation was the inevitable cost of attaining human emancipation. Martyrs sacrificed and redeemed their people, and though their bodies returned to the earth, their spirits rose to "supreme immortality." Key West's pantheon of martyrs deepened the community's sense of obligation to complete the task and ensure that the dead had not sacrificed their lives in vain. These included revolutionaries who had died during the Ten Years' War, such as Carlos Manuel de Céspedes, Francisco Vicente Aguilera, Perucho Figueredo, and Ignacio Argamonte, but local martyrs also joined the patriotic list.

Musical pomp and circumstance imbued these activities with further enthusiasm and sense of authenticity. When Cubans first arrived in Key West, they hired local bands for such occasions, but in time they formed their own band, called La Libertad, which included clarinets, flutes, drums, trombones, cornets, violas, and other instruments; eventually the band included some twenty-five musicians. José Rogelio Castillo, a Colombian tobacco worker and veteran of the war, directed the band for many years. It performed free of charge at political events, dances, and bazaars, and its rendition of Cuban songs such as "La Bayamesa," the Cuban nationalist composition by Perucho Figueredo, invariably stirred passions.[64] Culture and patriotic performance played an important role in keeping Cubans connected to their roots and to the political sensibilities of their community.

To ensure an independent Cuba for future generations, exiles worked to make sure that their children grew up in a foreign land with a strong sense of being Cuban and a powerful commitment to nationalism and independence. Poyo and others recognized that this required actions and events that celebrated Cuba and education that taught children the island's history, culture, and traditions in their native tongue. Parents and other adults were aware that exile could become a multigenerational experience, and they wanted to ensure that the community's children would identify as Cuban. Though Key West established its first public schools in 1870, Cubans preferred their own academies that taught their children in Spanish and socialized them to the broader world of Cuban life and culture.

At the initiative of Reyes, Poyo, close colleague Martin Herrera, and others gathered on November 11, 1871, to inaugurate the Sociedad de Instrucción y Recreo San Carlos (San Carlos Educational and Recreation Society), named after Carlos Manuel de Céspedes, the first president of the Cuban revolutionary government. The new society replaced Ateneo Democrático Cubano (Cuban Democratic Athenaeum), which had been established in 1869. Poyo joined in the inaugural speeches and celebrations, which included comedic sketches, singing, and performances of Cuban *guaracha*, a popular dance form.

The board of directors (which the community had elected) hired Alejandro Menéndez as the first teacher. Menéndez oversaw the education of ninety students, including one of the board members, Eduardo Paredes, a black man who had never attended school. San Carlos Institute paid the teacher's salary and furnished school supplies using funds from a monthly fee levied on members and money raised through periodic bazaars and others kinds of activities. The institution included a theatre and also served as a center of political activism where the community heard speeches and offered support for the revolution.

Popular theatrical productions drew such enthusiastic and varied audiences that in 1883 secretary Antonio Díaz Carrasco published rules of conduct. In addition to banning smoking (a bold move in a cigar town), the rules prohibited whistling, interrupting the actors, throwing objects of any kind that might offend decency or distract the public or actors, and using indelicate language (*palabras indecorosas*). Violators would be dealt "with all the vigor of the law."[65]

San Carlos Institute often faced great challenges. An economic downturn that closed cigar factories and provoked a strike in 1873 forced the school to close, but not for long. When the crisis passed, Poyo, Reyes, and especially Martín Herrera worked to open the school again. Herrera was originally from Pinar del Rio, where he had worked as a barber. Herrera arrived in 1869 and over the years ran a café, a restaurant, a hotel, and a meat market. He was tall and skinny like Don Quixote and disheveled and he was verbose and used crude language. But he constantly worked with nervous energy for independence and his work consumed his personal finances. San Carlos Institute was his most prized community cause. Herrera raised money for the school by organizing groups of women to knock on doors of homes and visit business establishments. He was sometimes demanding in his efforts to raise money, and often people avoided him on the streets. They knew that he would relieve them of their money, and if not their money, then items that could be sold at the school bazaar.[66]

In 1874, Herrera finally was able to purchase a building on Green Street for $150 and reopen the school. He put the deed in the names of Poyo and two other community members. The boys' section was called Carlos Manuel de Céspedes, and the girls' section took the name of Francisco Vicente Aguilera, who had recently visited Key West. The school board hired two new teachers, José García Toledo and his wife Elisa Figueredo (the daughter of Perucho Figueredo). Both taught at San Carlos Institute for many years and became beloved figures in the community. They taught Celia, América, Blanca, and Francisco Poyo and hundreds of other Cuban youth. Despite the fact that the community's children were raised in exile, they remained Cuban in language, culture, identity, and inspiration.[67]

The school faced other periodic closings, but each time the community, especially the alumni, rallied to bring it back.[68] In April 1886, a fire destroyed about a third of the city, including San Carlos Institute. It devastated the cigar industry and caused hundreds to leave for Havana, Tampa, and other places in search of work. Once again Martín Herrera sprang into action to resurrect the school, aided by Poyo and others. The school reopened in January 1888. In late November 1886, for example, Herrera collected $166.50 from factories and individuals. Carolina "La Patriota" gave him $1.60 from the tobacco strippers of the Canales factory; Trujillo factory workers contributed $7.05; workers in the Nichols factory donated $4.70; the Morilla factory gave $10. Workers in the Gato, Pérez, and Seidenberg factories also contributed, as did individuals and businesses such as United States Cleaners, Juan Terry, Dr. José Armona, the E. H. Gato Company, and the Cayetano Soria Company. This income from the community and resources collected at special fund-raising events maintained San Carlos Institute.[69]

The economic enterprises, social composition, and cultural environment of Cayo Hueso created and perpetuated a revolutionary community that remained loyal to nationalist ideals. Many workers arrived simply looking for work and did not have much political sensibility or consciousness, but the community's nationalist traditions usually won them over to its guiding nationalist purpose.

Perhaps Puerto Rican nationalist Eugenio María Hostos best expressed what people thought about Key West. He arrived in New York in 1869 and helped edit the revolutionary newspaper *La Revolución*.[70] He was disturbed by what he found in New York: a chaotic and politically divided exile community that was deeply influenced by conservative men associated with the island's elites. In 1874 Hostos described Cayo Hueso as the community in exile that best represented Cuban nationalist ideals and was fully committed to supporting the insurrectionary effort. Though he had never visited south Florida, Hostos seemed fully informed about the community, where support for revolution remained enthusiastic and fervent. The Paris community, he noted, was composed mostly of "refugees of pleasure" looking to replace in France the wealth they had lost in Cuba; Cubans in Puerto Plata (Dominican

Republic) had patriotism but had no plans; those in New Orleans had tired of failed efforts; and New York was a ruin. Only Key West responded without complaint to the needs of the revolution. Who are the Cubans of Cayo Hueso? he asked. They were not the richest Cubans; in fact, they were poor for the most part. Not one of them, he declared, had the resources of the least rich in other centers where Cuban exiles had settled. They were not numerous, educated, or rich like the Cubans in New York and some other centers. Their distinguished revolutionary activism came from their sense of duty and the ability to create a piece of independent Cuba in an alien land. Hostos deeply appreciated Key West's newspaper, political associations, educational institutions, mutual aid societies, and credit unions, which he saw as effective preparation for life in the new republic. Furthermore, he lauded the Cubans for their great service to the United States in building such a prosperous community.[71]

Early in the Ten Years' War, Poyo recognized that an effective revolutionary movement required a system of support organized in a space where it could take root and bloom, a safe community where activists could live and act freely. As early as the mid-1870s, Cayo Hueso had achieved a reputation as a working-class center for exiled Cubans that was fully committed to Cuba's independence and militantly supportive of the insurgency. Francisco Vicente Aguilera, the vice-president of the Cuban republic, called Key West the vanguard of the revolution, and in 1892, when José Martí arrived in Key West, he agreed.[72] Cigar workers and entrepreneurs were generous in their provision of economic resources and political activists led clubs and societies that kept the community mobilized and enthusiastic. Cubans in Key West believed that only by maintaining a powerful sense of culture and identity would they remain collectively committed to their goal of independence. For them, becoming Americans culturally, including forgetting the Spanish language and Cuban history and losing their sense of loyalty to their homeland, would have been a betrayal of their nationality and identity. They struggled mightily to remain Cuban and passed the identity on to the next generation, a process that was facilitated by Key West's relatively isolated location on the edge of the Florida straits.

In the 1870s, Havana was closer and easier to reach from Key West than any city in the United States. In Florida, only Tampa rivaled Havana for Key

West's attention after 1886. During the Ten Years' War, Poyo and his many colleagues and collaborators built a self-sustaining revolutionary community that became more radical, determined, and influential with the passage of time. There was nothing serendipitous about Key West's activism; it was intentional and determined.

2

NATIONALISM

> There is only one path to salvation: the establishment of the Cuban Republic where Cubans and Spaniards [can] find peace, work, and progress.
>
> *El Yara*, 1880

In late February 1870, shortly after the Castañon affair, José D. Poyo stood with a crowd at the Key West docks and greeted General Manuel de Quesada, the former commander in chief of the Cuban insurgent army, who was arriving on a steamer from Nassau on his way to New York.[1] Manuel Quesada, a charismatic personality who was originally from Camaguey, had migrated to Mexico in 1855 with his brother Rafael and fought with Benito Juárez against the French occupation. During his service Quesada had commanded a division, served as military governor of Durango, and participated in campaigns against Emperor Maximilian's forces. His brother Rafael rose to the rank of colonel in the Mexican army. When they learned of the Cuban rebellion, they organized the first military expedition to Cuba with the schooner *Galvanic*, which left Nassau on December 27, 1868, with eighty men, 3,000 rifles, and half a million rounds of ammunition. One of the few rebels with military command and combat experience, Manuel de Quesada immediately took a prominent role in the fighting.[2] In April 1869, insurgent leaders representing the various Cuban regions in rebellion convened at Guáimaro to establish a Republic in Arms. A constitution provided for a House of Representatives that elected Carlos Manuel de Céspedes president of the republic and Manuel de Quesada commander of the army. To avoid capture, the government moved frequently but maintained an active role in directing the insurgency.

From the moment of the establishment of the Cuban insurgent republic in April 1869, the legislative and executive branches of government fell into bitter disagreement, reflecting regional suspicions, racial fears, tactical

Figure 2. José Dolores Poyo, ca. 1880. Photograph courtesy of Wright Langley.

differences, ideological disagreements, and even personal rivalries that also permeated the centers where exiles had gathered. Quesada soon entered into a struggle of wills with the legislature, which rejected his aggressive military policies, claiming they violated the new republic's constitutional protections. The House of Representatives opposed the army's unilateral appropriation of food and other necessities of war from local plantations and farms under rebel control, the forced recruitment of soldiers, and what they viewed as the commander's insubordination. Quesada denounced what he saw as unnecessary constitutional limitations that impeded the effective conduct of the war and expressed disdain for lawmakers whom he believed were discrediting and undermining President Céspedes, his brother-in-law. Legislators viewed Quesada's actions as a prelude to military dictatorship, and after numerous disagreements, they dismissed him in December 1869.[3]

Differences over military strategy fueled this internal conflict, but so did ideology. The House of Representatives placed its confidence in a possible U.S.-mediated diplomatic solution with Spain that some hoped would lead to the annexation of Cuba. But after a brief flirtation with annexation, President Céspedes embraced independence and supported Quesada's ambition to defeat Spain on the battlefield.

During his brief stay in Key West, Quesada informed Poyo and others that President Céspedes had commissioned him to raise a large expedition to reinforce the insurgency. Poyo thought Quesada was an able commander with the militant ethos and military skills necessary to defeat Spain and agreed to act as his representative and advocate in Key West. In leading the local Quesadista faction, Poyo associated himself with the radical sector of the Cuban separatist movement. This group insisted on defeating Spain and rejected both a U.S.-mediated diplomatic solution or purchase of Cuba from Spain. This goal required an aggressive, well-conceived, and well-executed military strategy with support from the Cuban people, despite what the elite political and social sectors thought and did. For thirty years these ideas formed the cornerstone of Poyo's revolutionary nationalist political thought.

The Shaping of a Revolutionary

Poyo came of age during the 1840s and 1850s, a time when Cubans were increasingly questioning Spain's firm control over its colony and were experiencing a growing sense of Cuba's distinctive identity as a nation. In the late eighteenth and early nineteenth centuries, Enlightenment ideals and the appearance of cultural and economic societies and colleges produced a growing national identity among elites throughout Latin America. The independence wars (1810–1824) politicized nationalism in the region, but few Cubans supported separatist political movements similar to those on the continent. They mostly experienced nationalism as a cultural phenomenon; seeing themselves as a unique people with a distinct way of being that they expressed through literature, music, art, and Hispanic traditions that had been transfigured by their tropical environment. They also advocated greater autonomy for Cuba within the Spanish empire and embraced a liberal philosophy that embraced representative government, capitalist development, commercial freedom, and the eventual abolition of slavery. During the 1820s through the 1840s, a generation of Cuban leaders and thinkers, including José de la Luz y Caballero and José Antonio Saco, explored the meaning of Cuban identity, influencing subsequent generations.

The next generation (Poyo's generation), like Latin Americans in the 1810s before them, experienced the transformation of cultural nationalism into a powerful force for political separation through armed action. Poyo gradually came to believe that for Cubans to be fully Cuban, they would have to shed their identity as Spanish subjects. Poyo, a third-generation Cuban, lived the everyday existence of a Havana resident earning a modest living as a newspaper proof reader. His sense of place and belonging emerged from walking the narrow cobble-stoned streets; standing near the harbor entrance looking across to the Castillo del Morro, which Spain had built in the sixteenth century to defend Havana; feeling the winds coming off the Florida Straits; and enjoying the palms dotting the urban landscape. This was Cuba, not Spain. Instead of inspiring the island's inhabitants with pride and ensuring their comfort, Spain imposed hardships on her subjects.

Poyo's political discourses as a revolutionary usually expressed an anti-Spanish passion and militancy whose source is complex and not easy to fully know. His modest middle-class background suggests he did not share the feelings of personal privilege denied and the damaged economic possibilities that especially bothered the many disenfranchised non-sugar elites in eastern Cuba who instigated the insurrection in 1868. Poyo's anti-Spanish attitudes may have stemmed in part from personal unresolved anger, perhaps a reaction to an incident in 1854 when police arrested his father, Francisco Antonio Poyo, in Havana for reading in public a political broadside opposing a new conservative captain general. His father's fate is not known, but this experience may have contributed to his intense personal desire to help terminate Spain's rule in Cuba.[4]

Revolutionary leaders are often middle-class individuals with grievances and a sense of moral indignation that can be resolved only through radical action.[5] During the 1880s economic and social conditions confirmed Poyo's view of Cuba as a despotic and corrupt colony that was administered for the benefit of Spaniards. Poyo's rejection of an unjust colonial rule found support in the ideals of Freemasonry, with its distinct certainty of right and wrong, which he subscribed to throughout his adult life.

Masonic secret societies emerged in Great Britain during the early eighteenth century and spread throughout Europe and the Americas. They advocated "truth, morality, tolerance and charitable works." In 1804, the Grand Lodge of Pennsylvania chartered Havana's first lodge, Theological Virtues Lodge No. 103. The Cuban lodge spread the notions of liberty, equality, and fraternity for the free-born. The Grand Lodges of Louisiana and South Carolina also sponsored lodges in Cuba, and in 1821 the first Grand Lodge of Cuba appeared, which chartered sixty-six Masonic lodges across the island within two years.

However, the lodges slowly disappeared when the Spanish monarchy declared Freemasonry outside the law and began relentlessly persecuting Masons. Though the repression eased after 1830, Masonry remained illegal and no formal lodges existed in Cuba despite continued interest. Many joined lodges abroad and participated in organized clandestine movements against Spanish rule, contributing to a conspiratorial tradition that influenced Cuban filibusters such as Narciso López in the United States during the 1840s and 1850s.[6]

The rise of liberals in Spain during the 1850s and 1860s made it possible for Masonic lodges to reorganize in Cuba. The Gran Logia de Colón was formed in 1859 in the eastern region of Cuba, and a second lodge, the Gran Oriente de Cuba y las Antillas (GOCA), was formed in 1862. The conservative members of the Gran Logia supported Spanish rule, but GOCA disseminated sociopolitical goals aimed at promoting democratic and republican values and an independent Cuba. Vicente Antonio de Castro y Bermúdez, a longtime and distinguished Mason, founded GOCA. The clear political goals of the lodge attracted a new generation of Cubans who were tired of Spanish rule and ready to meet secretly and organize conspiracies.

GOCA's activities soon created tension with the Supreme Council in the United States. Although the American council disqualified its charter because the lodge was too political, GOCA remained organized and active. GOCA stood for Cuban sovereignty, freedom to work, religious and individual freedom, the right of association, and social equality. These goals incited condemnation from Spanish authorities, the Catholic Church, and elite members of Cuban society. GOCA members sparked the uprising in Oriente Province in 1868. When pro-Spanish *voluntarios* systematically and violently repressed the uprising in Havana and other cities in early 1869, they especially targeted Masons, who they regarded as some of their most dangerous opponents.[7]

It is not known when Poyo affiliated with Freemasonry, but he was about twenty-five when GOCA formed, and he was likely initiated soon thereafter. Poyo transported his commitment to Masonry to Key West; he and others founded the Dr. Félix Varela Lodge No. 64 there in 1972. Dade Lodge No.14, which had been founded by Anglo-Americans in 1845, sponsored the Félix Varela lodge, which was formed as a Spanish-language lodge for Cuban immigrants. Poyo served in various capacities, including secretary and later as Venerable Maestro, the senior leadership post. Fellow Mason Fernando Figueredo said that Poyo's altruism, persistence, talent, and dedication to the Order of Freemasons earned him a reputation as one of the most esteemed and distinguished Masons in Florida.[8]

The lodge's name indicates the political inclinations of Cuban Masons in Key West. Cuban priest Félix Varela had been an exile in Philadelphia, New York, and Florida since the 1820s. Despite the strong anti-Catholic traditions of Freemasonry, the Cuban masons honored Father Varela for a number of reasons. He ministered among the poor Irish Catholic immigrant community in New York for many years, and his newspaper, *El Habanero*, as well as his other writings publicly advocated Cuba's independence from Spain.[9]

After his death in 1854 at St. Augustine, where he had retired, Varela became a symbol of Cuban independence, especially among exiles in the United States. The devotion to Varela remained so strong that in May 1889, Manuel P. Delgado and Manuel Moreno, representatives to the Florida legislature from Monroe County, petitioned the bishop of St. Augustine to permit the transfer of Valera's remains to Key West. The bishop refused the request but suggested that Key West Cubans could repair the dilapidated chapel in St. Augustine where Valera's remains rested. *El Yara* endorsed the idea saying, "What say the respectable Cubans who 'saw the light' in Lodge Dr. Felix Varela, No. 64?" Whether they followed through is unknown.[10] Like many lodges in Cuba, those in Key West dedicated themselves fully to fighting Spanish rule in their homeland. Poyo used many aspects of Masonry, including its values, its symbolism, and its organization, in his revolutionary activities.

Liberalism and Governance

In addition to Masonic thought, the idealism of the Spanish revolution against Napoleonic occupation (1808–1814) informed Poyo's principles and liberal political instincts. Poyo was well versed in Spanish and Latin American affairs, and the pages of his newspaper frequently referred to these topics as Poyo challenged his readers to consider revolutionary action. King Fernando VII's forced abdication and replacement by Napoleon's brother helped instigate the Latin American wars of independence and inspired Spain's liberal Constitution of 1812, which Poyo considered the highest accomplishment of Spanish liberalism. After Spain's successful rejection of French occupation, Spanish liberals forced a constitutional monarchy on a reluctant Fernando when he returned to the throne.[11] "Recovering its dignity," *El Yara* explained to its readers, "the Spanish nation declared, 'down with absolute power!'"[12]

The Spanish Constitution was perhaps the most democratic of the many revolutionary documents of the era, which included a unicameral Cortes (legislature) with decisive power to make law. Though executive power resided with the king, he could not dissolve the Cortes or prohibit legislation. The Constitution mandated an independent judiciary and a decentralized system based on provincial deputies and elected municipal councils that were designed to replace hereditary elites. It guaranteed a free press, abolished the Inquisition, and restricted or dismantled seigniorial institutions, including tribute from Indians and forced labor in the Americas. All free Spaniards of both hemispheres became citizens of the new nation, a definition that included mestizos, Indians, and free blacks, who received the right to vote without the barriers of literacy or property requirements. Though a complex system of indirect voting ensured certain controls, no other constitution during that era of revolution opened citizenship and political participation to this extent.[13]

This did not last long. At the first opportunity, Fernando VII consolidated conservative support, and in 1814 he ordered the military to overthrow the constitutional regime and restored royal absolutism. Poyo lamented the transitory nature of this great accomplishment and that liberal governance in the Americas failed to materialize. Ultimately, explained *El Yara*, leaders in the Americas took matters into their own hands and rebelled. "Spain was justly punished for its exclusiveness," the paper informed its readers, and only Cuba and Puerto Rico remained firmly in Spanish hands.[14]

Spanish liberals again revolted in 1820, restored the 1812 constitution, and included West Indian representatives in the Cortes, thus providing an opportunity to transform Spain's remaining colonial system. But, *El Yara* declared, "a fatal predestination" seemed to dominate Spanish politics and the forces of reaction quickly returned the country to the "cult of selfishness and injustice."[15] In 1822, pro-absolutist opponents encouraged by Fernando and the church again overthrew the liberals with the support of a French army. Fierce persecution and executions of liberals ensued, and many liberals fled Spain.[16]

As part of the absolutist reaction, Fernando established a military commission in Spain to uncover and persecute liberal dissidents and authorized Captain General Francisco Dionisio Vives to do the same in Cuba, especially targeting separatist elements on the island inspired by the Latin American wars of independence. The commission essentially imposed a state of siege, and it remained in force in Cuba long after it was dismantled in Spain. Among those fleeing Madrid was Father Félix Varela, one of Cuba's representatives to the Cortes, who had argued for the elimination of the slave trade and slavery itself. Varela escaped to Paris, then moved to New York, where he began his calls for Cuba's independence.[17]

Even when in power, Poyo lamented, Spanish liberals took few steps to reform the colonial system and grant Cubans greater political and economic freedoms. After the death of Fernando VII in 1833, moderate liberals returned to office in Spain under a renewed constitutional monarchy, but they appointed General Miguel Tacón, a supporter of absolutism, to govern

Cuba. Tacón arrived in Cuba eager to reassure the peninsular and Cuban slaveholding elite and repress dissident elements on the island. He governed Cuba with an iron hand and did what he could to undermine the influence of Cuba's liberals, but he also oversaw the election of Cuban representatives to a constitutional assembly in Spain.[18]

Much to Tacón's dismay, Cubans elected four liberals, led most prominently by José Antonio Saco, who traveled to Madrid to take his seat. But in 1837 the Cortes voted against applying the new Constitution to Spanish colonies in America and Asia and did not seat its delegates. Instead they imposed *leyes especiales* (special laws), "in keeping with ... local conditions." This continued until the late 1850s and 1860s, when growing Cuban complaints about Spain's repressive rule finally prompted captain generals to support a measure of reform and liberalization.

Cubans formed a Reformist Club and published a newspaper, *El Siglo*, to advocate for greater political autonomy, greater political participation, abolition of the slave trade, and gradual abolition that compensated slaveowners. The Spanish government even invited a delegation of liberal Cuban sugar planters and slaveholders to a "Junta de Información" to discuss reforms in 1867. The delegates drew up a reform agenda that the Spanish government promised to consider, but it never did. Nothing changed, and *El Yara* noted Cubans remained "silenced by the whip of the Captain Generals" until they finally tired of repression and declared independence in October 1868.[19]

Poyo viewed Spain as a nation so traumatized by having lost its entire American mainland empire that its sense of honor necessitated unyielding and brutal control in Cuba. In his view, Spain's generally repressive instincts and lack of moral compass had become intolerable. It failed to recognize there was no honor in suffocating the aspirations of the Cuban people and lacked the wisdom to accept that colonies could not be kept under Spain's thumb in the name of that country's honor and national integrity forever. *El Yara* pointed to Great Britain's 1849 Acts of Navigation, which satisfied Canada's aspirations for free trade, even though Great Britain realized that this would lead eventually to effective independence for the colony. Spain could have avoided the Ten Years' War if it had followed Britain's example and gradually granted Cuba autonomy while maintaining Cubans as friends and allies. That would have demonstrated true national honor and earned the affections of Cubans.[20]

Poyo also highlighted Spain's determination to use political means to reap economic rewards in Cuba at all costs. In the 1880s, Spaniards controlled trade, banking, finance, industry, manufacturing, and property in Cuba. They also dominated the middle class as shopkeepers, merchants, artisans, government bureaucrats, and office clerks.[21] Poyo had no confidence in Spain's ability to rule the island wisely for the benefit of Cubans and felt that its colonial legacy was an island divided into two societies—Spanish and Cuban—that were inexorably locked in economic conflict. Spanish governance benefited the economic interests of Iberians and their Cuban collaborators, not most Cubans. The Spanish were motivated by pure greed, *El Yara* argued, otherwise they would have long before sought some political solution in Cuba.

Even if Cubans could be persuaded to abandon their legitimate political right to independence and overlook the past "horrors" of Spanish domination, their country was economically ruined, *El Yara* declared. The newspaper denounced Spain's destruction of the Cuban economy. This was clearly visible in stagnant production, ruined commerce, unproductive agriculture, and general bankruptcy. Poyo's newspaper characterized Cubans as beasts of burden in a system imposed with the heel of a boot and compared taxation in Cuba to the situation in the British colonies in 1776 that gave impetus to the independence movement. Inordinate taxation in Cuba maintained an immense army and a bloated administrative bureaucracy. There were enough Spanish bureaucrats in Cuba to fill all the government offices in all Latin America, the newspaper claimed. Political and administrative miscalculations and errors had combined with Spain's exploitative spirit to create such extreme economic ruin and disaster that no Spanish government could stem colonial disorder (*desbarajuste colonial*).[22]

Poyo also thought the Catholic Church provided support for colonialism and opposition to liberalism, reform, and Cuba's overall welfare. Bolstered by Masonic thought, Poyo condemned Spain for confusing the rights of the Church with the interests of the clergy, whom he believed represented a powerful corrupting force in both Spain and Cuba. He applauded the instincts of the authors of the Constitution of 1812, who were suspicious of the influences and intentions of the clergy and thus created a strong unicameral legislature composed of "the people."[23]

However, Poyo lamented, even in the Cortes, the clergy successfully defended the interests of the Church by heading off efforts to separate church and state. Delegates who were bishops threatened fellow representatives and government ministers with excommunication if they challenged the Church's authority and prerogatives. "The dominant and arrogant authority" of the Church that was imposed in ancient times, *El Yara* declared, was the same authority that was lording over the Spanish people in the late nineteenth century. "It seems incredible!" Poyo exclaimed.[24] The culture and forces of conservatism operated in similar ways in Cuba, where the Church remained loyal to Spain. Although the clergy never acted with the uniformity *El Yara*'s analysis suggested and many, especially during the Spanish war of independence against France, advocated liberalism within the context of Catholic tradition, Poyo insisted that Catholicism's instincts were inherently reactionary.[25]

This general sentiment marginalized Catholic Cubans in Key West, where a heavily working-class community mostly put religion aside in favor of labor ideologies, including socialism and anarchism. Those inclined toward Christianity worshipped mostly in Protestant churches, especially those in the Episcopalian and Methodist traditions. Cuban pastors led active Protestant congregations and regularly preached anti-Catholic sermons. Enrique Someillán, Juan Bautista Báez, Manuel Deulofeu, and Pedro Duarte were some of the well-known Protestant Cuban pastors of this era. Prominent revolutionary figures Fernando Figueredo and Carlos Manuel de Céspedes, for example, worshiped in the Cuban Episcopal congregation led by Duarte.

Deulofeu believed that evangelical Protestant traditions explained the true origin of the wealth and vigorous intellectual life Germany, Great Britain, and the United States had achieved. The great majority of Key West Cubans, he insisted, would never worship in a Catholic Church as long as bishops and priests in Cuba supported the Spanish government and the Spanish bishops of Oviedo, Valladolid, Madrid, Santiago, Sevilla, Granada, and Zaragosa presided over the commissions that organized the volunteer battalions sent to Cuba. The Cuban Catholic congregation in Key West remained small throughout the nineteenth century. St. Mary's Star of the Sea Catholic Church on Duval Street built a chapel honoring Nuestra Señora de la Caridad. The Sisters of the Holy Names of Jesus and Mary from Canada established a convent and a school for Cuban children, but it attracted only a few students.[26]

The general colonial experience, according to *El Yara*, illustrated the ineffective governance of a dishonorable nation that continually stymied the desires of Cubans to participate in their own destiny and produced an economic system that enriched the few, including mostly Spaniards, leaving Cubans in misery and culturally crippled for generations. Constant and often violent confrontations between absolutist and liberal partisans in Spain and their inability to deliver effective reform in Cuba convinced Poyo that Cubans had to strike out on their own if they ever expected to enjoy enlightened governance and a just distribution of material resources.[27]

Separatism

Poyo's precise intellectual journey to a pro-independence and revolutionary position is not documented, but his actions in Key West during the early 1870s left no doubt that his commitment to a liberal republic founded on democratic principles through revolutionary action was unambiguous. He believed that all nations had the desire to live as independent societies and that when they were blocked, they had the right to demand change and to revolt if necessary. Nothing should deter nations from this goal; to vacillate or retreat was to renounce their very personality and be subjugated to foreign influence. To accept this situation was the ultimate cowardice, something that was akin to suicide. Not defending a nation's right to exist—cost what it may—represented nothing less than "moral death."[28]

At the heart of Poyo's ideological vision were the values and virtues necessary for living in an independent republic. These included knowledge, honesty, equality, and morality. Independence presupposed a yearning for liberty, he believed, which revolutionaries had to properly understand. Ignorance, vice, moral laxity, and demagoguery were the legacies of slavery and repression and were antithetical to liberty. "If you aspire to enjoy a free nation," Poyo concluded, "don't forget that the virtues necessary to melt the shackles of moral slavery are just as important as the sharp blades needed to cut the chains of physical slavery."[29]

Poyo placed great stock in honesty and integrity. His daughter Celia once confided that she had often known her father to have sacks of money for the revolution in his bedroom while he looked for a piece of bread for dinner. She most feared that after such sacrifice he would not live to see an independent Cuba.[30] Many Cubans feared that these virtues could not be found in Hispanic American societies corrupted by centuries of Spanish rule, but

Poyo thought his countrymen perfectly capable of making the adjustments necessary to establish an independent nation guided by republican virtues.

Enshrining Cuba's independence as a nonnegotiable aspect of nationalist thought consumed Poyo during the 1870s. He admired the democratic political values and traditions of the United States, but he also recognized that nation's expansionist instincts. Had it not been for the United States, *El Yara* argued, Cuba would have been liberated in 1823, when Simón Bolívar organized an expedition to free Cuba from Spanish rule that was sponsored by Nueva Granada and Mexico. Before the expedition could depart for Cuba, the United States objected and the plan was abandoned. *El Yara* attributed U.S. opposition to fears that the South American liberator would abolish slavery and to concerns that Cuba might ultimately fall under the influence of Britain or Europe. Many in the United States preferred a weak Spanish sovereignty until annexation of Cuba became a viable policy option.

El Yara further explained that pro-slavery Americans and Narciso López had led an annexation campaign in the late 1840s and 1850s that ultimately failed in the face of strong opposition by northern interests concerned about the proposed division of Cuba into as many as three slave states. After the U.S. Civil War, the impetus for annexation shifted from slaveholders to those who wanted to advance capitalist expansion in Cuba. This group was the dominant annexationist force in the United States for the rest of the century.[31]

Concern about U.S. annexationist aspirations fueled Poyo's interest in a political formula that had been expressed in the 1860s and 1870s by various Caribbean intellectuals, especially Puerto Ricans Ramón E. Betances and Eugenio María Hostos. In 1867 Betances and others issued a manifesto calling on Cubans and Puerto Ricans to join in revolutionary action against Spain and work for a future Antillean confederation that could withstand the annexationist aspirations of many in the United States. During his residence in New York in the early 1870s, Hostos supported the Cuban insurgency and spread his ideas about Antillean unity in *La Voz de la Patria*, a newspaper Cuban exiles founded in 1875 to advance the independence of Cuba. Hostos called for representative democracies in Cuba, Puerto Rico, and the Dominican Republic and the formation of a confederation of the Antilles in collaboration with Latin American nations to create an international power capable of countering U.S. influence in the region. Fully in support, Poyo submitted a list of seventy citizens of Key West committed to these propositions to *La Voz de la Patria*.[32] However, this vision never developed into a practical political movement.

Poyo never doubted that powerful interests in the United States wanted to annex Cuba for their own purposes. This he could not influence, but he regularly challenged the numerous Cubans who routinely urged the United States to purchase the island from Spain or even acquire it by force. For several decades, some Cubans had considered annexation to the United States the only viable alternative to Spanish colonial rule. Initially only the boldest envisioned an independent Cuban republic, and it took the Ten Years' War for the great majority of insurgents to fully abandon the idea of exchanging Spanish colonialism for annexation. As a newcomer to exile politics, Poyo cut his political teeth in the 1870s on the issue of annexation: he opposed exile annexationists in New York who influenced the Cuban insurgent government, supported General Quesada, and led the anti-annexationist campaign in Key West.

When Poyo came to the United States in early 1869, Cuban novelist and longtime exile activist Cirilo Villaverde and his wife Emilia Casanova had already engaged the debate about Cuba's political future. In the 1840s and 1850s, those who favored separation from Spain did not usually draw a sharp distinction between independence and annexation, and most agreed on the legitimacy of both options. Separatists generally admired the United States and most believed that Cuba could prosper well as part of the union. Joining the United States offered protection against a potentially catastrophic slave insurrection, as had occurred in Haiti half a century before. Such an event was a real threat in Cuba in 1812 during the Aponte rebellion. Most exiles in the mid-nineteenth century wished for an eventual abolition of slavery but advocated a gradual process over the course of decades that required the oversight of the United States. They were confident that despite the severe divisions over slavery in the United States, it would find a peaceful and constitutional way to abolish slavery.

Annexationists also considered Cubans incapable of effective democratic rule and looked to the United States to provide an enduring civil society. They pointed to the political instability, civil wars, dictatorships, and economic chaos that enveloped a great deal of Latin America after independence, and they believed that Cubans faced the same challenges. Annexationists often warned that a protracted war of independence threatened to destroy the island's economy and produce dictators and military leaders who would bring tyranny to Cuba.[33]

The idea of an independent republic gained favor among some exiles in the mid-1850s after Narciso López's revolutionary initiatives. His efforts to ignite an annexationist insurrection on the island failed miserably and received little support from the U.S. government, which preferred to acquire Cuba through direct purchase from Spain. Most Cubans viewed the sale of their homeland as anti-democratic since it circumvented popular debate and discussion about the island's future and undermined self-determination. Some even called for independence, criticizing the United States for manipulating the Cuban question for its own reasons and not because of concern for the welfare of Cubans.[34]

Villaverde, who was one of López's strongest supporters, also experienced a change of heart in the mid-1860s (and perhaps before) and called on Cubans to defeat Spain in a popular and self-sufficient war that drew in all sectors of Cuban society, including slaves.[35] This radical idea terminated any possibility of cooperation with annexationists and provoked lively and often vitriolic debates throughout the 1870s. This development fractured insurgent unity and influenced Poyo's thinking about military strategy, democratic aspirations, slavery, race relations, and Cuba's place in the Caribbean and Latin America.

At the start of the war, annexation remained a popular goal among Cuban elites who had abandoned reform and joined the rebellion. Many members of the Cuban Republic in Arms and its representatives in the United States supported the idea. In 1869, wealthy Cuban José Morales Lemus served the Cuban government as chief agent in charge of organizing the exile communities and as diplomatic envoy to gain U.S. support for the insurrection. Wealthy planter Manuel de Aldama and prominent attorney José Antonio Echeverría aided Morales Lemus in New York and Washington, D.C., and were known collectively as the Cuban Junta. In 1870, Morales Lemus died and Aldama replaced him as chief agent and Echeverría as diplomatic envoy. These men followed a long tradition of reformist and annexationist thought, always skeptical of independence as an option. Villaverde characterized these government representatives in exile as aristocrats who were mostly concerned with their own interests and rejected their goal of encouraging the United States to purchase Cuba from Spain. He and his followers founded the mostly working-class Sociedad de Artesanos Cubanos de New York (Cuban Workers' Society of New York) to reject anything less than absolute independence.[36]

In Key West, Poyo sided with Villaverde and convinced the Club Patriótico Cubano to send its monthly contributions to the Sociedad de Artesanos, which supported Manuel de Quesada rather than the official junta. Annexationists in Key West opposed Poyo. Initially Quesada accomplished little, provoking a frustrated and impatient President Céspedes to dispatch Vice-President Francisco Aguilera to facilitate Quesada's expedition. Aguilera urged exiles to set aside their differences and sent representatives to various communities, including Key West, to promote reconciliation. Poyo responded by organizing and leading a new unity association called Asociación Patriótica del Sur in November 1871. In addition, as editor of *El Republicano*, he placed the newspaper at Aguilera's service. But after a brief honeymoon, political infighting returned in Key West. Suspicions and discord also divided exiles in New York, New Orleans, and other cities, paralyzing efforts to send expeditions with weapons and ammunition to Cuba.[37]

At the end of 1871, a desperate President Céspedes recalled Aguilera, fired Aldama and Echeverría and named Quesada to represent the government in exile, urging him to send much-needed war supplies as soon as possible. This action further heightened tensions between the president and the Cuban House of Representatives, which interpreted Quesada's appointment as an effort to gain partisan support in the exile communities and facilitate a much-feared military dictatorship. Finally, in November 1873, Quesada hired the *Virginius* to transport men, weapons, and ammunition to reinforce the insurgent army in Cuba. The Spanish navy captured the ship on the high seas and escorted the vessel to Santiago, where the authorities began a systematic execution of the expeditionary contingent that continued until the U.S. government threatened to intervene and stopped the slaughter. The men and large cache of arms the *Virginius* was carrying never reached the insurgent forces.[38]

In early November, before the culmination of these events, exiles learned that the House of Representatives had removed Céspedes from the presidency on October 27. Even though the action of the legislature was constitutional, Poyo considered this a significant blow to the insurgency. The head of the legislature, Salvador Cisneros Betancourt, became interim president while the government waited for Vice-President Aguilera's return to Cuba to take charge. Cisneros immediately fired Quesada and sent letters to leaders of the exile community, including Poyo, that sought advice about who to name as official government representatives in exile. Although Poyo lamented the actions of the legislature in his response, he did suggest the names of two strong supporters of Céspedes and Quesada to head a new junta in New York, advice he surely knew Cisneros would dismiss out of hand. Poyo informed the Quesada group in New York of his correspondence with Cisneros and promised to find out more about the motives for the "scandalous" removal of the president.[39] Cisneros was certainly not interested in affirming Céspedes's supporters, and he reappointed Aldama and his colleagues, who remained as the government's official representatives for the rest of the war.

Poyo's influence in Key West waned somewhat when the Aldama faction in New York returned to power. In 1874, when popular labor organizer Federico de Armas became Aldama's representative in Key West, he used the leverage of the appointment to displace Poyo as president of the Asociación del Sur and editor of *El Republicano*. Poyo remained intransigent and founded an opposing organization, the Comité Revolucionario Cubano, with the help of a new arrival to Key West, Carlos Manuel de Céspedes y Céspedes.[40]

Céspedes, the son of the former Cuban president, left Cuba shortly after his father's death in a Spanish ambush in March 1874. The House of Representatives had rejected the former president's request to leave Cuba after his removal from office and failed to provide a formal escort for his protection. Resentful that the new Cisneros-led government had not properly protected his father, the younger Céspedes made common cause with Poyo against the Aldama faction in Key West and New York. With annexationists back in positions of influence, Poyo organized the Sociedad Independencia de Cuba and used his platform as reader in the Martínez Ybor factory to urge workers to combat annexation and support independence.[41] Annexationist leaders condemned Poyo's aggressive politics. One critic, alluding to the deep divisions, declared that those who thought Cuba could be happy as an independent nation should live for a time in Key West and would be convinced about the need for annexation.[42]

Despite the damaging ideological divisions, debates about Cuba's political future could not be avoided since they went to the very heart of the rebellion's purpose. Advocates of independence such as Poyo simply could not countenance the possibility of annexation. Poyo insisted unconditionally on Cuban independence achieved through a self-sufficient and uncompromising war against Spanish authority. Poyo's campaign against Aldama's representatives in Key West created controversy, but for him a war that ended in U.S. annexation of Cuba was not a nationalist struggle and annexation had to be prevented at all costs. When the Ten Years' War ended, Poyo maintained his staunchly nationalist posture and never hesitated to confront anyone on this matter.

Social Questions

Economic and social dislocations were perhaps the most dramatic consequences of the Ten Years' War. They disturbed existing arrangements and set in motion a process of slave emancipation that accelerated until final abolition in 1886. Economic distress, particularly in the rural areas, left many without a way to make a living. In addition, labor ideologies gained popularity and Cuba's liberal elites increasingly challenged the Spanish oligarchs who firmly controlled the nation's destiny. Social issues became a central feature of nationalist thought as discussed in the pages of *El Yara*.

Poyo understood the intimate connection between the political and the social. During the 1870s Poyo realized that the exclusive class and racial definitions of national identity that most of Cuba's cultural nationalists advanced worked against independence. Poyo knew that leaders of Latin America's wars of independence had learned very quickly that a successful effort to defeat Spain would mean recruiting free and enslaved Africans, Indians, and mestizos into a unified and effective military force.

Similarly, the fact that Cuba was deeply marked by racial and class divisions meant that it was necessary to build a shared national identity for a coalition of Cubans of all social groups and races. Reformists preferred a compromise arrangement with Spain and annexationists looked to the United States for a political and economic framework capable of providing Cuba with a measure of autonomy, peace, and stability without disturbing the social order. *Independentistas* relied on a heterogeneous Cuban population that was willing to overcome their differences and create new economic and social relationships that would be compatible with a republic.

Poyo believed that Cuba's future as an independent nation would be stillborn without policies that provided economic opportunity and guaranteed political participation for all social sectors. *El Yara* expressed this in terms of the integration of politics and work. In the "old societies," the newspaper explained, "these powerful aspects of the human experience—politics and work—had always been divorced." The privileged castes managed politics while the humble classes provided riches and luxury for the powerful with their labor. This supremacy of the rich continued until the French Encylopedists raised awareness that the humble too had a right to improve their lives and "were equal in the world of humanity." The greatest triumph of the French Revolution, *El Yara* declared, was that it "highlighted and justified" the rights of the working classes.[43]

El Yara informed readers of Poyo's view of the political developments of the last century. Despite the advances in forms of government the Age of Revolution brought, reality did not change and societies remained divided by class. Though constitutional monarchy displaced absolutism in Europe, liberalism atrophied there. In the Americas, "a world of unusual conquests and extraordinary inequality" led to wars dedicated to overturning privilege, and only Cuba and Puerto Rico remained in a colonial system in which exploitation by the masters became even more marked than before the wars. In 1868, Cubans finally rose against colonial rule to eliminate caste differences and unify the nation under the egalitarian principles "of the Nazarene and the liberalism of the French revolution." The desire to create a nation and a spirit of self-preservation inspired Cubans to revolt against Spain. "That is why we are exiles," Poyo concluded.[44]

Well into the Ten Years' War, the fear of slave insurrections that might unleash mayhem and terror remained intact among many liberal cultural nationalists, who still imagined Cuba as a white nation steeped in tropically influenced Hispanic traditions. They were suspicious of a broad-based multiracial popular movement that sought to transform slaves into free citizens, but this was precisely what was needed to break from Spanish control, resist U.S. annexation, and create a unified nation. Villaverde's political group had embraced this view in 1866 and 1867 in their New York newspaper *La Voz de America*, and they influenced Poyo's thinking when he arrived in the United States. Only the immediate abolition of slavery, *La Voz* reasoned, could rally blacks and mulattoes, slave and otherwise, in the numbers necessary to launch an insurrection.⁴⁵ This issue became more urgent after the outbreak of the insurrection in October 1868, but rebel leaders in Cuba moved toward abolition quite hesitantly.

The Constitución de Guáimaro that rebels wrote in April 1869 declared that all Cubans were free, but the newly formed Cuban House of Representatives still feared slave unrest and passed laws to restrain the free movement of slaves and control the emancipation process. Although the same legislature abandoned these laws as unworkable the following year, many white insurgents continued to fear the consequences of a liberation army filled with blacks and mulattos. The percentage of soldiers of color in the rebel army grew, and at the end of the 1870s this group constituted a majority and included many generals and officers. Spain cleverly manipulated the fear of whites that the revolution was deteriorating into a race war, and many whites were convinced to surrender for this reason.⁴⁶

These developments fostered mutual suspicion among blacks and whites in Key West. Though they interacted fluidly, they generally lived in their own neighborhoods, and Cubans of color did not always consider the nationalist agenda to be their highest priority. When Francisco V. Aguilera visited Key West in early 1874, he noticed that few Cubans of color participated in fundraising activities. Aguilera learned that many people of color in Key West questioned whether the revolution served their interests. Many thought that their real revolution would come later, according to Aguilera, "to redeem all the offenses they had suffered under slavery, especially the crimes perpetrated in 1844." This was a reference to the response of Spanish authorities to the purported Escalera slave conspiracy led by free blacks and mulattoes; hundreds were tortured, executed, or deported. Aguilera reassured Afro-Cuban leaders in Key West that the insurgency supported unconditional abolition of slavery and complete racial equality. They responded by hosting a grand banquet to honor the vice-president that Poyo attended.⁴⁷

Taking his cue from Aguilera, Poyo struggled to convince Cubans of color that they could count on Cuban whites to defend their rights in the context of local U.S. politics during the 1870s. The highly politicized Cuban community overwhelmingly supported the Republican Party, the party of Lincoln. The ideals of that party seemed more in tune with pro-independence and anti-slavery rebel politics than the ideas of the Democratic Party, especially in the South, where the Democrats were associated with slavery and racism. When

Cubans arrived in significant numbers in the early 1870s, they entered a community deeply engaged in post–Civil War Reconstruction politics. Until the end of Reconstruction in 1876, Republicans in Florida and other southern states relied on former slaves and carpetbaggers from the north, and some white southerners known as scalawags, to consolidate their control. In Key West this included organizing black immigrants from the Bahamas as well as white and black Cubans, but the racial inflections of U.S. politics divided Cubans.

Early in 1876, Aldama used his influence as head of the Cuban junta in New York to encourage Cubans to vote for the Democratic candidate for president and denounced President Ulysses Grant and the Republican administration for doing nothing to help the Cuban cause. Some in Key West heeded his advice and created a Club Democrático Cubano (Cuban Democratic Club), but most Cubans remained Republican and vowed never to support the openly racist southern Democrats. Even Cubans who were strong supporters of Aldama in Key West refused to obey the directive, which they knew hurt the interests of their compatriots of color and alienated them from Cuban revolutionary politics.[48]

Enrique Carrero, one of Poyo's colleagues, celebrated the contribution of the highly organized black community to the revolutionary movement, pointing out their love for learning and progress. Their school, Colegio Unificación, prepared blacks to take their place as free citizens in an independent Cuba. To make their point even stronger, Key West annexationists and pro-independence leaders dissolved the Asociación del Sur and replaced it with a new association called Constitución de Guáimaro that was led by Antonio Rios, who served as president, and Carlos Borrego, a black community leader, who served as vice-president. In this way Key West's separatist community emphasized their support for a constitution that guaranteed full citizenship to all Cubans.[49]

Poyo actively supported minority rights. He pointed out the importance of constitutional protections in a liberal republic. Democracy required majority rule, Poyo noted, but only explicit constitutional protections ensured the rights of minorities.[50] Firsthand observations of southern politics during the mid-1870s reminded him that even with rights fully enshrined in a constitution, black minorities could be forcibly repressed by a determined white majority. In November 1876, Poyo founded a new (though short-lived) newspaper, *La Igualdad* (Equality), whose title suggested his commitment to equal rights for all citizens. At that moment, when Democrats were poised to retake control of the U.S. South, Poyo and others understood the plight of blacks and opposed any tampering with the Cuban constitution that diluted their rights as equal citizens.

If Key West was to be viable as a revolutionary center, Poyo and other non-black revolutionary leaders would need to convince Afro-Cubans that they faced a better future in an independent Cuba than one controlled by the Spanish. It was thus necessary for them to counter frequent Spanish claims of racial benevolence. For example, the outcome of the U.S. Civil War had inspired the creation of a Spanish Abolitionist Society in 1865 that gained considerable support on the peninsula, especially among liberal politicians. In 1870, the Spanish liberal government that gained power in 1868 enacted the Moret Law, a free-birth law for its colonies that initiated gradual emancipation. All slaves born after September 17, 1868; slaves who served in the Spanish army; slaves over the age of sixty; and government-owned slaves received their freedom. Owners received a small compensation for each slave that was freed. The process accelerated in 1880 with another law approved in the Spanish Cortes that abolished slavery, but provided eight years of *patronato* (tutelage) for former slaves.[51] The 1880 law led to full emancipation in 1886, but Poyo assured blacks that despite this legislation, their situation had changed little. He asked Cubans of color to consider the magnitude of the mistreatment they had endured under Spanish colonial despotism, including the "horrible hecatomb of 1844," when Captain General Leopoldo O'Donnell tried to destroy an emerging leadership in the Afro-Cuban community; this was a response to the Escalera conspiracy. He compared this to the "distinctions meritorious men of color have received from us, during the Ten Years' War, in the émigré communities, and everywhere." Poyo urged blacks to avenge the ignominious past, break ties with Spain, and support an independent Cuban nation.[52]

Overall, however, like most white nationalists, Poyo did not often raise sensitive and potentially divisive race issues. He assumed that the process of nation building would eventually produce an integrated Cuban nationality. Better to deemphasize a subject that Spain had cleverly and effectively used during the Ten Years' War to divide the insurgency and instead express a discourse of unity that characterized all Cubans as slaves. Poyo's argument was that all Cubans constituted the nation and were obliged to support the revolutionary movement.[53]

Poyo more frequently and eagerly engaged the problem of class, proposing that a successful republic would provide opportunities for Cuba's multiracial proletarian workers. Although artisan associations existed in Cuba during the 1840s and 1850s, a proletariat comprised of cigar workers did not appear with a distinct identity until the 1860s. This coincided with the shift in Spain's policies that was designed to attract the alienated liberal elites who had flirted with the annexationist politics of the late 1840s and 1850s. Reforms of the 1860s provided greater freedom of association and press, producing many organizations and newspapers that encouraged public discussion of political, economic, and social matters. Saturnino Martínez's *La Aurora* successfully promoted artisan organizations, education, and the *lectura*. The newspaper attracted a large following, especially in western Cuba.[54]

Opposition to this liberalization materialized among conservative Spanish loyalists in Cuba. In 1866, this contingent forced a reversal of some policies, including the abolition of the *lectura*.[55] From New York, *La Voz de America* called on workers to resist the ban: "No! Obedience in this case is humiliation.... Do not obey." It told workers to gather in private places to read and to defend themselves and even rebel if they were challenged.[56] *La Voz* urged cigar workers, who were emigrating to the United States in large numbers, to remain in Cuba and struggle against Spanish colonialism. "What we advise the tobacco workers," the newspaper concluded, "applies equally to all the artisans of our country."[57]

Fifteen years later, in this same vein, *El Yara* directly addressed tobacco workers in Cuba, many of whom regularly migrated back and forth between Key West and Havana looking for work. The newspaper complained of a great apathy among the island's tobacco workers; they did not fully recognize the extent to which Spanish policies negatively affected the working class, especially in the tobacco industry. Though the cigar industry was one of Cuba's great resources, *El Yara* charged that Spanish mismanagement had reduced the country to exporting its best tobacco leaf to growing Cuban manufacturing centers such as Key West and New York. Furthermore, the cigar industry reserved most jobs for Spanish and Chinese workers, who the newspaper noted with some exaggeration, dominated trade and commerce in Havana, while Cuban cigar makers routinely left Havana and Vuelta Abajo, Cuba's most important tobacco-growing district, for the United States. They left for many reasons, some natural and some caused by Spain's imperial policies. Droughts could not be controlled, but Spain's "barbarous" taxes and attempts to pit black against white and Cuban against Spaniard were largely responsible for mass outmigration of skilled workers.

Ultimately, *El Yara* declared, only the eviction of Spain could remedy these ills, and the newspaper remained confident that in time workers would join the revolutionary effort: "The mass that represents an important segment of the Cuban nation cannot remain indifferent to the cause of their country's regeneration."[58] Poyo regularly reaffirmed his belief that the working class could be counted on to take disinterested action for patriotic causes, while the rich usually acted in their own interest. In 1886, for example, *El Yara* reported on the reluctance of wealthy Cuban liberals in Paris to contribute to a mausoleum for José de la Luz y Caballero, who was considered a foundational educator and early advocate of liberalism in Cuba. Their ostentation and wealth was notorious, *El Yara* declared. They saw themselves as the equals of landed aristocrats, but they contributed only 589 francs: "How poor these rich [¡Que ricos tan pobres!]." In contrast, Juan Gualberto Gómez, a mulatto activist who had been deported to Madrid with few resources, contributed as much as the rich in Paris. "What a contrast! How rich this poor man! [¡Que pobre tan rico!]."[59]

Autonomy

On February 10, 1878, the insurgent government signed the Zanjón Pact with Captain General Arsenio Martínez Campos. During the previous two years under his leadership the Spanish army had slowly worn Cubans down in a war of attrition and had isolated them in the eastern portions of the island. Cubans accepted Spain's promises of autonomy as an alternative to their increasingly untenable situation, but the Spaniards did not commit to the immediate abolition of slavery. For Cuban liberals, autonomy meant at the very least a legislative body in Cuba that would be empowered to develop economic and social policies in coordination with Spanish officials, but instead the colony gained only the right to send representatives to the Spanish Cortes. The powerful captain general remained in charge of day-to-day governance.

Despite their disappointment, liberals founded the Partido Liberal Autonomista (Autonomist Liberal Party), contested elections, sent delegates to the Cortes, and lobbied for an eventual home rule arrangement. The conservative pro-Spanish Partido Unión Constitucional (Constitutional Union Party) defended the continuation of Spanish supremacy. The electoral laws written in Spain gave conservatives a decided edge, and they won elections handily; sixteen conservative unionists and only six liberal autonomists were elected to represent Cuba in Madrid. As a minority within the Cuban delegation and a miniscule element within the Cortes, Autonomists exerted little influence in the 1880s.[60]

Immediately after the Zanjón Pact was signed, Poyo launched a decade-long propaganda assault on the notion of political autonomy for Cuba, which he thought was a serious threat to independence. He characterized the new electoral system as an illegitimate farce that had nothing to do with the interests of the vast majority of Cubans who were excluded from participation. During the 1880s, many nationalists flirted with the new political system and considered Autonomists to be patriotic Cubans who approached problems with different strategies. Poyo considered autonomists little better than Spanish conservatives and made clear his contempt for those who accepted the Zanjón Pact, especially the insurgent "traitors" who had signed the document.

When Antonio Zambrana, one of the authors of the Constitución de Guáimaro and a prominent leader of the insurgent legislature during the Ten Years' War, became an Autonomist in the late 1880s and declared that Cubans enjoyed freedom under Spanish rule, *El Yara* responded with outrage. It wondered whether Zambrana thought Cubans were "imbeciles" who would accept such a fabulous story and castigated him for his sad history of changing positions. The newspaper also reminded readers that Zambrana had once referred to Carlos Manuel de Céspedes as nothing more than *un abogado de manigua* (a country lawyer), a deep insult to the memory of Cuba's most honored martyr.[61]

Conservatives and Autonomists, *El Yara* declared, competed in Cuba, not for supreme power but for the ability to manipulate (*mangoneo*) local administration. Defending Spanish interests, Conservatives enjoyed all the advantages and used their significant resources to undermine Autonomists, who attempted without success to gain the upper hand. All the Autonomists gained for their efforts was the ability to lament their own situation and the difficult situation of the country. Conservatives were little more than the master who assaulted Autonomist slaves, who simply endured and begged for their rights.[62]

The goals of the Autonomists, *El Yara* argued, were shameful, including their plans for a Cuban legislature, or Cámara Insular. Under this scheme a Council of Government (Consejo de Gobierno) that would be named and presided over by the Spanish captain general would oversee an assembly composed of representatives of the various Cuban provinces. This, the newspaper declared, offered little improvement over existing conditions, especially since the proposal gave the captain general and the Consejo de Gobierno the power to veto the Cámara's legislative decisions. The unreliable and untrustworthy Autonomists pursued a limited participatory system that ensured their control of an assembly they could use to negotiate for their policies with the captain general, leaving most Cubans on their own.[63]

El Yara also pointed out that the Spanish constitution of 1874 promised a free press in Spain, but Cuban editors were required to submit their published newspapers to government officials (*fiscal de imprenta*) for inspection; these officials often confiscated entire editions or simply initiated judicial proceedings against newspaper publishers who printed controversial views. Whether the publishers were convicted or not, the newspapers suffered severe economic consequences that produced a culture of self-censorship. *El Yara* also denounced limits on freedom of association, noting that meetings of four individuals or more required a license.[64]

The class privilege and pretensions of Autonomists especially bothered Poyo. He believed that reformist elites could not be counted on to advance the interests of ordinary Cubans. Although Poyo recognized many Autonomist leaders as distinguished and accomplished individuals, he saw them as a class apart, disconnected from the economic and social realities of common people; he hardly considered them Cubans at all. He insisted that although Autonomists were Cubans in their private lives, they were clearly Spaniards in every other way and that this made them enemies of most Cubans, especially separatists. Autonomists could never effectively represent the Cuban people because their very existence required the goodwill and permission of the Spanish government. Only the separatist party represented the interests of the Cuban people. History taught and daily practice confirmed, *El Yara* declared, that "people cannot expect economic and political benefits of any kind they do not conquer for themselves."[65]

Autonomists made little headway in their efforts to change Cuba in the 1880s, and many became disenchanted, especially after their constant electoral defeats. In 1886, Poyo reprinted an article from the liberal Havana newspaper *Diario de la Tarde* that called for Cubans to boycott the inherently unfair elections. He congratulated the newspaper for its forthright stand but lamented that when the Autonomists found themselves in such a difficult predicament they had little choice but to embrace prudent abstention, since they had rejected rebellion.[66]

When Autonomists failed to produce modest reforms through the rigged electoral system orchestrated by the Spanish government, all they could do was complain. Calling them *llorones* (crybabies), *El Yara* often reprinted portions of speeches of distinguished Autonomist leaders punctuated with editorial comments and biting sarcasm. The newspaper characterized Antonio Govín as discouraged and as a man who had little faith that his political ideals would triumph. It described Rafael Montoro as a correct and elegant and enthusiastic speaker, a doctrinaire person who was full of theories, but it claimed that his pronunciation of the Spanish language, his tastes, his education, and his cultivated preferences deprived him of any real understanding of Cuba's needs. And it characterized Carlos Saladrigas's words as an eloquent but discouraging patchwork of complaints. Although they confirmed his reputation as an orator, his "excellent and graphic portrait of the country's bleak situation, and his lack of confidence in its future" always concluded by ignoring the premise and attempting to whip up the enthusiasm of his listeners.[67]

El Yara's assaults on the Autonomists appeared in virtually every issue in the 1880s. "We have begged enough, asked enough, and been mocked enough since 1868," the newspaper declared. Also mocked were those who became Autonomists after the Zanjón Pact in the naïve belief that they could achieve effective political representation. *El Yara* called on Cubans to forget the "utopian theories of impossible evolutions" that only served to benefit Spanish control.[68] "There is only one path to salvation," the newspaper insisted: "the establishment of a Cuban Republic where Cubans and Spaniards find peace, work, and progress."[69]

In the 1870s, Poyo learned the rudiments of revolutionary work as he supported the insurgent army in Cuba through his newspaper and through his activism in the United States. He emerged during this decade as the ideologue of Key West's revolutionary community. He defined nationalism in only one way: Cuba's absolute independence. His nationalism included a social dimension that called for the abolition of slavery, the integration of people of color into Cuban society and identity, and the empowerment of the working classes by encouraging them to organize and demand their rights. He also consistently argued for a revolutionary rather than an evolutionary end to Spanish colonialism. Spain had demonstrated little interest in moving toward an Autonomist solution during the first half of the nineteenth century, and after the outbreak of the Ten Years' War, Poyo rejected reforms as irrelevant.

Cuba's pacification after 1880 did not change his mind. Autonomy would never work because of the configuration of established interests in Spain and in Cuba. Poyo also recognized the desire of some in the United States to annex the island and the desire of a minority of Cubans with political influence and diplomatic connections to have this happen. He remained vigilant and attacked annexation whenever it surfaced in public discourse. *El Yara* disseminated these messages throughout the exile communities and in Cuba, where the newspaper gained a reputation as a militant nationalist and popular voice in support of immediate insurrection.

3

REVOLUTION

Liberty is not requested, it is fought for!
El Yara, 1881

On March 11, 1878, José D. Poyo, Carlos Manuel Céspedes y Céspedes, son of Cuba's first president, and Martín Herrera organized a mass meeting in Key West to protest the Zanjón Pact. A revolutionary committee was organized at the meeting. Céspedes was elected as president and Poyo as secretary.[1] This reaffirmation of revolution occurred as Miguel de Aldama and the other official representatives in exile of the defunct government in arms accepted the peace treaty and prepared to return to Cuba. The spirits of the exile activists in Key West and New York took flight several days later, when General Antonio Maceo met with General Arsenio Martínez Campos of the Spanish forces to discuss the terms of the pact. Instead, Maceo rejected the treaty altogether, reaffirmed the insurrectionists' goals of independence and the abolition of slavery and continued the fight. The meeting became known as the Protesta de Baraguá.

Antonio Maceo was born in Santiago de Cuba in 1845 to a small landowning free couple of color. He joined the insurrection in 1868 as a soldier, but in just weeks his bold battlefield actions and leadership earned him a promotion to lieutenant. Maceo learned guerrilla tactics and soon became the most feared of the Cuban warriors under the command of General Máximo Gómez. The general, who was originally from the Dominican Republic, gained combat experience in the Spanish army when it quelled a Haitian invasion of his country in 1855. In 1875, with Brigadier General Maceo by his side, Gómez organized an offensive into Cuban sugar country in Las Villas and Havana, but his advance stalled in the face of internal divisions among insurgents that in part were related to racial concerns that paralyzed military operations and eventually contributed to the Zanjón Pact. Both of these men were of humble origins, were unrepentant insurgents, and were fixated on continuing the fight. Both also emerged from the war as prestigious commanders who were widely admired among Cuba's popular classes.[2]

The surviving white elites who had initiated the war in 1868 had for the most part returned to the Spanish fold, leaving the field to revolutionary activists with a strong inclusive vision, including Poyo in Key West. In April 1878, in probably his first communication with Maceo, Poyo congratulated him for his bold stance and expressed the hope that rebellion would regain strength with the traitors out of the way. Key West intended to support the liberating army, he said, and his "Cuban-radical newspaper," *El Patriota*, was fully at his disposal.[3]

Poyo's optimism proved unfounded. In June the new provisional government created at the Protesta de Baraguá also surrendered and the remaining forces in the field gave up the fight. But this second defeat did not discourage Key West revolutionaries any more than the Zanjón Pact had.[4] Poyo characterized the Ten Years' War as simply the first phase of an extended struggle for independence. The "soldiers of liberty" had capitulated but remained undefeated, he claimed. They returned to their homes to reflect, cure their wounds, recover their strength, and wait for another chance to "throw themselves into the unequal fight."[5]

Radicalization

Throughout the 1880s, Cubans in Key West debated the question of how to revive the rebellion. They routinely urged new strategies and tactics when previous ones seemed unworkable. After the Zanjón Pact, major insurgent initiatives on the island seemed unlikely since most of the important leaders were dead, exiled, or resigned to working for autonomist rule. Key West leaders believed that new efforts would have to originate from outside Cuba, and they remembered Narciso López's bold attempts in the late 1840s to incite insurrection. Like López, they were men of action, committed to insurrection in the immediate future. Achieving this goal required audacious and courageous men who were capable of inspiring the Cuban people to undertake concrete acts of rebellion, not timid elites and intellectuals interested in writing, persuading, and waiting. Though few in Cuba had supported

Figure 3. The leading exile newspapers of the 1890s represented a variety of political views. *El Yara, Patria,* and *El Porvenir* were the most widely read and most respected. From Guillermo de Zéndegui, *Ambito de Martí* (Havana: P. Fernández y Cia, 1954).

López, many exiles believed that this was because his military contingent was mostly American filibusters and because of his annexationist politics. A nationalist, self-determinist, and fully Cuban initiative, they believed, would fare differently.

In 1880, the last insurgent newspaper in New York, *La Independencia,* ceased publishing, leaving *El Yara* as the only printed source that was still calling for revolution. Poyo emerged as the most recognized revolutionary figure in Key West because of his consistent and unwavering commitment to action. His advice was much respected because of his meticulous and methodical style.[6] Poyo knew that interesting the Cuban people in another insurgency would not be easy, but he was determined to try. He thought Cubans would not tolerate the continuing tyranny of the postwar era for long. "One would have had to be blind not to understand," he wrote, that "the promises of letting bygones be bygones and seeking reconciliation between [Spanish] *victors* and the *undefeated* [Cubans] would soon collapse." The devastation created by the war and Spain's continuing policies of domination and assertions of supremacy could not defeat the sense of worth and dignity Cubans had acquired in their bruising battles for freedom. The old master would never accommodate the demands of the now "grown and mature servant."[7] Revolution would occur, Poyo knew, but not without instigation, leadership, strategizing, and determination. "No, Cubans, liberty is not requested, it is fought for," he declared in 1881.[8] The only way for the Cuban people to achieve independence was through armed revolution, cost what it may. Cubans had to reject the promises of the autonomists, which always looked to some future time instead of delivering in the present. "Down with the Spanish government! Forward the revolution!" Poyo wrote.[9]

During the Ten Years' War, the south Florida Cuban community became known as the *baluarte cubano* (Cuban bulwark), a term that described the community's coherence as revolutionaries and the influence that stemmed from its militancy and the willingness of cigar workers and manufacturers to commit resources to the cause. Poyo used the image of the *baluarte* to inspire and exhort Key West to revolution, which required first of all reorganizing the community in new ways. He and his colleagues believed that properly organized, determined, and experienced military leaders who had learned from the mistakes of the past and had full confidence in the Cuban people could revolutionize the island.

Poyo and other nationalist leaders had gained valuable experience about raising money and organizing expeditions during the Ten Years' War. During the war, news would spread quickly in the neighborhoods and factories when prominent revolutionary figures arrived. Welcoming contingents would gather at the docks to greet the visitors and parade through the streets to San Carlos Institute for a ceremony, accompanied by the Libertad band. After meetings with local political leaders, the visitors would usually tour cigar factories and political clubs, where they exhorted people to contribute funds to revolutionary efforts. Receptions in the large factories with two to five hundred workers could be breathtaking as workers welcomed visitors with the sound of their *chavetas* (tobacco knifes) hitting the top of the wooden work tables in unison. The best patriotic speeches opened pockets, and Cubans gave generously from their hard-earned wages, routinely contributing from a few thousand to tens of thousands of dollars. The visits generally lasted a few days, but sometimes they continued for several weeks, during which the visiting revolutionaries raised nationalist fervor in the community and strengthened the political reputations of the local leaders.

In early 1869, Ambrosio Valiente, representing the insurgent government, was the first to organize support in Key West. After his visit, a company of forty-two men, the Rifleros de la Habana, left for Nassau and joined the *Salvador* expedition commanded by Rafael de Quesada. Manuel de Quesada visited in 1870 and 1874. In 1871, José María Izaguirre arrived on a mission from Vice-President Francisco V. Aguilera. Later that year, Carlos García, a controversial bandit-turned-commander appeared with funds from the New York junta to outfit an expedition to Vuelta Abajo. Soon after that, insurgent Melchor Aguero came to raise money for a new expedition. In 1872, Thomas Jordan, a well-known American general who was the former chief of staff of the insurgent army, visited Key West. Also in 1872, General Bernabé Varona received a warm welcome in Key West; later in the year, he lost his life commanding the ill-fated *Virginius* expedition. Vice-President Aguilera visited in 1874. More revolutionaries came to Key West, including Colonel Fernando López de Queralta and Commander Pio Rosado, all determined to do something to defeat Spain. In July 1877, General Julio Sanguily and his brother Colonel Manuel Sanguily also came to raise funds.[10] Most of these revolutionary figures received resources and left with a high regard for the intensity and effectiveness of this community's support for the independence cause.

Maintaining the revolutionary infrastructure was not always easy, and the means of doing so changed in response to shifts in ideology and strategy. Poyo believed that the new circumstances in 1878 required the building of a more secretive revolutionary operation, one that could consolidate the town's decade-long militant tradition, would ensure that the leadership would be stable, would have a long view of the task ahead and would be willing to rethink and redirect the movement whenever necessary. On August 4, he invited five friends to his home and proposed a charter for a clandestine organization called Orden Cosmopolita del Sol (Cosmopolitan Order of the Sun), which was committed to propagating the principles of "Liberty, Fraternity and Union." They discussed the revolutionary mission, approved the constitution and bylaws, and made a solemn vow to observe the principles of the order.

The next evening at least four others joined them, and they formally founded what became known simply as Orden Del Sol. Each member selected a secret name; Poyo's was Pollo. The group elected officers, including Poyo as president. Between meetings, a steering committee directed secret activities of the full membership, which grew to thirty-seven individuals in 1883 including Poyo's two future sons-in-law. The secretiveness of the order and its use of aliases, symbols, insignias, and ritualized meetings were reminiscent of the methods of Masonic lodges. These customs not only created a brotherhood of like-minded revolutionaries, but also made infiltration difficult by spies from the Spanish consul.[11]

Poyo secured a measure of political cover for his activities when he became consul for Peru in Key West. This appointment stemmed from the visit to Key West in February 1878 of Leoncio Prado, son of Peru's president. Prado admired Cuba's struggle against Spain, and in late 1876, he spearheaded the hijacking of the Spanish passenger steamer *Moctezuma*, which he proposed to convert into a gunboat to harass Spanish shipping vessels in the Caribbean.[12] Prado's agents in New York, who were seeking funds to convert the ship into a war vessel, asked Poyo to serve as their representative in Key West.[13] He agreed to do so, but in February 1877, the Spanish naval ship *Juan Jorge* found the *Moctezuma*, which had been renamed the *Céspedes*, on the Honduran coast. Unable to escape, Prado and his crew disappeared into the brush, leaving the *Céspedes* in flames.

That same month, Cuban authorities capitulated at Zanjón, and Prado made his way to Key West. He vowed to raise money to reignite the rebellion and recruited Poyo as his local agent, promising him an appointment as Peruvian consul.[14] On November 23, 1878, the U.S. State Department received notice of Poyo's appointment as the Peruvian consul in Key West, and throughout the 1880s, this position offered him the partial protection of the Peruvian flag.[15] Despite constant complaints from the Spanish consul, Poyo only occasionally experienced threats of arrest and legal complications from U.S. authorities.

Two men of particular significance emerged with Poyo as the primary nationalist leaders in Key West. José Francisco Lamadriz and his wife Rosario arrived from New York in late 1878, where Lamadriz had resided as an exile for many years. Born in Havana in 1814, Lamadriz was among the first generation of exiled separatist activists. During the Ten Years' War, he was associated with the Villaverde faction in New York. He enjoyed tremendous prestige as a revolutionary, and Key West received him with great acclaim.[16]

Fernando Figueredo Socarrás arrived in 1881 with his wife Juana and family. Born of two prominent Camagueyano families in 1846, Figueredo attended university in the United States and returned to Cuba to fight in the Ten Years' War. Figueredo had a distinguished military career. He had served as secretary to President Céspedes, as chief of staff to General Manuel de Jesús Calvar, as a delegate to the rebel legislature, and as a comrade of Antonio Maceo at the Protesta de Baraguá. In 1878, he and a large group of Figueredo and Socarrás family members sought refuge first in the Dominican Republic and then in Key West, where Fernando worked as bookkeeper in cigar factories and pursued a career in local Key West politics. The death of many comrades in the frightful war, who often fought *al machete* (with machetes), inspired him to present a series of highly attended lectures about the conflict at San Carlos Institute that were later published as *La Revolución de Yara*, one of the first and classic accounts of the war.[17]

Lamadriz, Poyo, and Figueredo experienced the Ten Years' war in New York, Key West, and Cuba, respectively, and the diversity of their experiences with the rebellion prepared them for a decade-long collaboration as the ruling triumvirate of the Key West revolutionary community. Lamadriz generally played the role of senior statesman; Figueredo became the intermediary between the local Cuban and Florida political establishments; and Poyo was the ideologue and practical revolutionary activist. Together they strategized and maintained the community's thinking about the best way to revolutionize Cuba.

Poyo's rationale for insurrection became increasingly radical during the decade. "Before the cold and calculating Reason of State," he wrote in 1884, "the politics of sentiment is a dead letter." The idea of Reason of State, originally introduced by Niccolo Machiavelli in late-sixteenth-century Italy, justified advancing state interests without consideration for religious or moral constraints. The Reason of State constitutes "the supreme law of modern politics," Poyo declared, and "principles, men, morality, and everything, is subordinated to its power." "Each person for himself," he argued, "or he perishes."[18]

Poyo believed Spain used the concept of Reason of State to justify its policies of self-interest, and he believed that these policies had to be confronted with similar determination. Rights in the modern age had to be achieved through force; nothing else would succeed. Only through a commitment to self-determination and resistance, without waiting for the intervention of foreigners, could the Cuban victims of oppression establish their rights. "The victim is obliged to annihilate the victimizer, no matter how," or join him in the rubble trying, he declared. Poyo did not think anyone had the right to condemn a people that used all the means at their disposal to overcome oppression, especially if no one offered a helping hand. Since those who used Reason of State to justify their acts had no heart or sentiment, those fighting for their rights had to proceed in a similar fashion.[19] Because the struggle was so unequal, Cubans had a legitimate right to consider all tactics and strategies in their struggle to destroy Spanish colonialism.

Poyo also believed that Key West's small Cuban community was fully capable of nurturing and instigating revolution. Skeptics saw revolution as an overwhelming task that required more resources than the community could muster, but Poyo believed that all they needed was sufficient resources to transport and support the most prominent and experienced chieftains for a short period while they recruited an army.[20] During the Ten Years' War, Cuba's army fought a well-supplied and well-armed enemy for long and difficult periods without much support from the outside. If Cubans could do that then, they could do much more in the future with first-rate military leaders who had already been tested in battle.

This thinking relied on a belief that Cuba's unstable rural districts were ready for revolution, which was not unrealistic. A significant portion of the sugar plantations were in ruins or were bankrupt, and their recovery was undermined by a decline in sugar prices throughout the 1880s as European production of beet sugar increasingly competed with cane sugar. The efficiencies needed to compete with European sugar required capital investments in new machinery that many Cuban producers simply could not afford. Cuba's share of the sugar market declined, businesses closed, banks failed, and unemployment increased.

Furthermore, in 1880 the *patronato* accelerated the emancipation process, and over 100,000 slaves gained their freedom in the period before final abolition in 1886. These former slaves began their lives as free citizens in a Cuba that was ill-prepared to absorb them economically. The economic and social dislocations, which the political system managed poorly, produced many disaffected people—black and white alike—who had limited opportunities and strong anti-Spanish attitudes. Many turned to banditry, including veterans of the war of independence. Groups of bandits operated with impunity in regions where they focused their attentions on large landholders that benefited from the colonial state.[21] Some justified their activities in the name of "Cuba Libre," while others became bandits simply to make a living.[22] Poyo believed that it was the common people in Cuba's rural areas and small towns that had the most revolutionary potential and that if properly encouraged and organized they would provide the spark of insurrection.

Poyo was confident that even if military leaders did not spark an immediate large-scale revolution, they could conduct well-conceived guerrilla operations, especially if they were supported by new technologies of warfare. In February 1884, an inflammatory and controversial article publicly associated Poyo with a new and radical approach to fighting the Spanish. *El Yara* declared that although Cubans had launched a sustained war against Spain in 1868 with thousands of men armed mostly with machetes, now the approach had to be different. Poyo argued for a kind of "scientific war" in which armed fighters used the latest technologies to disrupt daily life on the island. Just a few men with the aid of dynamite, he argued, could destroy entire Spanish military contingents or naval vessels. "We had nothing like that during the Ten Years' War," Poyo noted. "The campaign of 84 will be decisive since the Spanish government lacks the strength to resist the system of warfare we are about to launch."[23]

A critical component of this strategy included establishing insurgent cells on the island with reliable supply lines abroad that had the ability to provide ammunition and explosives for specific missions. Tactics would include burning sugar fields and mills, raising money by kidnapping and holding prominent supporters of the colonial regime for ransom, and even destroying offices and public buildings associated with Spanish rule.[24] These small groups of insurgents would create havoc, deepen general discontent, and prepare the way for prominent military leaders such as Gómez and Maceo.

Poyo, Figueredo, and others helped organize a special revolutionary cell known as the Nihilistas Ubiquitarios Cubanos de Key West (Ubiquitous Cuban Nihilists of Key West) to take charge of organizing many of these activities. Similar clubs existed in New York, New Orleans, and other cities. Federico Gil Marrero headed the Key West cell, which included cigar manufacturers Cayetano Soria and Enrique Canals, labor leader Manuel M. Escassi, Orden del Sol member Manuel Cordero, and several others. Public notice of this strategy first came to light in *El Ubiquitario*, a newspaper issued by the nihilist organization's central committee in November 1883. The newspaper, which was published to coincide with the arrival in Cuba of a new captain general from Spain, informed the new ruler that Cubans were determined to be free, "cost what it may."[25]

In the 1870s and 1880s, revolutionary groups throughout the western world, especially in Russia, embraced the term nihilism to signal their commitment to unorthodox armed action; the term in this context had nothing to do with the philosophical nihilism of later years. Cuban nihilists embraced the term in this spirit and *El Ubiquitario* put officials in Cuba on notice that they would be everywhere (ubiquitous) until Spain surrendered the island. It demanded Spanish withdrawal from Cuba within one year, including surrendering all public properties without any claim to indemnification; the release of all political prisoners; and recognition of Cuba's national sovereignty.[26]

The Nihilistas Ubiquitarios Cubanos de Key West also announced the existence of an affiliated club in Havana that was waiting for a signal to unleash the destructive work. "Cubans, the hour has sounded," declared *El Ubiquitario*. Club members planned to use dynamite to destroy their enemies "in their entrenchments, in their camps, in their stores, in their houses, in their palaces; while dining, sleeping, working, during leisurely walks, resting; basically, wherever they can be attacked." These tactics mirrored the actions of the Spanish, the newspaper claimed, and club members encouraged their compatriots to launch assaults on their oppressors everywhere, promising that if they did so, they would soon secure their nation.[27]

The Havana cell organized other clubs that were capable of launching attacks on Cuban sugar wealth especially in Güines, Madruga, Jaruco, and other small towns south of Havana. On December 9, 1883, the Spanish consul in Key West reported that insurgents had bribed customs officials in Havana and unloaded several boxes of dynamite hidden in barrels of thread.[28] In May 1884, Poyo wrote to a sympathetic customs agent at the port of La Machina, on Cuba's southern coast in Pinar del Rio, to alert him to the arrival of barrels of flour with dynamite.[29] With all the correspondence and flow of commerce back and forth between Cuba and Key West, Spanish authorities had little chance of sealing Cuba's borders against infiltrators. While there is no evidence that the Key West radicals ever launched a campaign of indiscriminate dynamiting in Havana or any other Cuban city, they certainly prepared and supported infiltration by fighters who intended to use unorthodox methods in their attempt to destabilize Spanish rule in Cuba.

Key West coordinated with New York militants to investigate the latest in explosive technology. During August, members of the Club Independiente in New York accompanied a "chemist" to Hunters' Point to view tests of explosives. In October, a spy hired by the Spanish consulate reported that an arms manufacturer and dealer sold to four Cubans eight "infernal" explosive devices that looked like a cigar box 16 inches long by 4 ½ inches wide. The device was made of galvanized sheet iron and had an attached timer. It could be set to explode within eight minutes or eight days. It contained the power of 3,000 pounds of explosive powder and could destroy buildings, machinery, or even a fort. The manufacturer of these devices also claimed to have made explosives for "Haytian insurgents, Peruvians, Fenians and many others" and had gone to New York for the purpose of getting orders from Cubans for more explosives.[30]

Insurgents purchased weapons in New York and sent them to Key West in small shipments. The Spanish consul in New York reported in the first week of March 1884 that two cases of arms had been shipped to Poyo on the vessel *Alamo*.[31] Because of the immunity his position as Peruvian consul in Key West provided, Poyo stored the weapons in his home without fear of interference by county or state officials.[32] Spanish consular officials in New York consulted with the U.S. district attorney and learned that no law allowed authorities to seize the weapons; only if weapons were found on board a vessel whose passengers were planning hostile actions against a friendly nation could they be confiscated.[33]

Some militants disagreed with aspects of this radicalization, including Gómez, Maceo, and other prominent military leaders. Journalist Martín Morúa Delgado made his opposition to the use of dynamite clear, claiming that liberty had to be achieved through "noble and dignified" means. A patriot, he thought, could use a bomb to destroy a fortress but not a column of soldiers. Even Zulus did not use dynamite in warfare, he added.[34] He frequently spoke against the use of dynamite but admitted that he was in the minority among the militants.

Men of Action

When Key West revolutionaries held their mass protest of the Zanjón Pact on March 11, 1878, they did this in solidarity with their colleagues in New York, who had met the previous day for the same reason. The enthusiasm among exiles inspired many, but the new initiative lacked a military chief until General Calixto García arrived in New York in September 1878. García, who had been released from a prison in Pamplona, Spain, as part of the Zanjón Pact, was one of the best known and most respected commanders, especially after he survived a self-inflicted shot to the head as Spanish forces surrounded his position in 1874. He was much admired for this act of bravery and defiance, and Cuban exiles quickly tapped García to reorganize the rebellion. In New York, he established the Comité Revolucionario Cubano, and Cubans in the United States, Mexico, and the Caribbean responded with a network of revolutionary clubs that accepted García's authority.[35] Key West of course was part of the new network; revolutionaries there gathered at San Carlos Institute and established Club Revolucionario Cubano #25 in November 1878.[36]

In August 1879, insurgents in Oriente Province rose in revolt, even before securing significant weapons and ammunition from abroad. They included Ten Years' War fighters Flor Crombet, Emilio Núñez, Ramón Bonachea, Carlos Aguero, Serafín Sánchez, José "Mayía" Rodríguez, and Rafael "Tuerto" Rodríguez. The exile community immediately mobilized to support the Oriente revolutionaries by sending as many expeditions led by experienced commanders as possible. However, the two most important commanders did not participate in these expeditions.

Although Máximo Gómez refused to participate because he thought the effort premature and too disorganized, Antonio Maceo expressed his eagerness to take charge in Oriente Province. Initially García chose Maceo to lead the first expedition, but he later changed his mind when a Spanish propaganda campaign that characterized the new insurgency as essentially a black and mulatto rebellion activated race-based distrust and jealousy in the ranks of the rebels. García decided to use a white commander, a decision that angered Maceo, who remained on the sidelines while the relatively unknown General Gregorio Benítez led the expedition. Benítez received little support in Oriente, where the rebels had expected Maceo, and he died fighting sometime later in Matanzas.[37]

Despite this ominous beginning, Key West supported the insurrection and sent resources to New York. Lamadriz and Poyo organized speeches and fund-raising in the factories and at San Carlos Institute when García visited in mid-November 1879. After García's visit, he wrote to Poyo from Jacksonville to tell him that he was delayed in joining the fighting and asked for more resources to hasten his departure.[38] In the meantime, another commander, Brigadier Cecilio González, arrived in Key West with orders from the New York junta to outfit another expedition and proceed to Cuba as soon as possible.

González was a black commander who was known as *el oscuro* (the dark one). He had fought under Máximo Gómez and Antonio Maceo during the Ten Years' War. Like García, he wanted to reach Cuba quickly. The revolutionary committee in New York, which had obviously had second thoughts about their racial calculations, asked Key West to help González. Poyo and Lamadriz secured arms and a small vessel and sent him with a group of fighters to western Cuba in late December.[39] His fighting force of about forty men ranged the Havana countryside, but the jurisdiction where he operated contained close to 3,000 Spanish infantry and cavalry garrisoned in farms and towns. In March, González reached the Matanzas region, where he received additional military supplies from a local revolutionary club, but he too fell in battle sometime in June 1880.[40]

Finally, after several false starts, García and eighteen others reached Oriente Province on May 7. Poor coordination resulted in a skirmish with Spanish soldiers rather than the anticipated welcome of Cuban forces. Unaware of García's tenuous situation, ten days later revolutionaries in Kingston announced his safe landing and the establishment of a revolutionary government under his presidency. In Key West, Lamadriz became the revolution's official agent in the United States; he was responsible for sending weapons and establishing supply lines.

García's group survived their initial skirmish with the Spanish military, but they never raised a viable fighting force, and as they began their operations various other insurgent bands surrendered in the face of a strong response from the Spanish military. On August 3, 1880, with only three men left, García finally ended the short-lived campaign and returned to prison. Some 6,000 ill-equipped insurgents rose against Spain in 1880, but they faced a Spanish force of 25,000 well-trained and well-armed soldiers who defeated them quite easily, band by band.[41]

Hundreds if not thousands of Cuban military veterans scattered throughout the Caribbean after 1880, seeking places to live and work, including Honduras, the Dominican Republic, Haiti, and Jamaica. Veterans also moved to Mexico and numerous cities in the United States. Many chose Key West because of its stellar reputation as a revolutionary hotbed and a center of cigar production. "Welcome, brothers!" declared *El Yara* as the arrivals strengthened the south Florida isle's militant tradition. The new arrivals included military veterans Figueredo, Gerardo Castellanos, Alejandro Rodríguez, José Rogelio Castillo, Teodoro and Enrique Pérez, Enrique Canals, Francisco Lufríu, Francisco Urquiza, and José R. Estrada.

The fighters reunited with their families and became tobacco workers, newspaper editors, shop owners, union organizers, and entrepreneurs. They joined revolutionary organizations, including Orden del Sol, strengthening the community's commitment to renewed revolutionary action.[42] These bruised, battered, and sometimes shattered men shared the goal of reigniting revolution as soon as possible. Lufríu, for example, arrived paralyzed from the waist down, and people recalled him working at the factory, crutches at his side, with a sad, languid face and profound expression. As he rolled cigars in constant pain, they supposed him to be absorbed in thoughts about the "enslaved homeland" and "glorious remembrances of bygone days," fully prepared to continue the struggle.[43]

Tired of war, the Cuban people did not respond as expected to what became known as The Little War (La Guerra Chiquita), and those that did were inadequately armed and supplied. Ill-organized rebels learned that an assault on Spanish power required resources and leadership that was not available or effectively used in 1879–1880. For most Cubans, expectations of independence in the near term ended; the matter seemed closed for the foreseeable future. But in Key West and New York, an activist minority still encouraged by *El Yara* insisted on a practical reassessment, not an abandonment of the goal.

In November 1882 the former interim president of the defunct Cuban republic, Salvador Cisneros Betancourt, organized a committee in New York, urged Máximo Gómez to lead a new effort, and asked Poyo to provide the necessary war matériel. Poyo agreed to do so and communicated with insurgents in Jamaica, Mexico, and the Dominican Republic.[44] *El Yara* also supported and highlighted the guerrilla activities of a number of commanders who were still operating after pacification, especially Ramón Bonachea and Carlos Aguero. Poyo did not consider these operations to be an immediate threat to Spanish rule, but he saw them as a powerful symbolic resistance and a testimony of the colonial system's inability to provide peace and order. Both of these experienced fighters independently headed guerrilla bands in 1882–1883, and both slipped out of Cuba to seek resources for their struggle.

Bonachea reached Kingston, Jamaica, in early 1883, and after a quick visit to Cartagena, Colombia, he traveled to Key West in May to confer with Lamadriz, Poyo, and Figueredo. They agreed to help him, and at a mass meeting attended by cigar workers and many manufacturers on the evening of June 11, Bonachea raised $10,000 in an event punctuated by Cuban flags and the martial sounds of the Libertad band. According to the Spanish consul, Bonachea's success in Key West was an important development that demonstrated the growing power of the veteran leadership there.[45]

The guerrilla leader then departed for New York in July, where about seventy-five persons, two-thirds of whom were black and mulatto according to the Spanish consulate's spy, had recently formed Club Independiente under the presidency of Juan Arnao. Born in 1812, Arnao had participated in conspiracies since the 1840s and had cooperated with Narciso López and helped organize various expeditions in the 1870s. In addition to Cisneros Betancourt, other important members included Juan Bellido de Luna, an important separatist journalist in New York for twenty years, and Cirilo Villaverde and many of his followers, including Ramón Rubiera de Armas, a vocal nationalist labor leader. Journalist Martín Morúa Delgado, who had recently arrived from Key West, helped found a revolutionary newspaper, *El Separatista*, which he edited along with Rubiera.[46]

Despite initial enthusiasm and Club Independiente's support of Bonachea, it soon became evident that exiles in New York remained skeptical about the possibilities for revolution in the 1880s. One activist wrote Poyo to complain that most in New York opposed launching revolution in Cuba, and indeed, after three months Bonachea had raised only $4,000. Bonachea inspired little confidence, and New Yorkers suggested that he wait for the two most important military leaders, Gómez and Maceo, to commit.[47] From Honduras, Maceo likewise counseled Bonachea to wait for Gómez's lead, arguing that he did not have enough prestige to launch a revolt on his own. The two generals also criticized the exile centers for excessive propaganda campaigns, particularly *El Yara* and *El Separatista*, which they believed alerted Spanish authorities to the plans of insurgents unnecessarily.[48] Although this criticism made sense, Poyo believed that propaganda played an important role in keeping communities mobilized and financial contributions flowing. Spanish consuls throughout the United States and the Caribbean kept very close tabs on Cuban activists and little escaped their vigilant spy networks, regardless of what did or did not appear in the newspapers.

Bonachea, who referred to himself as chief of the vanguard (*El jefe de la vanguardia*), proceeded anyway with the goal of establishing a revolutionary foothold in Cuba. *El Yara*, which supported him fully, maintained a barrage of propaganda that described Cuba's economic and social situation as worse than ever and emphasized Bonachea's credentials as a veteran. The newspaper also countered characterizations in the Spanish press of insurgents as bandits and Bonachea as having fled the island. "It is all a lie," proclaimed *El Yara*, insisting that a popular uprising would make Cuba free and destroy slavery. In August 1883, Poyo assured Bonachea that the revolutionary call had been disseminated to the island and that "our greatest desire is to already see you in Cuba." "The unity of all who conspire for the good of Cuba," *El Yara* emphasized, "is necessary now, more than ever." On September 15, 1883, Bonachea left New York for Kingston, Jamaica, where he made final preparations for his expedition.[49]

In the meantime, Carlos Aguero, who was known as "Aguerito," continued his guerrilla activities in the Cuban countryside. He joined the insurgent army in 1870 at only fourteen years old. He served with commanders Gómez, Julio Sanguily and Cecilio González; participated in the Little War; and finally ended up in prison for a year before escaping. Impetuous, fearsome, undisciplined, and bold, Aguero returned to action in 1882 with a small guerrilla band and raised resources by raiding plantations and kidnapping wealthy planters in Matanzas. Spaniards referred to Aguero as a bandit despite his well-established credentials as an insurrectionist and organized a force to track him.[50]

When Aguero arrived in Key West unannounced on November 16, 1883, rumors spread that he too had surrendered and agreed to leave the island. That evening at San Carlos Institute, 600 excited people who were eager to see the insurgent cheered as Aguero assured Cubans that he had not capitulated. His forces remained well organized and were under the command of competent *jefes*, but he needed resources to continue the increasingly difficult fight against the large and well-supplied Spanish forces.[51] Poyo assured him of Key West's support.

Aguero then went to New York, where on December 1, 1883 he met with around twenty-five members of the Club Independiente, but like Bonachea, he encountered ambivalence. He returned to Key West and worked closely with Poyo and Figueredo, who made final preparations for his departure for Cuba. This involved collecting additional funds, purchasing armaments, manufacturing explosives, and urging the community to support the enterprise. As head of the initiative, Poyo even commissioned Aguero as general of the army of insurrection.[52]

The Spanish consul, sensing a heightened level of activity in the local community, mobilized his spies and warned authorities in Cuba to dispatch gunboats and intercept the insurgent chief, but the expedition launched undetected on April 4, 1883. Forty well-armed men accompanied Aguero, including war veterans Rosendo García and Perico Torres as his second and third in command. García, who was born in Puerto Principe in 1855, had joined his parents in the countryside at the outbreak of the Ten Years' War at the age of eleven. After they were killed, he fought under General Julio Sanguily and Máximo Gómez. He seconded Maceo's Protesta de Baraguá in 1878.[53]

Aguero and his men reached Cuba's northern coast in Matanzas, near Varadero, and skirmished with Spanish forces as they marched inland. They escaped but sustained casualties and found themselves short of weapons and supplies. The remaining members of the band, who included Aguero, García, Torres, Casimiro Sotolongo, José Alvarez Arteaga (known as Matagás), and José Morejón, kidnapped a sugar mill owner, whom they ransomed for 3,000 pesos, which gave them sufficient funds to continue their operations.[54]

Key West supported the insurgent band by preparing explosives for transportation to Cuba. This involved obtaining the raw materials from the nihilist organization in New York and manufacturing the dynamite in Key West. Gil Marrero did most of the work of transporting materials and Poyo and others stored the explosives. Poyo kept Aguero informed of activities through *El Yara*, which was regularly smuggled into Cuba. Bonachea, in the meantime, remained in the Caribbean, where he was still organizing his return. Another small group led by Pancho Castro left Key West for Cuba in early May. In New York, two other war veterans, Panchín Varona and Limbano Sánchez, prepared yet another expedition with the support of Juan Arnao and Club Independiente.[55]

In the midst of his activities with Bonachea and Aguero, Poyo finally received a communication from Máximo Gómez in August 1883, announcing that he and Maceo would join the insurrectionary activities. This was exciting news, since Gómez and Maceo provided a level of revolutionary legitimacy that Bonachea and Aguero could not. During the previous year a core of rebels had gathered around the two in Honduras, including Eusebio Hernández, a doctor; military veterans Flor Crombet, Tuerto Rodríguez, and Carlos Roloff; and Tomás Estrada Palma, former president of the Cuban Republic in Arms and now a schoolteacher. Gómez had turned to agriculture near San Pedro Sula, while Maceo had secured an appointment as a commander in the Honduran army at Puerto Cortés. They waited on developments in Cuba and in exile.[56]

Shortly after his letter to Poyo, Gómez almost died of pneumonia. Hernández skillfully nursed the general back to health, but Gómez did not make his move until the next year, after he received an offer of $200,000 from a wealthy Cuban in New York. The prospect of a down payment of these funds and the enthusiasm of the exile communities for the organizing to benefit Bonachea and Aguero as reflected in *El Yara* and *El Separatista* convinced the two men that the moment to act was nearing. In the middle of June 1884, Maceo wrote Poyo warning of obscure machinations between Spain and the United States. "Cuba will be free when the redeeming blade" throws Spaniards into sea, but not through arrangements with the United States, Maceo wrote. Be sure, he emphasized, that "anyone that tries to possess Cuba and does not perish in the struggle will find its soil soaked in blood. Cuba has many sons that have given up their families and welfare to protect their honor and the homeland." This passion and impatience strongly suggested that he too was ready for action.[57]

Gómez and Maceo finally reached Key West on September 18, 1884, after a brief stay in New Orleans, a train trip to Cedar Key, a small boat ride to Tampa, and finally a steamer to the city. They happily encountered many former military comrades, including Figueredo, Enrique and Teodoro Pérez, Enrique Canals, José R. Estrada, and José Rogelio Castillo, and for the first time they greeted Poyo personally. Gómez revealed his revolutionary program to these men and numerous cigar manufacturers. The plan called for the creation of a *junta gubernativa* (governing body) composed of five men to oversee the movement in exile, including raising funds and reinforcing the insurgent army.

The program placed the military firmly at the helm. During the Ten Years' War, military men such as Gómez had learned that trying to fight an insurrection with direction from a divided civilian base was folly. Although ideology had divided Cubans, so had the structure of the insurgency, which had placed authority for the war in the hands of civilian leaders in the executive and legislative branches of the Republic in Arms. Political conflicts in the government took attention away from the military project, and everyone remembered how Gómez's 1875 military campaign into the western provinces had been frustrated by political disruptions among the insurgents, which had undermined the seriousness of the rebels' final military threat to Spanish rule.[58]

Determined to avoid similar problems, Gómez's plan placed all authority in the hands of a capable commander in chief concerned exclusively with defeating the Spanish. The movement's *jefe superior* (military chief), to be named by the exile communities, would be responsible only to a governing junta, from which he would receive ample power to organize the army and authority to formulate regulations and general orders. The program explicitly rejected a civilian government in arms that might weaken the effectiveness of the military.[59]

Poyo and Lamadriz fully backed Gómez, as did Figueredo. Poyo had admired the "enthusiastic legislators" of 1869 who had produced the Guáimaro Constitution, which he had also celebrated at the time, but he too learned the bitter lessons of the Ten Years' War. He compared the rebels in 1869 to children without experience who understood politics through the idealistic speeches of French republicans and believed themselves capable of "herculean tasks with infantile strength." But experience with revolution had provided the wisdom that war should be in the hands of warriors, not those of politicians. Poyo believed that during times of revolution the complex process of representative democracy had to give way to the simplified governance of militarism.[60]

The two chiefs introduced their program to Poyo, Lamadriz, Figueredo, and a group of twenty or so others at a cigar factory. Poyo had full confidence that Gómez and Maceo, with the assistance of adequately equipped rebel fighters, would be able to spark rebellion and lead a victorious war against Spain, but unlike Bonachea and Aguero, they intended to proceed more systematically. They would land in Cuba only after securing a substantial expedition of men who had enough arms to establish a territorial foothold and mobilize an immediate full-scale insurrection. Their approach was more like an invasion than a guerrilla war, and it required significant funds and meticulous preparation.

The Key West revolutionaries formed a secret club named Club Máximo Gómez, which later became Club Carlos Manuel de Céspedes, to spearhead the new effort. Its inspiration was similar to that of the Orden Del Sol, and all members agreed that it should remain secret as a way of protecting the work. Its officers included Ten Years' War veterans Enrique Pérez and Figueredo, cigar manufacturers Carlos Recio and Teodoro Pérez, and Poyo. The group also formed a public political arm, the Sociedad de Beneficiencia Cubana de Cayo Hueso, which received direction, financial resources, and moral support from the secret club. The officers of the publicly constituted *sociedad* remained subordinate to the leadership of the secret club, and they encouraged the founding of new clubs to raise funds for the Gómez-Maceo project.[61]

New York

With the new revolutionary organization in place and $5,000 in hand, the two generals left for New York on September 26. Besides looking forward to receiving the $200,000, Gómez and Maceo expected the full support of the New York's Cuban society. Instead, like Bonachea and Aguero had, they ran into problems immediately. The promised funds did not materialize, and they soon learned that the small group associated with Club Independiente had little support in the broader community.

Unlike Key West's largely multiracial working-class nationalists, most of New York's prominent Cuban political thinkers and activists were socially conservative white middle-class professionals, merchants, doctors, journalists, writers, and intellectuals embedded in a cosmopolitan and sophisticated Hispanic American community that was suspicious of Latin America's multiracial working classes. They frequented literary societies and salons and attended social engagements that were known for their refinement and diversity of political ideas. Most rejected armed movements organized from abroad and put their faith in the power of propaganda to eventually mobilize Cuban opinion. Some were still willing to contemplate an autonomist compromise with Spain or annexation of Cuba to the United States. Soon a debilitating fault line in the ranks of the nationalists became evident.

One of the most talented nationalists in New York was José Martí, a young intellectual, writer, poet, and activist. Born in 1853, Martí had established his nationalist credentials early. At the age of sixteen, he suffered imprisonment and exile to Spain. After the Zanjón Pact, Martí returned to Cuba, where he immediately joined a revolutionary committee and eventually ended up in New York as part of Calixto García's revolutionary central committee. Except for a brief time spent in Venezuela in 1881, Martí remained in New York. In 1883 and 1884, he worked for *La América*, a commercial and literary magazine owned by Rafael Castro Palomino, a man with nationalist sympathies but conservative instincts.

Like most of his colleagues in New York, Martí had little confidence in a new revolutionary push, but his reasons differed from those of his more conservative friends. An intellectual of the first order who questioned many of the positivist assumptions of his middle-class compatriots, Martí did not fear revolution but doubted that Cuba could be liberated without much patient preliminary work. The failures of the 1870s convinced him of several things: that only movements initiated and organized in Cuba could inspire confidence and revolution, that this would only happen when Cubans united behind a political program that offered a viable and clear alternative to Spanish rule, that a revolution based solely on military leadership was dangerous to the nationalist movement's democratic goals, and that a failure of the autonomist political experiment was a prerequisite for revolution. In the meantime, nationalists had to patiently rely on propaganda and persuasion to unify Cubans behind the idea of another independence war, which he felt had a better chance of provoking rebellion than invasions.[62]

Martí first articulated his reservations to Máximo Gómez and Antonio Maceo in 1882 in letters that counseled against ill-conceived actions. He also made these concerns public during Aguero's visit on October 10, 1883, at a meeting of nationalists at Clarendon Hall. Martí characterized Aguero's plan as premature, and later he wrote to Bonachea to try to dissuade him from implementing his plans.[63] One observer at Clarendon Hall paraphrased Martí, saying that Cubans worked for the same end but along different paths. Some thought revolution could be launched without sufficient preparation, while wiser voices cautioned against action "without arms that are loaded and prepared." At the right opportunity, the observer quoted Martí, "the work of the latter will be seen."[64]

Despite his reservations, Martí met with Gómez and Maceo in October 1884 to learn their plans. Among other things, Gómez explained his intention of sending agents to Mexico, Paris, Santo Domingo, Kingston, and Key West to gather support and funds. He instructed Maceo to travel to Mexico and asked Martí to go along, knowing he had spent time there in the 1870s. Martí immediately agreed, but when he excitedly offered suggestions about possibilities in Mexico, Gómez gruffly interrupted. "What is to be done there will be agreed to calmly," he told Martí. "For now, prepare to leave as soon as possible." Offended by Gómez's remark, the sensitive Martí abruptly left the room and then withdrew from the movement.

Martí told Gómez in a letter that he could not participate in a movement that would saddle Cuba with a "personal despotism" and declared that "founding a nation is not like commanding a military camp." Martí reiterated his commitment to a war initiated by the Cuban people with a clear plan and ample resources, but not a "personal adventure" by a handful of "caudillos" whose own ambitions obscured the movement's glorious ideals. Martí's offended and bitter tone aggravated the rupture and Gómez responded in kind. But this was more than a personal dispute; it reflected a sharp and broad-based disagreement among nationalists about strategy that led to political distance between New York and Key West.[65]

Key West nationalists saw their New York compatriots as bourgeois and a distracting force from revolutionary action. Certainly they recognized Martí and his colleagues as talented intellectuals and elegant writers with worthwhile ideas, but they felt that they lacked the courage or determination to undertake necessary action. In April 1885, Lamadriz wrote the head of Club Independiente to try to persuade him that Gómez was the "man of the hour" who could lead Cuba to independence. He urged his colleague to convince New York's Cubans to overlook the general's harshness, lack of social graces, and undiplomatic manner and support the revolutionary initiative. Follow the example of Key West, he urged. But this was not a convincing message to most in New York.[66]

Only a few in New York responded to Lamadriz's exhortation, and only *La República*, which replaced the defunct *El Separatista* in 1885, supported Gómez and the Key West plan. Its labor leader editor, Ramón Rubiera, had strongly backed General Quesada in the 1870s and was active in New York's Club de Artesanos. He and contributing writer Morúa Delgado followed the militant line that insisted on immediate revolutionary action, but *La República* made little headway in mobilizing New York, and it ceased publishing in 1886, once again leaving only *El Yara* and *La Propaganda* in Key West to continue the revolutionary campaign.[67] The revolutionary clubs in New York dissolved, and many of the city's militant leaders, including Arnao, Morúa Delgado, and Rubiera, eventually moved to Florida. Cisneros Betancourt, who was not convinced of the viability of revolution, returned to Cuba.

Gómez lost little time refocusing his attention on the racially diverse community of Cuban workers and manufacturers in Key West. He lamented to Juan Arnao about the indifference he had encountered in New York and described the revolution as having two faces: one face was aristocratic and the other was democratic, supported by the poor classes. It was the workers who would give him and his companions the means to reach Cuba's battlefields, Gómez argued. "I will go to the factories," Gómez declared. There, "you do not need to address letters to the cigar workers; there is no need to speak with them in secret since their interests are tied only to the homeland."[68]

El Yara also expressed its disappointment about New York's ambivalence toward revolution and questioned those who always found pretexts to avoid committing to action. They used excuses to justify their status as mere spectators with expressions of hesitation and the use of the word *"but."* The newspaper offered an example: "We desire the independence of our nation, *but* do not support revolution because the people are not prepared." Others feared slave uprisings and some wanted guarantees of democracy from Gómez and Maceo. Those who continually offered excuses, *El Yara* concluded, would never find a way to abandon their hesitant attitude, one that condemned them to spiritual poverty and expressed a lack of patriotism.[69]

During one moment of particular frustration, *El Yara* speculated that perhaps those who were unwilling to act suffered a paralyzing passivity that had been instilled in them through the oppressiveness of Spanish colonialism. Centuries of Spanish tyranny and colonial control, he noted, had cultivated a "lamentable heritage": a belief that liberty would somehow be freely given without the need for extraordinary action by Cubans themselves. To achieve liberty, Cubans had to think of it as a necessary good, a right to be acted upon. But the life of tyranny, the newspaper feared, had created laziness among Cubans that the despots counted on. Spain's economic monopoly and the imposition of a slave system had infused the Cuban people with a lazy conscience, a lazy sense of reason, and a lazy heart, all of which inhibited redemptive struggles for freedom. Overcoming obstacles was a lot of work, and Cubans preferred to submit peacefully. That, *El Yara* insisted, was a lamentable, wicked fruit of Spanish colonial domination.[70]

In the second half of the 1880s, Martí was the most eloquent opponent of armed action in the near term. He was supported by his close friend Enrique Trujillo, who edited *El Avisador Cubano*. Trujillo declared that revolution would not be instigated in exile, only advocated. He believed that disseminating propaganda, not sending expeditions, was the proper role of the community in exile.[71] At a well-attended commemoration of Grito de Yara at the Masonic Temple in New York on October 10, 1887, Martí recognized that many Cubans were impatient for war but emphasized that "aching hands" needed to restrain them from "inopportune valor." If the communities in exile had not yet sparked war, perhaps it was because the time had not yet arrived; there were many sensible men who preferred that historical circumstances dictate the appropriate moment rather than premature action. "We are not judges, but servants!" he declared. It would be unjust, he thought, to launch a war on an unprepared people who were guilty only of forgiving despots and believing in their promises of justice.[72]

Martí never advocated autonomy, but for many he was a closet autonomist.[73] According to one observer at the Clarendon Hall meeting of October 10, 1883, Martí's "views reflected those of the Liberal Party of Cuba" [the Autonomists].[74] His speeches sometimes hinted at the possibility that an autonomist solution might one day appear that Cubans would accept. During the 1888 commemoration of Grito de Yara in New York, one activist publicly accused Martí of timidity and lack of patriotism, perhaps in response to a recently published book that claimed that Martí would accept autonomy under certain circumstances.[75] Comments he made in a speech the year before had not helped. In calling upon revolutionaries to be patient, he said that in the unlikely event that others found a successful compromise and Cubans ended up having "wait[ed] in vain" for revolution, this would have to be accepted: "It is not important that we triumph, but that our homeland be happy."[76] In Key West, *El Pueblo* accused Trujillo's *Avisador Cubano* of promoting autonomist propaganda and published a letter accusing Martí of making pro-autonomy statements. The newspaper's editor, Morúa Delgado, received a bitter complaint from Martí denying the charge.[77] In Florida most Cubans considered Martí a nationalist, but not a revolutionary nationalist.

Failure

In December 1884, after the disagreement with Martí, Goméz concluded that little could be expected in New York and went to New Orleans. Maceo traveled as planned to Mexico. Gómez instructed Poyo to continue supplying "Aguerito" with arms and ammunition. He encouraged Aguero to carry on with guerrilla warfare in Cuba and announced that he too would soon be there. In early February 1885, Gómez traveled to Key West and appointed individuals to the revolutionary movement's central committee. The members were Lamadriz, Poyo, Figueredo, Enrique Pérez, and Francisco Lufríu.[78] But news from Cuba brought disappointment.

Over a year after his fund-raising visit to Key West, Bonachea finally arrived on the coast of Cuba on December 3, 1884, close to the port of Manzanillo. He was detected immediately. Local authorities captured the insurgent and his comrades and took them to Santiago de Cuba for trial. In a letter to Poyo and Figueredo dated the day before his execution, March 6, 1885, Bonachea asked that they care for his family. Bonachea's wife and four children were living in Mexico City with his mother-in-law. They had few resources and Bonachea hoped that the "heroic Key [West]" would provide his children with an education.[79] Women set to work raising funds for the family, and even Gómez, who did not much like the revolutionary leader, contributed $10. In late August, a deputation of leading citizens in Key West received Mrs. Bonachea and her children at the wharf. The community provided the family with a house, enrolled the four children at San Carlos Institute, and honored Bonachea as a martyr for the revolution.[80]

Bad news continued to arrive. In March, shortly after Bonachea's execution, news arrived in Key West of Aguero's death. He and his men had been persistently pursued by the Spanish Civil Guard. The group had dwindled to only eight men, although Aguero had accepted two new recruits. One day as they carried out an assault on a farm, a contingent of the Civil Guard suddenly appeared and ordered them to surrender. When Aguero refused, one of the new recruits, a government agent as it turned out, killed him instantly with a *machetazo* (machete blow) to his head. Several of Aguero's men escaped, including García, Torres, and Matagás. Spanish officials found papers on Aguero's body that revealed his relationship with the Key West and New York leadership, but they never made this evidence public since they preferred to characterize him as a brigand rather than a revolutionary leader.[81]

On March 22, 1885, hundreds filled the hall at San Carlos Institute to capacity to commemorate the deaths of Aguero, Bonachea, and the others who had been killed in battle or executed during the previous weeks. According to a correspondent for the *New York Herald*, emblems of mourning draped the building. Inside the hall, a flower-strewn catafalque was decorated with a skull and crossbones. For several hours the Libertad band played dirges, the audience sang hymns, and leaders dedicated eulogies to the nationalist martyrs.[82]

In mid-May, veterans Limbano Sánchez and Panchín Varona landed close to Baracoa with a group of militants, but they too failed to attract recruits, and every one of them was dead or captured within weeks. Revolutionaries expected setbacks. They had little time to ponder the deaths of their comrades except to praise them as martyrs whose sacrifices would eventually be recognized and celebrated. Support for Gómez and Maceo's activities proceeded uninterrupted. Gómez traveled to New York to purchase arms, which he shipped clandestinely to Santo Domingo, while from Jamaica Antonio

Maceo and his brother José organized a new expedition. Other veterans did the same in other locations. Emilio Núñez, a doctor and a resident of Philadelphia who had collaborated with Gómez and Maceo in the mid-1880s, planned an expedition from that city, while Flor Crombet waited in Panama for arms from New York. Tuerto Rodríguez organized another expedition in Key West in coordination with Poyo and the local leadership. Gómez coordinated the various expeditions and, having learned from the failed haphazard efforts of the Little War, cautioned insurgents in Cuba not to move until the expeditions arrived.[83]

The generals relied heavily on resources from Key West. In early 1884, Gómez received $25,000 from that community with promises of another $30,000, which he thought would be enough to launch his expedition. In October 1885, Maceo and Eusebio Hernández traveled to Key West for another fund-raising visit. They encountered an enthusiastic community waiting for them at the docks. Loud cheers, a 21-gun salute, and procession to San Carlos Institute led by the Cuban band in a drenching rain initiated a week of activities. At San Carlos Institute, Hernández took the podium and explained why the insurrection had not yet begun, but the crowd did not need explanations. After Maceo spoke, those in attendance contributed cash and jewelry to the fund-raising committee, leaving him amazed and grateful for the community's strong support. The two generals spoke at many cigar factories, where they raised $10,000 during the *semana patriótica* (Patriotic Week).[84] While they waited for Gómez and Maceo to act, Rodríguez, Poyo, and other revolutionary leaders made sure that the community remained alert, mobilized, and responsive and counseled patience as they hoped for the final drama to unfold. *El Yara* remained enthusiastic and denounced autonomism, those who were timid, and those who questioned the revolutionary movement.

Unfortunately, the optimism in Key West was not enough to overcome many problems and bad luck. On February 6, *El Yara* announced that Gómez had been arrested in Santo Domingo, where he was suspected of conspiring against the Dominican president. He was soon released when this proved false, but Dominican authorities confiscated his entire stockpile of armaments. Nevertheless, the general traveled to Jamaica to encourage the revolutionaries and insisted that plans move forward with the weapons secured by Maceo, Núñez, and others.[85]

Then an even bigger disaster happened while Gómez was contemplating more fund-raising events in Key West. On March 30, 1886, at 1:30 a.m., a fire began in a café at San Carlos Institute on Duval Street. Dry wooden buildings, inadequate fire-fighting equipment, and a strong southerly wind combined to produce an uncontrollable blaze that spread quickly from the center of town in a swath toward the docks, consuming homes, businesses, public buildings, and warehouses. Firefighters finally gained control of the fire at dawn, but not before the six wharves, a cigar-box factory, a warehouse containing stores of imported tobacco from Cuba, and at least eleven cigar factories had been destroyed. The burned factories included Seidenberg, Soria, Canals, Ellinger, Martinez Ybor, Kelly, Gregory, Angulo, Alfonso, and Barranco. Few owners had insurance and many faced immediate bankruptcy. Among the largest, only the Gato factory survived. Overnight more than 3,000 workers lost their jobs.[86]

El Yara denounced Spanish authorities for immediately sending the Spanish naval vessel *Juan Jorge* to transport workers back to Havana. It called on Cubans to remain faithful to revolution, stay in their place, and reject the Spanish government's cynical help, which was designed to destroy the revolutionary center. Members of the Partida la Tranca (a vigilante group often armed with cudgels that was led by Federico Gil Marrero for many years) walked the docks, trying to dissuade Cubans from joining the exodus, efforts that provoked confrontations and fights. The membership included Ten Years' War veterans and members of the Nihilist club such as Rosendo García, Perico Torres, Emilio García, and Salomé Escassi. The Spanish consul warned authorities in Cuba to watch carefully for members of revolutionary groups who might take advantage of the confusion to board the ship and infiltrate Cuba.[87]

Despite efforts by Poyo and others to maintain a patriotic spirit, unemployment and homelessness destroyed the most important source of financial support for the revolution. After agonizing reflection, the revolutionary leadership in Key West in May urged Gómez and Maceo to suspend the revolutionary campaign. Gómez wrote Poyo: "My friend: I can't tell you to work harder because you worked when no one else did. Only you could be heard from that miserable Key back then preaching: Revolution!" "When everyone seemed asleep," he reemphasized, "only you wrote proclaiming and defending the rights of the oppressed and so all I can say to you and the other patriots like you is that I will never abandon you."[88]

Even after Key West bowed out, the military chiefs gathered in Jamaica and waited for Maceo's weapons to arrive from New York. In the middle of July 1886, as the steamer *Morning Star*, which was carrying the armaments, passed near Cuban waters, a Spanish war vessel approached. The captain of the ship panicked and ordered the cargo thrown overboard to avoid confiscation of his vessel. That was the last straw. After two years of organizing and fund-raising, the revolutionary movement had lost the arms and ammunition purchased mostly with the resources of Key West's manufacturers and workers.

In August, Eusebio Hernández again traveled to Key West on behalf of Gómez to assess the situation and reported that the town was still in shambles. Workers had lost confidence in Key West's ability to revolutionize Cuba and were in no mood to cooperate with the nationalists. They turned to other matters and the military leadership, including Gomez, Maceo, Crombet, Rodríguez, and Núñez, finally gave up, at least for the time being.[89]

In the first half of the 1880s, Key West became the center of organized revolutionary activism and established a distinct revolutionary nationalist identity, ideology, and strategies. Throughout the previous decade the insurgent government in Cuba had looked to middle-class professionals and even wealthy Cubans in New York for leadership and guidance. After the Little War, most in that city lost confidence in any immediate revolutionary solution to the Cuban problem. Well-educated Cubans in New York, many of whom had considerable resources, remained in dialogue with their colleagues on the island, and many remained open to a variety of solutions, including autonomy and annexation. The pro-independence activists among them watched developments, and published their nationalist discourses in newspapers and pamphlets, and tried to convince their colleagues in Cuba that Spanish colonialism simply had no future. But except for a handful who were associated with revolutionary clubs in New York, New York Cubans rejected the militant posture of Key West, and they rarely provided funds for the ongoing efforts to send armed fighters to Cuba.

In addition to concerns about strategy, many Cubans in New York viewed with apprehension the social rhetoric of the revolutionary nationalist ideology espoused in Key West and the unpredictable consequences of mobilizing blacks and workers. Máximo Gómez observed this distinction between the two communities and often said that only the workers of Key West could be counted on to support his initiatives. Poyo and the leadership in Key West supported Gómez and Maceo unconditionally, and despite the setbacks of 1886, they continued to recognize them as the legitimate and natural leaders of the Cuban independence movement. At the same time, Key West's revolutionary nationalist community faced new challenges that threatened its very existence.

4

PRESERVATION

> After so much work and so much hostility from Spaniards in Cuba, how are we to be indifferent when those very same Spaniards come to Key West to take possession of the fruits of our labor and reduce us to misery and impotence?
>
> *El Yara*, 1888

In late 1888, Poyo warned about an imminent danger to Key West's nationalist community. Building a revolutionary capability took time and determination, but defending its cohesion and integrity proved equally challenging. Although the tight-knit town and its cigar industry expanded substantially in the 1880s in response to a booming demand for Cuban cigars in the United States, growth brought unexpected consequences. Cubans still dominated the migratory stream to Key West, but they did not necessarily always share the enthusiasm for nationalism of those who had landed a decade earlier. Increasing levels of unemployment in Havana's cigar industry pushed thousands of workers to the United States, and they arrived with a sharp sense of social grievance. Labor issues increasingly captured the attention of workers and threatened to displace the nationalist issues of the past, which many considered to be anachronistic. Nationalist traditions that had regularly produced excitement and substantial funds for the insurgent cause now seemed less appealing.

The pacification of Cuba and the gradual abolition of slavery there intensified the migration of Spaniards to Cuba, and beginning in 1886 Spain subsidized the cost of travel for many Spaniards seeking employment there. This reduced unemployment in Spain and increased the number of residents of Cuba who were loyal to that nation. These migrants, who were mostly from Asturias and Galicia, were generally destitute, but they were determined to start a new life and were willing to work for little. Many settled in Cuba's rural districts, replacing freed former slaves who had abandoned the sugar plantations. Others became small farmers. Some moved to towns, where they earned livelihoods as storekeepers and merchants. Cigar factories in the cities, especially Havana, also provided opportunities for new residents from Spain. Like Cubans, some of these cigar workers eventually sought opportunities in Key West and Tampa.[1] Spanish workers generally had little sympathy or were at best ambivalent about Cuban independence. They also subscribed to labor philosophies, especially anarchism, that rejected political movements for ideological reasons.

Poyo turned his attention to both of these challenges. He increased his efforts to encourage the cause of nationalism and at the same time tried to discourage Spanish workers from emigrating to Key West. "After so much work and so much hostility from Spaniards in Cuba," Poyo argued, "how are we to be indifferent when those very same Spaniards come to Key West to take possession of the fruits of our labor and reduce us to misery and impotence?" "How could we not try to prevent this [from] happening?" he declared in 1888, warning that a mass immigration of men with "confused ideas" would threaten the nationalist movement.[2] Poyo understood that nationalists had to combat such threats with vigorous action. Building a unified nationalist movement that included the collaboration and good will of workers and manufacturers had never been easy; it required stubborn determination, considerable negotiation, and even occasional coercion and violence.

Labor, Capital, and Nationalism

During the Panic of 1873, Poyo heard workers' complaints about poor wages and labor conditions as he sat at the reader's podium. Cigar workers organized into a union during this national financial crisis. Two years later, in 1875, workers went out on strike when the largest manufacturers announced a significant wage reduction and laid off employees.[3] Federico de Armas and Manuel Escassi, officers of the Asociación Patriótica del Sur, led the strike. They denounced manufacturers in *El Republicano* and threatened to cripple the industry unless owners accepted an appropriate settlement. The strikers published *La Huelga* (The Strike) to keep the workers informed, established a strike fund (*caja de ahorros*), and even sent a committee to New York to request financial support from the separatist junta there. Junta members refused help, provoking one Key West labor leader to say that separatists had forgotten the many services Key West had provided for the nationalist movement. However, the cigar workers' organization was weak and lacked adequate resources to sustain a long strike, and the workers returned to the factories. But the issue did not end there. Knowing that many labor leaders also worked as separatist activists, several angry manufacturers retaliated and refused to allow them to enter the factories to raise funds for the revolution. This was a sign of the potential difficulties and contradictions in the relationship between nationalist activism and labor interests.[4]

Poyo sympathized with the workers and supported labor organizing and unions, not only because they paid his wages as *lector* but out of his sense of justice. However, he urged labor and cigar factory owners to avoid sharp confrontations for the sake of unity among nationalists. Poyo supported practical labor actions that promoted negotiation and resolved specific grievances of workers within a reasonable time frame, but he cautioned against utopian ideas that might lead to extended strikes and might damage ongoing nationalist operations.

Predictably, stresses in relations between management and labor increased as the cigar industry grew. When thousands of workers in Key West lost their jobs in 1878 during another difficult economic downturn at the tail end of the depression that began in 1873, fund-raising for the Little War was affected. Poyo reported to Lamadriz, who was in New York, that a lack of worker contributions had made it impossible for him to raise the $2,000 Lamadriz had requested. Another strike in 1979 also affected fund-raising efforts. This strike was settled when General Calixto García and Lamadriz arrived in Key West and interceded in the dispute. Workers compromised and agreed to smaller wage increases than they had asked for in return for recognition of their union. When García landed in Cuba the following month, the Unión de Tabaqueros participated in the street parade organized by the insurgent community, revealing that workers remained strongly in the revolutionary camp.[5]

Yet another strike in 1885 disrupted fund-raising for the nationalist cause during the Gómez and Maceo campaign. Workers and manufacturers both supported the nationalist agenda and cooperated regularly in political clubs, but they could not resolve their labor differences. A committee of workers visited the factories and explained the reasons for the action from the reader's *tribuna*. Manufacturers Teodoro Pérez, Carlos Recio, and Enrique Canales responded by withdrawing financial pledges they had made to Máximo Gómez. Hundreds of cigar workers returned to Cuba to look for work. Seeing an opportunity to weaken both the Key West cigar industry and the nationalist movement, Spanish authorities in Cuba sent vessels specifically for the purpose of transporting them. Tuerto Rodríguez, Gómez's aide, who was deeply concerned about the loss of income to the nationalist movement at a crucial moment, joined the negotiations, urged both sides to work toward a solution, and served as a witness to a compromise agreement.[6] Once again nationalist and labor interests had found tenuous common ground, but only because nationalists intervened and pressured all parties concerned to reach an accord.

Nationalism versus Worker Solidarity

Unfortunately for the nationalists, the 1885 strike marked a watershed moment in their relations with labor in Key West. Labor leaders had anticipated a great victory and resented what they saw as interference by nationalists. From their perspective, nationalist politics had stymied the efforts of organized workers over and over. When workers raised concerns in public about the efficacy of the Gómez-Maceo plan, *El Yara* warned them not to undermine the moral authority of the military leadership because of impatience or lack of confidence in the ability of nationalist leaders. In February 1886, when the leaders of Federación de Tabaqueros Cubanos proposed that a portion of the union's strike funds be donated to the Gómez-Maceo expedition, some workers lost their patience. They denounced the idea, bolted from the union, and joined the Knights of Labor, an emerging force in local organizing.[7]

The Knights of Labor had first organized U.S. workers in 1869, but it began to gain traction in 1886, when its membership skyrocketed to over 100,000 nationally. The organization was open to all and was structured along territorial rather than trade union lines. The Knights created a reformist movement that urged harmony between labor and capital, but they also emphasized worker solidarity across trades, ethnicities, and races.[8] Many Cuban workers who were disillusioned with the nationalists embraced this full commitment to labor issues and worker solidarity, even if that solidarity meant including the growing number of Spanish workers arriving in Key West. This rankled Poyo and other nationalists who opposed mixed assemblies of Cuban and Spanish workers.

A small proportion of Spanish workers supported the nationalist aspirations of their Cuban colleagues, but most did not. This posed a threat to the revolutionary community, which depended on an enthusiastic Cuban working-class constituency. Nationalists decided to intimidate Spaniards and discourage their entry to Key West, a policy they initiated at the end of the Little War. A November 1883 article in *El Ubiquitario* excoriated Spanish immigrants. Though the author of the article recognized that immigrants had the right to live in Key West and that all should respect the legal system that provided each person with rights before the law, he (or she) declared that Cubans should not feel obligated to embrace the "poisonous serpents" (Spaniards) and feel their "tainted and darting tongues."[9]

Cubans had the obligation, *El Yara* argued some years later, to confront Spaniards who entered their communities of exile to displace them again after having done so in Cuba already. Cuban tobacco workers emigrated from their homeland under economic duress, *El Yara* insisted, sometimes leaving behind family members and loved ones, and exposed themselves to innumerable difficulties such as alien climates, languages, religions, and customs in their new homes. They emigrated to avoid dying of starvation, the newspaper insisted, "because the Spaniards control everything and they are a plague."[10] "Cuban manufacturers," *El Ubiquitario* said, "be warned!" If you hire Spaniards, "yours will be the responsibility. Do not forget; only you will be at fault." The newspaper did make exceptions for Spaniards who supported the Cuban cause, but it cautioned that "he who does not support the cause will always be our enemy."[11]

In 1880, the Unión de Tabaqueros, urged on by *El Yara*, prohibited Spanish and Chinese workers from joining, closing the door to possible jobs for workers in these groups in unionized factories. This action, *El Yara* argued, simply mirrored the policies in Cuba, where Spanish-controlled factories preferred immigrants from Spain and China to Cubans.[12] Key West factory owners who were sympathetic with the nationalists mostly refused Spanish workers, but as the Cuban-dominated unions grew stronger, they pressured the more reluctant non-Cuban manufacturers to do so as well.

Unions controlled hiring through an intricate apprenticeship system that required each worker to have approval to work in union factories. For example, one of Gómez's aides, military veteran José Rogelio Castillo, who arrived in Key West in 1885, worked for a time as typographer for *El Yara*. Later he applied to work as an apprentice in veteran Alejandro Rodriguez's cigar factory. His companion in arms, Francisco Javier Urquiza, did the same in the Teodoro Pérez factory. After six months Castillo's mentor pronounced him a skilled cigar selector, and he sought work in the Pérez factory, only to learn he needed union authorization as well as certification. He passed an exam administered at the Diego López factory and gained the right to work wherever he wanted. The union-controlled apprenticeship system provided a mechanism for incorporating nationalists into the factories, thus strengthening the pool of available resources for the nationalist cause. It also ensued that those who were uninterested in or opposed to nationalist politics did not take jobs from those willing to contribute to fund-raising.[13]

Spanish workers in Key West who were undeterred by these obstacles and worked in non-union factories often faced direct intimidation and occasional violence from members of the Unión de Tabaqueros and Partida la Tranca who watched the docks for arriving Spaniards. In April 1885, members of the cigar selectors' union warned a Spaniard named Manuel Renducles to leave the city. When he refused to do so, he was struck across the head with a bar. The Spanish consul pressured the district attorney to investigate union leader Luis Valdés in connection with this incident and filed assault charges against him on Renducles' behalf, but he expressed little optimism about a guilty verdict "because the courts here have always sided with the Cubans on this island."[14]

Cuban labor leaders finally rebelled against nationalist constraints in 1886. These men, who included Ramón Rivero, Carlos Baliño, Francisco Segura, and Guillermo Sorondo, supported labor solidarity and denounced policies that attempted to shut out Spanish workers from Key West. "It is not possible with one daughter to have two sons-in-law," declared Rivero, meaning that workers in the factories could not worry about labor and political issues at the same time. In the workplace, he argued, workers should worry only about the problem of poverty; political matters should be managed in the patriotic clubs outside the factories.[15] As the Spanish consul gleefully explained, the "unfortunate tobacco workers muzzled by those who live off of them" finally dared to challenge the nationalists.[16] Similar strains between workers and nationalist leaders appeared in New York, where the Unión de Torcedores (Cigar Makers' Union) criticized the nationalist newspapers *La República* and *Avisador Cubano* for opposing a strike in January and February 1886. One labor leader published a manifesto that characterized nationalists as hostile to labor and urged workers to stop donating money to political clubs and the nationalist press.[17]

The Knights of Labor benefited from these disruptions and grew rapidly in Key West. In 1886, Rivero and Baliño organized Spanish-language assemblies of the Knights, and in May they reported that four of the seven assemblies in the district assembly were comprised of Cubans and Spaniards. These included Progreso (No. 4672), Cuba (No. 5695), Perseverancia (No. 6079), and Igualdad (No. 6165). Baliño, who was originally from Guanajay, west of Havana, migrated to New Orleans in 1869 after his father was arrested for insurgent activities. After working there in a cigar-box factory and then a cigar factory, he moved to Key West in 1882 and took a job in the Gato establishment.[18]

Baliño immediately helped organize the tobacco wrapper selectors' union, and four years later the 38-year-old activist was unanimously elected as Gran Maestro Obrero (Grand Labor Master) of the district assembly of the Knights of Labor. His colleague Rivero, who was twenty-eight in 1886, was a leader of the cigar classers' union and became editor of *El Ecuador*, a two-page Spanish-language insert for the English-language newspaper *The Equator*, which was owned and edited by Charles B. Pendleton, a prominent local leader in the Knights. *El Ecuador* focused almost exclusively on labor interests, strove for solidarity among all workers, and disseminated Knights of Labor ideology in south Florida's Hispanic community.[19]

The Knights sought solidarity and harmony with manufacturers through negotiation and rejected class-based socialist and anarchist ideologies as divisive and destructive. Sorondo and Segura often made statements based on these principles in Key West, arguing that the Knights of Labor offered an alternative to the "social plagues" of communism, anarchism, and nihilism that were exploding spontaneously across the world. In the United States, the Knights offered the possibility of fending off such explosions by seeking harmony between antagonistic elements and encouraging them to resolve their differences by finding solutions to the nation's social problems.[20]

In the mid-1880s, the breach between Cuban nationalists and labor leaders in Key West was wider than it had ever been. It was aggravated by the Key West fire of March 30, 1886, which threatened the very survival of the nationalist community. *El Yara*, whose offices were spared the fire's destructive path, sprang into action. It took an optimistic attitude, predicting that Key West would rise from the ashes like the fabled phoenix. Poyo expected that it would not take long for generous gifts to arrive from all regions of the nation. But all Cubans, including capitalists, industrialists, storeowners, professionals, and workers, had a moral duty to unite and rebuild their adopted town.

This was not the time, the newspaper insisted, for manufacturers and store owners to maximize their profits at the expense of the poor to make up for their damaging losses or for workers to engage in labor actions and disrupt the little production that existed. The burden of reconstruction had to be shared by all, including those with accumulated capital and those who worked with their hands. In the middle of April, *El Yara* announced that the sounds of axes and hammers, carts transporting supplies, and the voices of workers signaled that reconstruction had started in earnest. Several factories had already opened and others were prepared to do the same, as were many other commercial establishments.[21]

The impact of the fire on the nationalist cause was never far from Poyo's thoughts, and he insisted that Cubans remain patriotic. Only a rebuilt Key West could ensure the survival of a nationalist Cuban community whose members remained committed to revolution and independence. Poyo went so far as to politicize the disaster, suggesting that Spaniards might have had something to do with the fire. He argued that Cuba's conservative press, which constantly railed against Key West as a nest of vermin, may have fueled the "treacherous hand of some malicious, anxiety crazed persons." It was quite a coincidence that the fire began at San Carlos Institute, the community's most glorious institution, and destroyed the school where for fifteen years Cuban children learned "the sublime maxims of Christian morality and enlightenment for a life of law and liberty."[22]

He admitted that such thoughts were speculative, but he still wondered whether the Cuban community's implacable foes would stoop to such a moral low. If so, they underestimated the determination of Cubans to struggle without reservation like the "great Bolívar." Poyo also charged that Spain's offers to repatriate Cuban workers amounted to a cynical plan to further weaken the nationalist movement. He urged workers to stay in Key West, help with reconstruction, and prepare for revolution. "Only in that way," *El Yara* declared, "will we extract the claws of the ancient Castilian lion from the Pearl of the Antilles."[23] Poyo lobbied forcefully and frequently for resources and labor to reconstruct the San Carlos community center and school. At the end of May, *El Yara* called on the board of directors to take the lead, call a meeting, and raise the necessary funds. The newspaper promised to publish the names of donors. "Let us not lose more time. Build San Carlos; get to work [*manos a la obra*]."[24]

Ybor City

Nationalist fund-raising was out of the question for the foreseeable future, but Poyo and his colleague Estrada were determined not to cede ideological ground. *El Yara* and *La Propaganda* rejected *El Ecuador*'s support for the Knights of Labor as unpatriotic. In the period after the fire, both editors continued to condemn Spanish colonialism and encourage the community to stay true to revolution, even if only in rhetorical and moral terms given the current circumstances.[25]

Efforts to inspire the community, promote nationalist solidarity, and convince workers to stay in Key West while it was being rebuilt were not enough to not stop thousands from seeking work elsewhere. Some returned to Havana, but most traveled up the Florida coast to the Tampa neighborhood of Ybor City, where Vicente Martinez Ybor and two Spanish manufacturers from New York, Serafín Sánchez and Ignacio Haya, were founding a new cigar-making center. Having tired of the constant labor agitation in Key West over the previous fifteen years, Martinez Ybor decided to relocate after his factory burned to the ground.

Many other factories opened in the vicinity in subsequent years, transforming Tampa into a major cigar-making center that competed with Key West as Florida's most prosperous city. Workers streamed to Tampa from Key West, Havana, and New York, and it was not long before the nationalist community recognized the possibility of creating a second *baluarte cubano*. Poyo, who had visited Tampa's new Cuban community in July, made the move to Ybor City in September 1886 and returned to his place as *lector* in the Martínez Ybor factory.

Although Poyo needed work, that was probably not the main reason for his departure to Ybor City since he could have easily found work in Key West as the factories reopened. It is more likely that during this time of economic difficulty, when active revolutionary organizing in Key West seemed out of the question, his move reflected a decision to transform Ybor City into a second militant revolutionary center. An anonymous columnist for Havana's *El Español* wrote that workers in various anti-nationalist factories in Key West whistled rudely at "Don Dolores," knowing that he was moving to Tampa with "arms and military baggage."[26]

On September 26, 1886, Poyo published the first issue of *El Yara* in Ybor City, the only Spanish-language newspaper in Tampa. In a rare reference to himself, he thanked his many friends in Key West for a generous sendoff as well as *El Ecuador* for a heart-felt dedication to Poyo for his years of journalistic service. Despite their differences regarding strategy Poyo saw Rivero, Baliño, Segura, and others who worked on that labor newspaper as committed patriots. Poyo also begged his readers in Ybor City for patience and asked them to forgive whatever faults they noticed in the issue since the printing press had been damaged on the trip from Key West, making the already difficult publishing circumstances even more challenging. Poyo explained that *El Yara* intended to be a community newspaper dedicated to a strong cigar industry and the rights of workers; but, with this said, Poyo wasted no time in reminding Cubans of their obligations to help Cuba gain independence from Spain.[27]

Drawing from their experience in Key West, Cuban nationalists infused their new community with patriotic symbols and commemorative events. On November 27, nationalists gathered at Teatro Ibor to remember the execution of the Cuban medical students in 1871. The main speaker, nationalist labor leader Santos Benítez, sketched the history of the most prominent events of the Cuban revolution and concluded with a call for unity so that nationalists could complete the "redeeming work." Several other speakers, including Poyo, took the stage and developed the theme, all of which "paid a much-deserved tribute of admiration and appreciation to the memory of the glorious martyrs of the Cuban Revolution."[28]

Even as Poyo was settling into his new surroundings, he recognized the toughest challenges for nationalists in Ybor City: the number of Cuban workers who were exchanging nationalist activism for labor activism and the arrival of many Spanish workers. Even in mid-May 1886, before he left Key

West, Poyo had received correspondence from nationalists in Tampa that lamented the declining interest in Cuban politics there. Perhaps taking advantage of this sentiment, the Martínez Ybor factory hired a Spanish foreman in June, but the manufacturer had miscalculated. Workers protested, declaring that the "indestructible principle of political antagonism" between Cubans and Spaniards meant that only a Cuban factory foreman was acceptable to them.[29] Martínez Ybor quickly defused the situation by firing the Spaniard and hiring Santos Benítez.

In Ybor City, *El Yara* quickly returned to the discourse of the early 1880s and challenged Cubans to reject solidarity with Spanish workers. Cuban workers, it declared, should not be expected to unite with those who had abused them in Cuba. Furthermore, they did not need the solidarity of Spanish workers, since in Key West Cubans had already demonstrated their ability to carry out strikes and defend their interests without anybody's help. "Why call on them now?"[30] Experience demonstrated that when Cubans gave in to their generous impulses and invited Spaniards into their factories, they always regretted the results. In Vera Cruz, New Orleans, New York, and other cities where Cubans arrived before Spaniards, *El Yara* insisted, they were eventually displaced by the Iberians, not because the Spaniards were better workers but because of their large numbers.[31]

Almost as if to prove the newspaper's point about the displacement of Cubans in the cigar factories, the community soon learned that the Sánchez-Haya factory had hired thirty Spanish workers directly from Havana. *El Yara* cautioned that when enough Spanish workers arrived, the manufacturer would announce to Cubans: "Gentlemen (*Caballeros*), we don't need you anymore. Leave."[32] Poyo and others protested and made speeches against the arriving workers, but for the moment matters did not escalate.[33]

Instead, Cuban workers organized a union. On December 2, Ramón Rubiera, the nationalist editor and labor leader from New York, arrived in Tampa and founded a branch of the New York–based Federación Cubana de Tabaqueros (Cuban Federation of Tobacco Workers). The new union elected Manuel P. Delgado as its first president. The nationalists faced immediate resistance from leaders of the local Knights of Labor assemblies, who characterized the Federación as nothing more than a political group designed to instill hatred against the Spanish. Delgado rejected this and said that their union recognized all workers as brothers and did not reject members on the basis of nationality, race, or color. But while Federación leaders struggled against the monopoly of the wealthy, they also defended nationalist ideals. The only division, Delgado declared, is the "natural one" between the Cuban and Spaniards who controlled the cigar-making trade in New York. But, he hastened to add, Spaniards would not be permitted to dominate the industry in Ybor City.[34]

A similar debate erupted in Key West when Rubiera urged that another branch of the Federación be established to counter the growing influence of the Knights. An especially sharp exchange between Rubiera's *La República* and Martín Morúa Delgado's *El Pueblo* almost resulted in a dual of honor between the two men, who had previously cooperated as editors of *El Separatista* in New York. Morúa Delgado, like Rivero and Baliño, defended the Knights and supported the notion of worker solidarity across skills and ethnicities, while Rubiera, like Poyo, promoted the orthodox nationalist agenda.[35]

The competition between the Federación Cubana de Tabaqueros and the Knights of Labor soon led to bitter competition in Tampa's factories, and before long a relatively minor incident sparked an outburst. On January 17, Santos Benítez dismissed a Spanish worker from the Ybor factory, some said for his political opinions. The worker, who was a member of the Knights, complained to his assembly, which took up the case. Though the majority of the workers in the factory were members of the Federación, of which Santos Benítez himself was an honorary member, the district assembly of the Knights demanded that the Martínez Ybor factory reinstate the worker or face a strike action. This statement was applauded by the mostly Spanish workers in the Sánchez-Haya factory who were affiliated with the Knights of Labor. The workers in the Martínez Ybor factory voted against a strike, including most of the Cuban Knights in the factory, who felt that the district assembly's response was exaggerated.

On January 19, a delegation of Knights arrived at the door of the Martínez Ybor factory. The only factory employee in the delegation, Cayetano Troncoso, gained entrance and Poyo ceded the reader's *tribuna* to him. He announced the strike, which would continue until the dismissed worker was rehired and foreman Benítez was fired. Troncoso also instructed all the Knights in the factory to attend a meeting in ten minutes at Mascotte Hall, a community center, or be in violation of union regulations. The Knights remained divided between Spaniards, who supported the strike, and Cubans, who opposed the action. A special commission was appointed to find a solution that included members of another Knights assembly that was composed mostly of Anglo-Americans.

The next day the Knights invited Benítez to a meeting on the upper floor of Mascotte Hall to discuss the situation. The Knights proposed that in exchange for rehiring the dismissed worker and pledges to stop discriminating against Spanish workers, the Knights would abandon their demand that Benítez be fired. Benítez responded that those terms were contrary to what he felt was just, since the majority of workers in the Martínez Ybor factory did not want to work with the dismissed Spanish worker or others like him.

As Benítez was preparing to leave the meeting, shots rang out in the downstairs bar. Believing that he was being ambushed, Benítez escaped down the back stairs as the shots continued. When the smoke cleared, four men lay wounded, two Cubans and two Spaniards. One of the Cubans, Manuel F. Martínez, secretary of one of the Knights assemblies, lay critically wounded with two shots to the chest. The other Cuban, Carlos V. Quijano, was shot in the leg. Friends promptly took him to the office of *El Yara*, which was nearby. The two Spaniards suffered non-critical gunshots, one in the arm and the other in the lumbar region. But Martínez died the next day, and a Spanish worker of the Haya factory accused Cubans Emilio García and Isidoro Leijas of murdering him. Both men were committed nationalists who were members of the Federación Cubana de Tabaqueros and were active in the Black Guard, a vigilante group that had been formed to intimidate Spanish workers. After they were arrested, they declared that they were innocent and were freed on $5,000 bail that was provided by Vicente Martínez Ybor.[36]

This incident deepened divisions among Cuban nationalists. *El Yara* supported the defendants, as did Estrada's *La Propaganda* in Key West, but Rivero's *El Ecuador* and Morúa Delgado's *El Pueblo* sided with the Knights. Morúa Delgado declared that a crime had been committed and the guilty had to be punished, blaming intransigent nationalist politics for the spectacle. He also published an article from the *Tampa Tribune* that characterized the shootings as a "cowardly ambush" against members of the Knights by members of the Federación.[37]

The violence also caused considerable distress among Tampa's Anglo-Americans, and Spanish manufacturer Haya skillfully used this to his advantage. Under pressure from the Knights, Haya, and members of the broader Tampa community who wanted an end to the conflict, Martínez Ybor finally dismissed Benítez. Furious Cubans blamed Haya for this, and some threatened to burn his factory and other Spanish-owned business establishments. Spaniards armed themselves, and events threatened to get out of hand, prompting the Anglo-American Tampa Board of Trade to intervene. The board compiled lists of nationalist "agitators" and threatened seventy-five with lynching if they did not leave town. Most men whose names were on the lists left Ybor City in February and March. Supporters in Key West, especially Estrada, raised funds in the factories to purchase steamer tickets for those who needed to leave. Benítez left for California or Mexico, while Poyo, Delgado, and many others returned to Key West. Emilio García and Isidoro Leijas remained in Tampa for their trials.[38]

The efforts of nationalists to convert Ybor City into a hotbed of patriotic activism failed, at least for the moment. Their strategy of discouraging immigration of Spanish workers and denying them access to the Ybor City factories fell short for a variety of reasons. Too many Cubans had become loyal to the Knights and rejected the politics of exclusion that the nationalist unions promoted. In addition, many Tampa manufacturers, who were no longer under the same constraints as they had been in Key West, refused to cooperate with the nationalists. But the decision of the Anglo-American Board of Trade to take action against the nationalists proved to be the most important factor. Labor radicals held sway in Tampa for at least two more years, and Poyo's departure signaled the nationalist community's decision to reconsolidate in Key West. But even this would not be easy.

Anarchism

The immigration of Spanish workers and the new trend toward ideological diversity in Key West both constituted threats to the nationalists. After 1886, another even more dangerous challenge emerged in the form of anarchism. Anarchist ideas not only reinforced the call for worker solidarity but also included a radical analysis of class and an absolute rejection of nationalism that was absent in the discourse of the Knights of Labor. In Key West, anarchist organizations rapidly displaced the Knights in the late 1880s.

In the mid-1880s, workers in Cuba grew tired of the reformist traditions of their labor associations that advocated cooperative relationships between workers and manufacturers. Reformist unions that had been established in the 1860s lost ground to anarchist organizations, which tobacco workers played a central role in founding. In 1887, the various unions sponsored a Congreso Obrero de Cuba (Cuban Workers' Congress) that issued a document of principles, including a prohibition against supporting political or religious doctrines. Anarchist leader Enrique Roig de San Martín's *El Productor* quickly became the most influential labor newspaper in Cuba. For the first time, workers organized strikes and challenged capitalists with a radical ideology that called for a socialist transformation of Cuban society.[39]

Anarchist thought also influenced workers in Key West, where radical thought was not new. Federico de Armas, a member of the Socialist International in Madrid, had disseminated socialist ideas in Key West in the early 1870s and, according to one critic, had turned *El Republicano* into a *"gacetilla socialista"* (socialist newsletter). These developments paralleled similar developments in New York, where many workers associated with the Villaverde, Quesada, and Sociedad de Artesanos faction sympathized with the Socialist International and the Paris Commune.[40]

Socialism remained popular among Cuban exiles in the late 1880s. Martín Morúa Delgado's *El Pueblo* and Pedro Pequeño and Néstor Carbonell's *El Cubano* sympathized with the increasing labor activism of workers. Two radical labor papers began publishing in 1888: Federico Corbet's *La Justicia* and Carlos Baliño's *La Tribuna del Trabajo*. That same year, Ramón Rivero and Francisco Segura moved to Tampa and filled the void left by *El Yara*'s departure with *La Revista de Florida*, also a labor newspaper. All these editors supported the right of workers to organize, rejected the anti-Spanish discourse of the nationalist press, and generally supported socialist ideals.[41]

Those who promoted anarchism found a sympathetic hearing in this environment. In addition to fighting for higher wages and other labor issues, anarchists offered a broad critique of the basic organization and culture of modern industrial society. After the Key West fire, manufacturers rebuilt according to the "company town" model that was so often used in the late nineteenth century. At least four factories, of which Gato was the most prominent, moved outside the city limits, where owners purchased large tracts of land and built factories. Around the factory buildings they constructed hundreds of small "shotgun" cottages, which they rented to the workers. According to Havana's *El Productor*, which regularly published letters from an anonymous Key West correspondent, the creation of this "feudal estate" was designed to further exploit the workers and control every detail of their lives.

Located in *el monte* (outside the town), the factories were surrounded by swamps that the correspondent sarcastically referred to as beautiful lakes that were reminiscent of Venice. In addition to being plagued by inadequate sidewalks and dangerous hygienic conditions for workers, including mosquitoes and other insects that caused fevers, *El Productor* argued that the environment in *el monte* was designed to distract workers from labor activism. Manufacturers relieved workers of their hard earned wages and assaulted their integrity and moral fiber by installing "el bar room" and encouraging gaming, lotteries, and all manner of corrupt practices.[42]

More critical for nationalists was *El Productor*'s advice to workers that they abandon political activism altogether and turn to labor and social questions exclusively. The newspaper told workers to be socialists, since this idea, not nationalism, confronted the "bourgeois regime that enslaves us."[43] Many workers in Key West agreed. They remained Cuban, they wanted independence, and they vowed to support revolution when the time arrived, but until then they would fight in the factories to defend the rights of workers, imitating the factory owners, "who before being nationalists are members of the bourgeoisie."[44]

Anarchism acquired an official presence in Key West on October 11, 1888, when Havana-based Alianza Obrera leader Enrique Messonier organized a new Unión de Tabaqueros. The first meeting featured radical oratory that alienated nationalists such as Manuel P. Delgado. At the next meeting, Delgado proposed a resolution prohibiting the union from maintaining formal relations with associations in Havana, obviously meaning the Alianza Obrera. The group voted down his proposal, but the discussion became heated. *El Productor*'s anonymous Key West correspondent charged that Delgado had threatened to discredit the union if it affiliated with Havana's anarchists, launching a war of words between *El Yara* and the Havana anarchist newspaper.[45]

Earlier in the year another incident dramatized the divisions in the community. When a meeting was held to support a fund-raising drive for General Flor Crombet, someone nominated Carlos Baliño as recording secretary for the meeting. Manuel Escassi denounced Baliño for his activism with the Knights of Labor and his "disloyalty" to Cuba. Baliño defended himself, saying that he loved Cuba as much as any man; he and his denouncer almost came to blows. Crombet defused the situation, and the meeting selected Teodoro Pérez as secretary instead.⁴⁶

Strike

The social and political tensions in Key West's Cuban community boiled over into open confrontation in 1889. In February, workers in the Del Pino factory struck for higher wages, the third such strike action in Key West that month. Workers also struck the José Toledo and Teodoro Pérez factories in July, and in September, they walked out of the Ellinger factory. Finally in October, workers walked off their jobs at the Gato factory. The manufacturer refused to negotiate, declaring that his business offered adequate wages. Workers had been happy with the wage rates, Gato claimed, until radical organizers convinced them to demand increases. He called the strike leaders "restless creatures" who would never be satisfied and charged that "they have infected the others!" After ascertaining that Gato had not violated industry wage standards, the Key West manufacturers' association representing most factories declared a general lockout across the industry. When owners finally agreed to reopen the factories, workers stayed away.⁴⁷

Preparing for an extended action, labor leaders Messonier, Eduardo Pajarín, José de Castro Palomino, Julian Martínez, and several others formed a Comité de Recursos y Arbitrios (Resource and Welfare Committee) and called for support from Havana's anarchists. Workers persisted with their strike throughout October, November and December, demonstrating an unusual solidarity. The profits of Key West manufacturers tumbled as Tampa manufacturers filled the huge Christmas season orders, and Key West owners faced the prospect of losing their markets permanently to the manufacturers in the Tampa Bay area. Sensing their advantage, workers remained intransigent.

When the strikes in the tobacco industry accelerated in September 1889, *El Yara* repeated its determination to defend nationalist traditions from Spanish anarchist influence. Poyo insisted that Spaniards were the problem and reaffirmed the nationalist line about their presence in Key West. "The patriotic organization of Key West's Cuban immigrants," it declared, "would have lacked substance from the first moments if they had not acted in every way to discourage Spanish immigrants from Cuba."[48] Exiles had transformed what was an arid and solitary island into a prosperous population free of Spanish influences, and the community had always provided hospitality to Cubans fleeing tyranny and misery, *El Yara* claimed. Cubans knew that tolerating Spanish immigrants would have threatened their privileged place in Key West factories and would have resulted in their "eternal enemies" living among them. They would have ended up overwhelmed by Spaniards just like their compatriots in Havana, New York, and Tampa.

However, Poyo was aware that this strike was led by Cuban anarchists, not Spaniards. The same Cubans who called themselves anarchists and left their homeland overwhelmed by poverty would not have found work and comfort had Key West not remained eminently Cuban, Poyo reminded his readers. Did the anarchists think they could destroy the work of so many years by appealing to "an impossible socialism?" Poyo advocated negotiation and compromise between labor and capital and objected vociferously to the anarchists' strategy of urging workers to abandon Key West until the manufacturers relented.[49]

El Productor's anonymous correspondent in Key West responded in kind. Although he conceded that Poyo was usually a pragmatic influence during strikes, sometimes supporting workers and other times supporting manufacturers, depending on the issues and the circumstances, in this case, the newspaper noted, Poyo had sided with the capitalists. Soon after the strike commenced, the correspondent charged that *El Yara* had sold out to the owners. He said that he had never seen money change hands, but the relationship was clear as day. Poyo's appeal to "patriotism, dignity, and the impregnable bulwark" served only to distract workers and keep them in misery. In addition, he observed that *El Yara* would not hesitate to oppose the workers' most effective strategy—abandoning Key West—because it hurt the manufacturers, the business community, and property owners that constituted the bourgeois class, which *El Yara* served.[50]

This cynical attack did not consider that Poyo had always opposed this strategy because it disrupted the community's very fabric. In the early 1880s, striking workers often returned home, but they acted on their own and not as part of a strike strategy organized by local labor leaders. In fact, it was a strategy promoted by the Spanish consul and authorities in Cuba who sent vessels to return the workers home. A mass departure of workers risked destroying a coherent community that was in touch with its historical traditions and favored Cuban independence. Labor leaders with a nationalist bent had also understood the potential consequences of mass departure for the revolutionary movement, but in 1889 things changed. Strike leaders, no longer interested in nationalist politics, now actively urged workers to leave for Havana.[51]

The situation became even more grave when nationalists learned of the Spanish consul's collusion with the strikers. Within days of the strike, Consul Luis Marinas and anarchist leaders asked Havana authorities to provide transportation for hundreds of workers waiting to return home. Gato, Poyo, Lamadriz, and others believed that Marinas had actually instigated the strike in the first place and made a complaint to this effect to the Key West Board of Trade. An investigative committee eventually concluded that he had indeed encouraged the workers not to settle their grievances and instead leave for Havana. Marinas admitted that he had urged workers to defend their rights but blamed the entire affair on "a handful of separatists" who depended on the cigar makers to fund their revolutionary mischief in Cuba. He also boasted to his superiors that cigar production had fallen precipitously, leaving the nationalist trouble makers crippled. The U.S. ambassador in Madrid called for the removal of Marinas, and the Spanish government complied, fearing an international diplomatic incident.[52]

Throughout 1889, *El Productor* had spent considerable energy trying to discredit the nationalist leaders, especially Poyo. It maintained a barrage of personal attacks in its attempts to counter *El Yara*'s hard-hitting articles and further undermine Poyo's traditional influence among workers. In April, the Key West correspondent in *El Productor* renewed its criticism about the proliferation of lotteries and other forms of gambling among the workers. Although these activities were often sponsored by the manufacturers, he was particularly concerned about *El Yara*'s support for this "corruption." In early May, the same critic suggested that *El Yara* had received funds from the manufacturers to sow discord among workers. In August, he charged Poyo with using his influence to advance the interests of the factory owners, including the owner of the Ellinger factory, where he worked as *lector*. He accused Poyo of being in league with the foreman, lording over the workers, and foisting injustices on the workers that he kept secret so not to lose his job as reader.[53] Another attack in Havana's *El Español* claimed that the influence of the patriot leaders had declined sharply and that wherever Poyo and his lackeys walked, they received rude whistles from the striking workers.[54]

Angered and frustrated by these personal attacks, Poyo refused to read the anarchist newspaper from the *tribuna* any longer "because it is a Spanish newspaper and those who send [critical] correspondence from here [Key West] are of doubtful nationality."[55] This angered the workers at the Ellinger factory, who voted to replace him, believing that they had a right to hear from any newspaper they wanted. Poyo was dejected to see workers increasingly abandon the nationalist credo that he had carefully cultivated and defended for twenty years. In need of work, insulted, and under constant assault, Poyo considered leaving Key West. Knowing of Máximo Gómez's strong connections in Honduras, Poyo asked the general about the possibilities of establishing a Honduran consulate in Tampa. His Peruvian consulship had never included a salary and he seemed determined to abandon the *lectura*.[56] But this was only a passing frustration, and Poyo quickly resumed his defense of the nationalist community. After the strike he found work reading in the Gato factory, and eventually he returned to the Ellinger factory. However, Poyo was emotionally bruised from his battles with the anarchists.

Finally, with no settlement in sight, the manufacturers capitulated in early January.[57] "Complete Triumph," declared *El Productor*.[58] At the end of the month, strike leaders in Key West called a meeting at the Salón Progreso (Hall of Progress) to offer an accounting of the committee's work and issue a vote of thanks to supporters in Havana and Tampa, including *El Productor* and *La Revista de Florida*.[59] The workers returned to their jobs, but the strike had created deep and painful animosities that divided the nationalist and working communities as never before.

Nationalists did not abandon their aggressive stance, confident that most workers remained committed to Cuban independence. Using a carrot-and-stick strategy, they reiterated their support for worker organizations and labor rights but again insisted that actions be taken in harmony with the interests of the revolutionary movement. When the local manufacturers' association provided funds for steamer fares, hundreds of workers returned to Key West from Tampa and Havana, but nationalists continued to demand that Cubans and not Spaniards fill the factory jobs.

On January 13, 1890, over 200 people gathered at San Carlos Institute with labor leaders Messonier, Castro Palomino, Izaguirre, and Corbet. After some debate, the assembly petitioned the factory owners not hire to Spaniards. *El Yara*'s report that labor agreed to cooperate with the nationalist community brought a sharp condemnation from *El Productor*, which now referred to the union leaders as *former* socialists: "They have fled the socialist party."[60] One labor leader explained that he did not in fact support the petition and rejected the idea that Spanish workers threatened the nationalist cause in Key West. But he acknowledged that most Cuban workers shared strong patriotic feelings and supported banning Spaniards, a reality that could not be overcome. Another worker complained to the Havana newspaper *El Español* that cowardice had won the day and that workers had delivered themselves with their feet and hands tied "to the party of exploiters led by the 'eminent' José de los Dolores de Pollo [sic]."[61]

Those associated with the Havana anarchists who remained unmoved and insisted on worker solidarity at all costs faced hostility and intimidation from the nationalists. When Enrique Creci, the editor of *El Buñuelo*, a labor newspaper, reaffirmed anarchist propositions and claimed that workers received his newspaper with enthusiasm, nationalists threatened him. On the evening of March 10, 1890, while Creci was riding in a coach on Farola Street, four members of the Partida la Tranca ordered him to leave town. Later, from Tampa, where he was working with *La Revista de Florida*, Creci criticized workers in Key West who claimed to be socialists but actually supported the expulsion of Spanish workers. He called Key West a political town and refused to recognize those supporting the nationalists as socialists.[62]

El Yara raised new concerns after the founding of a new socialist-oriented labor organization in Key West, Círculo de Trabajadores in March 1890. It cautioned the organization that as long as the Cuban people were without a nation and lived in slavery, the nationalist cause remained the predominant commitment of the Cuban exile community. The *Círculo de Trabajadores* responded with a flyer the next day asserting its goal of supporting the labor groups, education for workers, and workers' rights without diminishing support for the concepts independence and liberty. Somewhat defensively, the flyer appealed to the public for its verdict on the value of the work of the *Círculo de Trabajadores*: were its goals noble and edifying or was it a dangerous and divisive force in the heart of the community?[63]

In the meantime, conditions in Cuba for the anarchist labor movement changed quite significantly beginning in 1890. As May 1 approached, labor organizations in Cuba called a general strike to celebrate workers' day. Even though few workers supported the strike, it provoked repressive actions by the government. The situation worsened when General Camilo Polavieja, a conservative, became captain general of Cuba soon after these events and promised to destroy all opposition to Spanish rule. Arrests and prosecution of seventeen well-known anarchists soon followed. One of the arrested individuals was Messonier, who had returned to Havana. Though the anarchist leaders were ultimately released, they recognized that the colonial state would no longer tolerate their ideology and activities. As a result of this development, they developed a new appreciation for the nationalist movement.[64]

Most labor leaders eventually accepted the reality of nationalist ascendency. Over the next two years, labor leaders and propagandists Messonier, Baliño, Rivero, Sorondo, Segura, and even Creci, who had always sympathized with the idea of an independent Cuba but who prioritized labor concerns, returned to nationalist orthodoxy as a renewed patriotic enthusiasm gripped Key West and Tampa.

The mass immigration of Spanish workers and radical labor ideologies constituted serious threats to the integrity of the community that necessitated strong responses. Poyo's experience in Tampa, where nationalists failed to gain a foothold in 1886–1889, deepened his certainty about this. Key West nationalists managed to minimize the arrival of Spaniards using outright intimidation, some violence, and pressure on manufacturers to hire only Cubans, and they fought successfully to undermine labor leaders who promoted anti-nationalist discourses. Although the Knights of Labor and anarchists gained the upper hand for a time, the constant push-back by *El Yara*, *La Propaganda*, and political clubs eventually wore down these groups, and their leaders recognized that most workers sympathized with the nationalist agenda. When Cuban radical labor leaders in Key West finally accepted the primacy of nationalism over cross-ethnic solidarity with Spaniards, the political leaders returned to the business of organizing their community.

Poyo and his colleagues believed that the future of any independence movement required the survival of Key West as a militant revolutionary center. While Spanish reform policies in the 1880s caused many Cubans to change their perspective on armed revolution, attitudes among nationalist leaders in Key West remained steady. Although they had strategic disagreements about how to respond to changing situations, they remained committed to the idea that independence would never be achieved without a firmly militant center capable of maintaining a consistent message and providing resources for those willing to fight. This is why they defended the *baluarte cubano* at all costs.

5

PERSISTENCE

> I think that if through a discrete, prudent, and cautious plan we decided to take from Spaniards in Cuba the money needed to commence, we would save time and prevent difficulties that today seem insurmountable.
>
> José D. Poyo, 1888

One evening in late August 1887, José D. Poyo and Ten Years' War veteran General Juan Fernández Ruz, a newcomer to Key West, met with a group of conspirators and made final preparations for a small expedition. In the name of the Key West revolutionary committee, Poyo and Ruz commissioned Manuel Beribén (aka Quiebra Hachas, a hardwood tree known colloquially in Cuba as "axe-breaker") and Manuel García as commanders of around forty-five fighters. Few in Key West contributed to this small operation, but funds arrived from Cuba. Although the Spanish consul tried to monitor the group's comings and goings, all he could tell his superiors in September was that an expedition had left for Cardenas. Hearing that yet another contingent was preparing to depart, concerned authorities in Cuba dispatched a warship to patrol the waters around Key West. A Spanish vessel was also docked at Key West, and rumors circulated that it brought agents intending to kidnap Cuban American citizens involved in the latest activities. However, these rumors proved to be false.[1]

Key West Cubans persisted in fomenting revolution despite difficult circumstances. In addition to the disastrous fire that destroyed the community's financial base, New York Cubans remained opposed to insurgency, the autonomist liberals in Havana continued to seek accommodation, workers seemed disengaged from nationalism, and military leaders had not yet recovered from their latest defeat. Gone were the days of patriotic enthusiasm when manufacturers and workers conspired together and donated funds to the cause.

One correspondent in New York declared that patriotism was on the decline and that financial contributions had dried up.[2] However, the local nationalist leadership in Key West adjusted. *El Yara* and *La Propaganda* continued the nationalist drumbeat, and Manuel Beribén and Manuel García offered new ways of challenging Spanish power. Poyo pursued these strategies with his usual determination.

Politicized *Bandoleros*

During the mid- to late 1880s, difficult economic and social conditions in rural Cuba gave rise to a grave problem with marauding bands that the Spanish government referred to as *bandoleros* (bandits). Dozens of independent bands roamed the countryside, forcing the Spanish government to establish a Civil Guard that was capable of tracking them down. But not all were purely bandits. Many were bandits turned patriots who justified their activities with nationalist rhetoric and financial donations to the independence cause. Regardless of their motivations, the bands shared a similar modus operandi that included attacking military outposts, farms, plantations, and small towns and confiscating supplies and livestock. Kidnapping and ransoming prominent plantation owners or their family members proved the most lucrative. For example, in 1885 and 1886, abductions in Matanzas produced 70,000 gold pesos. Plantation owners even paid annual levies to avoid kidnappings or having their fields torched. In 1884, authorities provided the Rural Guard with permanent garrisons, especially in the sugar zones, forcing many of the marauders to depart for Key West, a close and hospitable safe haven. Others took advantage of a Spanish policy that provided safe passage if they agreed to cease operations. Key West authorities bitterly complained about this policy.[3]

Among the fighters being organized by Poyo and Ruz to embark for Cuba in 1887 were veterans of Carlos Aguero's guerrilla operation and a number of recent bandit arrivals to Key West. Some, like Aguero's and Bonachea's men in the early part of the decade had clear nationalist credentials and goals and were seen by many Cubans as patriots. Perico Torres, Rosendo García, and José Alvarez Arteaga (Matagás), members of Carlos Aguero's expedition, remained in Cuba after their leader's death. Torres and Rosendo García joined Lengüe Romero, a notorious bandit in Havana Province, and

Matagás established his own group in Matanzas. Before joining Aguero in 1883, Matagás had traveled around Cuba's countryside robbing travelers, but he soon committed to the separatist cause. He remained in action until he was killed in 1896. Throughout 1885 both groups participated in kidnappings and robberies, all the while proclaiming "Viva Cuba Libre," presumably waiting for the arrival of Máximo Gómez and Antonio Maceo.[4]

When Torres slipped out of Cuba on the steamer *Mascotte* in early 1886, he was accompanied by another member of the Romero group, Manuel García. Other insurgent bandits, including Manuel Beribén, Emilio García, Isidoro Leijas, Victor Fragoso, Domingo Montelongo, and Salomé Escassi, settled in Key West with their families and found jobs in the cigar industry. Beribén and Emilio García had accompanied Maceo for a while before infiltrating Cuba and then fleeing to Key West. In 1884, Emilio García regularly smuggled correspondence from Gómez and Maceo to Julio Sanguily, Carlos Aguero, and others.[5] According to the Spanish consul, *bandoleros* arrived regularly in Key West, and in July 1887, he reported that "four individuals of Matagás' group, three blacks and a white," disembarked from the steamer *Mascotte*.[6]

The arrival of these tough characters in Key West coincided with Tuerto Rodríguez's efforts to organize a fighting contingent and leave for Cuba at the appropriate moment. Rodríguez, who was born in Puerto Principe, Dominican Republic, in 1846, fought with a cavalry unit in Camaguey in 1868. He fought in many of the important battles and rose to brigadier general before leaving Cuba after the Zanjón Pact. He joined Gómez in Honduras in 1883 and accepted his assignment in Key West two years later.[7] Rodríguez had operated with some patriot-bandits in Cuba for a time and asked the group in Key West to support his expedition, but he abandoned the enterprise after the fire and a significant shift in the mood of workers regarding revolutionary action.[8]

Disappointed with Rodríguez's departure and especially angry when Gómez and Maceo quit their activities, Rosendo García and Perico Torres took charge of organizing the expedition. More *bandoleros* arrived and joined their efforts with the expedition. Many of those who lacked a political consciousness or experience with nationalist activities soon imbibed the patriotic atmosphere. They listened to the *lectores* in the factories, heard community orators, and participated in political clubs, activities that fused their complex bandit origins with nationalist enthusiasm. But they made little progress with the expedition.

The difficult situation in Key West after the fire forced patriot-bandits to earn wages. Rosendo García and Torres found work at the Martínez Ybor factory in Tampa along with Manuel García, Isidoro Leijas, and a number of others. Emilio García opened a bar in Ybor City. These men played a leading role in the Black Guard vigilante group in Tampa, which was much like the Partida la Tranca in Key West, and several participated in the violent confrontation at the Mascotte bar. They returned to Key West in February and March 1887, when the Tampa Board of Trade threatened the safety of the Cuban nationalists. Only Emilio García and Leijas remained in Tampa. They had been charged with the murder of a Knights of Labor activist and had to stay in the city until their trial the following year. A jury found them not guilty due to the contradictory testimony of eyewitnesses.[9]

General Juan Fernández Ruz, Poyo's collaborator in dispatching the Beribén-García expedition, arrived in Key West March 1887. Ruz was a Ten Years' War veteran who had settled in Barcelona after the Zanjón Pact. He made his way to New York in mid-1886, when the Gómez-Maceo initiative offered the strong possibility of another insurrection. Despite the demise of that initiative, Ruz continued to Key West, where he joined the Rosendo García-Perico Torres group and quickly became their leader.[10]

Apparently, Poyo's role in all of this was to offer encouragement and insist on the political legitimacy of their activities. Poyo was especially intrigued with Manuel García and suggested he lead the planned expedition along with Beribén, Ruz's favorite. Beribén, who was originally from a well-to-do family in Biscay, in the Basque region of Spain, had arrived in Cuba fifteen years earlier and had joined the insurgent forces during the Ten Years' War. In 1887, he was thirty-three years old. The six-foot-tall, 240-pound man with blue eyes and wide whiskers possessed charisma, clear revolutionary credentials, and republican ideals.[11]

Manuel García was a less obvious choice as a leader. Poyo no doubt saw in 37-year-old García the silent, uncultured man of rough aspect and poor manners who was also the practical, consumed, bold, cunning, and generous man that one historian later described. In addition, he was a good shot. In 1871, García had murdered his stepfather for beating his mother and turned to rural banditry.[12] Despite García's less-than-appealing style, Poyo recognized that like Aguero before him, he had intense anti-Spanish attitudes, well-honed fighting skills, and considerable experience with kidnapping and ransoming prominent wealthy figures, a practice that could provide resources that were not available in the exile communities.

This new revolutionary strategy built on Aguero's guerrilla experience and for the time promised to spread some measure of havoc and insecurity in Cuba's already turbulent rural districts. Though the operations of bandits promoted instability and the impression of ongoing insurrectionary activity, they also had the potential to inspire a revolutionary vanguard, not unlike what Bonachea had envisioned. The Spanish consul viewed the *bandoleros* with great concern and warned his superiors to prevent them from reaching Key West. The next year the consul confirmed the growing success of nationalists in politicizing bandits, declaring that "banditry can no longer be considered a common crime, it is responding to a political plan, which promotes independence as well as annexation."[13]

After landing in Matanzas, Beribén and García marched with their forty or fifty fighters for six days into the Morejón Mountains, where they encountered a large Spanish force. Newspapers in the United States initially reported that Spanish forces had killed García but later clarified that Beribén, not García, had fallen. The Spanish captured seventeen fighters, but the rest reached the mountains and regrouped. García and the remaining men then made their way toward Havana Province and rejoined Lengüe Romero. When Romero died in action in January 1888, García took charge and in the next months gained considerable notoriety for two kidnappings that raised at least $17,000, a portion of which made its way to Key West.[14] As García's fame grew, he began referring to himself as Rey de los Campos (King of the Countryside) and publicizing his goal of *Cuba libre*.

Disputes and Divisions

Despite the promising collaboration between Ruz and Poyo and the renewal of revolutionary activism in Key West, personal differences and disagreements about strategy split the community there. Ruz was a rather flamboyant and charismatic character with a considerable ego who presented himself as the natural and obvious successor to Gómez and Maceo. Because of his distinguished career fighting in Cuba in the Ten Years' War, Ruz believed that he was the man of the hour, the one who was capable of uniting Cubans behind a new effort to revolutionize the island. Ruz's plans included building a coalition of revolutionary groups in the various exile communities. He visited New York in October 1887, where he met with a group that José Martí had convened to listen to his propositions. While the New Yorkers listened politely, they were not impressed, and Ruz returned to Key West with only vague promises of support that never materialized.[15]

Back in Key West, Ruz sensed a change in attitudes about him. Ruz had badly mishandled his relations with the nationalist leadership there, beginning with Poyo. His pompous manner and his clear desire to command alienated Poyo, who remained loyal to Gómez. Ruz especially erred in publicly accusing Gómez of not accounting for the thousands of dollars he had raised in Key West, a criticism that circulated in the community after the general abandoned his plan to invade Cuba. Lamadriz and Figueredo also considered Gómez the movement's indisputable leader and followed Poyo's lead. In January 1888, these three men and several others formed a group called Los Diez (The Ten) that worked to discredit Ruz's activities.[16]

To further complicate matters, the popular and charismatic General Flor Crombet arrived in Key West in February. Thirty-eight-year-old Crombet, who was born to a French family of color that was probably originally from Haiti, joined the Ten Years' War in 1868 and demonstrated a tenaciousness that gave him a reputation as one of the best guerrilla fighters. He participated in many battles, rose to the rank of general, and joined Maceo's protest against the Zanjón Pact. During the Little War he suffered arrest, but in 1881 he escaped and joined Gómez and Maceo in Honduras.[17]

Crombet initially agreed to Ruz's plan for revolution, which involved an expedition composed mostly of the patriot-bandits in league with Manuel García who had provided funds for the enterprise. But relations between the two men soon soured. Ruz informed Crombet that he had offered General Julio Sanguily the military leadership in Vuelta Abajo and wanted him to direct operations in another region. Offended by Ruz's presumption, Crombet responded that he had not gone to Key West to place himself under Ruz's orders, especially since most military chiefs remained loyal to Máximo Gómez. Ruz responded clumsily by reminding people that Crombet was black as a way to discredit him. He also accused Crombet of being Gómez's puppet and even perhaps an undercover autonomist intent on denouncing revolutionary plans and turning Ruz over to Spanish authorities.[18]

Crombet lashed out in kind, calling Ruz immoral for relying on bandits to spark a revolution in Cuba, a strategy he would never support. This sealed the breach between the two men. The Key West nationalist leadership not only applauded this conflict but helped instigate it. The consul speculated that Ruz's lack of tact and inability to get along with the revolutionary leaders in Key West was attributable to his personal vanity and lack of education.

Nevertheless, Ruz remained active and gathered followers. Not dissuaded by his inability to win a firm commitment from New York's nationalists or by his lack of success in Key West, he continued to work with the patriot-bandits and gained backing from a small group in Key West led by Federico Gil Marrero, who reestablished the nihilist club that had been founded in 1883. This time it was called El Nivel (Level or Even or Equality). Throughout 1888, Ruz acted as Manuel García's point man in Key West and received considerable sums of money from him. He also developed relations with numerous groups in Cuba, including a revolutionary committee in Havana.

In August 1888, Ruz received notice that armed groups were ready and waiting in Santiago de Cuba, Puerto Principe, Santa Clara, Remedios, Cárdenas, Cienfuegos, and Matanzas, but he failed to convert his plans into concrete revolutionary action. His conflicts with the leading nationalists left him without enough legitimacy to lead, and eventually even many of his close supporters abandoned him. In November, Ruz finally quit altogether and went to New York, where he published a manifesto before returning to Barcelona. He blamed the nationalist leaders in Key West for his failure, especially Poyo, Lamadriz, Figueredo, and several others.[19]

Meanwhile, with the full support of key nationalist leaders, Crombet continued to try to energize workers in the factories in Key West and Tampa, but with little success. Few workers attended a mass meeting in Key West on March 7, 1888, a sign of their continuing reluctance to contribute their wages to another nationalist enterprise. Workers were focused on labor activism and for the moment were more drawn to anarchist than nationalist ideals. At an earlier meeting of the Cuban black community's Sociedad el Progreso, numerous welcoming speeches extolled the glories of the past war. Noticing that nobody mentioned Máximo Gómez, Crombet reminded the audience that he represented the veteran general, but he had misread them. Labor activist Carlos Baliño openly declared that ideas, not men, inspired him and that he might even reconsider his attitudes about Spain should labor policies in Cuba change to allow greater freedom of action. Baliño's comment provoked a rebuke from *La Propaganda*, which insisted on independence before everything.[20] This kind of challenge to the nationalists had been unthinkable before 1886, but in 1888 it was not uncommon.

Another meeting on March 11 produced a similar result, leaving Crombet discouraged and some in the Cuban nationalist black community furious because they perceived the lack of response to Crombet from workers a racial slight to their community. The Spanish consul saw it otherwise: "The truth is, even if Crombet was as white as snow the result would have been the same since no one is now disposed to give more money to the freeloaders."[21] In a final effort, the nationalist community met on April 11 at the Odd Fellows Hall on Caroline Street. Nearly all of the nationalist leaders attended, including Lamadriz, Figueredo, Herrera, Morúa Delgado, and about fifty others, and issued a manifesto that called on Key West to support the visiting revolutionary leader.[22]

The meeting produced some enthusiasm, but few in the community donated funds, confirming that even respected military leaders could not overcome popular disenchantment. A discouraged Crombet left for New York in July but fared no better there. Finally, in a controversial move, he gave up and returned to Cuba, taking advantage of an amnesty that Spanish authorities had offered to former insurgents who faced legal sanction.[23]

Poyo did not attend the April 11 meeting, reflecting his skepticism about the possibility of raising funds for the nationalist cause. Throughout these months Poyo had been silent, refusing to take a public stand about the personal controversies between Ruz and Crombet. This was a striking contrast to his behavior in previous years, when he had publicly exhorted Key West Cubans to contribute to the Gómez-Maceo initiative. Experience had taught Poyo that a revolutionary should be circumspect, prudent, careful in communication, and not boastful. A revolutionary had to keep the enemy ignorant of his activities and maintain the element of surprise. For that reason *El Yara* did not discuss organizing activities or strategies. It focused on condemning autonomist, annexationist, and anarchist challenges to the ideal of independence. Poyo knew that constant public disagreements hurt the community's reputation, since it suggested a lack of capability and seriousness and gave its enemies important information. Others could do what they wished, but Poyo had learned the importance of discretion from repeated failures and bitter experience.[24]

Privately, however, he let his colleagues know that neither Ruz nor Crombet offered a viable alternative at the moment. While Poyo shared Ruz's vision of filling Cuba with an endless parade of guerrilla groups who could create generalized disaffection with Spanish rule and raise funds, he rejected what he saw as Ruz's grandiosity, immoral character, and refusal to accept Gómez and Maceo as the revolution's natural leaders. Poyo acknowledged Ruz's brave career during the Ten Years' War but characterized him as "dead, morally and politically."[25]

Although Poyo admired Crombet and supported him unconditionally as Gómez's comrade, he argued that Key West was not ready for new fund-raising drives. Too many in Key West were still angry about the failed Gomez-Maceo campaign and too distracted with labor ideologies and working-class activism. One observer criticized Poyo for discouraging fund-raising efforts in the factories, saying, "Poyo always the same—waiting for another day," but Crombet's inability to create enthusiasm and raise funds for his enterprise proved Poyo's point.[26]

Poyo nevertheless remained enthusiastic about infiltrating Cuba to promote unrest and rebelliousness. *El Yara* supported Manuel García, who could raise the resources he needed where they existed, among Cuba's wealthy, especially since revolutionaries in exile could not expect help from anyone.[27] Poyo became Manuel García's primary contact in Key West after Ruz left. In a letter to Máximo Gómez, Poyo argued that "if through a discrete, prudent, and cautious plan we decided to take from Spaniards in Cuba the money needed to commence, we would save time and prevent difficulties that today seem insurmountable."[28]

As Poyo had hoped, the kidnapping and extortion activities of Manuel García and many others transformed the rural districts around Havana into a virtual war zone. The government's inability to guarantee peace in the countryside frightened planters, who wondered whether authorities could provide a stable environment. This situation had serious political implications for Spain. Things became so difficult that in April 1888 the captain general imposed martial law in the provinces of Pinar del Río, Havana, Matanzas, and Santa Clara, placing the administration of justice directly under military control. Poyo believed that this action would foment rebellion. "We accept the challenge," *El Yara* announced.[29] Emergency governance remained in force through 1889 without much success, but the capacity of the military was strengthened in 1890, when the new captain general, Camilo G. Polavieja, dispatched 10,000 soldiers to rural districts in a clearly military operation. Although Spanish troops killed, captured, or executed many, this effort was still not sufficient, and bandits remained a dangerous threat to the established classes in the rural areas.[30]

In January 1889, García ordered his followers in Key West who were under the leadership of Bernardino Trujillo (aka José Rodríguez) to heed Poyo's instructions. "Poyo is so intent on organizing this latest movement," noted the Spanish consul, "that he did not attend the inauguration of the San Carlos."[31] Instead, the consul continued, that evening he met with "el negro" (Trujillo) for several hours to discuss preparations for another expedition. Several days later, Poyo again met with Trujillo and Emilio García to resolve an apparent disagreement over who would lead the guerrilla contingent; both Trujillo and García wanted to be the *jefe* of the expedition.

The consul was suspicious about the enterprise. He speculated that this activity was perhaps a decoy because preparations suffered "certain defects." In fact, the consul told superiors that Poyo had received a letter from Havana reporting that Manuel García had attempted to leave the island several times without success and asking that Poyo send a guerrilla contingent as a distraction. The consul did not consider the expedition a threat, but he warned authorities in Cuba that if these bandits were not eliminated they could well serve as the basis for a future revolutionary movement, which, of course, was precisely Poyo's goal. In May 1889, Poyo received another $1,140 from García's kidnapping activities in Cuba.[32]

Poyo's support of García and his willingness to use explosives created considerable controversy in Key West throughout the 1880s. In fact, none of the other important Key West leaders except Poyo's son-in-law Delgado and Dr. Manuel Moreno figured in these activities with García. Some opposed these strategies as too radical and inherently immoral and viewed Poyo and his group as fanatics.[33]

In 1884, a friend of Poyo's reported on his activities to the Spanish consul, saying that he considered himself a Cuban patriot but felt that Poyo's activities were criminal. Another critic, Néstor Leonelo Carbonell, a Ten Years' War veteran who arrived in Key West around 1886 and later became a leading nationalist leader in Tampa, refused to participate in Poyo's activities with the patriot-bandits and argued that the end did not justify the means. Pedro Pequeño, editor of Key West's *El Cubano*, for which Carbonell also wrote, also publicly condemned efforts to organize "bandit expeditions." Pequeño was so opposed to these strategies that in late 1889 he returned to Havana as a converted autonomist after publishing a proclamation denouncing the "immoral practices" of the separatist party. Morúa Delgado was also disillusioned with nationalist politics of exiles and returned to Cuba in 1889, where he published *La Nueva Era* and participated in autonomist politics.[34]

The Spanish consul reported that even Lamadriz and Figueredo expressed doubts about Poyo's activities and did not take part, but this may have been less out of principle than because of personal considerations. Lamadriz, an attorney, had to consider the effects of associating with patriot-bandits on his professional standing, while Figueredo, a local political figure, had to protect his reputation with the voting public. In the 1880s his public service included representing Monroe County in the Florida Assembly, working as customs inspector, and achieving election as Superintendent of Public Education.[35]

In contrast, Poyo's work as *lector* and as editor of his own newspaper left him quite free to act. In an irony of history, only his local ideological nemesis, Manuel Moreno, a representative of Monroe County to the Florida Assembly, also supported García, but for different reasons than Poyo. Moreno was an annexationist who believed that if guerrilla groups caused enough chaos, the United States might be persuaded to intervene and take control of the island. This was certainly not the goal Poyo had in mind. Poyo's radicalism often left him "alone, abandoned, scorned, [and] accused as demented," according to Figueredo, but he "maintained faith and heart."[36]

Poyo was simply advocating on a smaller scale what the army of insurrection would do in a grander fashion when the independence war erupted. Máximo Gómez, Antonio Maceo, and the liberation army implemented guerrilla warfare, used scorched-earth tactics, and extorted plantation owners; these were indispensable strategies for keeping the Spanish army at bay.[37] Poyo did not view insurgency and war as a romantic adventure; he saw it as a brutish affair to be pursued with all available methods. He had made this clear in 1883 and 1884. From his point of view, the war had not ended in

1878 or even in 1880; he rejected the Zanjón Pact and continued the struggle without compromise. The revolutionary party—a party of action—was invariably obligated to try every strategy, and as far as Poyo was concerned, "the measures available to carry out the work are as many and varied as may fit in the abstract idea of the revolutionary."[38]

Convención Cubana

In December 1889, in the midst of frustrating divisions about nationalist strategy and leadership and challenges from Havana anarchists that included the strike that closed down the entire industry in Key West, a group of nationalists gathered to evaluate the situation. They agreed on the futility of broad-based fund-raising efforts and decided on an approach that relied heavily on organizing revolutionary sympathizers in Cuba. They returned to the model of the secret organization, Orden Cosmopólita del Sol, that Poyo had introduced in 1878 and Club Máximo Gómez had used again in 1884. They called the new organization the Convención Cubana. A political arm, Club Luz de Yara (Light of Yara Club), issued public pronouncements and instructions, but the two organizations had the same officers: Lamadriz (president), Poyo (vice-president), and Figueredo (secretary). Each of the Convención Cubana's twenty-five members was sworn to secrecy. They organized as much of the community as possible through additional clubs that were subordinate to the Convención. The two main objectives of the organization were raising funds to purchase and store weapons and promoting revolutionary cells in Cuba. The first goal was postponed until a more propitious time, but organizing Cuba was immediately feasible and became the organization's primary preoccupation.

Four committees spearheaded activities: War, Treasury, Propaganda and Correspondence. Manufacturers Gato, Recio, and Soria took charge of the Treasury Committee, and military veterans Figueredo, Gerardo Castellanos, and José Rogelio Castillo led the War Committee. Poyo and Manuel P. Delgado handled the Correspondence Committee. Initially, at least, the correspondence and war committees played the most important roles of establishing contacts with insurgent elements in Cuba, beginning with messages to Máximo Gómez and Antonio Maceo, who were at their headquarters in Santo Domingo and Jamaica, respectively.[39]

Figure 4. Membership of the Convención Cubana de Cayo Hueso, a secret patriotic institution. *Top Row:* José Martí, Carlos Roloff, José D. Poyo, and Tomás Estrada Palma. From Juan J. E. Casasus, *La emigración cubana y la independencia de la patria* (Havana: Editorial Lex, 1933).

Other revolutionary contacts in Cuba included Guillermo Moncada and Bartolomé Masó in Oriente; Manuel and Ricardo Sartorio in Holguín; Luaces and Mola in Puerto Principe; Luís Lagomasino and Federico Zayas in Las Villas; Julio Sanguily, Juan Gualberto Gómez, and others in Havana; and, of course, the many other veterans scattered in the communities where exiles had gathered. In Villa de Placetas in the province of Las Villas, Luís Lagomasino, who owned the newspaper *El Cubano* and was head of a revolutionary club, Provisional de Cinco Villas no. 2, responded positively to Poyo and Figueredo, with whom he had collaborated since 1883. He attributed his own expertise in revolutionary work "to the indefatigable propagandist José Dolores Poyo, Director de 'El Yara' de Key West, Fla."[40]

In early February 1890, around the time the new secret organization was formed, news arrived in Key West that Antonio Maceo, like Crombet, had accepted an invitation from Cuba's governor to discuss his reintegration into Cuban society. Although he was not serious about renouncing revolution, Maceo saw the opportunity for gathering firsthand information about the state of affairs in Cuba. He traveled to Havana and checked into the Hotel Inglaterra, in the heart of the city. Immediately he convened clandestine meetings with dozens of sympathizers of the insurgency, many of whom were already in contact with the revolutionaries in Key West. He also met with associations of working-class Afro-Cubans who were linked with anarchists, a demonstration of the growing convergence of separatist and labor interests.[41] He traveled throughout the provinces of Havana and Pinar del Rio and across the island to Oriente and sent agents to places he did not visit to determine the general state of intent and readiness.

In a letter to Convención leaders, Maceo characterized the revolutionary situation in Cuba as positive but not quite ready for action. He designated the Convención as the chief revolutionary center in exile and named Máximo Gómez the military leader. Two prominent intellectuals coordinated Maceo's plan in Havana. One of them was Juan Gualberto Gómez, a well-educated journalist who was the best-known nonwhite Cuban intellectual. He had suffered arrest and imprisonment in Ceuta for a time during the Little War, but he was given probatory release in Madrid, where he stayed until 1890. He returned to Cuba in time to accept Maceo's offer to coordinate revolutionary activities in Havana, which he shared with Manuel Sanguily, a colonel during the war whose intellectual talents became evident in writings and speeches throughout the 1880s. Maceo and the island rebels finally set October 10, 1890, the anniversary of the Grito de Yara, as the date for launching the insurrection.⁴²

In April, Convención representatives traveled to Cuba and met with Maceo and a group of insurgent leaders, probably to discuss funneling resources to the rebels and preparing an expedition. A week later the Spanish consul reported the formation of several new revolutionary clubs, including the Liga de Cubanos Independientes (League of Independent Cubans), which was headed by Juan Arnao, who had settled in Key West after decades in New York. Like other new Key West organizations, the League of Independent Cubans was subordinate to the Convención. It took charge of training and equipping recruits for the expedition. Members of this group included Rosendo García, Perico Torres, Bernardino Trujillo, and numerous others.⁴³

In theory, the Convención did not intend to support guerrilla operations of the type Poyo advocated or support the activities of Manuel García, but activities quickly moved in that direction. From New York, manufacturer and Convención member Eduardo H. Gato shipped rifles to several different people in Key West so not to raise suspicions; including five to Francisco Ybern (*El Yara's* office manager), five to Carlos Recio, and more to Emilio García and Juan Arnao. Gato also sent $200 toward the purchase of the schooner. A very concerned consul sent a telegram to Cuba's captain general on August 31: "Expedition of bandits organized to join Manuel García in Cuba. Schooner purchased. Possess 30 rifles. Waiting for orders to launch." He followed with the information that the expedition would depart at night under the command of Torres or Rosendo García and coordinate with Manuel García.⁴⁴

In Cuba, Maceo also contacted Manuel García through General Julio Sanguily, Manuel's older brother. Born in 1846, Julio had studied in the United States and had joined Manuel de Quesada's *Galvanic* expedition in 1868 and had fought on Cuba's battlefields in the Ten Years' War. He led a lethal cavalry unit from Camaguey. In short order he rose to the rank of general, and he served with Gómez.⁴⁵ Sanguily had emerged from the war with a stellar reputation as a fierce fighter and remained in Cuba, where he instigated and supported conspiracies in the 1880s. He had secured Carlos Aguero a safe conduct pass from Spanish authorities to Key West in 1883, and now he served as intermediary between Maceo and García. In summer 1889, García had again achieved headlines with a series of kidnappings, and he returned briefly to Key West before meeting with Sanguily and Maceo.[46] Maceo instructed García about what to do when the rebellion erupted, but while he was waiting for things to begin, the Rey de los Campos continued his normal activities.

In the late afternoon of June 20, 1890, armed with rifles, machetes, and revolvers, García's group attacked the town of San Nicolás, southwest of Havana. They targeted a store, taking all available cash as well as supplies, and kidnapped the merchant and another resident of the town. While waiting for a ransom of 8,500 gold pesos for the two men, he extorted the railroad companies for 15,000 pesos with threats to derail trains, kill mechanics, and burn stations. The threat to the transportation system may have been made in coordination with Maceo, who continued to travel the island making connections with insurgent groups. In August, Maceo contacted the Convención about the status of the expedition.[47]

Not surprisingly, Spanish intelligence learned of Maceo's plans, and the government acted. On August 29, 1890, police surrounded his hotel and ordered him and his family to leave the very next day on a steamer for New York. Days later, many of the leaders of the conspiracy, including Flor Crombet, suffered the same fate. In New York, Maceo informed nationalist leaders in Key West of his optimism and intention to continue and said that he would soon visit them. Convención leaders urged their networks in Cuba to be patient and cautious, especially the enthusiastic Lagomasino group in La Villas. The League of Independent Cubans, which had 327 active members and almost $14,000 in cash, remained ready.[48]

However, many rank-and-file fighters in Key West lost patience and gathered at Emilio Garcia's bar to lament the delays. García declared himself fed up with the waiting, and others agreed. They should forget the local *jefes* in Key West and immediately join Manuel García in Cuba, commented one man. Another disagreed, counseling patience, while yet another wondered when final instructions would arrive from Cuba. Meanwhile, instead of going to Key West, Maceo departed immediately for Honduras to prepare his landing in Cuba, where two thousand men waited his arrival to initiate operations. He told Poyo to remain expectant and asked for any available funds.[49]

The Spanish consul remained vigilant and reported that despite Maceo's departure from Cuba the rebels in Key West remained active and continued to accumulate funds. He provided Spanish authorities with a list of twenty-nine "*dinamitistas*," by which he meant the activists of the League of Independent Cubans. According to the consul, these men included seven "bandits, thieves and murderers"; four cigar manufacturers; four merchants, two tobacco workers; four *lectores*; three journalist/printers; two government employees; one bookkeeper; a pharmacist; and a barber. He said that they usually met at the Gil Marrero or Cecilio Henríquez cigar factories or at Poyo's home, which was still protected because he was the Peruvian consul.[50]

Everything remained quiet throughout October and November as the insurrectionists waited for developments in Cuba, but the news was not encouraging. Maceo had not arrived, and Spanish authorities increased their pursuit of the other conspirators across the island. They also pursued Manuel García, who was desperately trying to get out of Cuba. Julio Sanguily in Cuba, who was trying to help García, cautioned Rosendo García and Torres in Key West to remain still, by which he meant that they should not send the expedition or try to contact Manuel García, since this might alert authorities to his whereabouts.[51]

García appeared again briefly in Key West in March 1891 and likely consulted with Poyo and Manuel Moreno, among others. But García tired of waiting for Maceo and returned to the island in April, where he made the bold step of declaring war on Spain. In a manifesto dated April 27, García proclaimed himself general of the Occidental Department of the Island of Cuba and rejected the legitimacy of Spanish rule. Listing a litany of grievances, including unfair taxes, government corruption, personal insults, and abrogation of civil rights, he proclaimed independence and the creation of a republic. Curiously, a version of the document appeared in English that also called for Cuba's annexation to the United States. The origin of that document is a mystery, but it may be that while García was in Key West, Manuel Moreno persuaded him to include the annexationist passage to encourage the United States to intervene. Poyo and the great majority of Key West nationalists would never have consented to such a proclamation; it suggests either some duplicity on García's part or a less-than-sophisticated understanding of the political implications of such a statement.[52]

García's action was perhaps designed to force the hand of many conspirators, including Maceo, who had informed supporters in Santiago de Cuba, Baracoa, and Holguín that he would soon leave for the island from Costa Rica. Nobody in Cuba responded to García's call, and Maceo remained in exile, but the King of the Countryside continued his raids and kidnappings. In Key West, nationalists again lowered their visibility to await another opportunity while organizing insurrectionists in Cuba and receiving funds from patriot-bandit groups who continued to create a climate of unrest.[53]

If nothing else, Maceo's activities in 1890 and 1891 and the Convención's preparations in Key West stirred nationalist enthusiasm. This was highlighted at the October 10, 1890, commemoration of the declaration of Cuban independence. The nationalist community gathered at eight in the morning and the La Libertad band led students carrying the Cuban and American flags in a large parade down the principal streets to the cemetery. Behind them followed members of the Círculo Cubano, Liga de Trabajadores Cubanos, Club Patria y Libertad, Club Independiente, Liga de Cubanos Independientes, and the Afro-Cuban group Sociedad el Progreso, among others, carrying banners and images of Carlos Manuel de Céspedes, Francisco V. Aguilera, and other martyrs.

At the cemetery, Methodist pastor E. B. Someillán led his church choir in hymns. Speeches followed, and the venerable exile veteran Arnao condemned the autonomists, whom he held responsible for delaying the inevitable revolution in Cuba. Representatives of the various clubs spoke, as did Flor Crombet, who was representing military veterans. Poyo closed the ceremony by reciting an "epic poem" dedicated to Carlos Manuel de Céspedes, the martyr he held in special regard. That night Arnao presided at another meeting at San Carlos Institute, where spectators listened to two more hours of speeches promising a free Cuba.[54]

The failure of the Gómez-Maceo initiative, the Key West fire, and the rise of labor ideologies that were attractive to Cuban workers in Key West made mobilizing nationalists in the Key West community very difficult in the late 1880s, but nationalist leaders changed their strategies to meet the new circumstances. Few residents of Key West continued to provide resources, and the practice of raising funds in the factories no longer worked. But Poyo recognized an alternative in the mid-1880s when Cuba's patriot-bandits began their operations. The considerable experience of these men in kidnapping and ransoming wealthy planters and raiding small towns offered a new source of funds. Poyo and other nationalists helped politicize those without nationalist consciousness, and many infiltrated Cuba as small bands of guerrilla fighters determined to cause whatever havoc they could. They raised money for themselves and for the revolutionary treasury in Key West. Manuel García and Matagás proved the most successful, and they both continued their activities until the outbreak of the second war of independence.

Some nationalist leaders in Key West expressed ambivalence about and others expressed outright opposition to this turn in the strategy of the nationalists, characterizing it as immoral and not in keeping with the noble goals of the nationalist movement. But Poyo viewed this as the only viable approach, at least until the workers regained their enthusiasm for the cause. These *bandoleros* took on patriot identities—some sincerely and others as a way of justifying their banditry—and gained a kind of political legitimacy in Key West and Cuba. They cooperated with the Convención's conspiracies, became important allies in spreading nationalist sentiment, and helped create an environment conducive to revolution.

6

MARTÍ

> Let's help this man by offering him our patriotic support and our cooperation.
> José D. Poyo, 1892

On Christmas Day 1892, José F. Lamadriz and José D. Poyo, president and vice-president respectively of the Convención Cubana, stood on the waterfront in Key West, accompanied by a young tobacco worker, Genaro Hernández, the head of the community's organizing and invitations committee for this event. Other local revolutionary leaders, a large crowd, and the Libertad band waited with them as the steamer *Olivette* from Tampa eased toward the dock. Visible on the vessel's deck was a fragile, serious-looking 39-year-old man with a receding hairline and a moustache who was wearing a black suit and tie and a white shirt. José Martí was distinct and unforgettable, and Poyo recognized him immediately. As Martí disembarked from the ship, Lamadriz, Poyo, and Hernández approached him. The crowd cheered and the band played. "I embrace the past revolution," Martí said emotionally as he embraced Lamadriz. "And I embrace the future revolution," Lamadriz responded. Poyo also embraced Martí, as did Hernández. Fernando Figueredo, the third-ranking Convención leader, was conspicuously absent; he opposed the visit.

The crowd escorted the four men to a coach for transportation to the Duval House, but even though he was suffering from severe bronchitis, Martí refused to ride. He excitedly walked the couple of blocks to the hotel, where young Hernández stood on a chair in the lobby and gave Martí the official welcome from the organizing committee. Martí said that he already felt better, referring to his bronchial illness, because "this is my medicine, Cubans; here is the comforting medicine of the soul, which like the body also suffers illness." That evening at a banquet, Martí sat between Lamadriz and Juan Arnao, the two most prestigious elders of the revolutionary community. Feeling inspired, he offered toasts on three separate occasions before retiring for the night. The next day he awoke exuberant but even more sick, and Dr. Eligio Palma ordered a strict regimen of bed rest and quiet.[1]

This encounter initiated Poyo's and Key West's relationship with Martí. The Florida group lacked one individual who was capable of rising above the rest and claiming overall leadership of the revolutionary movement. In fact, there had never been such a leader in the communities in exile, which in part explained their inability to work in concert. Poyo and his colleagues brought many talents to the task of revolution but not the characteristics and skills necessary to defuse competing interests and unify a diverse community for a final assault on Spanish rule in Cuba. The Key West community had experience, organization, and commitment, and its members had helped create revolutionary cells in Cuba, but it lacked the charismatic leadership Martí revealed in Florida. Poyo's friendship with Martí symbolized the integration of talent, skills, and plans required to finally spark a revolutionary movement of national proportions.

Tampa

This was Poyo's second encounter with the prominent revolutionary orator and writer from New York, whom he had met briefly just weeks earlier in Tampa. But he had been well-acquainted with Martí's writings and erudition since his first speech in New York in early 1880, which had been sold in pamphlet form for ten cents a copy in Key West. Poyo no doubt read that speech at the Martínez Ybor factory, introducing workers to the thinking of this young agitator.[2]

Poyo watched throughout the decade as Martí's nationalist reputation grew, especially at the Pan-American Conference in 1889 in Washington, D.C. Secretary of State James G. Blaine convened this conference to consider economic relations and reciprocal trade agreements between the United States and Latin American nations. Martí attended as Uruguayan consul in New York and caused considerable controversy when he expressed doubts about the wisdom of linking Latin America's destiny with the United States too closely.

Martí and his friend Enrique Trujillo also wrote eloquently against the renewed pro-annexationist propaganda of prominent exiles Juan Bellido de Luna, José Antonio Rodríguez, José Ambrosio González, Fidel and Adolfo Pierra, Manuel Moreno, and others.[3] In 1888, Martí helped found a new nationalist club in New York, Los Independientes, in response to this resurgence of support for annexation and what seemed to be the final failure of the autonomist experiment in Cuba. However, unlike the Convención Cubana's strategy of fomenting revolution in Cuba, the New York club limited its activities to discussion and promoting nationalist propaganda. Poyo appreciated Martí's standing as New York's most prominent leader, orator, and writer, but like most in Key West, he saw him as too moderate and timid.[4]

Poyo briefly corresponded with Martí in December 1887 when Martí reached out to build bridges with Key West. Although Martí disagreed with Poyo's radical views, he lauded him as one of the most respected revolutionary figures in exile. He acknowledged Poyo's role in keeping nationalist sentiment and discourse alive in the 1880s, "during times of least faith among our compatriots," and saluted him as a man of great energy and dedication to the cause who could be counted on to help prepare the approaching grand but difficult times in Cuba.

Martí also knew of the animosity many in Key West felt toward him and the community's strong dedication to Máximo Gómez, but this did not detract from his respect for the "exemplary Cubans of Key West." He assured Poyo of his own complete commitment to armed revolution, which many doubted, but he insisted on a carefully prepared struggle accompanied by a reasoned, convincing program that would be capable of inspiring the Cuban people. The time had come to provide the means to convert growing dissatisfaction with Spanish rule into a confident and well-organized revolution and to avoid the errors of the past, Martí wrote. In this tactful letter, Martí courted Poyo and the Key West community while simultaneously but carefully restating the arguments he had made to Gómez in 1884: that a successful revolution needed more than expeditions and well-known military veterans.[5]

While Martí did not say so concretely, Poyo knew that his letter stemmed from Juan Fernández Ruz's October 1887 visit to New York. Martí did not see Ruz as a serious revolutionary leader, but he drafted a statement with a committee of prominent New York nationalists that outlined ideas for uniting the communities which they distributed to many of the veterans, including Gómez and Maceo. They called for action that would convince Cubans of the need for revolution and a republic. They also wanted members of communities in exile to prepare a capable military; unify in a spirit of equality and democracy; avoid allowing any class, racial, regional, or group interest to dominate; and combat the debilitating effects of annexationist thinking.[6] Gómez and Maceo responded positively, but Martí's statement and his letter were not well received in Key West. Poyo likely responded to Martí's letter, but perhaps not with enough encouragement for their correspondence to continue. In April 1888, Poyo reported to Gómez that the "New York Directory [Martí's group]—as far as I know—has failed to obtain any followers here, though they have tried."[7]

In late 1891, Poyo learned that Tampa nationalists had invited Martí to be keynote speaker at their annual November 27 celebration. Tampa's independence activists, especially labor leaders Ramón Rivero and Néstor Carbonell, had finally succeeded in overcoming radical labor opposition and had formed nationalist clubs just a year earlier. Rivero and Carbonell were not associated with Poyo's brand of intransigent nationalism, which had failed to consolidate workers in Tampa in 1886. They approached the workers less stridently and at a time when Spanish repression of anarchists in Cuba provided new incentives to support independence. They founded a literary and cultural center called the Liceo Cubano whose members formed the Liga Patriótica Cubana to invigorate nationalist agitation. In 1892, Eligio Carbonell, Francisco Lifruíu, José D. Ramírez, and numerous others founded Club Ignacio Agramonte, which was named after a prominent martyred Ten Years' War veteran. For the commemorative event in 1891, club members wanted "an orator of renowned eloquence" from outside the community, and Néstor Carbonell suggested Martí because he believed Martí's recent notoriety and inspiring nationalist oratory could encourage Tampa Cubans to greater activism.[8]

Sufficiently intrigued with Martí's growing prominence, Poyo accompanied his friend Francisco María González, a stenographer and a *lector* at the Gato factory whom Carbonell had invited to transcribe the speeches. González was one of the most talented and respected readers in Key West. He had organized the selectors' union in the early 1880s and had worked with *El Yara*. He was also well known in Tampa. Poyo went as a journalist, and though he too was well known in Tampa, his historical differences of opinion with Carbonell and Rivero, prominent political leaders in Tampa, may explain why his involvement at the November 27 event was only marginal.

On November 25, a large crowd met Martí at the railway station, and the next evening he gave his first speech at the Club Ignacio Agramonte. Rivero introduced González, who recited a patriotic poem, and then Martí spoke. Before retiring for the night, González prepared the speech for distribution the next day, and news of Martí's extraordinary performance spread throughout the community. About a thousand filled the hall that next evening. After comments by Rivero and González, Martí delivered a solemn commemoration of the medical students who had been executed in 1871.[9] The next day he visited factories, where he was well received and demonstrated an extraordinary ability to inspire and mobilize workers.

Poyo remained an observer until Carbonell asked him to introduce Martí at the Enrique Pendas factory, which presented a particular challenge. The factory employed about 800 mostly Spanish workers, most of whom were probably aligned with anarchist unions. However, nationalist leaders thought they might be ready for a new message given the recent repression of anarchists in Havana. After greeting Pendas in his offices, Martí, Carbonell, Poyo, González, and the rest of the entourage entered the gallery on the second floor, where the workers waited silently. In the center of the gallery, a table bordered with flowers and filled with foods and fine liquors signaled a special event. Poyo took his place behind the *lector*'s podium and introduced the featured speaker to the large audience of cigar workers, "explaining that Martí came to pay a debt of gratitude to his loyal friends, the sons of labor."[10]

Quickly sizing up the challenge, Martí replaced Poyo at the podium and launched into an emotionally charged oration that celebrated the value and dignity of manual work and of those who earned their daily bread through the sweat of their brows, unlike those who happily lived off the work of others. The fate of workers was the same everywhere, he declared, which is why the oppressed from Spain had immigrated to Argentina, Mexico, and other Latin America countries and were contributing to the progress of those nations. Then, "with exquisite tact," he wondered how it was that Spanish workers who loved liberty and justice contested the aspirations of Cuban workers who were fighting for a nation "with all and for the good of all." He concluded "with soft and moving accents," remembering his isolated exile in Madrid as a teenager, where a seventeen-year-old never had a better friend than a frank and loyal working-class member of the Civil Guard. At that moment an elderly cigar maker close to the front, who had been listening intently, suddenly stood from his bench with tears streaming down his cheeks and declared that he was that Civil Guard. Whether the exclamation held metaphorical or literal meaning is not clear, but the cigar maker approached Martí and they embraced, most certainly with the enthusiastic acclaim of the tobacco workers. They then gathered around the decorated table, toasted, and ate.

Martí's performance in Tampa left Poyo and González amazed. His spellbinding oratory, intellectual gifts, and political astuteness impressed them immediately, but his ability to excite Tampa' working-class community, including the Spanish anarchists, was his most impressive accomplishment. He mobilized the community with an enthusiasm not seen in south Florida in many years, especially with his acute sensitivity to the culture, economic concerns, racial realities, and political perspectives of cigar workers. Despite the anarchist ideals and ambivalence about nationalism of many workers in the second half of the eighties, Tampa's workers responded to Martí's oratory and the allure of his message of political unity and racial and social justice.[11]

Martí's message was not much different from the nationalist ideas Poyo had been expressing for twenty years, but his eloquence and emotional appeal revived and invigorated excitement for the patriotic message. Poyo had always challenged the anarchists in a no-nonsense, often harsh way, believing that they presented the most immediate threat to the community's nationalist solidarity. But Martí used his oratorical talents and genial gift with the Spanish language to court the workers. Poyo believed that Martí would be equally effective in Key West and could ignite passions there that would fuel the long-stagnant fund-raising activities needed to stockpile weapons and ammunition. The only question was whether Martí could be counted on to support revolution in the immediate term. Poyo must have talked with him enough to come away with the idea that he was less moderate than his reputation suggested.

Partido Revolucionario Cubano

When Poyo returned to Key West, he wasted little time publishing a special supplement of *El Yara* with a highly laudatory description of the events in

Tampa, including an enthusiastic review of Martí's speeches. González spoke of the Tampa meetings at the Gato factory and throughout the community.[12] Soon after the November events, Martí wrote to Poyo to express his appreciation for Poyo's supportive remarks and an anxious desire to visit Key West "on some respectful occasion." Martí expressed his readiness for revolution: "It is the hour of the furnaces," he declared, "and only the light [goal] should matter."[13]

Poyo shared the letter with members of the Convención and published it in *El Yara*. A group of young Key West tobacco workers met at San Carlos Institute, excited by the accounts of events in Tampa and little concerned about the past rivalries and resentments of the older generation. They agreed to invite the New York orator and formed a fund-raising committee to pay expenses. The Convención discussed whether to endorse the visit, knowing full well Martí would not come without their consent.[14]

Many in Key West remained resentful of Martí, especially Figueredo, who could not forgive him for his disrespectful opposition to Gómez. He thought him either a sincerely committed nationalist whose skills were limited to emotional oratory or a man who was politically opposed to revolution and was intentionally creating disunity. Arnao also opposed him. Poyo disagreed with his colleagues and thought Martí could be counted on or persuaded to promote the kind of revolutionary action that was advocated in the Florida communities. Another member of the Convención, Serafín Bello, also spoke for Martí. He had shared the podium with Martí and others during the October 10 commemorations in 1887 and 1888 and knew of his extraordinary ability to move audiences. He had also participated in Martí's meeting with Ruz in October 1887 and had signed the subsequent letter Martí had written to the military veterans asking for their collaboration.[15] After moving to Key West in 1889, Bello became a *lector*, maintained a correspondence with Martí, participated in the founding of the Convención Cubana, and most likely influenced his colleagues to give Martí a chance.[16]

Perhaps Lamadriz's support for the visit settled the matter. He was likely convinced by the various testimonials and the spontaneous actions of the young workers. With a 15–2 vote, the Convención sanctioned the visit, and Bello and González joined the official invitation committee organized by the workers. In the middle of December, tobacco worker Angel Peláez cabled Martí on behalf of the committee to invite him to come to Key West. He received a quick response: "I accept with great enthusiasm." But Martí did not begin his journey until he received reassurance from Lamadriz that he would be given a fair hearing in Key West. He left New York on December 22, traveling on a steamer to Jacksonville, where he caught a train for Tampa.[17] There several of Ybor City's nationalist leaders joined him on the *Olivette* for the final leg of the journey to Key West.

During his six-day convalescence from his bronchial illness, Martí eagerly met some of Key West's leading personalities in his hotel room, many of whom he knew only by reputation. Lamadriz, Figueredo, and Poyo visited the day after his arrival. As Martí later wrote, these three men, "a patriarch, a warrior, and a journalist," assured him that Cubans were of one mind and wanted their country to be happy.[18] Before the three men left, Martí asked for Manuel P. Delgado, who had stepped in to edit *El Yara* while his father-in-law helped organize the visit. Poyo said, "Manolo, Martí says he knows you don't love him; that you should go see him; he is sure you will love him." When Delgado and Poyo went to the hotel, Martí exclaimed, "See me, see me, see how I am, and love me!"[19] The three men talked about revolutionary matters, and on December 30, *El Yara* announced that Martí would be among them on the streets in the next day or two. And perhaps anticipating some opposition, Poyo also made the point that Martí would surely be received in the way a distinguished visitor deserved to be received.[20]

On New Year's Day, Martí began his activities, starting with a great reception at the Gato factory. Workers presented him with an album containing *pensamientos* (thoughts) penned by the workers to honor the distinguished visitor. Poyo's 19-year-old cigar-maker son, Francisco, made a notation reflecting the general tone of the entries: "To be free, it is necessary to comprehend the rights and duties that liberty requires, and among the apostles that teach these [rights and duties], you, illustrious Martí, are one of the best."[21] This and other comments demonstrated workers' familiarity with Martí's writings and the nationalist thought that had been read in the factories for years. Throughout that day and the next, Martí gave speeches, met with several patriotic associations, and began the process of convincing the community of his capacity to lead the revolutionary movement.

Lamadriz, Poyo, and Figueredo again met privately with Martí on January 3 in his hotel room. They listened as Martí discussed plans for a Cuban revolutionary party that he had initially sketched out with Tampa's political leaders. Satisfied with what they heard, the three men invited him to meet with the Convención the following day. At Gerardo Castellanos's home on Duval Street, the full membership listened, reviewed the text for the revolutionary party, and offered suggestions. The next day the triumvirate again joined Martí at his hotel to review the final revisions he had made throughout the night and agreed on a charter document for the Partido Revolucionario Cubano (PRC; Cuban Revolutionary Party), whose membership would draw from the grassroots clubs in the communities in exile.

The PRC sought to unify all the émigré associations and clubs and vowed to struggle for Cuban independence by organizing "a generous and brief war" aimed at bringing peace and prosperity to the island's inhabitants. This involved dismantling Cuba's authoritarian and bureaucratic colonial system and founding a new democratic nation with an economic system that benefited all its citizens. The PRC's strategy for revolution emphasized mobilizing exiles to common action, promoting cooperative relations among those outside and inside Cuba who were willing to contribute to a rapid and successful war, educating Cubans about the spirit and method of the proposed revolution, and raising funds to support all these activities and to purchase war matériel.[22]

Poyo felt that this document aligned well with the activities of the Convención. The charter document blended Martí's concerns for unity and a fully developed political platform with Key West's insistence on activism aimed at insurrection in the near term. While the document stated that the PRC would act only when Cuba was ready, it also declared an intention to prepare for the revolution immediately.[23] The PRC's desire to organize all the communities in exile in support of one program certainly broadened the Convención's work, and Martí's ability to mobilize the workers promised even greater opportunities to raise funds.

After this meeting, as Lamadriz, Poyo, and Figueredo left the hotel and walked down Duval Street discussing the encounter, Poyo said, "Let's help this man by offering him our patriotic support and our cooperation," and Lamadriz agreed. The still-skeptical Figueredo also agreed but added, "If he fails, let it not be said that the Convención was to blame."[24] After this meeting, Poyo saw Martí as a natural leader who would intensify and advance the revolutionary work with the guidance of the Florida leadership. Seeing Martí's performance in Key West, which generated even more enthusiasm than his speeches in Tampa, cemented Poyo's determination to back his plans.

With the approval of the Convención's leadership in hand, Martí presided on January 5 over a broader meeting of community leaders to propose the formal establishment of the revolutionary party. Twenty-seven, including Martí, gathered at San Carlos Institute. The group included representatives of Key West and Tampa nationalist clubs and of various sectors of the community, including military veterans, labor activists, and Afro-Cubans. Only women were missing, but this was consistent with the tradition of gender segregation in the revolutionary clubs. Martí read the PRC charter to the group, and González acted as recording secretary. Because the charter had already been vetted by the Convención, whose members constituted about half of those in attendance, the assembly moved quickly and approved the document without further significant analysis and discussion.[25]

It remained only to write the PRC's governing statutes, including rules, offices, and procedures, which the assembly charged Martí with drafting, subject to the approval of the revolutionary clubs. The next evening a general community *despedida* (farewell) for Martí at San Carlos Institute included the first public reading of the PRC charter. This was the first step in the community's acceptance and approval of the new revolutionary organization.[26]

However, the Spanish consul reported in mid-January that some militant leaders remained unconvinced of Martí's leadership abilities and actively worked to block the community's acceptance of the new party. They apparently believed that Martí's discourse still favored political work and theory over immediate revolutionary action. "Filibusterers" who had opposed "the theories of peace advanced by Mr. Martí" continued their opposition and published propaganda that opposed his ideas. The consul felt that although Martí's well-articulated and emotionally charged nationalist speeches had the power to persuade, they were less threatening than the practical revolutionary activism that mobilized insurgents in Cuba for which Key West was so well known.[27]

At the same time, the consul had few illusions that the prominent local leaders like Poyo who were embracing Martí had become less militant. In fact, he argued, Martí's speeches in Key West had a more inflammatory flavor than those he had delivered in Tampa the previous November, an indication of his need to gain the support of Poyo, Lamadriz, Arnao, and others.[28] The consul also reported that *El Yara*, which in the past had wanted little to do with Martí and had criticized his ideas, now supported him, which raised serious doubts about perceptions that Martí was a moderate. Poyo "does not accommodate with anything that is not revolution," he noted.[29] Even Figueredo and Arnao, though still not convinced about Martí, did not block the formation of the revolutionary clubs that were needed to approve and legitimize the PRC.

In the next months, Poyo and *El Yara* supported and defended Martí and the PRC against a series of attacks. A first challenge appeared from veterans Enrique Collazo and several others in Cuba, who published a letter-to-the-editor in the Havana newspaper *La Lucha* on January 6 questioning Martí's capacity to lead the movement of revolutionaries in exile. Whether the letter was in inspired by or encouraged by PRC opponents in Florida is unknown, but the response in Key West and Tampa left little doubt of Martí's popularity and of his acceptance in those two communities. Martí had inadvertently fueled his decade-long feud with veterans by criticizing a book that Havana resident and veteran Ramón Roa had recently published in Cuba that described the difficulties and hardships of the Ten Years' War. Martí interpreted the book as a discouraging message at a time when organizers sought to encourage a new generation to embrace revolutionary struggle and even ill-advisedly suggested that many Ten Years' War veterans in Cuba were now in the pay of the Spaniards. Collazo's letter defended his friend Roa's book and launched a sharp personal attack against Martí, repeating the many familiar charges that had been lodged against him over the years.

The Key West community mobilized to defend Martí even before he learned of the criticism. It is not likely that many shared Martí's views of Roa, but they thought Collazo's assault an overreaction that was especially divisive at the very time when they hoped to encourage unity. On January 11, 1892, Poyo, González, and Bello presided at a public meeting to discuss Collazo's letter, which they read aloud. Heated discussion resulted in an official *acta*, or declaration, from the Key West revolutionary community that reaffirmed their support for Martí and the PRC. They encouraged Martí to respond to the letter on his own behalf, but the Key West revolutionaries took it upon themselves to contradict an insulting passage in Collazo's letter that characterized Martí's work in Florida as little more than a calculated flattering of a "naïve people in order to grab their savings." The accusation that Martí had tried to extract the savings from "naive" émigrés was "false and calumnious," they declared.[30] Martí did respond to Collazo, but the Key West leadership intervened to defuse the increasingly bitter exchange to avoid further damage in nationalist ranks. Two Key West representatives visited Collazo in Havana while Figueredo wrote to Martí, and the two agreed to put their dispute aside.[31]

Revolutionary clubs in Tampa and New York quickly approved the PRC charter, but Key West leaders moved slowly and carefully to circumvent the still-considerable opposition to Martí and ensure broad support. On March 2, Martí wrote to Poyo to express his anxiety about the delay in ratifying the charter and proclaiming the birth of the PRC.[32] Martí also wrote to Bello and González to encourage them to prod the clubs forward and to skeptics such as Figueredo and veteran Gerardo Castellanos, hoping to assuage their concerns.[33] He told Poyo that it would be "a real crime" if war broke out in Cuba and exiles remained unorganized, but he did not want to insert himself too much since this might incite his opponents. He hoped Poyo would help move matters along.[34]

Two weeks later, the presidents of all the Key West clubs finally met at San Carlos Institute in a session presided over by Castellanos and González to ratify the PRC. They read the names of fifteen clubs who had ratified the charter, but some demanded a delay in the ratifying vote, saying that at least four of those clubs had not yet formally consented. Bello proposed another meeting for March 26. On that day, only presidents of twelve clubs accepted the PRC, revealing continuing resistance to Martí, but on April 8 the clubs in the various exile centers unanimously elected Martí to the post of *delegado*, leader of the party, and confirmed his candidate for treasurer, Benjamín Guerra. Guerra, an employee of the Manuel Barranco Tobacco Company in New York, was a prominent member of the Spanish-American Literary Society with Martí and served as vice-president of New York's Los Independientes nationalist club.[35]

On the evening of April 8, the Key West community gathered at San Carlos Institute to celebrate the birth of the new revolutionary party. Poyo inaugurated the activities. The PRC, Poyo argued, represented the aspirations of a nation that had long been engaged in a brutal struggle to achieve its freedom. The party was not interested in invading the island but wanted to organize and foment armed rebellion and accumulate the weapons and other resources needed to support the war at the appointed time. As the PRC revealed its existence, Poyo called on "all men of good will" to support the cause of liberty without regard for race or nationality. The new organization dignified the "innumerable sacrifices and torrents of blood" as well as the spirit of the Guáimaro Constitution, which had been ratified on April 10, 1868.[36]

Many club presidents followed with speeches that declared their allegiance to the PRC, and the meeting ended with a cable sent to *El Porvenir* and Martí's newspaper, *Patria*, proclaiming the existence of the PRC in Key West: "Viva Cuba!—Poyo—González."[37] Two days later, thirty-four clubs in the various communities publicly endorsed the PRC, including clubs in Key West, New York, Tampa, Kingston, Philadelphia, Boston, Ocala, and New Orleans.[38] The final institutional step was the creation of local PRC governing councils, the Cuerpos de Consejo, which were composed of the presidents of the affiliated clubs, to advise the *delegado* in revolutionary matters. The Key West *consejo* elected Poyo president and Gualterio García secretary.

As skepticism toward Martí slowly dissipated in Key West, new resistance to the PRC emerged from another source in New York where critics felt that Martí and the PRC were influenced too much by the radical communities in Florida. These included moderate nationalists as well as prominent annexationists such as Juan Bellido de Luna and José Ignacio Rodríguez. Martí expected attacks from annexationists and autonomists but not from fellow nationalists such as Enrique Trujillo, who tried to block approval of the PRC at a meeting of Los Independientes, the most influential Cuban nationalist club in New York.[39] The club's members dismissed Trujillo's concerns and joined the PRC, as did the other New York clubs. Trujillo responded by initiating a vigorous anti-PRC campaign in his newspaper.

Some may have attributed Trujillo's opposition to the PRC to a personal estrangement between him and Martí. Trujillo had secretly helped Martí's wife obtain permission from the Spanish consul in New York to return to Cuba with her son. Though Martí's marriage had been troubled for some time, he never forgave Trujillo for what he saw as a terrible betrayal. Manuel P. Delgado remembered a conversation with Martí as he boarded the steamer after his last visit to Key West in October 1894. When Delgado asked him if there was some way to mend fences with Trujillo, Martí responded emotionally, "Manolo, this is not possible! What he did to me is too deep; I can't, I can't, I can't. Leave me now. Leave me." They embraced and Delgado returned to shore.[40]

Trujillo's opposition went much deeper than the estrangement with Martí; he expressed substantive concerns about Martí's plans that were consistent with his moderate nationalist beliefs. Trujillo and many of his colleagues believed that Martí had embraced the radical perspectives of Florida's working-class communities and that the PRC did not represent the political values of the New York community. Trujillo supported the idea of a separatist party of exiles dedicated to attracting as many dissident voices as possible, including annexationists, but he could not support a party dedicated to instigating revolution, which he did not believe was the responsibility of exiles. This had been the predominant attitude of New York Cubans throughout the 1880s, and Trujillo insisted that this had been Martí's position as well. Trujillo also condemned what he saw as the PRC's highly centralized and dictatorial structure. An organization led by a charismatic leader who could not easily if necessary be removed by the local *consejos* and whose roles were consultative rather than legislative. It was "dictatorial and excessively reliant on one personality" and sinned against democratic principles.[41]

El Yara defended the PRC and debated *El Porvenir* on many occasions. Poyo rejected Trujillo's suggestion that the organization be called a separatist party, since this would have legitimized the participation of annexationists, which Poyo opposed outright. The term "revolutionary party" was adopted because "that is the environment in which it moves," but the real name was the Cuban Nationalist Party, Poyo said. He also rejected Trujillo's characterization of the PRC as an organization whose goal was to invade the island; that was a strategy of the past, he insisted. While the PRC would help prepare and support insurrection, its primary activity would be to organize revolutionary cells in Cuba that would ignite the revolt.

Poyo also supported the centralized structure of the PRC, which he believed appropriate for conspiratorial activities. This was consistent with his long-established support for vertically structured revolutionary organizations. Poyo encouraged Trujillo to take his concerns to his local party and seek reforms, knowing full well that Trujillo had already attempted to do so but had failed.[42] Trujillo made little headway in his efforts to stall the PRC, but the episode taught Martí that his most supportive allies lived in Florida, not in New York.

Probation

Despite the Key West leadership's support and enthusiasm for Martí and the PRC in early 1892, this did not signal the wider community's unconditional acceptance or eliminate concerns many had about his commitment to revolutionizing Cuba in the near term. In effect, Key West placed him on probation while he revealed his intentions and demonstrated his capabilities. The death of José Francisco Lamadriz on February 2 may have facilitated things for Martí. Poyo, his strongest supporter among the main revolutionary leaders in Key West, became president of both the Convención and the Cuerpo de Consejo, the community's two most important revolutionary organizations.[43] But Martí still had to prove himself to the community, and while his dance with Key West continued, the Convención resumed its normal and secret activities, about which Martí knew little, if anything.

Poyo and Figueredo had for some time felt that the Las Villas region of Cuba was most prepared to spark the insurrection, and they continued to encourage the work of Luis Lagomasino and his revolutionary group, which remained in continual communication with Key West leaders, especially Poyo.[44] In early 1892, Lagomasino, in coordination with Key West revolutionaries, contacted Máximo Gómez about an uprising he was planning for later that year. About the same time, Serafín Sánchez, an important military veteran from Las Villas and a former aide of Máximo Gómez, arrived in Key West to see for himself the nature of these preparations.

Though Sánchez, who was born in 1846, was much younger than Lamadriz, in some ways he replaced him in the leadership triumvirate with Poyo and Figueredo. He was an accomplished veteran; he had joined the Ten Years' War as a lieutenant but rose to lieutenant colonel under Gómez's command. Later he fought with General Carlos Roloff and participated in the Little War, but he left Cuba in August 1880 as resistance to Spanish rule crumbled. After a short residence in New York, he joined Gómez in the Dominican Republic, where he lived for eleven years. In 1891, he again moved briefly to New York and established a relationship with Martí before moving to Key West, where he joined the Convención and played an important role, especially with military matters and plans. He worked in a cigar factory and settled down in Key West with his family. He and his wife, Pepa, became close with Poyo and his family; in July, Sánchez was one of the official witnesses at the wedding of Poyo's son, Francisco.[45]

Believing that the revolutionary moment was almost at hand, the Convención asked Lagomasino to come to Key West to personally report on conditions in Las Villas and discuss plans for the insurrection. On the evening of June 21, Poyo, Sánchez, and Rosendo García greeted the Las Villas conspirator as he disembarked from the *Mascotte*. Lagomasino explained the plans of his groups, which included recognizing Gómez as overall military leader of insurrectionary efforts and Sánchez as head of military operations for Las Villas. They then met with the full membership of the Convención at Figueredo's home. Poyo opened the session by explaining Lagomasino's plan in general terms. Sánchez followed by announcing his—and by implication—Gomez's support for the initiative. Lagomasino then explained the details of the plan, indicating he had at least 200 armed men who were ready to act. The Convención approved of this plan and vowed to send weapons and ammunition as soon as possible. It also informed Lagomasino of ongoing activities in Oriente and Matanzas and instructed him to coordinate with these groups while maintaining contact with Key West. Finally, before returning to Cuba, Lagomasino met with the Convención's War Committee, which was led by Sánchez, to develop plans for strengthening the insurgent forces. They set August 25, 1892 as the day of insurrection.[46]

Even before Lagomasino's visit, Poyo, the *consejo*, and leading personalities had learned that Martí also possessed practical skills for transforming the theoretical PRC into an effective revolutionary organization. Key West received a frenzy of correspondence from Martí expressing his ideas for organizing the party's work. On May 13, Poyo and the Cuerpo de Consejo received their first official communication from Martí. He outlined the work ahead under various categories, including communications, war, and organization in exile and in Cuba, giving direction to the new revolutionary movement.[47]

The presidents of the revolutionary clubs in Key West received another missive that was written on May 16 in which Martí asked them to work with great secrecy and discretion since the Spanish consular offices watched closely and adeptly used spies to infiltrate the clubs. This was certainly not new information for the Key West conspirators, but it revealed Martí's understanding of the situation. Another letter dated May 27 outlined the rules and procedures for handling the funds raised by the clubs. And yet another letter dated June 9 asked the *consejo* to prepare a report on how many Ten Years' War veterans were in Key West and what their disposition was toward a new insurgency; Martí also requested information on other patriots who were willing to support the war effort.[48]

Finally, the Key West leadership heard from Martí what they saw as their first priority: he announced the need to send agents to Cuba to open channels of communication and asked the *consejo* to provide the necessary funds. The need for dispatching agents, he insisted, was urgent and extraordinarily important, but he also cautioned against premature action. His language suggested that he knew something about the plans in Las Villas. "Let us wait," he urged, "like giants working quietly" while developing information and the necessary forces on and off the island to launch the insurrection.[49] If his agents were to be successful, they would need as much information as possible about revolutionary groups and plans in Cuba. Armed with that information they would travel more quickly, with less danger, and with the likelihood of fewer mistakes. Martí also told Poyo that he had "valuable information, some alarming" about certain elements in Las Villas that could compromise the revolutionary movement.[50]

Martí also wanted to organize military veterans publicly and affirmatively under the banner of the PRC; Serafín Sánchez became his primary military correspondent in Key West. He wrote to Sánchez about military strategy, highlighting unity as the top priority, and encouraged him to write Gómez about the PRC. Martí also emphasized the need for accumulating adequate military resources to support the eventual conflagration. Martí thanked Poyo for the list of military veterans he had sent, and in July he made a second visit to Florida to court them. Key West Veterans remained fundamentally loyal to Gómez and Maceo, and without their backing Martí had little chance of building the revolutionary party.[51]

In Tampa, Martí spoke with General Carlos Roloff, who had arrived from Honduras with his family. Originally from Warsaw, Poland, Roloff immigrated to the United States around 1862 and joined the 9th Ohio Regiment. Shortly after the end of the Civil War, Roloff went to Cuba to work as a bookkeeper in the Bishop Sugar Importing Company and became active in the Masonic lodge in Caibarién, Cuba. When the Ten Years' War erupted, insurgent leaders who were looking for experienced military personnel made Roloff a major general of the rebel forces in Las Villas under Gómez. In 1876, he replaced Gómez as commander of the province's forces, and he continued the struggle until the Zanjón Pact. During the Little War, he worked with the revolutionary committee in New York, where he first met Martí. Later, he joined with Gómez and Maceo during the activities of the mid-1880s.

After several days of activities in Tampa, Roloff went to Key West and again demonstrated the prestige military veterans enjoyed. Roloff's arrival inspired celebrations, parades, meetings, and patriotic events in his honor as he toured the factories. Several days later, Martí came to Key West, where on July 6 he met formally with eleven veterans, including Roloff, Sánchez, Tuerto Rodriguez, Rogelio Castillo, and Francisco Lufríu. The veterans agreed on a document that declared their faith in the PRC.[52]

At a meeting at San Carlos Institute on July 12 that was "ably prepared by his friends," Martí delivered an inspired oration, but before the event ended someone rose to challenge him, making allusions to rumors that were still circulating about him. The Spanish consul reported that Martí rose to the challenge, and "making use of his ostentatious language and high-sounding phrases disputed the doubts expressed by his countryman." Thunderous applause disarmed his challenger and all seemed to embrace Martí as the leader of a new revolutionary movement.[53]

Martí's month-long visit to Florida finally convinced the Convención and military veterans that his priorities did in fact mirror their own and that he had the qualities that were needed in a leader. The urgent tone of Martí's correspondence in May and June and his success in wooing military veterans left little doubt about his energy, revolutionary intentions, political skills, and extraordinary ability to persuade. Convención leaders recognized the usefulness of PRC's structure for coordinating the insurgent elements across the island and in exile, and the long-standing perception that Martí's revolutionary politics were timid disappeared and was replaced by a perception of him as a bold, energetic leader who was dedicated to insurgency in the near term. Martí had also added a broader programmatic dimension and attracted a mass revolutionary constituency in all the exile centers, a development that went far beyond what the Convención had considered possible. After Martí left Key West, *El Yara* declared that the task of convincing the community of his leadership capabilities had been accomplished. "So logical was Mr. Martí," it noted, that "he rooted in the spirit of the people a profound conviction that today, at least, the PRC fills all the necessary qualities of a sensible, intelligent and practical revolutionary movement."[54]

It was likely during this trip to Key West that the Convención formally revealed its plan for the August 25 insurrection in Las Villas to Martí. In a meeting with Poyo, Roloff, Sánchez, and Gerardo Castellanos at a local restaurant, Martí predictably expressed his opposition to the uprising. Martí had declared on many occasions and perhaps repeated there that revolutions had to be carefully planned and brewed in their own time and the local leaders now fully agreed. During Martí's visit, *El Yara* published an editorial that argued that the revolution had to be prepared carefully in Cuba with sufficient support to be viable.[55] Then, Poyo remembered, "Martí said that he needed a prudent, civic-minded, patriotic man to go to Cuba to hear opinions, organize revolutionary clubs, and preach."[56] He and his colleagues recommended Castellanos on the spot and Martí agreed.

Forty-eight-year-old Castellanos had joined the insurrection in February 1869 and operated in Oriente and Camaguey Provinces under General Carlos Roloff and others. He reached the rank of commander before he was taken as a prisoner, but Spanish family members helped him escape to New York. After the war he settled in Key West, where he learned to make cigars and then established a modest factory. It earned him a living, but most of his profits went to support revolutionary activities.[57]

Soon after leaving Key West, Martí informed Poyo that in two days' time, Castellanos and other agents would leave on his mission that would be facilitated with the valuable data Key West provided about conditions in Cuba. Martí encouraged Poyo to use the Convención's influence to ensure that groups in Cuba came to an agreement with his agents.[58] On Martí's instructions, Castellanos offered Juan Gualberto Gómez the leadership of the PRC in Havana and recruited Julio Sanguily to manage military matters in the province. Castellanos met with conspirators in Matanzas, Las Villas, and Camaguey, introducing them to the new revolutionary party and gained their general support. On August 13, 1892, invoking the Convención's authority, Castellanos instructed a reluctant Lagomasino in Las Villas and the Sartorio brothers in Holguín to postpone the planned uprising. On a subsequent trip Castellanos traveled to Santiago. Numerous other Key West Cubans accepted revolutionary missions to Cuba from Martí, including manufacturers Gato and Teodoro Pérez and cigar maker Juan de Dios Barrios.[59]

After Castellanos's first trip to Cuba, the primary authority for preparing the insurrection belonged to Martí and the PRC, but the Convención remained a critical component, and Martí became an official member. The local council of the PRC brought together the presidents of dozens of revolutionary clubs, but was too large to effectively carry out secretive conspiratorial work. Martí instead relied on the leadership of the Convención (or Club Luz de Yara, as it was mostly known), especially Poyo, Figueredo, Roloff, Sánchez, and Castellanos, to provide day-to-day advice and support for clandestine activities. This worked especially well because Poyo served as president of both organizations.[60]

To further allay suspicions about Martí's leadership, Castellanos—on Martí's authority—assured insurgents in Cuba that General Máximo Gómez was the military chief of the revolutionary movement. Though this was a premature statement, since Gómez had not yet formally agreed to participate, it confirmed Martí's acceptance of the legendary warrior as the undisputed military leader and headed off concerns that the delay he demanded was attributable to timidity. Instead, the delay was a strategy that was calculated to strengthen and consolidate revolutionary cells before the insurrection was launched.[61]

Mobilization

The new enthusiasm both workers and manufacturers demonstrated for Martí and the PRC encouraged Poyo and the local revolutionary leadership to resume the fund-raising activities that Key West had abandoned in the late 1880s in the face of worker ambivalence. As Martí took charge of expanding revolutionary networks in Cuba and devising the logistics for arming expeditions, Poyo turned to strengthening grassroots organizing and securing resources. This involved creating effective fund-raising mechanisms, insisting on revolutionary discipline, and maintaining enthusiasm for revolution through the pages of *El Yara*.

After Martí's second visit to Key West, when workers responded enthusiastically to his factory visits and speeches, Poyo, Roloff, Sánchez, and Tuerto

Figure 5. José Martí (*standing, center*) with cigar workers at the Martínez Ybor cigar factory in Ybor City, Florida, July 1892. José D. Poyo is second from Martí's right, and Serafín Sánchez is on Poyo's right. From Guillermo de Zéndegui, *Ambito de Martí* (Havana: P. Fernández y Cia, 1954).

Rodríguez accompanied Martí on a statewide fund-raising campaign that began in Tampa. On the afternoon of July 19, 1892, the PRC delegation visited Tampa's Pons, Fernández y Sabby, Haya, and Martínez Ybor cigar factories. After dinner they attended the general meetings of Club Ignacio Agramonte and the Cuban black community's Liga Cubana de Instrucción. The next morning the delegation visited individual homes; it returned to other factories that afternoon. Workers greeted Martí enthusiastically at each event. The crowd that gathered at the Martínez Ybor factory was so large that the delegation struggled to enter the large brick building, but as they entered the workers exploded in applause and shouts of "Viva!" while the Cuban band struck up the revolutionary anthem "Hymn of Bayamo." Introductory speeches by men who represented a broad political, social, and racial constituency prepared the audience. Poyo and Arnao spoke for the community's traditional political leaders; Roloff and Sánchez represented the military veterans; Ramón Rivero and Ramón Rubiera expressed the views of labor; Joaquin Granados and Cornelio Brito represented the Cuban black community; and even Spanish anarchists who were disgusted with Spanish colonial oppression offered Cuban workers their solidarity through the presence of José Pérez Molina and Silverio Gómez. Martí delivered the main oration to an enthusiastic working-class audience.

The day ended with a general community gathering at the Círculo de Trabajadores, where some 1,500 people set out in procession across town to the Liceo Cubano. As a correspondent for *Patria* noted, the march demonstrated "the unity of the oppressed, of the disinherited, of all free men." That evening so many went to the Liceo Cubano that the assembly moved outdoors. The following morning, Martí, Poyo, Roloff, Sánchez, and Rivero set off for Ocala and then Jacksonville and St. Augustine to spread the ideas that had been reaffirmed in Tampa and Key West.[62]

Baseball offered the PRC another source of revenue. Cuban baseball teams first organized into a semi-professional league in Key West in 1887. When Francisco Díaz Silveira, a young poet who published nationalist verses in *El Yara*, formed a baseball team called Cuba, Poyo's son Francisco joined as catcher. Another Cuban nationalist, Luis Acosta, founded the Esperanza baseball club, and Frank Bolio, who had been on the committee that invited Martí to Key West, organized three additional teams: Habana, Fe and the Key West Greys. The players on the Greys were Anglo-American.[63] War veteran and cigar selector Alejandro Rodríguez and his wife Eva Adan managed Fe. League organizers also approached Gato about using some of his land for a baseball field on the south side of the Key, close to the beach. He agreed, and they built stands for spectators, put up a fence, and launched the first formal baseball season in 1888/1889. Teams played on Monday afternoons, since local laws prohibited professional contests on Sundays.

On one of his visits to Key West, Martí accompanied Poyo to a game that pitted the Cuba baseball club against a team of Americans. At that game, 19-year-old "Tinti" Molina hit a home run that won the game for the Cubans. Martí congratulated Molina after the game, telling him that the victory was a good omen for the coming struggle. Martí so inspired Molina that the young player later smuggled messages to activists when he traveled to join a team in Matanzas.[64] In 1896, after war began, a community group, Sociedad de Instrucción y Recreo José Martí (José Martí Educational and Recreational Society), organized a formal championship designed to support the war effort.[65]

On November 7, 1892, Poyo, the PRC Cuerpo de Consejo, and an enthusiastic multitude greeted Martí at the docks as he arrived for his third visit to Key West. In September he had traveled to the Dominican Republic, where General Gómez formally accepted an appointment as the revolution's supreme military chief. The Key West *consejo* heard Martí's briefings about his conversations with Gómez and agreed to accelerate its fund-raising efforts. On December 4, Poyo announced to the community that Gómez had accepted Martí's offer to serve as commander in chief of the insurgent army. In his customary fashion, Martí moved with great intensity, convening meetings at many clubs and societies. He even delivered a speech in English for the Anglo-American community, which responded by declaring its sympathy for the Cuban cause. At another meeting the *consejo* ratified Martí's idea of asking workers to donate one day's wages each month in a plan called "Día de la Patria." This plan was implemented on December 6, the day before his departure. Later the contribution changed to 10 percent of weekly wages. Many factory owners agreed to contribute the profits of one day's work each week to the revolutionary treasury.[66]

With some alarm, the Spanish consul reported that "the persistent and active propaganda of the agitator Mr. Martí, helped by his accomplices, the director of El Yara newspaper, the so-called General Serafín Sánchez and various others, is producing favorable support for his ideas."[67] He complained that some of those who were contributing funds did so only out of a sense of obligation in order to keep their jobs and to avoid being called bad patriots or, even worse, pro-Spanish.[68] Indeed, like they had in the early 1880s, activists organized factory floors with the cooperation of unions. Factory managers were often reluctant to require workers to contribute to the weekly collections for the PRC treasury as a condition of employment, but they did so. Commissions formed in the factories that acted as courts martial to judge those who did not comply, and Key West became like a military garrison where veterans such as Sánchez sponsored formal military exercises and training in the use of firearms.[69]

This structure and discipline provided the local PRC with significant funds on a regular basis. A portion of what was collected made its way to a "war fund" in New York under Martí's control while the rest remained under control of the Cuerpo de Consejo in Key West as "action funds" to be spent on any number of activities, including support for agents who were traveling to Cuba clandestinely. This essential system remained in place through 1898.

At the end of 1892, Martí moved from theory to practice. According to the Spanish consul, at a meeting of the Cuerpo de Consejo held on November 11 and 12, Martí told the presidents of the affiliated clubs "that the time had arrived to purchase arms and ammunition."[70] Poyo was certainly satisfied. In less than a year after Martí's first visit to Florida, the local PRC and Convención had transformed the excitement of Martí's energy, charisma, and ideological program into a new and powerful revolutionary movement.

Martí's oratory struck a special chord in Florida that mobilized communities like never before. This was reflected in Key West's annual commemoration of October 10, 1892, which was celebrated in an unusually optimistic manner. The day began when men, women, and children representing clubs, societies, military regiments, and organizations of different kinds met at San Carlos Institute at six in the morning. The multitude extended for three blocks. Carrying aloft images of iconic personalities, banners, crowns of flowers commemorating individuals, and flags, the parade set out for the cemetery accompanied by two musical bands. It passed by thousands of spectators who were applauding from the sidewalks. An estimated 5,000 people eventually crowded into the cemetery around a stage erected next to a veiled monument.

Dignitaries mounted the stage and the crowd quieted as Martin Herrera, the president of the organizing committee, began the proceedings by introducing Poyo. At that moment the choir of the Cuban Methodist Church "La Trinidad" accompanied by an organ began singing a somber hymn. Since 1869, Cubans in Key West had honored dead patriots at the cemetery every year, but on this occasion the community unveiled a 21-foot granite and marble obelisk that was covered from the base to the top with the names of the Cuba's martyrs on the site of José F. Lamadriz's grave. Deeply moved, Poyo offered "a patriotic and soul stirring address listened to by every Cuban with enraptured attention," according to one reporter.[71]

Herrera followed with an improvised and extended keynote speech and concluded his comments with an admonition to his compatriots, the autonomists and annexationists. If their love of country had grown cold, he told them, they should come to the Key West cemetery to feel the heat of Cuba's dignity (*vergüenza*) in the monument's cold marble. After over a dozen speakers, including a granddaughter of Lamadriz, the parade retraced its steps to San Carlos Institute, where Poyo read cables of encouragement from Martí in Jamaica and Roloff in Tampa. This day "marks the beginning of a new era in our political life," *El Yara* declared. Everyone, the newspaper insisted, now had a moral obligation to show their children the monument. This may have been one of the largest nationalist events to date in Key West.[72]

As a new year commenced, Poyo and his colleagues focused on raising funds and remained in touch with the expanding revolutionary groups in Cuba. Martí relied heavily on Key West. In December, he wrote to Poyo of the affection, pride, and appreciation all Cubans owed the émigré community of Key West.[73] With Key West now firmly supporting him, Martí began stockpiling weapons and made progress convincing insurgents in Cuba to cooperate with the PRC. In June and early July of 1893, he traveled to the Dominican Republic to meet with General Gómez and to Costa Rica to meet with General Maceo. He remained in touch with Juan Gualberto Gómez in Havana and spoke with General Julio Sanguily, who traveled to Jacksonville to apprise Martí of the situation in Cuba.[74]

Poyo regularly received letters from Martí that reassured him of his organizing activities in Cuba and emphasized the need for resources for a clandestine expedition. He maintained close touch with Key West in 1893 and traveled there in February, May, September, and December. Regular collections in the Key West factories provided the bulk of Martí's funds, but he also wrote and met directly with manufacturers to make separate appeals for resources. In February, Martí arrived to encourage fund-raising, and in March, he instructed the Key West *consejo* to provide resources to support *El Yara*, which was rarely financially viable. He saw the newspaper as critical for keeping the community mobilized.[75]

None of this calmed the impatience of revolutionaries in Cuba, where many remained disgruntled with Martí's decision the previous August to postpone the uprising in Las Villas. This was particularly evident when Martí visited Key West in November 1892. He met with the members of the Convención and an envoy from Manuel and Ricardo Sartorio in Holguín who was carrying a letter demanding the weapons that had been promised when Lagomasino had visited Key West earlier in the year. After some debate in which Martí argued for more time, the Convención again agreed to wait and refused to provide the weapons. One member, Juan Calderón, angrily resigned from the Convención, complaining that the PRC had been foisted on the community under false pretenses. At the meeting that had approved PRC's charter, he claimed, a chorus of two or three had urged approval while the rest had said nothing and through their silence had sanctioned something they did not fully understand.[76]

Impatience grew. In late April 1893, the Sartorio brothers, acting on their own, launched an uprising in Purino in Holguín Province. Martí heard the news on his way to see Maceo in Central America and urgently diverted to Key West, where he arrived on May 3 after a brief stop in Tampa. A multitude met Martí at the docks, and after touring factories and making speeches, he met with Poyo, Figueredo, Sánchez, and Roloff to discuss the troubling developments. They opposed the uprising, believing that it was premature and perhaps had even been instigated by Spanish agents hoping to uncover the numerous revolutionary cells working on the island. However, they did agree to extend support if the uprising gained a foothold.[77] The uprising did not prosper, but it highlighted impatience in Cuba and the need to accelerate activities. It also created enthusiasm in Key West, where Martí raised over $30,000 during his two-week stay.[78]

The Spanish consul had trouble learning the details about the increasing pace of conspiratorial work. Although he knew that regular communications were arriving from Cuba that described preparations and growth in revolutionary sentiment, only Martí and Poyo read the secret missives and the consul's agents learned very little. Key West remained active while Martí was traveling to communities in exile and overseeing the purchase of arms. In August, Sánchez traveled to New York to meet with Martí, Roloff went to Nassau to confer with exiles there, and Figueredo remained in Key West to help Poyo with a local expedition that was being coordinated with Rosendo García. All the while more veterans made their way to Key West to await developments.[79]

In August 1893, Convención leaders received an urgent letter from Julio Sanguily requesting $4,000 and urging that the insurrection be launched immediately. They wrote to Martí in support of the idea, but the *delegado* again disagreed and assured them of the efficacy of his plan to launch an expedition with the most influential military leaders (Gomez, Maceo, Crombet, Roloff, Sánchez) and enough arms to establish a revolutionary foothold. Though revolutionary leaders in Cuba were enthusiastic, he argued, they did not have sufficient prestige and experience to lead a successful uprising. The Convención agreed, but perhaps it was not fully convinced. Martí made an unannounced trip to Key West in the first week of September. He revealed more details about his plan and extracted a pledge from the Convención not to support actions in Cuba without his approval. The Spanish consul also thought he planned to "meet an important person" from Cuba, perhaps Julio Sanguily.[80]

In early November, another unauthorized uprising occurred in Cuba, this time in Lajas, Las Villas. On November 7, Martí cabled Poyo from New York: "Be attentive, wait for news from me. Telegraph yours." The next day he cabled Poyo again: "So far there are [revolutionary] groups in Lajas, Cienfuegos and Santa Clara." Martí began a barrage of correspondence that warned everyone to be alert for what might develop. On November 10, he again headed for Florida.[81] After a couple of days in Tampa he moved on to Key West, where he met with the *consejo* to discuss developments.

The position of the *consejo* remained the same as before. If the new uprising took hold, they would mobilize to support it, but this initiative collapsed even more quickly than the previous effort at Purino. Rumors circulated in Key West that local revolutionaries had encouraged the uprising; if this was true, they remained anonymous.[82] Key West Cubans continued to train and prepare a fighting force while they waited for Martí to finalize other elements of the plan, but they now expected that it would be only a short while before the insurrection started.

Friendship

In 1892 and 1893, Poyo and Martí developed an effective working relationship based on the compatibility of their roles and goals. Martí saw in Poyo a dedicated and talented grassroots leader who had played a leading role in creating the most cohesive and militant nationalist community in exile. Since only Key West could provide him with the political legitimacy and economic resources necessary to organize the new revolutionary movement, Martí relied on Poyo to help open doors. As president of both the Cuerpo de Consejo and the Convención, Poyo kept the community organized, mobilized, and committed to the PRC and its leadership. He valued Martí's extraordinary intellectual and oratorical abilities and natural leadership skills and supported him as the obvious candidate to lead a united movement of revolutionaries in exile. Martí did not disappoint and likely performed even more brilliantly than expected.

They also became close friends. They corresponded regularly, and Martí wrote official and personal letters that expressed his admiration and affection for the Key West leader. Though this was not unique for Martí, whose prolific correspondence regularly poured out his feelings and anxieties to a variety of friends, the letters demonstrated an affectionate relationship. The letters became more personal after Martí's second visit in July 1892.

On one occasion in August he responded to a note from Poyo, who in his fastidiousness about proper handling of PRC funds had gently reprimanded Martí about some misstep. Accepting the criticism, Martí said, "I welcome this letter carrying your complaint because now I can tell you what I have wanted to say but could not for fear you might consider me parasitical or needy." He thanked him for his generosity and tenderness and said that the "loving pride with which you watched over me was like that of a father and a brother at the same time." He valued Poyo for his watchful prudence, the beauty and weight of his words, the reality and courage of his convictions, and his magnificent rebellious soul. Martí enjoyed Poyo's friendship; he saw truth embedded deep in his being (*entrañas*) and appreciated "the purity and pain of his glorious life, the finest seed of a rough strength, and the poetry and consolation of an affectionate brother."[83]

A graver moment again inspired Martí to further expressions of affection for Poyo and his family. After Martí's trip to Key West in November 1892,

Poyo accompanied him to Tampa, where they visited factories and clubs and raised funds. Roloff and well-known orator Carolina "La Patriota" joined them in Tampa, and they departed for Ocala on December 14, returning two days later. Poyo prepared to return to Key West the next day, but that night Martí fell ill after tasting a putrid glass of wine that he quickly threw away. Martí called for a doctor, who later confirmed that he had been poisoned, probably with acid. Though he did not consume enough to threaten his life, the assassination attempt affected his intestinal tract for many months.[84]

Poyo wanted to remain, but Martí insisted he return home to be with his family, who needed him more than he, especially since Francisco's wife Louisa was about to give birth. "There was certain poetry," he told Poyo, "in arriving in time to warm the new born to your heart." "That is Christmas," he exclaimed. Martí asked Poyo to keep a setting "for the absent one" at the holiday table, asked that Clarita send him thoughts to quicken his cure, and told Poyo to kiss the hands of his noble daughters.[85] "We have much to do together. The big moment is close," he emphasized. Though Poyo was a reserved person and did not have an effusive personality, his letters no doubt expressed similar warm and bonding sentiments of admiration and friendship for Martí, but the loss of his correspondence makes a precise exploration impossible.

When José Martí visited Key West in late 1891 and early 1892 he found a well-organized community with long experience and a tradition of nationalist activism led by a cadre of committed, experienced, and skilled insurrectionists. Key West had patriotic clubs and schools, secret revolutionary associations, a nationalist working-class constituency, ties with revolutionary groups in Cuba, a financial base in the cigar industry, a certainty that one day Cuba would be rid of Spanish rule, and a predisposition to immediate action. Martí had intellectual prowess, political genius, charismatic presence, oratorical skills, and an obsessive energy that was capable of mobilizing a working-class community that was ripe for revolution.

While Martí forged an émigré-wide political party with a clear and inspiring political platform, community members in Key West chipped away at Martí's traditional skepticism about mobilizing for insurrection in the near term. Leaders in Key West played a critical role in moving Martí from revolutionary theory to action. Poyo opened doors for Martí in Key West, where under his guidance the New York orator became a practical revolutionary organizer, a man of action. Poyo and Martí needed one another, and this mutuality enhanced their revolutionary aspirations and produced an affectionate friendship. In his visit to Key West in May 1893, Martí again expressed his heartfelt affection for Poyo in a dedication on the back of a photo: "Cuba's honor became man, and was called José Dolores Poyo: To your virtue, to your talent, eloquence, to your heart, I dedicate this tribute, your brother, José Martí."[86]

7

CRISIS

> Anyone who saw Key West last year and saw it again today would almost doubt that it was the same exuberant town that revealed life in all of its dimensions.
>
> *El Yara*, 1894

An angry multitude converged at the Key West docks on the morning of January 2, 1894. Leaders of a special crisis committee of the Partido Revolucionario Cubano comprised of José D. Poyo, Fernando Figueredo, Manuel Patricio Delgado, Teodoro Pérez, and Miguel A. Zaldívar led the crowd, which included Protestant ministers and their congregations, members of the Partida la Tranca, and dozens of war veterans, among others. They encountered an armed police contingent that was anticipating trouble connected with the arrival of a steamer from Havana. The Cubans kept their distance but shouted disapproval at approximately 100 perplexed Spanish strikebreakers on the deck of the steamer.

Anglo-American authorities in Key West had recruited the Spanish workers for La Rosa Española, a factory of the Seidenberg and Company, which was based in New York. William Seidenberg himself disembarked first, accompanied by a delegation of Key West dignitaries that included Board of Trade (Chamber of Commerce) members, the mayor, the customs collector, federal and county judges, and several prominent religious leaders. They had traveled to Havana in late December and negotiated with the captain general for permission to hire Spanish workers who were not sympathetic with the Cuban nationalist cause. The delegation guaranteed the strikebreakers its protection. It intended not only to break the unions but also to undermine the PRC's power in the factories, a goal that Spanish authorities interested in weakening the Cuban nationalist enclave applauded.

Spanish workers received a police escort to their quarters, which were located close to the Seidenberg factory, but the day did not end without confrontation and fighting. Authorities arrested numerous Cubans, including Rosendo García, the well-known leader of the Partida la Tranca, whom they held without charge as a warning to the Cuban community.[1]

Politics

Years of pent-up tension and frustration in Key West led to this unexpected crisis, which would have a significant effect on revolutionary preparations. In the last third of the nineteenth century, Poyo and other nationalist leaders walked a fine line between their revolutionary goals and the interests of their Anglo-American hosts. Whether or not Cubans could work effectively for insurrection locally depended heavily on the quality of Cubans' relationships with their American neighbors, who had the power to either turn a blind eye to their activities or cause considerable trouble. Many Anglo-Americans had resented Cubans for a long time; these feelings lay just below the surface. They viewed them as a generally inferior "race," infected by what they saw as an ultimately flawed Hispanic culture that had been debilitated by centuries of miscegenation. They often complained that Cubans had overwhelmed their community. "There are already far too many people on the island. Everybody is in everybody's way," complained one newspaper.[2] "Key West is doomed," lamented another. "The Cubans won't assimilate with us. They won't learn our language, and the saloon-keepers and monte-men [gamblers] control their votes. Is it any wonder we're a hundred years behind the rest of the country?"[3]

Americans also expressed resentment about the political influence of Cubans. In the midst of a hotly contested political campaign in 1876, for example, the *Key of the Gulf* declared that "the idea that foreigners, seeking a temporary refuge on our shores from oppression, should be allowed to control our State, is revolting and antagonistic to every feeling of free and popular government."[4] However, fearing political repercussions, Florida newspapers learned to be careful about how they wrote about Cubans. One editor felt compelled to clarify that his phrase "the scum of the contiguous West India Islands" referred to the "ignorant Bahamas Negroes" who were immigrating to Key West, not to Cubans who were not Negroes.[5] Anglo-Americans also benefited greatly from the wealth the cigar industry was creating, and they learned to tolerate their Cuban neighbors.

Cubans admired many aspects of U.S. life and culture and expressed gratitude for the refuge and highly prized jobs Key West provided, but they resented the racist attitudes of Anglo-Americans. One Cuban characterized the "Yankees de Cayo Hueso" as "old southern confederates, eternal enemies of the union, and inspired by a formidable and invincible hatred toward the colored race." He described how they prohibited marriage between whites and blacks. Ministers who broke this law had to pay a $1,000 fine and risked the loss of their right to perform marriages. The mayor of Key West, he added, had extraordinary powers to imprison people accused of public drunkenness and put them to work in chains on city streets without even making formal charges or going to court.[6]

Cubans frequently touted their role in creating prosperity in Key West. They believed that their ingenuity, investment, and hard work had transformed Key West from a backwater fishing village to a booming industrial town, an accomplishment that infused them with a sense of pride and belonging. Having played a critical role in building the city, they demanded the right to use their resources and influence to promote Cuban independence without undue obstacles from Anglo-Americans. And to ensure that they had some measure of influence, they participated in Key West and Florida politics. Some Cuban nationalists expressed concern that the enthusiasm with which Cubans participated in U.S. politics distracted them from revolutionary matters, but most leaders such as Poyo, Lamadriz, and Figueredo encouraged Cubans to vote as long as their participation in electoral politics advanced, or at least did not detract from, revolutionary goals.[7]

The Florida state constitution gave immigrants the right to vote in state elections after only six months of residence and a legal declaration of intent to become a citizen. Despite their resentments toward Cuban immigrants, local Anglo-American politicians had little choice but to compete for their votes. Initially, the Republican Party won the loyalty of Cuban voters by dint of strategic patronage appointments; party officials also encouraged Cubans to run for office. In 1870, the Republican governor appointed Alejandro Mendoza to the office of justice of the peace and Angel Loño as a county judge. The next year, he appointed Nito Reyes as a justice of the peace.

In the city council elections of 1875, Republicans nominated Carlos

Manuel de Céspedes for mayor when it became evident Democrats were poised to win. Emphasizing insurgent rhetoric, Céspedes won by mobilizing the Cuban vote. Cuban support for Republicans translated into federal appointments in the customs house for Céspedes (after his mayoral term) and Manuel Govín, another activist. With their compatriots involved in port vigilance, nationalist activists could more easily dispatch men, weapons, and supplies to Cuba without fear of confiscation and arrest.

Cubans did not remain blindly committed to the Republicans, however. During the electoral season in 1876, Angel Loño and Lorenzo Jiménez, a war veteran, formed the Cuban Democratic Club. Disgusted with the Grant administration's failure to help the insurgency in Cuba, these nationalists hoped to make the Republicans realize the political power of Cubans, but they also astutely realized that the political environment in Florida increasingly favored Democrats. The two men succeeded in splitting the Cuban vote, leading to a victory for the Democratic Party in local elections that year. When Democrats took power across the state, Loño regained his appointment as county judge, which he had forfeited for supporting the Democrats.[8]

In subsequent years, Cubans remained active in both political parties. During the 1880 campaign season, the Cuban Hancock and English Club of Key West, which had 150 members, supported the Democratic presidential ticket. *La Propaganda* editor José R. Estrada and others (including Loño) began publishing a new newspaper, *El Localista*, to rally Cuban support for the Democratic Party, while labor leader Ramón Rivero supported Republicans in *La Fraternidad*. The Democratic ticket achieved victory in city elections with less than a 200-vote margin, demonstrating the importance of the Cuban vote in shifting the electoral balance.

In November 1880, Manuel Escassi ran as a Republican for the Florida Assembly but lost with the rest of the party ticket; he was not successful in attracting Cuban Democrats, who in that election failed to vote along ethnic lines. When the Executive Council of the Democratic Party of Monroe County rewarded Loño with membership, other Cubans were drawn to the party, including prominent cigar manufacturer Teodoro Pérez and merchant Carlos Recio. Cubans even participated in other parties than the two major ones. In November 1882, for example, Fernando Figueredo stood for Monroe County representative in the Florida Assembly as candidate for a Republican breakaway Independent Party. The Independents, including Figueredo, lost to the Democrats, but they received more votes than Republican Party candidates, denying them victory.[9]

Strains and Stresses

Despite the resentful attitudes of Anglo-Americans, Cuban participation in local politics developed smoothly enough, but their continuing nationalist priorities at times caused tensions and friction. In 1884, Cubans tested their political influence in the face of reaction from local authorities to their routine violation of U.S. neutrality laws.

When Carlos Aguero arrived to raise reinforcements for his guerrilla band, the Spanish consul lost no time contacting his superiors, who submitted an extradition request to the U.S. government that characterized Aguero as a common bandit and charged him with "rapine, arson, highway robbery and murder." The administration of President Chester Arthur was involved in negotiations with Spain for a commercial treaty and was anxious to resolve this complication. It pressed District Attorney George B. Patterson in Key West to press an extradition case and arrest Aguero, an action that complicated matters for local Republicans. While Aguero languished in prison, an outraged Cuban community mobilized and flexed its political muscle to influence events.[10]

Knowing that Cubans represented perhaps a third to half of the voting constituency, local Republican officials had little interest in alienating that community. They had carefully cultivated the Cuban vote and had delivered patronage positions in local federal offices in 1883 and 1884. Customs collector Frank Wicker had recently appointed Cubans Ramón Alvarez to the office of deputy customs collector and Figueredo and Manuel Escassi as customs inspectors, but this was not enough to mollify a Cuban community that was angered over the Aguero case.[11]

Fearful of the local political consequences, politicians of all stripes worked for Aguero's release. Characterizing the extradition as a political matter rather than a criminal one, in February 1884 Democratic senator Wilkinson Call demanded that the president prevent Aguero's delivery to Spanish authorities, a request that was referred to the Committee on Foreign Relations. Another Democratic official, Livingston W. Bethel, a local attorney who was also lieutenant governor of Florida, agreed to defend Aguero. Not to be outdone,

Patterson argued that the Spanish government had not provided sufficient evidence to extradite Aguero. On February 21 Judge James Locke, a Republican, formally rejected the extradition request and freed Aguero.[12]

The Cuban community was jubilant. After a special lunch for Aguero that was hosted at *El Yara*'s office, Rosendo García, Perico Torres, Poyo, and numerous others led a large crowd to San Carlos Institute, where they celebrated the insurgent chief and *Cuba libre*. A representative from the sheriff's office, a former slave, spoke in support of Cuban freedom and against the "tyrannical Spanish government." The crowd then paraded through the streets, accompanied by the Libertad band, expressing its appreciation of the support local politicians had rendered. They stopped in front of the homes of Lieutenant Governor Bethel, District Attorney Patterson, and Customs Collector Wicker, among others. Aguero and others spoke from a stage erected on Front Street, and later, at San Carlos Institute, several Republican Party officials offered supportive thoughts about Cuban independence.[13] Throughout the day, the revolutionary committee received funds for Aguero's expedition, including $100 from Wicker. Manuel P. Delgado's newspaper *La Voz de Hatuey* declared that Aguero planned to leave immediately for Cuba to continue the struggle and that Gómez and Maceo would soon follow him.[14]

In a report to superiors on March 29, 1884, the Spanish consul was confident that with all the local publicity, Aguero would not try to launch his expedition from Key West. When Aguero's vessel slipped out of Key West on April 4, a furious consul denounced the total failure of local officials to enforce U.S. neutrality laws. He charged Wicker and his Cuban employees Figueredo and Escassi with complicity in allowing Aguero's expedition to depart. Unfortunately for Wicker, President Arthur's interest in negotiating the reciprocity treaty with Spain outweighed his willingness to support the Republican Party's interests in south Florida. A special agent from the Treasury Department arrived in Key West, temporarily took charge of the Customs House, and took steps to ensure that neutrality laws were properly enforced. After reviewing reports on Wicker's sympathies for Cuban insurgents and his weak enforcement of neutrality laws, the U.S. Senate removed him from office. The consul also pushed the treasury agent in Key West to pursue legal action against Poyo and Dr. Manuel Moreno for conspiring with Aguero, which they felt was the most effective way to "terrorize" the rebels, one that was even better than the U.S. navy.[15]

Pressure from Washington finally convinced District Attorney Patterson to charge all who were involved with the specific incident the Spanish consul had brought to the attention of the federal government. Aguero; Emilio Díaz and Bruno Alfonso, who sailed the vessel; Clinton Shavers, owner of the vessel, and Poyo, who oversaw the operation, were charged with violating federal neutrality laws in U.S. District Court. On June 16, 1884, Patterson asked for an arrest warrant for Poyo, which the judge denied without comment, perhaps because he was the Peruvian consul. The judge then dismissed Aguero's case since he had left the country, but he did authorize the arrest of Díaz, Alfonso, and Shavers. The jury found Alfonso and Shavers not guilty; it convicted only Díaz, who received a sentence of eight months in prison and a $500 fine.[16]

Additional actions followed against Cubans who were stocking arms, ammunition, and explosives. On June 11, 1884, the treasury agent arrested Federico Gil Marrero, president of the Nihilist Club, as he arrived on a steamer from New York after he found 100 explosive caps, 500 feet of fuse, and powder that was not properly packed and marked as required by law in his luggage. Marrero was also carrying twelve glass tubes, four thermometers, mercury, and alcohol, all things that were used in manufacturing dynamite. Marrero was charged and arraigned on July 2, but he posted a $1,000 bond. The jury acquitted him, and several days later Judge Locke returned all the seized items. The court also dropped charges against Poyo for storing a large cache of weapons, ammunition, and dynamite at his newspaper office, which doubled as the Peruvian consulate. The Spanish consul was not surprised at the verdict or by the fact that the judge returned Marrero's property. He commented to his superiors that "the court has yet to find anyone guilty of crimes committed against our government."[17]

Cubans recognized that these actions by local officials were a less-than-vigorous response to the pressure from Washington, and they rewarded them at the polls. Bethel won election as mayor of Key West and Locke won a congressional seat with the support of the Cuban bloc. But to highlight their continuing electoral importance, Cubans also elected Fernando Figueredo to the Florida Assembly; the first Cuban to sit in the legislature. During his term in Tallahassee, Figueredo sponsored a resolution that asked the U.S. Congress to protect Florida's cigar industry, which was threatened by the reciprocity treaty with Spain that President Arthur wanted.[18]

Diverging Interests

In 1884, Anglo-American politicians had finessed the complications arising from Aguero's activities and in return, the Cuban community had given them its political support. But attitudes and circumstances changed when numerous cigar factories moved up the coast to the Tampa Bay region. This exodus began with the fire in Key West in 1886 but continued through the decade. Important businesses that had contributed to the city's growth and development such as Martínez Ybor, Lozano Pendas & Co., Palacios, and Villamil Pino & Co. left Key West. In 1890, Ocala also promoted itself as an excellent site for cigar factories, and within three years seventeen factories were operating in a new area of Ocala known as Martí City. These factories employed 700 workers, many who had come from Key West.[19]

Key West residents worried that Tampa and to a lesser extent Ocala would overtake their city as Florida's most important tobacco center and blamed Cuban nationalist and anarchist radicals and other "bad elements" from Cuba. Especially vocal in this regard was Charles Pendleton, editor of the *Equator-Democrat*, who had no doubt that increasing migration from Cuba threatened to destabilize the city's economy. He and others did not yet fully recognize the comparative advantages Tampa offered; it was the better economy there that fueled the continual relocation of factories, regardless of whatever political activities Cubans might be involved in.[20]

Negative descriptions of Key West began to appear in Spanish-language newspapers in Cuba, some English-language newspapers in Florida, and even some New York newspapers. Referring to Key West as a *nido de sabandijas* (nest of vermin), one Spanish observer who had visited in 1889 thought he had entered some of the "most reeking neighborhoods in Havana." Uproar and disorder offended his sensibilities, especially the squalid, heterogeneous group of "men, women, youngsters, blacks, mulattos, undefined, and whites chattering endlessly at the docks." He completed his comparison of Key West's "low classes" with their similar types in Havana by observing that unemployed workers and vagrants in bars and on street corners "had identical language styles and absolutely similar vices." This was to be expected, he explained, since Havana was where these "low-class people" came from and where they would eventually return. Key West was unstable, he noted, because such people came and went at their whim. The only reason the visitor even bothered to disembark at Key West on his return to Havana from New York, he claimed, was to satisfy his curiosity, to see the place that was so well known in Cuba as a center of bandits and pirates.[21]

A New York journalist also gave Key West a less-than-flattering review. He described Cubans as living in small frame cottages filled with children and surrounded with chickens, palmetto trees, and bad smells. At night Cubans gambled to pass the time, and on Sunday they attended cockfights. "In preparing a fowl for combat," he noted with obvious distaste, "a Cuban plucks out the tail feathers, snips the red flesh under the beak, and then thrusts the bleeding head into his mouth. The salivated wound is afterwards sprinkled with black pepper." The Sunday battles began with spurs and ended with "gaffes"—contrivances designed to tear out a rooster's spine. There were never two survivors of a cockfight, he declared.[22]

The perception that crime was increasing especially bothered Pendleton and the business community. They condemned a drift toward lawlessness that seemed especially clear in mid-March 1888, when José Rafael Estrada, the editor of *La Propaganda*, was murdered. Many in Key West disliked the Cuban journalist's confrontational style and his support for the revolutionary militants, especially his support for the occasionally heavy-handed tactics they used to maintain discipline in the ranks of the nationalists, and they were perhaps not entirely surprised when he was shot in the head during a quarrel in a local café. Estrada had been influential in both nationalist and Democratic Party politics, and a large crowd attended his funeral at San Carlos Institute that included the mayor and other local dignitaries. The body of the popular leader lay in his casket dressed in his Ten Years' War military uniform, including his hat and sword. Eulogies by prominent citizens praised his commitment to Cuban independence and attested to his good character and reputation.[23]

Pendleton did not join in the adulation. He argued that Estrada had threatened his assailant and had gotten what he deserved. He accused Estrada's followers, including Emilio García and Isidoro Leijas, of intimidating witnesses for the defense to prevent them from testifying in court. At Pendleton's instigation, Key West's Board of Trade urged authorities to act against these bad elements and even hinted that the intimidation tactics (including threats of lynching), which had been effectively used in Tampa in 1887 against Cuban nationalists, might be necessary. After Celestino Palacio, a Spanish cigar manufacturer, complained that nationalists had demanded "loans or donations" from him and other manufacturers, which he characterized as blackmail, at least twenty-three Anglo-American members of the Board of Trade signed a resolution against such coercive demands and pressured authorities for "a most vigorous prosecution."[24]

In April and May 1888, the police arrested several of those who had already been accused of demanding contributions from prominent manufacturers, including Emilio Díaz and Emilio García, who were scheduled for trial in November. Perico Torres and some of his followers were also arrested, but they posted bond. Isidoro Leijas and Bernardino Trujillo left for Nassau before they could be arrested, and several others left for Tampa and Jacksonville. Pendleton reminded his readers that Spanish authorities actively sought most of these men. Certainly their experience with rebel groups in Cuba meant that they were operating in that the blurred border between nationalism and banditry.[25]

Pendleton continued his aggressive stance and reprinted a report that had appeared in a Havana newspaper that claimed that "the bandit Leijas [who] is in Key West" had threatened a Havana resident with kidnapping if he did not respond to his demands for money.[26] When *La Propaganda* vehemently protested and condemned the Board of Trade's threats to lynch Cubans, the *Equator-Democrat* declared that efforts to "borrow sympathy for these men" were unwise. "We are no advocate of [lynching]," it declared, "but these scoundrels have gone further than lynching, they have assassinated," referring to murder charges Emilio García and Leijas had faced in Tampa in 1887. (Both men were exonerated.) The focus on Leijas led British authorities in Nassau to arrest him at the insistence of authorities in Cuba, but Leijas hanged himself in his cell rather than face a Spanish prison and certain execution.[27]

The Board of Trade then turned against the labor radicals who had led the general strike of the cigar industry in late 1889. In early November, members of the Board of Trade representing the business community demanded to see strike leader Enrique Messonier at the Key West Bank. Former district court marshal Peter Knight, who was known in the Cuban community as the *capitán de los linchadores* (captain of the lynch mobs), met him at the bank door and "in a rude manner and [with] violent language" ushered him into a room, where he encountered Pendleton, John J. Philbrick, N. Maloney, and a few other members of the board. Philbrick was one of Key West's most prominent business leaders and Maloney was a member of an important local family. They handed Messonier a steamer ticket and ordered him to leave town, warning that they could not vouch for his safety if he refused. At first he resisted and went to City Hall to file a complaint, but the mayor, the chief of police, and the city secretary reiterated the order and the local militia escorted him to the docks. In a rare moment of converging interest among Cuban workers and nationalists, hundreds gathered to protest the expulsion, but Messonier left peacefully. Soon thereafter, other members of the strike organizing committee received similar warnings and departed.[28]

These actions in 1888 and 1889 represented a shift in the tolerant attitudes of the local Anglo-American political and economic establishment. Cuban workers resented and condemned the aggressiveness of Anglo-Americans, as did nationalist leaders, who expressed their dismay in *El Yara*. Even though the newspaper disagreed with Messonier's anarchist beliefs, it protested the injustice as an assault on the Cuban community, a violation of the laws of the United States, and a dangerous precedent. "From the moment a citizen is left at the mercy of a coterie [the Board of Trade] that arbitrarily pistol-whips the laws," *El Yara* declared, "there can be no liberty, security, no recourse in civil society, since arbitrary action against one is arbitrary action against all."[29]

The increase in ethnic tensions found voice in fall 1888 when Cubans reminded Anglo-American politicians of their ability to influence local politics. As in previous years, when the Cuban community sought to send a political message to the Republican and Democratic Parties, Cubans of both parties voted along ethnic lines. Nationalist leaders ran for the office of Florida Assembly representative: Manuel P. Delgado competed for one seat as a Democrat and Dr. Manuel Moreno ran for the other as a Republican. Cuban voters delivered both seats to the Cuban candidates, in the process sending a message to Anglo-American politicians who challenged Cuban nationalists.[30]

These events created a complex situation for Poyo and the nationalist leadership. While they opposed Cuban anarchists who placed labor issues above nationalist ideology, they could not accept the deportation of such men. In addition, Anglo-American leaders such as Pendleton were attacking and urging the deportation of nationalist activists whom Poyo relied on to send armed groups to Cuba. He could organize expeditions, but he had to be careful not to overreach to the point that would generate conflict with local authorities who could make life difficult for him. After all, Cuban nationalists also "pistol-whipped" the laws and they contended with bandits who were arriving from Cuba with little interest in revolutionary affairs. These men could not always be controlled and often caused conflict and used rough methods to settle accounts, which obviously disturbed the Anglo-American community. After the legal complications resulting from the Aguero affair, Poyo acted with greater discretion. This was evidenced in his less-visible relations with Manuel García, Perico Torres, and others. Local authorities could much more easily ignore these more discrete contacts if they wanted, and they usually did. Managing the political, economic, and social issues of the Cuban community that conflicted with Anglo-American interests locally proved challenging for Poyo and the nationalist leadership.

Confrontation and Conflict

The tensions between Cubans and Anglo-Americans finally exploded into open conflict when the national economic downturn of 1893 damaged the cigar industry in Key West. The local PRC's work with Martí to expand insurrectionist cells in Cuba and plan expeditions faced imminent retrenchment as cigar markets dried up, factories closed temporarily, wages declined, and laid-off workers provoked damaging strikes.

Acting on intelligence provided by the Spanish consul, authorities in Cuba moved to take advantage of the weakened Key West community. In early August they sent the steamer *Julia* to Key West to carry unemployed workers back to Cuba.[31] This caused alarm in the nationalist community, which opposed the repatriation of Cuban workers. Poyo had considerable experience with managing these kinds of challenges, but the economic climate in late 1893 threatened the Cuban community and the local PRC organization at a particularly sensitive time for the revolutionary movement.

As the end of the year approached, Seidenberg & Co. reopened after a brief period, but workers refused to return when they learned the company had recruited thirteen Spanish workers and a foreman in Havana, presumably at lower wages. The company appealed to the Key West Board of Trade and threatened to move its operations to Tampa if the board failed to use its influence with government officials to undermine the power of the striking workers. Business leaders were still smarting from the great strike in 1889 and the increasing competition from Tampa and other Florida cigar communities and convinced local authorities to act. In early January 1894, when Key West business and government leaders returned from Havana with a steamer filled with contracted Spanish workers, the stage was set for an unprecedented ethnic confrontation between Cubans and Anglo-Americans.

Cuban leaders fully understood that local authorities had flagrantly violated the Alien Contract Labor Law of 1888, which made it illegal for employers to contract with workers outside national boundaries. They called for a boycott of the Anglo-American community in every respect, which Cuban women took a lead in organizing. Serafín Sánchez referred to this as "peaceful warfare." Cubans refused to engage in commerce with businesses owned by Anglo-Americans, from butcher shops to carriage service. Even black American domestic workers suffered in this boycott. In addition, Carolina "La Patriota" took up guard at the Cuban monument at the cemetery after hearing rumors that it would be vandalized. After consulting the spirits she told the community not to worry "time is on our side."[32]

Poyo immediately sought a local attorney to challenge Key West authorities about what seemed to be a clear violation of the contract labor law, but no lawyer dared take the case. From New York, Martí arranged for a young lawyer named Horatio Rubens to travel to Key West, and Poyo assigned Delgado to work with him. Delgado had served in the Florida state legislature and was a notary public who was familiar with court proceedings. He also knew the local Anglo-American personalities well. Local authorities were disturbed by Rubens's presence in Key West, and noting his youth, local authorities tried to intimidate him. On his first night in Key West, several men entered his hotel room and urged him leave the next day. He received several more threats, but the Cuban community kept a close watch over him.

The first thing Rubens did was obtain the release of Rosendo García, who had been arrested the same day as the confrontations at the docks on January 2, 1894. Rumors spread that *linchadores* planned to make an example of García, prompting the Partida La Tranca to place a guard detail around the jail. When Rubens finally managed to secure a hearing with the county judge, he demanded that the prisoners be given a speedy trial or he would be forced to seek a trial in another city. Seeing that the determined young attorney had legal skill, the judge finally agreed to set a trial date. On the day of the trial, the Partida escorted García to court. It also ensured that his accusers and witnesses did not appear. After his release, García immediately boarded a steamer and joined Martí in New York.[33]

Rubens then turned his attention to the contract labor case, but he quickly concluded that local authorities planned to ignore what was an obvious violation of federal law. He filed a complaint with the superintendent of the Immigration Bureau at the U.S. Department of Treasury, who appointed a local board in Key West to investigate the case. The superintendent also dispatched a special treasury agent to Key West.[34] Martí remained watchful while Rubens sorted out the legal issues and Poyo managed the dangerous tensions that periodically erupted into confrontations on the streets as Cubans persisted in their boycott.

In mid-January, Martí went to Tampa. He was anxious to visit Key West. Many in the Anglo-American community knew Martí only as an agitator who had frequently disrupted business and politicized factory workers over the previous two years. In July 1892, for example, when Martí arrived in Key West, manufacturers braced themselves for interruptions in production. When he left, a local newspaper correspondent declared that "peace reigns at last" after three weeks of demonstrations and nationalist agitation.[35] Non-Cuban manufacturers, who particularly resented Martí for sending Rubens to Key West, warned the PRC leader not to land at Key West. Fearful of what might happen, Rubens, Poyo, Figueredo, and Sánchez sought to dissuade Martí from visiting; they were even concerned that he might be assassinated. But Martí did not abandon his plan to visit Key West until Rubens met with him in Tampa on his way to Washington, D.C.[36]

Rubens had traveled to Washington in response to a message from the superintendent of the Bureau of Immigration announcing a hearing of all parties involved in the contract labor case. The hearing was held on January 20, 1894. The superintendent ruled that a violation of the contract labor law had indeed occurred. The delegation of Anglo-American officials from Key West, which included the mayor, the collector of customs, and Seidenberg, refused to accept this decision and demanded a hearing with the secretary of the treasury and the attorney general one week later. Key West leaders contended their community's welfare was at stake and that cigar factories would close if manufacturers did not have access to foreign workers.[37]

In early February, all involved returned to Key West to wait for the decision of the Treasury Department. A large crowd met the Anglo-American delegation at the docks with signs that celebrated their return, but only one sign at the office of *El Yara* greeted Rubens, who arrived on the same steamer. An organized procession from city hall escorted officials to a nearby hotel, where they delivered speeches defending their right to hire Spanish workers. Pendleton declared that even if the government ordered the return of the Spanish workers, "we have sufficient force in Key West to resist." "For every ten they send back, one hundred more will come." The event drew a crowd of Cubans, and numerous fights broke out with Spaniards before the crowd dispersed.[38]

Soon thereafter, the Treasury Department ruled definitively that Key West manufacturers had violated federal law and ordered that the workers be deported. But defense attorneys immediately filed for writs of habeas corpus, which ended the matter for the immediate future. The workers remained at their jobs and the Cuban community felt betrayed. In response, the Treasury Department ordered the arrest of those involved in violating federal law, including Pendleton, Seidenberg, and several local officials. However, a visiting district judge from New Orleans dismissed the entire case, using the proceedings as an opportunity to criticize Cuban nationalists. The judge lectured the district attorney, declaring that Cubans, not Anglo-Americans, were the lawbreakers. He said that the district attorney had failed to do his duty when he had not charged Martí, Poyo, and others with violating neutrality laws. The judge said that raising funds to carry out a war against a nation at peace with the United States was a clear violation of these laws. Rubens objected, but the judge accused him of interfering in local matters and defending Cuban delinquents and lawbreakers. "You should all be in jail," he yelled at Rubens and the Cuban leaders sitting at his side.[39]

The judge's tirade was in step with the goal of local authorities of disrupting the PRC and its activities. And in this they were somewhat successful. When Poyo was threatened with arrest for trying to revolutionize Cuba and violating U.S. neutrality laws, he ceased his activities temporarily. Rubens informed Martí and Poyo that nothing in U.S. law prohibited the PRC's activities; the only thing that would be illegal would be actually attacking a friendly nation. Martí urged Poyo to reorganize at his own pace and with prudence, but he also suggested that PRC secretary Gualterio García take the lead initially so that Poyo would be less visible.[40] Some in Cuba also did what they could to discredit Poyo, publishing defamatory and personal accusations in the newspapers *La Discusión* and *Las Avispas*. In addition, Delgado was summoned to court for allegedly using his authority as a notary public to unlawfully certify a document. This accusation was likely retribution because he had assisted Rubens.[41]

A war of words embroiled the *Equator-Democrat*, José Martí's *Patria*, and *El Porvenir*, further aggravating matters. *El Porvenir*'s editor, Enrique Trujillo, who was still opposed to Martí, condemned the introduction of contract workers, but he also opposed revolutionary nationalism and held Martí and the local PRC responsible for the escalating tension. Trujillo particularly complained of Martí's article "To Cuba," which was reprinted in English in the *Equator-Democrat*. It reassured nationalist Cubans of the justness of their cause, provocatively criticized the Anglo-American community, and pointed to the recent events in Key West as further reasons for Cubans to secure their own country. Martí's inflammatory nationalist rhetoric condemned the "good [Anglo-American] men of Key West who yielded, from passion or ignorance, or from a false conception of their true convenience to an evident coalition of private interests, of demagogues deriving their living from catering to public prejudices, of pendants [sic] incapable of understanding the people they deride, of revengeful aspirants who in an hour of revolt satiated their anger, hardly unmasked through years, for having needed the people they scoff at [Cubans], for preying upon their favor, their friendship, and their votes."[42] The PRC's militant ethos, Trujillo argued, had fueled the violent confrontations. He condemned the politicization of cigar workers and the military-like organization on the factory floors that excluded Spaniards. Trujillo urged Cuban workers to respect the right of Spanish workers to work instead of rejecting and alienating them. Win them over to Cuban nationalism, Trujillo said.[43]

The *Equator-Democrat* called on Cubans to reject violence and respect constitutional procedures, declaring that "American liberty does not mean uncontrolled license." It also condemned what it saw as fanatical and incendiary articles that had been disseminated in *Patria*. These should be rejected by all good citizens, the newspaper proclaimed. It recommended Trujillo's articles, which insisted—as did Key West authorities—that the affair in Key West "is a local matter stemming from labor concerns, the ample liberty of its citizens, and having to do with order in the workplace and harmony among diverse elements of the city."[44]

Zaldívar, a member of the PRC's crisis committee, also entered the fray, reminding everyone that the manufacturers had precipitated the crisis with their unilateral reduction of workers' wages and illegal importation of Spanish workers. He also lamented the *Equator-Democrat's* attacks on the Cuban community, which were "so insulting they could not be repeated." "Mr. Pendleton," he said, "has always been an enemy of the Cubans; he was among those who went to Havana to ask the Governor for [pro-Spanish] *voluntarios* and expects us to be content and satisfied."[45]

Cubans debated about how best to respond on the local political front. Some Democratic and Republican Cubans wanted to exert pressure within their local parties. However, on February 6 Cubans gathered and wrote a platform for an alternative political party, the Partido Independiente. Several days later a public assembly ratified the platform. The Executive Committee of the new party included Fernando Figueredo (president), Martín Herrera (first vice-president), Manuel Moreno (second vice-president), and Manuel P. Delgado (secretary). The first three were Republicans and the last a Democrat, a reflection of Cuban dissatisfaction with both mainstream parties. Teodoro Pérez, another important Democrat, also joined the new party, but many Cubans did not want to break their ties with parties that they depended for patronage jobs in the customs house, the courts, and other offices.[46]

Cubans soon abandoned the new organization and took a more radical path: they relocated to the Tampa Bay area, highlighting their deep sense of betrayal. In January and February, hundreds of workers had left Key West for Havana, Ybor City, and Ocala in search of work, and the exodus spread to include manufacturers and important Cuban nationalist leaders. In early March 1894, a committee of Cubans closely associated with the PRC and the tobacco industry visited Tampa to explore the possibilities of moving there. The committee included E. F. O'Halloran, Teodoro Pérez, Manuel Barranco, Martín Herrera, Severo de Armas, F. Fleitas, and Fernando Figueredo.[47]

In 1892, Tampa entrepreneur Hugh Macfarlane had established another cigar town and courted Key West manufacturers. The new town became known as West Tampa. Because of the problems in Key West, he raised the stakes and offered cigar manufacturers land and even factory buildings free of charge if they would bring workers who would rent homes from his real estate company.[48] Martí City, near Ocala, also offered incentives to cigar manufacturers. These tempting offers made it economically advantageous for manufacturers to relocate, and many did. In addition to the 1,500 or 2,000 workers who followed the manufacturers, important PRC leaders relocated, including Figueredo, Martín Herrera, Juan Arnao, Gerardo Castellanos, and Gualterio García, secretary of the PRC. Among the major Cuban manufacturers, only Eduardo Gato did not consider moving. Workers in his factory issued an "Exposition and Petition" that denounced recent events in Key West and expressed their willingness to accompany Gato if he decided to relocate his factory to Tampa. Gato responded with gratitude but said that he did not intend to be driven from Key West and had in any case received economic incentives to remain that would benefit all in Key West.[49]

Poyo supported this exodus, but very reluctantly. In the first week of April, *El Yara* announced: "It is resolved." Seven or eight manufacturers had decided to transfer their factories to West Tampa. "The new Israelites," declared *El Yara*, "depart to plant their tents in less ungrateful lands. Let us take up the pilgrim's knapsack and prepare to leave."[50] After so many years of careful organizing and effort, the "Cuban bulwark" was on the verge of disappearing. But it seemed unavoidable. The coexistence Poyo had built with Key West's Anglo-American leadership seemed irreparably damaged, and the people who had so often expressed their support for the Cuban nationalist cause had become dangerous enemies.

Forging Ahead

The PRC experienced a difficult setback in the first half of 1894. Officials threatened to arrest its leaders, the mass exodus of manufacturers and workers left the party depleted, the number of nationalist clubs had declined, and contributions in the factories for nationalist projects had almost ceased. The structures the PRC had created in the factories, including the collection committees, disappeared or at least weakened as many manufacturers took advantage of the PRC's lower profile to establish greater control over hiring and over the factory floors.

Despite the bleak situation, Poyo remained in Key West, as did Delgado, and rebuilt the capacity for revolutionary action. So did Gato, in whose factory Poyo continued to read, and Serafín Sánchez, Carlos Roloff, and many of the military veterans who viewed Key West as strategically critical for communicating with insurgents in Cuba and staging an assault on the island. While the exodus continued, a few arrived to Key West, most prominently Fermín Valdés Domínguez, Martí's good friend who had been among the medical students who were arrested during the infamous Castañon case that was so closely tied to the city's patriotic traditions. Poyo and Delgado continued to publish *El Yara*. They began publishing an English-language version in March, hoping to open a conversation with the Anglo-American community. "The first issue in English is inspired and brilliant," observed *Patria*. "It is the soul of José Dolores Poyo, and the precise and sharp language of Manuel Delgado."[51]

An event that took place on March 20, 1894, marked the beginning of the easing of recriminations between Cubans and Anglo Americans. A labor dispute in the Seidenberg factory sparked a strike of the American and Spanish workers that had replaced Cubans in January and quickly escalated into violence. In December 1893, Seidenberg had thought Cuban workers were disruptive to the functioning of his factory, but his new workers stoned the factory, broke windows, and attempted to force their way into the building. Rushing to the scene, police pushed the protestors back but not before a stone struck and severely wounded the Spanish foreman who had overseen the importation of the Spanish workers. Outraged by the disturbance, Seidenberg declared this a great moral victory for the Cubans he had maligned and a humiliation for Anglo-Americans. The factory opened again after three days, but Seidenberg began making plans to relocate to Tampa.[52]

Key West's Anglo-American leadership realized their miscalculation. This incident sorely disabused them of the assumption that contracting workers in Havana who were influenced by anarchism instead of nationalism would resolve their labor-management problems. Their determination to destroy Cuban labor unions led to complications with the federal authorities and a wholesale flight of Cuban manufacturers. And their effort to undermine the PRC only reinforced the exodus. Furthermore, they harmed their relations with their Cuban neighbors, which had been for the most part cordial since their arrival in the 1870s. In the end, although some Anglo Americans changed their attitude, as reflected by the request in Pendleton's *Equator-Democrat* that Cubans reconsider their decision and remain in Key West where they could more effectively serve the Cuban independence movement, the Seidenberg factory left the area.[53]

After this episode, tensions declined and both sides made efforts to bring the conflict and animosity to an end. Poyo and the PRC leadership rebuilt their damaged fortunes. In early April, they celebrated the third year of the founding of the PRC and participated in unanimously reelecting Martí as *delegado*. The representatives of the nineteen clubs with enough members to warrant a vote in the PRC council reelected Poyo as council president and elected Ramón Rivera as secretary. Rivera replaced Gualterio García, who had joined the exodus to Tampa. PRC leaders, who no longer faced threats of arrest, organized a public celebration at San Carlos Institute, which filled to capacity.

Poyo opened the event with a fervent speech. He was flanked on the decorated stage by Sánchez, Figueredo, the presidents of various PRC clubs, and members of the Hijas de la Libertad dressed in "gala outfits." Sitting on Poyo's right, Fermín Valdés Domínguez waited to give the keynote address while various members of men's and women's clubs spoke. After poetry recitals by "the precious little girl Matilda Orta" and Melitina Azpeytía, "a genial orator," Valdés Domínguez stepped forward and was greeted with thunderous applause and cheers. He vowed to avenge the executed medical students and become a soldier for Cuba's freedom. Francisco María González, the popular *lector*, offered a summary of the evening and Poyo happily and with "brief and heart-felt words" terminated the celebration. As the crowd filed out of the building and made their way to their homes, they were accompanied by the martial music ("*músicas guerreras*") of the *Libertad* band.[54]

Poyo finally gave Martí the green light to visit Key West, and he arrived on May 15, 1894, accompanied by eighteen-year-old Panchito Gómez Toro, the son of the Dominican general. At a meeting of the Cuerpo de Consejo, the *delegado* urged the community to meet their financial obligations so that revolutionary work could continue. The next day he visited the Gato factory, where 500 workers received him enthusiastically. That evening at a public event at San Carlos Institute, Martí introduced Gómez, invoked his illustrious father, and reminded the audience of the importance of the PRC's work in preparing for the war. He then asked if he could remain confident "in my people, whose patriotism inspires me and whose voice encourages me to continue the journey?" Noisy exclamations of "*Vivas!*" resonated throughout the hall.[55]

Figure 6. José Martí speaking at a cigar factory in Key West, Florida. On Martí's right is José D. Poyo (with his arm crossed over his chest), and on Martí's left is Fernando Figueredo. On Poyo's right (facing forward) is Néstor Leonelo Carbonell. Oil painting by Juan Hernández Giró. From Guillermo de Zéndegui, *Ambito de Martí* (Havana: P. Fernández y Cia, 1954).

Though the community's enthusiasm was strong, all was not well. Even though tensions with the Anglo-American community had eased, the economic crisis persisted and the departure of factories in Key West reduced income for the revolution significantly. Other communities provided Martí with resources, but Key West remained indispensable. Its fund-raising system had always been the most formidable and reliable, and disruption threatened Martí's ability to continue his activities. Even before the political crisis with the Anglo-American community eased in April, leaders in Key West created a Comité de Colectas del Comercio de Cayo Hueso (Business Collection Committee of Key West) to supplement the weakened collection system in the factories. The committee received a letter from Martí asking for funds since the need "at every hour grows more urgent."[56]

Some tensions between Cubans and Anglo-Americans remained. Although Martí was welcome in several factories, others closed their doors. The management at the Falk and Mayer factory refused to allow him to visit, provoking a strike. But Martí intervened quickly, asking the workers to abandon the action since it might revive accusations that he was interfering in local affairs and create deeper strains. Despite some setbacks, Martí raised enthusiasm and obtained promises of financial contributions before he left on May 19.[57]

Martí was optimistic that the tide had turned and expected resources to flow again. From Jacksonville, on his way to New Orleans and Central America, Martí wrote Poyo, Sánchez, and Valdés Domínguez a letter that warned that expectations and tensions in Cuba could unexpectedly precipitate events at any time and emphasized that the communities in exile needed to be ready. Although the PRC had stopped demanding already promised funds in light of the pain and trauma in Key West, now, he wrote, "the needs of the homeland are greater than the afflictions of local communities." Though Martí recognized that what he asked was difficult and required sacrifices, "today, pledges need to be remembered: today, what was promised should be gathered: today, it is necessary to request, in good time, the help of those who have not yet given."[58] Several days later, Sánchez received another letter from Martí from New Orleans that asked him to contact certain people in various factories to help raise the funds. "Become the chief of police," he told Sánchez, who as a military veteran knew how to exert pressure.[59]

But Martí's badgering was not enough to overcome the depressed economic conditions in Key West. Poyo received another letter from the clearly frustrated *delegado* in early July, who by then was back in New York. Martí told Poyo of his trip to Central America and Jamaica, saying he had accomplished his goals and had even raised funds among the poor communities in those regions that made the centers of Cuban exiles in the United States seem rich in comparison. "And there, how are things going?" he asked. "Not one peso from the Key," he noted acidly, "and according to the records, over $3,000 had been promised." He would write a letter, he told Poyo. "Take it from house to house. Do it urgently, as urgently as it is." Recognizing his harsh tone, Martí then softened a bit saying, "I don't want to harass you. You will help me there, in whatever way possible." "Whatever is done there," he reassured Poyo, "will leave me as proud as I am of the timely and pleasurable efforts of the Cubans I just saw [in San José and Jamaica]." Martí closed by urging Poyo to pressure the community in the pages of *El Yara*: "You, pressuring with the press, is one of my constant visions. Love me a bit, as I love you."[60]

The events of the previous months had left Poyo pessimistic and dejected, and Martí's correspondence did little to raise his spirits. On the very day Martí wrote his demanding letter, Poyo revealed his mood in *El Yara*: "Anyone who saw Key West last year and saw it again today would almost doubt that it was the same exuberant town that revealed life in all of its dimensions." Empty factories were the most obvious eyesores. "Sad events we all lament led to their departure," Poyo said, and large numbers of workers had followed, as had many small business owners, merchants, and individuals. "And in the middle of this general chaos, not even a ray of consoling hope for the future is evident."[61] He too felt the economic constraints, since his own wages were linked to the fate of the workers. And of course Poyo missed many friends and confidants who had left, especially Figueredo and Herrera, on whom he had always relied for support and advice.

The rupture with the Anglo-American community and their threats against him and the community took their toll on Poyo's state of mind, even more than the strike of 1889 had. Martí had noticed this earlier in the year and expressed concern for Poyo's "quiet and profound pain." Martí wrote Gualterio García that Poyo must be suffering a heavy heart since "with full rights," he saw himself as "one of the patriarchs of the great work which brutal disorder is bringing down." Rumors spread that Poyo intended to follow his friends to Tampa. Martí told García, "I think often of Poyo and I am beginning to find happiness in the hope that he may move to a place where the anxiety quiets and the sadness, which now visibly dominates, lessens."[62]

On July 30, Poyo's frustration became especially evident. He warned that without contributions he could no longer afford to publish *El Yara* every day. "We could reduce publication to once a week" in order to continue serving the nationalist cause, he suggested. This however would not resolve the embarrassment he felt about the indifference of those the newspaper served. Poyo wrote that if he was unable to overcome the lack of interest he would cease publication altogether and move to another area. "We shall see what we do."[63]

His admonitions changed little, and in early August, perhaps because of depleted income or simply because he was exhausted from the stress of the previous months, Poyo traveled to Tampa, apparently expecting to stay among his many friends. But his self-imposed exile did not last long, and before the end of the month Poyo returned to Key West. He seemed to be reinvigorated. As Martí wrote, "He has returned to his constant arena, and out of the steamer came the old and beloved printing press to open all the doors to the light. He, on the wide table, again writes his punishments and scorn, his prudent counsel and his sadness, his language precise and real."[64] Valdés Domínguez commemorated his return in an article for *Patria*: "He could not stay there [Tampa]; the chief should be in the Cuban bulwark which is the Key." He welcomed him back in the name of the Club Luz de Yara.[65] Martí thanked Valdés Dominguez for supporting Poyo: "How much I esteem the love you give Poyo which provides him the strength that others steal!"[66] In his first editorial after his return, Poyo reaffirmed the important work of the PRC and José Martí and declared to his brothers in Cuba: "Order: We Will Obey."[67]

Except for his family, no one more than Martí recognized Poyo's material and psychological difficulties during this period. He acknowledged Poyo's struggle in an article in *Patria* entitled "Nuestro 'Yara'":

> It is beautiful to see an honorable man struggle; see him suffer, since from the spectacle of pain emerges the strength to oppose evil; see him rise triumphantly, with his face toward the sun, and from all the crossroads see him defend without pay and at the cost of his blood, the

medicine of his children, the shoes of his grandchildren, an idea that will only end when its defender, at the end of his life sees the welcoming brilliance of death. The spectacle of such an invincible man highlights the power of love. Jose Dolores Poyo is like that.[68]

Despite many difficulties and stresses, Poyo, Delgado, Sánchez, Roloff, Valdés Domínguez and many other activists slowly rebuilt the revolutionary community. Many years later, Delgado confessed that at the time he thought they had suffered a great loss. Seidenberg had moved his factory and the town was economically debilitated, but with hard work much of its strength returned. Slowly the factories began producing again, and within a year workers in the large establishments were contributing between $300 and $400 a week. Generals Roloff and Sánchez created a *lotería de la patria* (lottery of the nation) that was sponsored by the Key West Mutual Aid Society. With the help of Francisco Ibern, *El Yara*'s office manager, they sold tickets in Key West and Tampa and even in New York. The first drawing was held on August 28, 1894.[69] The lottery produced important income for the PRC. Some of the lottery income also supported Cuban families in need.

The number of clubs affiliated with the PRC in Key West declined considerably, but they persisted and survived. In April 1896, Poyo reported that twenty-six men's clubs and eight women's clubs were in operation. There were also thirty clubs in Tampa and eleven in West Tampa.[70] But the cigar industry in Key West never fully recovered from the crisis of the late 1880s and early 1890s, and Tampa took its place as the largest center of Cuban exiles. Though Key West's economic base and its population both declined, Poyo and the local leadership remained committed and succeeded in rebuilding a militant community in support of Cuban independence.

8

WAR

> Time passes, the winter campaign begins, and Spain prepares an army of 200,000 men, counting on the support of the free American nations, who trade with Spain and allow it to use their ports in the war of extermination against the Cubans.... It seems unbelievable.
>
> *El Yara*, 1895

On April 27, 1895, Máximo Gómez wrote Poyo, "Here come two lines from these liberated fields of Beautiful Cuba." Gómez, Martí, and Maceo had reached Cuba with little challenge, and the day before Cuban forces had driven back a Spanish column. "From here," Gómez declared, "you will see the brilliance of a beautiful aurora the day Cuba is redeemed." "Do not weaken over there," he told Poyo. "Work."[1]

Despite a strong relationship with Martí, Poyo never wavered in his support for Máximo Gómez. He firmly backed Martí and the PRC's activities to organize the rebellion, but he never doubted that once the war started the critical figures would be Generals Gómez and Antonio Maceo. In the 1880s, Poyo had remained in frequent correspondence with the Gómez, and in December 1893 he reassured Gómez that he could always count on him: "I am as loyal in my principles [to Gómez], as in my affections."[2]

Gómez's letter signaled the moment to begin delivering war matériel to revolutionaries in Cuba. Everyone knew that the outcome of the war largely depended on the effectiveness of exile communities' in providing enough arms, ammunition, and explosives to fight a large and well-equipped Spanish military. The failure to do just that had doomed the Ten Years' War almost two decades earlier. Thousands had volunteered to join the expeditionary forces, but more than anything else the liberation army needed weapons and ammunition. Poyo spent the next four years struggling to meet that objective.

Insurrection

In late 1894, while the PRC, through the *delegación* (the *delegado*'s office) and the Cuerpos de Consejo, labored to increase the number of revolutionary cells in Cuba and urged the exile communities to continue providing critical financial resources, Martí and a handful of men, in coordination with Key West, worked secretly on an expedition whose goal was to transport the revolution's primary military leaders to Cuba. Martí kept the preparations as close to his chest as possible, knowing that the fewer who knew of the plans the better, especially given the effectiveness of Spain's counterintelligence activities. He confided the details of the plans only to senior political and military leaders such as Poyo, Figueredo, Sánchez, and Roloff, who were in charge of Key West's portion of the plan.

Martí visited Key West for what turned out to be the last time on October 3, 1894. He checked on the status of the local expedition and then traveled to Jacksonville to confer with others involved in coordinating the vessels that would carry the military leaders to Cuba.[3] In the last days of October, Martí told Gato that all was now ready, but he still needed $5,000 to purchase more arms. "Since I have no more to request of the poor," he asked him for one more contribution, and Gato complied.[4] Martí finalized the preparations and gathered around him Mayía Rodríguez, Máximo Gómez's envoy; Enrique Collazo, who was representing Havana's insurgent groups; and Enrique Loynaz del Castillo, who had joined them from Maceo's camp in Costa Rica. In Key West, Poyo and his colleagues waited for word and continued to prepare the force assembled there.[5]

In January, Martí carefully activated what became known as the Fernandina Plan, which involved loading three vessels with enough arms, ammunition, and men to sustain an insurrectionary uprising for some time while leaders recruited an army and received additional supplies from abroad. Three ships planned to leave from New York and Boston and rendezvous in Fernandina, Florida, a small and isolated port just north of Jacksonville, to take on the war supplies. The vessel *Amadis* planned to pick up Generals Roloff and Sánchez and a contingent of some 200 in Key West and travel directly to Las Villas. The *Baracoa* would take Martí, Mayía Rodríguez, and Enrique Collazo to rendezvous with Máximo Gómez and 200 men in the Dominican Republic and then head for Cuba. The *Lagonda* prepared to sail for Costa

Rica to transport Generals Maceo and Crombet and another 200 fighters. The *Lagonda* arrived in Ferdandina first, followed by the *Amadis*. They were loaded with arms and ammunition while they awaited the *Baracoa*.[6]

On January 10, 1895, while Martí was in New York preparing last-minute shipments of military stores, he received a cable that informed him that customs officials in Florida had seized the ships. Martí rushed to join Collazo, Mayía Rodríguez, and others in Jacksonville, where he exploded into a despondent rage and protested that it was not his fault. He blamed Fernando López de Queralta, an aide recommended to him by Sánchez and Roloff, who had revealed plans to one of the captains of the vessels. The conspirators hid from the police while they considered their next move, but they realized that impatience among insurgents in Cuba could no longer be restrained and that raising another expedition was out of the question. "Don't worry about me," Martí reassured Poyo and the Key West community. "I know how to die and recover." Despite the setback and his continuing anxiety, Martí believed that the effort to mount the expedition had resulted in "greater respect and faith than ever."[7] The confiscation of three fully armed ships ironically confirmed the PRC's effectiveness and Martí's leadership of the revolution.

On February 17, Martí confirmed the bad news for Juan Gualberto Gómez in Havana and asked him whether insurgent leaders were nonetheless prepared to rise. Two weeks of frenzied correspondence determined the course of action, and Martí, Collazo, and Mayía Rodríguez—with the approval of Máximo Gómez and forces in Cuba—finally issued the order to begin the insurrection. PRC secretary Gonzalo de Quesada, one of Martí's closest aides, delivered the order announcing that the insurrection would begin on February 24 to Figueredo in Tampa and returned to New York with $2,000 for Martí. Figueredo ordered that the historic document be concealed in a large cigar, which Juan Dios de la Guardia, a Key West resident, delivered to Juan Gualberto Gómez in Havana. Meanwhile Martí, Collazo, and Mayía Rodríguez went to Haiti to wait for funds from Florida. On February 7, they joined Gómez at his home in Montecristi, Dominican Republic.[8]

Once a firm date had been set, Juan Gualberto Gómez began mobilizing the uprising. On February 23, he left Havana and headed for the rendezvous point, an abandoned sugar mill called La Ignacia not far from the city. General Julio Sanguily planned to meet him there, as would Manuel García who had remained active. In letters to Máximo Gómez in August and November

1893, Martí had described the Havana insurrectionist networks that were collaborating with the PRC. He mentioned García and numerous "young residents of Havana of good families, doctors, and country folk."[9] But things did not go well. On the day of the uprising, Spanish authorities arrested Julio Sanguily as he prepared to leave his home in Havana. They also arrested his aide, José María Aguirre, at the Havana railway station.[10] Other important Havana insurgents suffered the same fate.

Manuel García gathered his troops and set out on the same day to join Juan Gualberto Gómez; he was accompanied by an agent Julio Sanguily had sent. On their way to the rendezvous point, the force stopped at a small country store, where they confiscated supplies in the name of the Cuban Republic. But in a bizarre turn of events, a member of the group suddenly turned on García and Sanguily's agent, killing them both. The assassin escaped with money and documents and García's band dispersed, leaving the patriot-bandit's body sprawled on the ground after almost ten years of constant action against Spanish colonialism. Alone and pursued by the Spanish who had full knowledge of the conspiracy, Juan Gualberto Gómez surrendered a few days later.[11]

The Spanish stopped the Havana insurgency in its tracks. Las Villas remained quiet, as did Matanzas; only Oriente responded with enough enthusiasm to provide a possible foothold for insurrection. Groups of insurgents gathered at Baire, in eastern Cuba, and initiated sporadic guerrilla operations. They held their own while waiting for the arrival of the primary revolutionary leaders. In April, Martí, Gómez, Maceo, Crombet, and others landed, mobilized insurgent forces, and expanded the campaign.[12]

Enthusiasm in the communities of exiles turned to concern in May 1895 when devastating rumors circulated in Spanish and U.S. newspapers that José Martí had fallen in battle. Lacking confirmation, many denounced the news simply as Spanish efforts to demoralize the revolutionaries, but in mid-June confirmation arrived from rebel forces that Martí had indeed died in a skirmish at Dos Ríos in Oriente Province. General Flor Crombet had also fallen sometime later. Martí's most loyal constituencies in Key West and Tampa grieved hard. "One can't speak of our matters," Valdés Domínguez wrote in his diary. "One can't speak about politics without feeling the loss of the genius that took us to war, and taught us with his integrity and valor the road to honor and dignity." "We are with him," he declared, "he lives among us, he is our guide."[13] Martí's example inspired nationalists, and his death made revolutionaries in Key West even more determined.

Martí wrote his last letter to Poyo on February 19, 1895, from Santiago de los Caballeros in the Dominican Republic. He thanked him for a highly laudatory article in *El Yara*. "This may seem an exaggeration," he told Poyo, "[but] all my pain was worth having deserved that judgment [expressed in the article], for having moved your soul so sincerely. My delight is not for me, it's for you." In his own oblique way, Martí told Poyo of his imminent departure for Cuba: "Let me now leave you and travel on the sea. A day of peace will arrive and we will stand erect, and then you will know the pride your friend has in you."[14] In the following month Martí wrote many similar letters to exiled comrades, delivering farewells as if he believed he would not survive the war.

Poyo grieved the loss of his friend who was also a man he had come to regard as genuinely extraordinary. Martí was the key figure the exile communities needed to support a well-conceived uprising against Spain. When he embraced Martí in Tampa in late 1891 Poyo saw what his skeptical colleagues had not yet seen—Martí's extraordinary talent to excite and mobilize workers. Martí had charisma and astute political organizing skills that attracted tremendous loyalty. Two years later, on the occasion of the rededication of the improved and redecorated monument to Cuba's martyrs in the Key West cemetery, Poyo spoke of Martí as the teacher (*maestro*) and apostle (*apóstol*) of the new Cuban generation. Martí continued the work of Céspedes, he explained, and began the new revolutionary phase that "in these moments excites the admiration of the world for its heroic sacrifices." Do not mourn him anymore, Poyo told his community. "The immolation of the Just is the altar on which generations are blessed.... The Maestro died as do heroes, with his face to the sun, bordered with imperishable laurels."[15]

Immediately after Martí's death, Gonzalo de Quesada, Benjamín Guerra, Horatio Rubens, and others in New York turned their attention to the somber task of replacing him, as the party statutes required. On July 10, 1895, the PRC in New York announced the election of Tomás Estrada Palma as *delegado*. He was an intriguing choice and, one would have thought, somewhat controversial in Florida's militant communities, but the transition occurred quickly and without public discussion or dissension. Estrada Palma had been an insurgent during the Ten Years' War. He had served briefly as president of the Republic in Arms before being captured and imprisoned. He later settled in Central Valley in upstate New York, where he became a Quaker and established a school for boys. He was a man of great erudition and was highly respected in New York's Cuban community. Although he was conservative by temperament, admired the United States, and had supported annexation since the 1870s, Estrada Palma recognized that the vast majority of Cubans preferred independence and never spoke of annexation publicly. Most Cubans viewed Estrada Palma as an honest patriot with a distinguished revolutionary career.

Though the process by which Estrada Palma was selected to head the PRC is not known, one New York journalist who interviewed Benjamín Guerra reported that his election "had been all arranged for," which meant by the predominantly middle-class leaders in New York.[16] Although Martí owed his political legitimacy as leader of the PRC primarily to the Florida centers, New Yorkers Quesada and Guerra managed the transition. When he left New York for Santo Domingo, Martí had left these two men in charge of the party, and they remained in effective control after his death. They almost certainly played a crucial role in promoting the selection of Estrada Palma, but they must have at least consulted respected and experienced local PRC council leaders in Florida such as Poyo, Figueredo, and Rivero, who themselves could have been serious candidates for the job.

Perhaps as he left for Santo Domingo Martí had privately instructed his colleagues in New York to champion Estrada Palma in case of his death. Martí and Estrada Palma were quite close, and Martí instructed Quesada and Guerra about many other things, including how to handle his writings and personal papers should he not return.[17] Since Estrada Palma held no official position in the PRC and had a reputation as a long-time separatist, Martí may have thought him capable of maintaining party unity in the face of the traditional rivalries, especially between New York and Florida. Martí recognized the Florida leaders as excellent revolutionary organizers but may have considered them insufficiently prepared for the world of diplomacy that the *delegado* would undoubtedly face once the war began. Furthermore, logistically speaking, a *delegado* based in New York would be better situated for diplomatic and other kinds of business in support of the insurrection.

In any case, no evidence of opposition to Estrada Palma emerged, even in Florida, and Poyo had little ambition to exert leadership outside the Key West community. He would have rejected any political movement that challenged

Estrada Palma as a danger to the immediate task at hand. In September 1895, Poyo traveled with his son-in-law Delgado to New York to coordinate with the new head of the PRC. Estrada Palma sponsored a well-publicized dinner in Poyo's honor at the Martin Hotel in Manhattan to thank him for his years of dedication but perhaps also to consolidate his support. The dinner group included Poyo's ideological nemesis, Enrique Trujillo; Carlos Manuel de Céspedes y Quesada (son of the Ten Years' War leader), who had just returned from residence in Paris to support the insurrection; PRC attorney Horatio Rubens; Martí's aides Guerra and Quesada; leaders of the PRC's Cuerpo de Consejo in New York; and Delgado.

The group toasted Poyo's revolutionary career, beginning with Estrada Palma, who praised his patriotism and accomplishments as a revolutionary journalist. Trujillo proclaimed *El Yara* to be the very essence of nationality. Quesada said that Poyo symbolized the Key West community, whose patriotism was responsible for the strength of the current war.[18] Poyo expressed his gratitude and must have felt vindicated to be praised by many New York leaders that had in the 1880s generally viewed him as fanatic and even as immoral for his unswerving commitment to armed rebellion at all costs. He and Delgado returned home confident about the PRC's new leader.

Expeditions

From the moment Gómez and Martí began their journeys to Cuba, Poyo, Sánchez, Roloff, and the Key West PRC council set about reorganizing the expedition that had been stranded when the Fernandina Plan failed. About 100 fighters waited impatiently for a vessel and weapons. Their destination was Las Villas, a critical province in the middle of the island that needed revolutionary inspiration, leaders, and weapons. In addition to regular contributions, workers in the factories and wealthy manufacturers such as Gato contributed to special collections, and mass meetings drew multitudes that also contributed.

Speakers at one meeting at San Carlos Institute included Poyo, Quesada, Enrique Loynaz Del Castillo, Valdés Domínguez, and some of Martí's young tobacco worker followers, including Gualterio García and Angel Peláez. The audience quickly filled the contribution trays that were passed hand to hand. With these resources, the *delegación* in New York that Quesada and Guerra had coordinated in Martí's absence acquired weapons and searched for a vessel to transport the expedition.[19]

Poyo coordinated activities, and Roloff and Sánchez took charge of military preparations. The two generals explored the surrounding keys for a suitable encampment while Poyo and his aide, Angel Figueredo, son of Perucho Figueredo, the author of the "Hymn of Bayamo," quietly secured supplies and schooners to transfer men to the camp and then to the steamer when it arrived. In May 1895 a first contingent of forty-two men departed for Pine Key, some forty miles east of Key West, which was under the command of José Rogelio Castillo and Rosendo García. Pine Key was a desolate island where a few people earned a living burning wood to sell as charcoal. It provided isolation, but its mosquito-infested environment proved uncomfortable and unhealthy. The soldiers, who were mostly Key West Cubans who had waited for years for this opportunity to fight for Cuba's independence, trained and waited for the vessel that would take them to Cuba. Impatient to join the expedition, Valdés Domínguez grew anxious. He wrote that whenever "I was unable to hide my impatience from my good friend José D. Poyo, he always answered: the horse is about to arrive."[20]

While Key West prepared, the *delegación* in New York purchased the steamer, the *George W. Childs*, onto which they loaded arms, including some that attorney Rubens salvaged from the Fernandina debacle, and dispatched it to south Florida. Roloff, Sánchez, and another contingent of men hurried to Pine Key, but instead of the *Childs* a United States revenue cutter appeared and dropped anchor for some time. Unable to approach Pine Key because of the cutter, the *Childs* proceeded to the Dominican Republic. Roloff returned to Key West with several aides and continued for New York to consult with Quesada and Guerra while Poyo resupplied the fighters at Pine Key and Sánchez maintained discipline and a training schedule.[21]

The weeks passed and the soldiers on Pine Key continued to suffer from the punishing conditions. The heat, humidity, mosquitoes, and isolation caused many to wonder whether they would ever see their homeland. Some became ill and others deserted, but the vast majority waited patiently. Then unexpectedly, on July 15, 1895, a crippled *Childs* steamed into Key West. The ship had picked up Mayía Rodríguez and forty-seven men, thirty rifles, and 80,000 rounds in the Dominican Republic and headed for the Cuban coast. However, before it reached its destination, the vessel began taking on water and diverted to Key West, where it arrived, according to Poyo, "in a blatant violation of all the laws." Fearing that the military resources for the expedition would be seized, he quickly transferred the men and the cargo to a schooner that conveyed them to Sánchez's encampment on Pine Key.[22]

Soon, the insurgent contingent learned of the approach of a vessel under Roloff's command, the *James Woodall*, which the New York *delegación* had purchased two weeks before. The *Woodall* anchored near Pine Key, and a fleet of small boats immediately transported about 150 men and weapons and supplies to the steamer, which the fighters renamed the *José Martí* in honor of their fallen leader. The vessel left Pine Key on July 18, and on July 24, the ship dropped anchor on the south coast of Las Villas, landing the first, largest, and most important expedition of the war.[23]

With this landing, the war in Las Villas gained momentum and opened the way for Cuban forces led by Gómez and Maceo to move steadily westward across the island in 1895 and early 1896. Their demands for weapons and ammunition increased accordingly, but the successful expedition was not easily replicated. The rush to send expeditions inevitably resulted in disorganization, poor timing, and competition for resources among leaders of expeditions. The second effort to launch a major expedition from Key West illustrated these problems.

Before Gómez and Martí left for Cuba from Montecristi on April 1, 1895, they commissioned General Collazo, who was with them, to return to the United States and organize an expedition to Vuelta Abajo. After conferring with Estrada Palma, Collazo proceeded to Tampa, where he worked with Figueredo. At the end of July, he met with Poyo and others in Key West to plan the expedition.[24] Collazo dispatched his fighters to Cudjoe Key in the Florida Keys. Like their predecessors in the Roloff-Sánchez expedition, they trained and waited for a ship to transport them to Cuba.

During his trip to New York in September 1895, Poyo received funds for Collazo's enterprise and promises that a steamer would soon arrive to transport fighters, but authorities confiscated the vessel before it could reach Florida.[25] While the *delegación* in New York sought another ship, Poyo maintained the supply line to the over 100 expeditionaries waiting in the Keys, with the help of Guerra, who had arrived from New York. As the weeks passed, the situation became tense. Unlike Roloff and Sánchez, who had faced similar circumstances, Collazo was a bit of a prima donna with a difficult personality and little tolerance for discomfort. During his stay in Tampa and Key West, Collazo alienated both Figueredo and Poyo with his incessant and bitter complaints about the long wait, poor food, inadequate logistics, and generally difficult conditions.[26]

Finally, in early December, the steamer *Horsa*, under the command of Emilio Núñez, arrived from New York near the expeditionary encampment, only to learn that Collazo had tired of waiting. No doubt unaware of the *Horsa*'s approach, Collazo had sent half his contingent back to Key West on the schooners Poyo had provided for loading men, arms, and ammunition onto the arriving vessel. Collazo sent Poyo a terse note demanding that he provide for the fighters in Key West while he decided on his next move. Without schooners, the *Horsa* could not be loaded because the waters around the key were too shallow. On learning this, and fearing the arrival of Coast Guard cutters if they remained too long, Núñez ordered the vessel out of the area and proceeded to Key West in a small boat to confer with Poyo. Poyo and Núñez sent Collazo a message suggesting an alternative plan, but the temperamental general ordered the rest of the fighters to Key West and left for Tampa to begin anew.

In the meantime, Poyo provided for the more than 100 members of the expedition in Key West who had no jobs, lodging, food, or supplies of any kind. He offered steamer passage to anyone who wanted to leave and contacted Estrada Palma about what to do with the rest of the soldiers, who were depleting the local PRC treasury a little more each day. It took several months to disperse the soldiers, many of whom eventually rejoined Collazo when he finally launched an expedition from Jacksonville in mid-March 1896, successfully landing near Varadero. Soon after Collazo reached Cuba, General Calixto García landed there from New York. Finally the critical trio of generals—García, Gómez, and Maceo—was in place.[27]

The work that was done to organize expeditions attracted the attention of U.S. authorities. While the relative isolation of hundreds of keys and their proximity to Cuba made it seem that south Florida was a perfect location for training soldiers, the Spanish consul kept his superiors in Washington well informed. Official complaints from the Spaniards to the U.S. government resulted in a strong response from President Grover Cleveland. On June 12, 1895, the president issued a formal proclamation that reaffirmed the nation's neutrality laws, condemned filibustering activities, and called on federal officials to prevent violations of the law and prosecute offenders. Within days, the secretary of the treasury had ordered the Coast Guard cutter *Raleigh* to Key West, and in July, after the launch of the Roloff-Sánchez expedition, four more cruisers were patrolling the waters from Pensacola to Key West, including the *Wiona* in the waters between Key West and Biscayne Bay.[28]

Poyo continually expressed frustration about the Cleveland administration's effectiveness in seizing expeditions and prosecuting leaders. Usually, authorities dropped charges or doled out light sentences, but the time and money expended on avoiding the authorities, recovering seized weapons, and defending those who had been charged drained resources from the insurrection. When President William McKinley took office in early 1897 and reaffirmed policies to prevent expeditions from leaving United States in violation of neutrality laws, *El Yara* condemned the obstructionist policies. If the United States really respected international law, the newspaper declared, it would not side with an abusive Spanish power and prevent the shipment of arms and supplies to the revolutionary forces fighting in Cuba.[29]

In effect, *El Yara* called for the United States to grant the Cuban government the status of belligerents. Under international law, belligerency status can be given in a situation of civil war when insurgents occupy and administer a significant portion of territory and establish a responsible leadership committed to the international rules of war. As belligerents, Cubans would have been recognized as legitimate political actors and as a sovereign people involved in a war with Spain. Arms merchants could have sold war matériel to the rebels without interference from authorities, in the same way that they sold arms to Spain. This would have greatly facilitated matters in Key West for Poyo, who could then have operated openly and without the vigilance of the coastline that made expeditions from south Florida impractical. In Washington, the *delegación* lobbied the congress to obtain the status of belligerents for Cuban rebels, but the McKinley administration refused the request.[30]

In addition, the Spanish government increased its diplomatic presence in Florida. Spain had always limited its representation in Florida to a consul in Key West, but now it wanted enhanced vigilance. The longtime consul in Key West, Pedro Solís, established his headquarters in Tampa and oversaw an enhanced consular presence that included new consuls and vice-consuls in Key West and Jacksonville and a vice-consul in Tampa.[31]

Increased vigilance by the Coast Guard, active spy networks organized by

Spanish consuls, and a large Cuban population with little discipline for keeping secrets made Key West and Tampa less than ideal places for organizing expeditions. Local Anglo-American politicians generally sympathized with the Cuban cause and could often be persuaded to ignore the organizing activities, but matters changed when President Cleveland declared his intention to stop the expeditions to avoid complicating relations with Spain. Coast Guard officials and naval personnel did not face the political constraints that local politicians did and constituted the greatest threat to the organizing of Cuban expeditions. Poyo did what he could to convince local Anglo-American authorities to be tolerant, but he advised Estrada Palma that these delicate matters relied on the goodwill of many who could easily denounce the activities: "Matters of this magnitude, so unpredictable, cannot remain secret from local authorities or anybody else here."[32]

This reality and the initial disorganization and frequent lack of coordination among leaders of expeditions prompted the *delegado* to create a Department of Expeditions under the command of General Emilio Núñez in February 1896. The 40-year-old Núñez, who was originally from Cienfuegos and was a veteran of the Ten Years' War, had settled in Philadelphia, where he worked as a dentist and cigar entrepreneur. He had also cooperated with the Gómez-Maceo initiative. Núñez asked Estrada Palma's secretary, Joaquín Castillo, to join him, and they gathered a competent group of military veterans and mariners. They also coordinated closely with Poyo in Key West, Figueredo in Tampa, and Alejandro Huau, one of Jacksonville's most prominent Cuban citizens. Since the Coast Guard was focused mostly on Key West and Tampa, Núñez organized expeditions mostly along the Atlantic coast, especially near Jacksonville, where Huau played an important role.[33]

In March 1896, Estrada Palma also authorized a special committee in Key West that was separate from the Núñez group. Its task was to send small contingents with military supplies to the insurgent army. Cuban secretary of war Roloff encouraged the idea of an ongoing supply program by which schooners would travel regularly from Key West to different locations in Cuba. This committee, which was headed by Francisco Chenard, a Havana conspirator who had moved to Key West, coordinated its work with Poyo. Numerous veterans in Key West offered their services, including Fernández Ruz, Tuerto Rodríguez, Perico Torres, and less well-known men such as Ricardo Trujillo and Juan Monzón.[34]

Poyo and the committee launched various expeditions. At the end of March 1896, journalist Sylvester Scovel, who worked for Joseph Pulitzer's newspaper *The World*, came to Key West and asked Poyo to smuggle him into Cuba, offering to pay half the expenses for the *Marta* expedition, which was about to leave with eleven men and a cache of weapons. Poyo agreed, knowing that the well-known journalist could provide good publicity for the insurgency. As the *Marta* approached Cuba, a Spanish gunboat gave chase. The crew panicked and immediately headed away from the coast, throwing their weapons overboard in case they were overtaken. Furious over the loss of the weapons, Poyo ejected the leader of the expedition from the PRC, telling Estrada Palma that he deserved more "but here it is not possible." In Cuba, he said, he would have paid "with his head for disposing of weapons destined for the defense of the homeland."[35] In April, Poyo and the committee dispatched several shipments of weapons and explosives that had been purchased with funds from the PRC treasuries in Key West and Tampa. A first expedition delivered 150 rifles, 172,000 rounds, and dynamite. When a British warship from the Bahamas apprehended a second schooner loaded with weapons, Poyo sent Angel Figueredo to Nassau to recover what he could.[36]

In the meantime, Maceo and a 2,500-man force had reached Pinar del Rio, Cuba's western province, but only about a third of the troops had firearms. On April 20, 1896, Colonel Juan Monzón left Key West on the *Competitor* with a complement of forty-five fighters, 100 revolvers, dynamite, medicine, and other supplies. Five days later, they reached Cuba and delivered supplies to Maceo's forces. Shortly before the *Competitor* group arrived, an expedition had delivered 150 rifles, 80,000 rounds, and dynamite.[37] Maceo used most of the Florida ammunition in the battle of Cacarajícara, which forced the Spanish to retreat but left Cuban forces again starved for military stores. In June, Maceo complained to Gómez about a lack of resources, but in July he declared to Poyo that "it is not necessary for me to tell you of the even greater advantages we will have in the future from the many war elements we are receiving, thanks to your activities." As long as supplies continued to reach insurgent forces, Cuba "will soon be free without the need for outside help."[38] Despite some successes with Maceo, Poyo advised Estrada Palma that the small expeditions were too intermittent and insignificant, and they agreed to disband the Key West committee in favor of diverting all resources to Núñez's operations, which could deliver many more weapons at a time.[39]

Figure 7. Members of a Cuban expeditionary force, ca. 1897.

Hoping to spur further expeditionary activity, General Gómez sent Secretary of War Roloff to the United States. He lived secretly in New York for a couple weeks in July, presumably preparing his expedition, then he traveled with Quesada and Guerra to Key West, where an extraordinary reception greeted him. Cuban flags and banners adorned houses and businesses, and a large crowd paraded to a meeting at San Carlos Institute, where Roloff updated the community on the state of the insurrection. He visited factories, raised money for his expedition, and then spent time with his wife and children, whom he had not seen since leaving Key West the previous year.

Poyo brought together leading Anglo-American politicians to honor the Polish general at a banquet at a restaurant appropriately named El Polaco (The Pole). This event demonstrates how hard Poyo worked to repair his relations with the local political establishment. Clearly he hoped to win their tolerance for the PRC's less-than-legal activities. Roloff sat between Poyo and the mayor of Key West and heard a speech by Hunt Harris, a representative from Monroe County to the Florida legislature. Harris condemned President Cleveland for his hostile attitude toward the Cuban insurgents and for his refusal to grant the Cubans the status of belligerents so the exile communities could send war supplies in larger quantities without harassment. In collaboration with Núñez and Poyo, Roloff completed his preparations, and on August 13 the steamer *Dauntless* transported the expedition to the southern coast of Oriente Province.[40]

Poyo, Figueredo, and Huau oversaw logistical and numerous other tasks for the expeditionary department in Florida, including handling legal matters and bribing officials when necessary. After delivering the expedition, the *Dauntless* returned to the United States, where authorities arrested Roloff, Núñez, and Castillo in different locations for violating neutrality laws. Poyo, Figueredo, and Huau immediately provided legal resources and political influence to secure their acquittal. From Jacksonville, Huau suggested that the matter could be resolved in Key West if influential men approached Judge Livingston Bethel and convinced him to drop the charges. In a letter to Estrada Palma, Poyo enclosed almost $2,000 that had been raised in Key West, but he set aside funds for Castillo's legal costs. He informed the *delegado* that the local judge had let Castillo out on bail, which had been posted by local merchant Carlos Recio, and that Huau arranged to move the case to Jacksonville, where he thought matters would be worked out more easily. "Remain confident, you, as well as the friends and family of Mr. Castillo," Poyo told Estrada Palma, "that all efforts and necessary expenditures will be mobilized to ensure his freedom without consequences."[41] In due time, the government dropped its cases against the three men.

Sending help to Cuba required huge resources and the commitment of many individuals, but they provided only a small portion of what was needed. Key West and the other communities of exiles could only deliver so much. While tobacco entrepreneurs such as Gato and Teodoro Pérez and cigar workers continued to contribute, they too had limited financial capacities, and the needs of the liberation army far exceeded available resources. The *delegación* in New York sought additional funds and coordinated with the government in arms and military leaders to extract funds from the island's sugar planters. At the end of May 1896, Estrada Palma had raised about $60,000 from planters, but he needed more than $250,000 in the next two months to provide enough resources to fight the war. Estrada Palma reported to Gómez that while he had received funds from some planters, many others had not honored their promises to deposit payments in New York banks.[42] Finding the funds the expeditions required was an ongoing challenge throughout the war.

The PRC also experimented with a strategy to create chaos in Havana and force authorities to redirect resources from the battlefields. In April 1896, a young Key West–born Cuban, Armando André, received permission from the *delegación* in New York to begin acts of sabotage. André smuggled dynamite into Cuba provided by activists in Tampa, but the revolutionary junta in Havana diverted the explosives to other uses. A frustrated André returned to Key West, where Poyo gave him additional funds and more dynamite. "We'll see if he performs well," Poyo wrote to Estrada Palma.[43] On returning to Havana, André and two others set out to assassinate the captain general by setting off explosives in his official palace. André's reconnaissance of the building revealed they could access only the toilets in the basement just under the governor's offices. On the appointed day, André made his way to the bathrooms, set the fuse, and exited quickly. After the explosion, he returned to the scene and discovered that while the bomb had demolished the toilets and had lightly wounded a guard, it had not affected the upper floors. André and his colleagues then set another bomb at the city's principal gas works that failed to explode and was discovered and removed before André could return. Exiles abandoned further sabotage campaigns in Havana.[44]

Revolutionary Unity and Discipline

From the start, obtaining resources to conduct a war against Spain proved to be an overwhelming task. The task required a unified, organized, motivated, and disciplined community. The divisions that had developed in the Cuban exile community during the Ten Years' War and subsequent experiences in the quest for revolution had highlighted for Poyo the indispensability of the unity Martí had achieved. Poyo vowed not to duplicate the factional disputes of the 1870s that had paralyzed reinforcements to the insurgent army; these now had to be avoided at all costs. Cubans were now losing their lives, and he asked exiles to sacrifice and conform to revolutionary requirements, even including restructuring the PRC.

Poyo argued for a stronger hierarchy of authority in the PRC at the local level. After the successful landing of the Roloff-Sánchez expedition, he pointed out to Estrada Palma that as president of the Cuerpo de Consejo in Key West he did not technically have the authority to oversee organizing for expeditions or other delicate activities and asked to be appointed as an official agent of the New York *delegación* in Key West.

In this way he could act with greater effectiveness and when he was needed independently of the Key West Cuerpo de Consejo over which he presided as an elected leader. Estrada Palma not only made the appointment but concluded that this structure was necessary for all the revolutionary centers and appointed Fernando Figueredo agent for the peninsula of Florida, which included Cubans in Ocala and Jacksonville.[45] As official agents of the New York *delegación*, Poyo and Figueredo acted decisively to implement policies or even head off divisive opposition within the local *consejos*.

Authority and hierarchy became even more defined in September 1895 with the establishment of a government in arms known as the Consejo de Gobierno de la República (Government Council of the Republic in Arms). President Salvador Cisneros Betancourt named Estrada Palma diplomatic representative in the United States. Poyo and Figueredo received official appointments as subagents of the revolutionary government in Key West and Tampa. They were directly responsible to Estrada Palma, which strengthened their local authority even more. Recognizing a potential conflict of authority between the PRC *delegado* and the official representative of the government if at some point different men occupied the positions, Poyo and the Key West Cuerpo de Consejo submitted a resolution to the PRC calling for suppressing elections for the *delegado*, an action all the *consejos* approved.

This resolution actually transformed the nature of the PRC from a grassroots and democratic organization to an arm of the revolutionary government, which had direct influence over the party through its exile representative. Poyo remained insistent that insurrectionists should operate with a clear line of authority to avoid discord and division, even if that meant undermining the authority of local councils.[46] Local *consejos* continued to have the right to elect their presidents, but as agents of the *delegación* and the Cuban government in arms itself, Poyo and Figueredo remained in charge of their *consejos* for the duration of the war.

Poyo's insistence on a clear chain of command also became evident in his relationship with the small expeditions committee Estrada Palma established. While the *delegado* appointed Chenard to lead the committee and authorized him to act independently, PRC funds remained under Poyo's authority. Poyo was unhappy with this arrangement because it blurred the channel of authority, but he agreed to it. However, Estrada Palma had done this without consulting Poyo and the local party, with whom Chenard had no formal ties. Poyo's relations with Chenard were fraught with complications and they continued to deteriorate. Finally, to register his dissatisfaction with Estrada Palma, Poyo resigned as a PRC agent in Key West. The *delegado* relented and dissolved the independent committee, placing all organizing for expeditions in the hands of Núñez. He asked Poyo to continue his work, especially his work to strengthen the treasury.[47] Satisfied with this arrangement, Poyo worked closely with Núñez. Chenard moved to New York, where he soon became president of the Cuerpo de Consejo in that city.

Although Poyo became an agent of the Consejo de Gobierno de la República he would have preferred a military government headed by Gómez. In fact, the structure of the revolution had been a top priority of discussion when Martí, Gómez, and Maceo met in Cuba for the first time in April 1895. Still suspicious of Gómez and Maceo's military backgrounds, Martí had insisted on a civilian government, but the issue was not resolved before his death. In September 1895, representatives of the various army divisions met at Jimaguayú and debated the merits of military versus constitutional government. They finally decided on the latter and the Consejo de Gobierno de la República, but predictably, the senior generals, including Gómez, Maceo, and Calixto García, viewed civilian government as an obstacle to military efficiency and strategy. They often ignored the government, but they tolerated it to ensure favorable international opinion about the democratic nature of the struggle.[48]

Support for the generals from the exile communities in Florida became evident in April 1897, on the eve of new elections in Cuba, when the Consejo de Gobierno de la República published a decree instructing the exile communities to elect two representatives to join its ranks in Cuba. In Key West, this caused considerable commotion, confusion, and even premature announcements of candidacies, prompting the *delegado* to issue a circular outlining possible electoral procedures, but leaders of the exile communities in Florida objected to the concept of representative elections with multiple parties. Poyo, Figueredo, and Rivero remained skeptical of representative institutions as long as the war continued and believed that maintaining unity and a focus on the revolution was difficult enough without infusing divisive elections and politics. Florida's Cuerpos de Consejo held public meetings and passed resolutions urging the exile communities to abstain from elections. In New York, this decision was not supported until it became clear that the exile communities in Jacksonville, New Orleans, Galveston, Mexico, and other places agreed with the position of Key West and Tampa leaders.[49]

Even with more centralized PRC authority, Poyo spent considerable time dealing with disagreements and divisions. Tens of thousands of refugees sought safety in the United States in the years after the outbreak of the insurrection. The communities became increasingly heterogeneous and brought political, class, and racial tensions to the forefront in a variety of ways. The new exiles included many middle- and upper-class Cubans, including scholars, poets, doctors, lawyers, merchants, and journalists who had been associated with the autonomist movement or had remained politically neutral but now supported independence.[50]

Some middle-class newcomers to Key West had little appreciation for long-established community traditions and had difficulty living in such close quarters with the working classes. For example, Esteban Borrero, a poet and writer who arrived in 1896, complained to Estrada Palma about the *turbas* (multitudes) in Key West who railed against the middle and upper classes and intellectuals. Calling them *mala gente* ("bad people"), Borrero said that they lived by "an anarchic concept of social life" and scoffed at their claims of patriotism. He described a black man at an event commemorating Martí's death. The man unleashed a barrage of racially based insults against the predominantly white audience, whom he called cowardly. He also predicted the triumph of his race in Cuba. "What is this, dear God?" Borrero declared. "It is pernicious for our cause; and gives you a sense of the intellectual and moral capacity of these people."[51]

It was probably not a coincidence that this incident occurred at the same time as a court-martial removed from command a popular black general, Quintín Banderas, for a variety of charges that included allegedly bringing disrepute to the honor of the Cuban liberation army. Banderas claimed that racism and social tensions had increased in Cuba as the struggle wore on, and these tensions also rippled through the exile community.[52]

Longtime Key West resident and PRC activist Ramón Dobarganes characterized the new middle-class immigrants as cultured but suffering from defects that were characteristic of colonialism; that is, they had a sense of social superiority and condescension and recoiled at the harsh verbal confrontations, intransigence, stubbornness, and military-like authoritarianism that was often characteristic of Key West's revolutionary leaders. They considered themselves better suited to leadership positions in the PRC than those who were already in charge.

Poyo agreed with Dobarganes, and when ambitious newcomers threatened PRC unity, he dealt with them directly, often with little tact and diplomacy. In September 1896, *El Yara* harshly accused some new arrivals to Key West of undermining the welfare of the revolution and criticized wealthy Cubans who contributed little. Even his associate Dobarganes sometimes considered Poyo's approach to be tactless and counterproductive. "Poyo has a dry character and I really lament that he is not more worldly," he wrote a colleague in Tampa, "and [I] especially [wish] that he were a bit courteous to maintain the harmony that should rein among us."[53] Dobarganes also wrote Estrada Palma about the tensions, hoping he could smooth over the situation, but the *delegado* stayed clear of such local conflicts.[54]

For Poyo, these newcomers represented more than a challenge to his political authority. Their elitist attitudes brought into question their commitment to the revolutionary credo and ethos that Martí had articulated. In March 1897, *El Yara* declared that the revolution had placed all Cubans on the same level and that the goal was not only to be independent but to rid Cuba of colonial habits. He told Cuba's elites to forget their corrupt sinecures and to earn their reputations, titles, and honors, which the Cuban nation would now distribute to deserving people. In October, *El Yara* published another article that obviously targeted the newcomers. In words that were reminiscent of Martí's language, it declared that the revolution was for the good of all Cuba's citizens and not the few.[55]

Poyo and *El Yara* remained absolutely loyal to the PRC and did not challenge its official institutions even when they seemed to embrace the new immigrants and their elitist ethos. In New York, for example, Rafael Serra, a black activist who had been a friend of Martí, established a newspaper, *La Doctrina de Martí*, in part to challenge the recent autonomist converts to independence and remind the revolutionary leaders in New York of Martí's popular ideology of social inclusion. Sotero Figueroa, who had edited *Patria* under Martí's leadership, wrote an editorial in *La Doctrina* accusing José Enrique de Varona, the new editor of *Patria*, of being totally out of step with PRC revolutionary ideology. As a former autonomist, Varona had infused

Patria with a more conservative tone and more conservative politics than had been the case when Martí edited the newspaper. Working-class and black community leaders in Key West and Tampa supported Serra and *La Doctrina*, and while Poyo may have shared their critique of wealthier Cuban immigrants—which he expressed with regard to similar social elements in Key West—he refused to criticize the New York PRC. He remained committed to Martí's ideal of revolutionary unity as the first order of business.[56]

Some challenges with raising funds among the working classes had always plagued the revolutionary community and this remained the case, causing an experienced Poyo to act cautiously. Workers complained that the funds they contributed never accomplished anything concrete. They remembered the failures of the 1880s. In November 1892, the Spanish consul had reported that some club presidents who were impatient for revolution had refused to turn their funds over to Martí until his intention to act became clear. Then there were those who were not interested in movements of any kind who simply resented giving their hard-earned money to anyone; they wanted to live their lives in peace and be left alone by political and labor agitators alike.[57]

As before, during periods of labor unrest and strikes, *El Yara* counseled negotiation and a return to work as soon as possible for the good of the cause, expressing impatience when strikes lasted too long. In November 1897, during a strike in the Gato factory, *El Yara* sided with the workers when a dispute with the foreman could not be resolved. The newspaper counseled the foreman to resign, and he did. Much relieved, *El Yara* hoped that workers and owners would maintain good relations for a long time to come, "which is what is convenient for everyone and for those in Cuba spilling their blood to give us a nation."[58] That same month, a strike at the Villamil factory prompted *El Yara* to intervene again; it urged workers to resolve the conflict. But a newly founded labor newspaper, *El Vigía*, pushed back, saying that while workers fulfilled their patriotic commitments, factory owners exploited their employees.[59] *El Yara* worked carefully and tried to minimize the number of strikes without entering into harsh debates similar to the debates of 1889 and 1890 that had alienated workers from the nationalist movement.

In fact, Poyo and his colleagues frequently supported labor issues and ideologies that did not conflict with nationalism. In February 1896, for example, *El Yara* welcomed well known socialist activist Diego Vicente Tejera, who had moved from New York, to Key West. Tejera admired what he called the raw radical instincts of Key West's cigar workers but believed that they needed direction. Poyo participated in a "political-patriotic event" with labor leaders, writers, and other well-known community figures to honor Tejera and applauded when the socialist intellectual delivered a series of presentations at San Carlos Institute on politics, race, labor and numerous other topics in late 1897. "He has awakened much interest, principally among our working class," noted *El Yara*. "So on to San Carlos!"[60]

El Yara also praised the establishment of a Socialist Club that aspired to be a political party in an independent Cuba. The club formed to encourage workers to participate in popular movements that would carry out the general reconstruction of Cuba, but organizers carefully emphasized that independence was a prerequisite, since a socialist party was impossible under Spanish rule.[61] Poyo encouraged workers to defend their ideas, rights, and interests, but he watched closely to make sure that these activities did not deflect from the priority of raising funds for the revolution.

Sometimes workers objected to the 10 percent the PRC deducted from their wages and took concrete steps to avoid paying. Some opposed the requirement altogether while others thought it too steep, especially since the PRC regularly asked for additional contributions for other things such as the Comité de Auxilio de Familias (Family Support Committee), a community welfare fund. Some insisted that the PRC deductions should be voluntary. Even though Poyo objected, workers in the Gato and Nichols factories voted in June 1896 to reduce the contribution to 5 percent. Some revolutionaries criticized Poyo for failing to block the move in the very factory where he read, while others believed that *El Yara*'s articles denouncing the reduction were too strong. They accused Poyo of being overbearing and lacking sympathy for the workers.[62]

The decision to reduce the percentage of PRC contributions in these two factories attracted the attention of workers in other factories, and in July 1897 black cigar workers at the Gabriel H. Gato El Modelo factory in Jacksonville demanded that the contribution be eliminated altogether. A writer in *Patria* blamed Spanish machinations but this demand was more likely further evidence of continuing racial strain and revealed a rebellious streak among some Cuban blacks who did not feel that the war was in their interest.[63]

Some in Key West sought creative ways to weaken the local PRC Cuerpo de Consejo and perhaps Poyo for his sometimes heavy-handed approaches.

At the Villamil factory in 1896, for example, some workers proposed sending funds directly to New York rather than giving them to the local party, which Poyo interpreted as a ploy to make collections more difficult to account for. He also viewed this as a strategy to undermine the authority of the local *consejo* and disrupt revolutionary discipline. Poyo asked Estrada Palma to reaffirm that funds were to be deposited in the local councils, which he did. The *delegado* expressed his support for Poyo and rejected any challenge to party discipline.[64]

It is possible that those who were trying to divert the money to New York questioned how funds were being used in Key West. One controversy was related to the stipends the PRC provided to people in the community for different reasons. At the outbreak of the war, each community faced the logistical problem of providing resources for those who were volunteering to fight. When Collazo's Key West effort failed, for example, Poyo suddenly had to provide room and board for over 100 men without jobs while they waited for new orders. In addition, individuals periodically approached Poyo who offered to command expeditions and sought stipends while they developed their plans and raised resources. In some cases, Poyo provided money while they organized their expeditions. This provoked some workers to accuse Poyo of wasting resources. "If Poyo wants a general staff," one critic declared, "he should pay out of his pocket."[65]

Aware of the sensitivity about what amounted to forced taxation, Poyo meticulously accounted for the funds, so obsessively that even his good friend Figueredo in Tampa complained to Estrada Palma. Figueredo said that Poyo consistently sought reimbursement from the Tampa *consejo* whenever he provided funds for activities in Tampa; he thought this behavior was too much since they were all working for the same goal.[66]

Poyo also sought ways to raise funds for the Comité de Auxilio de Familias, whose needs increased throughout the economic downturn of 1893 and 1894. In July 1896, Estrada Palma authorized the use of a larger portion of the local PRC treasury for the needy and agreed to a PRC-sponsored lottery in Key West to raise more funds. The *delegado* told Poyo that in principle he opposed lotteries and all resources derived from gaming, but since Cubans already spent their hard-earned money on the large Spanish raffles in Cuba they should be encouraged to support the PRC lottery in Key West. He authorized Poyo to promote the lottery in the clubs, presumably through *El Yara* and in official PRC communications. The need for assistance increased even more after the outbreak of the war. Juan Ramón O'Farrill, a talented doctor from Havana, directed the committee and spent his days collecting and distributing food. In May 1898, O'Farrill secured help from Clara Barton, who traveled to Key West and Tampa and directed her local Red Cross operations to provide much-needed help to Cuban refugees.[67]

Initially, the welfare committee also provided stipends to families whose wage earners had gone to fight in Cuba. As needs increased, Poyo felt that this policy created too much of a drain on resources. In 1896 he recommended to Estrada Palma that only single men be encouraged to fight, since married men left their families without resources, who eventually became burdens for the welfare fund. In addition, the PRC needed the earning power of married men in the cigar factories more than their presence on Cuba's battlefields, where plenty of men waited for arms to join the fight. Key West's primary activity, Poyo thought, should be to ensure a supply of weapons and ammunition for the liberation army. Estrada Palma issued the order that only single men should be encouraged to fight in Cuba and emphasized that only under extraordinary circumstances would financial help be provided to families of fighting men.[68]

Despite the many challenges, the great majority of Cubans in Key West remained committed to the PRC and Poyo's leadership. In late 1897, one newspaper edited by newcomers who were interested in minimizing animosity between leaders and the new arrivals declared that everyone needed to accept the established revolutionary leadership. There was no reason, declared *El Intransigente*, why newcomers, former autonomists, those who were originally opposed to revolution, and even those who had served Spain could not now belong to the revolutionary party, but not as leaders. That right belonged to men such as Estrada Palma, Poyo, and others, including the humble tobacco workers who for years served as the base of the revolutionary movement.[69] Overall, workers supported PRC leaders, who after all were mostly workers themselves who were sympathetic to labor interests. But at this historical moment, the leaders' primary concern was to wage war against Spain.

U.S. Intervention

From the beginning of the war, Cuban insurgents fully intended to defeat the Spanish on their own terms, requesting only the status of belligerents from the United States to facilitate the task of supplying the liberation army. They did not know what to expect, but they quickly learned the United States had no intention of facilitating victory. In November 1895, Poyo complained that despite the aspirations of the Cuban people and the insurgent army's great gains, the "Great American Republic" refused to grant insurgents the status of belligerents. In the meantime, "time passes, the winter campaign begins, and Spain prepares an army of 200,000 men, counting on the support of the free American nations, who trade with Spain and allow it to use their ports in the war of extermination against the Cubans. It seems unbelievable [*parece mentira*]!"[70]

Although Cuban troops defied the odds and spread revolution across the entire island in 1895 and early 1896, things turned difficult when the Spanish government sent General Valeriano Weyler to defeat the rebels. Weyler, who had extensive experience with counterinsurgency in the Philippines, initiated an offensive in the second half of 1896 that included a brutal strategy of concentrating the rural population in camps close to the towns and cities. The goal was to put an end to the support they were providing for the rebels. The general also consolidated the scattered Spanish forces into large field armies and began a systematic sweep of the island, beginning in Pinar del Rio and moving eastward. He used aggressive and ruthless war tactics that included treating captured rebels as bandits and thieves and executing them on the spot, and the Cubans responded in kind.

Weyler forced Gómez to retreat eastward and cut off Maceo in Pinar del Río. When Gómez urgently asked Maceo to join him, the mulatto general set out with a small force. As Maceo rode across Havana Province on the afternoon of December 7, 1896, Spanish troops ambushed and killed him along with Panchito Gómez, the son of General Gómez. Just three weeks earlier, General Serafín Sánchez, who had been operating in Las Villas, also died in battle. Fatally shot several times, he famously declared, as blood spurted from his mouth, "They have killed me. It is nothing. Continue the charge."[71]

These losses were ominous. Though he had only met Maceo on two occasions, Poyo had corresponded with him for almost twenty years and knew the irreplaceable quality of his leadership. The loss of Sánchez was more personal for Poyo, and he and Clara consoled Sánchez's wife, Pepa. As usual Poyo remained stoic in the face of martyrdom but these deaths must have shaken him and made him realize that the insurrection still faced great challenges. Cubans had lost Martí, Flor Crombet, and now two of their beloved and talented generals, and Weyler's campaign had succeeded in forcing Cuban forces eastward. The war became a brutal struggle of attrition as tens of thousands of Cubans died of disease and starvation in the concentration camps.

August 1897 brought another unexpected turn. An Italian anarchist assassinated the hardline conservative prime minister of Spain, Antonio Cánovas del Castillo, who had sent Weyler to Cuba. This resulted in new elections and the ascendancy of political liberalism. Tired of the war, liberals decided to negotiate with the Cuban insurgents. In a show of good faith, they recalled Weyler, granted Cuba an expanded autonomy government, and declared a unilateral cease-fire. The new Cuban government was established on January 1, 1898. It consisted of a two-house parliament, one elected and the other appointed by the captain general. A cabinet composed of the autonomist leaders of the 1880s also advised the captain general.[72]

These Spanish reforms were too little, too late. Insurgent Cubans remembered bitterly the promises of autonomy Spain had made in the Zanjón Pact twenty years earlier and vowed not to be misled again. Taking advantage of the Spanish cease-fire, the liberation army regrouped and launched a new offensive in the fall of 1897. Calixto García attacked and captured Las Tunas, a town of 4,000 in Oriente Province. The town had little strategic importance, but it provided an important moral victory that gave the exile communities new hope and demoralized the Spanish army.[73]

Meanwhile, Estrada Palma and his diplomatic team in New York and Washington initiated a public relations campaign against Spain's new reformist initiative, which owed a great deal to diplomatic pressure from the United States. In exchange for reforms, the McKinley administration promised Madrid that it would pressure representatives of the insurgents in the United States. Rumors of this bargain began circulating, and in August Poyo traveled with his son Francisco to New York to participate in PRC talks about how to respond. They agreed on mass meetings and public condemnations of the new autonomy government in Cuba.[74]

Poyo organized the campaign in Key West, and on October 4 the *consejo* passed a resolution rejecting any negotiation with Spain that was not based on Cuba's absolute independence.[75] Other communities followed suit. *El Yara* also denounced the appearance of an autonomist newspaper in New York, declaring that if its editors were Cuban born, "may the curses of the nation be with them."[76] In early November, Estrada Palma publicly delivered the PRC's official rejection of autonomy, and the exile communities reaffirmed the speech in a joint manifesto.[77] Any illusions the U.S. government harbored that Cubans might seriously negotiate with Spain quickly dissipated.

At another level of discussion, the ongoing tragedy of the war, which was more difficult and brutal than most had expected or even imagined, raised questions in the minds of many exiles about future military prospects. It became increasingly evident that despite their best efforts the exile communities could not provide the insurgent army with sufficient resources to win the war outright. Shortages of funds and the U.S. policy of harassing expeditionary forces deprived the Cubans of enough rifles, ammunition, dynamite, and other supplies to definitively defeat and expel the Spanish. Cuban exiles had dispatched sixty-four expeditions from the United States in 1895–1898, but only around 60 percent had reached their destination and their cargoes did not nearly meet the need.[78] The liberation army clearly did not have the resources to defeat the Spanish in the short term.

The logic of direct intervention by the United States became increasingly difficult to resist and planters, businessmen, and even many autonomists in Cuba slowly concluded that Spain could not defeat the insurgents and that the rebels could not be persuaded to negotiate for anything less than independence. In the final months of 1897, Estrada Palma and his associates in New York and Washington concluded that only U.S. intervention could end the destructive war, protect Cuba's wealth, and alleviate the suffering of its people. This was not a difficult conclusion for Estrada Palma and many of his advisors who had always admired the United States. Even Guerra and Quesada, who had been among Martí's closest colleagues accepted the idea, along with many Cubans in New York.[79]

Annexationists Fidel Pierra and his brother Adolfo, longtime New York residents who were close to the *delegación*, did what they could to convince Cubans in Florida to accept U.S. intervention. Fidel argued that there was no money, ammunition, uniforms, or food in Cuba and that exile resources had run out.[80] In a letter to Key West's *Vigía* newspaper, Adolfo argued that direct intervention would bring the war to an end in a matter of weeks and that those who knew the "spirit of the institutions and the people of this great Republic" realized it would never force annexation; this would happen only if Cubans wanted it.[81] Even the stridently nationalist PRC leaders in Florida watched silently as the diplomatic representatives in New York encouraged direct U.S. involvement, recognizing the United States would no longer tolerate the destructive war in Cuba.

Relations between the United States and Spain deteriorated as the possibility of resolving the Cuban war in the short term faded. U.S. public opinion strongly favored some action, as did the "yellow press" that sensationalized every aspect of the Cuban problem. McKinley concluded that short of granting Cuban insurgents the status of belligerents so exiles could support the insurrection more freely and effectively, which he would not do, only direct intervention could bring the affair to an end. Events soon unfolded that facilitated intervention. In early February, riots in Havana led by *voluntarios* opposed to Spain's new politics of accommodation threatened American lives and property, prompting McKinley to make a show of force. On January 25, 1898, the USS *Maine* entered Havana harbor and put down its anchor.

On February 13, Poyo organized a great reception in Key West for Estrada Palma and PRC secretary José Antonio González Lanuza, who arrived for what had become an annual Florida visit to inspire exiles and touch base with the most enthusiastic revolutionary communities. Like Martí before them, the two New York leaders made the obligatory visits to cigar factories, where they heard and made speeches, enjoyed beer and other treats, and watched children enact patriotic sketches.

At a mass meeting at San Carlos Institute, they lauded the importance of Key West to the revolutionary enterprise. González Lanuza, who had been arrested and sent to prison in Spain at the beginning of the war, escaped, and then joined the PRC in New York, said that the revolution "had been born in Key West" and that without the critical help of the émigrés there the first fighters would have failed. Estrada Palma continued in the same vein, emotionally declaring that his audience was like his children and he would converse with them as if with family. Poyo concluded the event, declaring that this annual meeting with the *delegado* would be "the last in a foreign territory" because the moment of the great victory was near.[82]

Little did Poyo imagine the accuracy of this statement, which he had made so often before during patriotic occasions. Two days later, a tragic report from Havana disrupted the celebrations. The USS *Maine* had exploded and sunk in Havana harbor, killing hundreds of sailors. The next day, Estrada Palma and González Lanuza hurried to Tampa, where they canceled the planned activities and proceeded to New York. Tampa's *consejos* encouraged Cuban homes and places of business to fly flags at half-mast for three days. They also sent a cable to the U.S. secretary of state with condolences from the Cuban people and ordered a mass meeting to memorialize the victims.[83]

Before anyone determined the cause of the explosion, tensions escalated as the U.S. press pointed to Spain. It did not take long for Cubans to do the same. In its first mention of the disaster, *Patria* offered condolences to the American people for the tragedy but commented on the suspicious circumstances of the event that accused Spain of exercising "unimpeachable force."[84] Cubans in Key West also implicated Spain in the disaster, which suggests that the community now viewed U.S. intervention as their only hope of defeating the Spanish. The *New York Times* reported that Cubans in Key West encouraged suspicions of foul play in Havana and believed that the disaster would in some way resolve the Cuban war. Emotions overflowed in Key West when ships carrying the dead sailors arrived at the docks and people crowded the sidewalks to observe caskets carried single file in horse-drawn hearses make their way to the cemetery where they were buried.[85]

El Yara also instigated animosities by publishing a mysterious report from Havana (probably written by independence sympathizers) claiming that a Spanish agent had placed an underwater mine on the hull of the USS *Maine*. After the ship was destroyed, the report claimed, Spanish authorities then murdered the perpetrator. Newspapers all over the country, including the *St. Louis Republic*, promoted the conspiracy theory, which drew upon the testimonies of surviving sailors that an explosive on the outside of the hull had done the damage, and cited the report *El Yara* had published implicating the Spanish. Tensions increased, and in March a large U.S. fleet gathered in Key West, followed by news that a Spanish flotilla had left the Canary Islands for the Caribbean.[86]

At the end of March 1898, the much-awaited USS Maine Court of Inquiry released its findings, affirming that the ship had been sunk by a mine. In Key West, Cubans became so agitated that the Spanish consul and vice-consul packed their official archive, boarded the *Mascotte* for Tampa, and never returned. According to one report, the consular officials feared "the storm" that was brewing among Cubans. Soon, hundreds began arriving in Key West from Cuba, including American tourists and Cubans with U.S. citizenship who anticipated violence from the pro-Spanish *voluntarios*.[87] No one in Key West doubted that war between the United States and Spain was near.

Finally, in April 1898, President McKinley requested a congressional joint resolution authorizing him to intervene in Cuba and pacify the island, without recognizing the legitimacy of the Cuban insurgents or their aspirations for independence. The attorney for the Cuban diplomatic team in Washington, Horatio Rubens, immediately notified congressional leaders that without a clear recognition of the Cuban Republic in Arms, insurgents would not only oppose intervention but even fight U.S. troops. Highly critical news accounts about Rubens's statements caused dismay among members of the Cuban diplomatic team in New York and Washington, including Estrada Palma, Guerra, Quesada, and Fidel Pierra, who reprimanded him for his comments. They were committed to U.S. intervention under any circumstances, and they believed that his extremely impolitic rhetoric lost them friends. Rubens, in turn, castigated Estrada Palma for not representing the ideals of the Cubans fighting on the island.[88]

Despite the concerns of Estrada Palma and others, Congress heeded Rubens's warnings, and on April 20, McKinley signed a resolution authorizing him to enter Cuba. An amendment to the resolution proclaimed that the "people of the island of Cuba are and of right ought to be free and independent." The amendment, which was drafted by Senator Henry M. Teller of Colorado, renounced any intention on the part of the United States "to exercise sovereignty, jurisdiction, or control over said island except for pacification thereof, and asserts its determination, when that is accomplished, to leave the government and control of the island to its people." But it did not recognize the Cuban government in arms or any other authority on or off the island.[89] It demanded that Spain relinquish control of Cuba immediately and directed McKinley to use force if necessary.

In Key West, schools closed, and throughout the day the streets were filled with excited Cubans shouting "Cuba Libre" and discussing the congressional action and its implications. Some 200 residents headed by the traditional Cuban band marched through the streets in defiance of Spain; speeches praising

McKinley followed the parade. Poyo was out of town (possibly in New York), but the *consejo*, led by interim president Juan Calderón and secretary Rivera, organized a community meeting on April 22 and gave "cordial and sincere" thanks to the United States for its "generous and humanitarian support" and reassured Estrada Palma of the personal commitment of each member of the community for whatever might be necessary in the upcoming war.[90]

Gómez received news from Poyo about these events in late April and expressed satisfaction "of the recognition by the people of the United States and its government of the Cuban people's rights and capacity to control its own destiny."[91] But the Cuban government and Gómez knew nothing of the details that Estrada Palma had omitted. He did not share them until May 10, when he informed Cubans that the United States had withheld recognition of all island authorities and that he had unilaterally agreed to place the Cuban military under the authority of the United States. The Cuban government and Cuban generals reacted angrily and censured Estrada Palma for overstepping his authority, but they soon accepted what was a fait accompli.[92]

Poyo had always argued for a self-sufficient revolutionary movement dedicated to Cuba's absolute independence. Since the 1860s, the militant nationalist wing of the separatist movement Poyo belonged to and provided a mouthpiece for in *El Yara* had promoted a self-sufficient and self-determining movement for Cuban independence. The most the militants were willing to accept from the United States was recognition that Cuban rebels had the status of belligerents, which would have legalized their reinforcement of Cuban insurgents from U.S. shores, but this never came.

When the war began in 1895, the rapid movement of Cuban forces from east to west and the energetic organizing of expeditions in the United States created optimism that the liberation army would soon defeat the Spanish. Enough Cubans were ready to join the army, but they lacked arms, ammunition, uniforms, and other supplies. Exiles struggled mightily for three years to support these efforts, and though over half of the expeditions reached Cuba, the cargoes they delivered were never equal to the need. The cigar-making communities of Key West and Tampa sent what they could, but their capacity was insufficient. Even after the liberation army taxed the wealthy plantations and farms in the areas they occupied, funds still did not meet the battlefield requirements. Vigilant Spanish consuls, local customs officials, and the U.S. naval vessels that patrolled the shores made things even worse. Legal expenses for those who were arrested and for lawsuits to recover arms from confiscated ships and from federal authorities constantly depleted the already limited resources.

General Weyler's counteroffensive in 1896 and 1897 produced a stalemate that doomed the Cuban army's ability to end the war in the immediate term. Cuban troops maintained constant guerrilla assaults on the better-equipped and better-trained Spanish forces but rarely conducted conventional attacks that were capable of inflicting defeats that might convince Spain to release its "ever faithful isle." Though Cuban soldiers were ferocious fighters, those without rifles were forced to depend on machetes and often even lacked the most basic footwear. The war's frightful human cost, especially in the rural concentration camps, and epidemic diseases distressed everyone involved, especially those who believed—as Martí had—that a war against Spain would be generous and brief. It was neither, and exiles must have felt despair about the consequences to Cuba's people and society.

After three years of uncompromising and bloody warfare, Cubans did not yet seem on the verge of victory and the exiles had lost confidence that they could reach a short-term victory.[93] Cubans could still defeat the Spanish, but probably only through a longer war of attrition that Spain would eventually quit. This was a situation the United States had no intention of accepting in 1898. Acting in its own self-interest, the U.S. government prepared to intervene, and the best Cubans could do was persuade the Congress to adopt the Teller Amendment that would guarantee the eventual independence of Cuba.

Poyo may have had qualms, but he remained insistent on revolutionary unity and regularly censured anyone who challenged the authority and hierarchy of the PRC. In any case, as a practical revolutionary, Poyo knew the reality of the situation and recognized that the die had been cast. No amount of protesting would now prevent the United States from intervening, an action that most observers, Cubans and others, believed would end the war quickly. When intervention seemed inevitable, Cubans of all political stripes finally accepted the reality and hoped that the United States would honor its commitment to Cuban independence. The U.S. navy quickly disposed of its Spanish counterpart in late June, and followed with a landing of American forces near Santiago de Cuba that was facilitated by General Calixto García and his troops.

Cuban exiles remained determined to participate in and influence events the best they could, even as the United States took charge of the war. Poyo immediately helped organize and supply a local military contingent of two or three hundred men that Núñez transported to Tampa in early May to join a Cuban brigade that was already forming. At the end of May, the steamer *Florida* landed a contingent of 400 mostly Cuban soldiers twenty-five miles east of Havana. Another expedition landed in mid-July with another 400 mostly Cuban fighters and a large cache of arms and supplies.[94]

After U.S. intervention, the integrity of the PRC's fund-raising infrastructure began to disintegrate. Leaders exhorted their constituencies to continue providing resources, but contributions declined. Poyo informed Estrada Palma in late July that workers no longer contributed as they had before, a development the *delegado* lamented bitterly.[95] Workers no doubt lost their enthusiasm and thought carefully about contributing their hard-earned money to support a cause whose outcome now seemed totally unpredictable. Shortly after this, Spanish forces in Santiago surrendered, and on August 12 the United States and Spain signed a peace protocol.[96] Though Poyo privately lamented the intervention, he celebrated Spain's defeat, a goal he had worked toward for thirty years.

As he watched the frenzy around the USS *Maine* crisis that virtually guaranteed direct U.S. involvement in the Cuban insurrection, Poyo wrote Máximo Gómez expressing his regret that he had not accomplished more, that his efforts had fallen short. Gómez told Fermín Valdés Domínguez, his chief of staff, that Poyo was one of those who was fated to suffer, a soldier of honor who knew nothing of cowardice.[97] In May 1898, even before U.S. troops landed in Cuba, Gómez paused to recognize Poyo's years of commitment to Cuban independence, especially noting *El Yara*'s enduring militant nationalism. He directed Valdés Domínguez to prepare an album for Poyo with *pensamientos* (thoughts) about the war and Cuba penned by the army's general staff as an *ofrenda* (homage). A *cuaderno* (writing book) illustrated with a palm tree and the words "Cuba Libre" contained the inscriptions. Gómez added his own dedication to *El Yara* and Valdés Domínguez concluded the album with his own dedication to "the first of our newspapers: which has been and is a flag of combat, which as enthusiastic soldiers we honor and hold high."[98] Humbled by this homage, Poyo simply thanked them. As U.S. troops landed in Cuba, the struggle for independence entered a new phase that required careful vigilance.

9

LEGACY

> Clarita: we are now free! Long Live Cuba Libre!
> José D. Poyo, 1902

José D. Poyo gathered a large PRC-affiliated multitude at San Carlos Institute on December 30, 1898 for a final meeting of the Cuerpo de Consejo. As the audience settled, he read aloud a communication from Tomás Estrada Palma. "Having achieved the goal of Cuban independence," the *delegado* proposed the dissolution of the organization. With little discussion, the assembled quickly accepted the proposal and passed several resolutions thanking the "meritorious patriot Mr. J. D. Poyo" for competently managing his double role as PRC agent in Key West and president of the Cuerpo de Consejo. The assembly also thanked the New York Delegación and General Gómez for his services on Cuba's battlefields. Another resolution ordered the publication of a remembrance for the PRC's first leader, José Martí. Poyo in turn expressed his appreciation, especially for the work of the *consejo* to which he would always remain grateful.[1] Sometime in the next weeks, Poyo and his family boarded a steamer for Cuba after thirty years in exile.

The Poyo family never doubted that they would eventually return to Cuba. Poyo and his wife Clara raised their family and saw numerous grandchildren born in Key West, but they never considered staying there permanently. Their son Francisco and his wife, Louisa, along with their daughter Celia and her husband, Manuel P. Delgado, returned also, perhaps with them or shortly after. Francisco, a baseball player of prominence in Key West, joined a team in Havana called Cuba as player and manager and later as part owner. Although Francisco's sister América and his brother-in-law Francisco Alpízar did not return immediately, they moved to Havana within a few years.[2]

His sister Blanca and her husband also returned to Havana, although Blanca passed away in 1900.

The return of the entire family reflected the depth of its commitment to nationalism and its optimism about Cuba's future. As Poyo's grandson Raoul Alpízar Poyo explained, they "were going to have a free nation, independent, honest, worthy in every way of the efforts expended." "Judging from the fantasies turning in the minds of the returning travelers," he continued, "the desires of the old Cuban revolutionary émigrés was becoming a reality."[3] Although the family gladly transitioned back to Cuba after their extended exile, the legacy of the revolution fell short of their expectations.

Limits of Revolution

Thousands of Cuban returned home, but many more lacked the resources to do so. In fact, one reason that fund-raising in factories deteriorated badly after the United States intervened was the illusion many Cuban exiles had that Americans would provide everything, including the means for them to go home.[4] As early as October 1898, representatives of Cuban workers traveled to Havana seeking funds for workers interested in returning. In mid-January, through the mediation of Estrada Palma, the U.S. secretary of war provided limited resources, a token really, to purchase tickets for Cubans who wanted to return. But the U.S. government did not favor a mass relocation of unemployed Cubans to the island, and it authorized only 100 tickets, causing considerable frustration.[5]

Most Cubans in Florida never returned at all. In addition to Poyo, the activists who did go home in 1899 included Gerardo Castellanos, Fernando Figueredo, Martín Herrera, Teodoro Pérez, Néstor Carbonell, Juan Arnao, Francisco María González, and many others. Labor leaders Carlos Baliño, Ramón Rivero, and Enrique Messonier returned and engaged in anarchist and socialist activism. Later Baliño helped establish the Cuban Communist Party. Most found the economic situation in Cuba more depressed than they had imagined. As one returning exile noted, repatriated Cubans had to compete with "autonomists, reformers, aristocrats, and members of the [pro-Spanish] Constitutional Union" for jobs in the occupation government.[6]

As Poyo prepared for his trip home, his thoughts, like those of many other Cubans, focused on the intentions of the United States. He hoped the

U.S. government would honor the commitments it had made in the Teller Amendment, but he remained skeptical, especially in light of its refusal to recognize the Cuban government in arms. In early July 1898, *Patria* noted that this situation created confusing sentiments and ideas that mixed the joy of Spain's imminent defeat with doubts about Cuba's future under U.S. control.[7] It pointed out that outright recognition of Cuba's insurgent authorities would have defused growing tensions between Cubans and Americans on the island.

Poyo wrote an editorial in *El Yara* warning of the annexationist intentions of many in the United States and many Cubans and called on his compatriots to prepare for serious and difficult discussions and negotiations. Gonzalo de Quesada, in Washington, assured Poyo that President McKinley supported Cuban independence and congratulated him for his analysis. "Everything depends on our seriousness," Quesada said, "as you so well express."[8]

But doubts persisted, and clues about the intentions of the United States became evident very soon after July 16, 1898, the day when Spanish military leaders formally surrendered Santiago de Cuba to U.S. generals. Even before Cubans had finished celebrating Spain's defeat, they learned to their amazement that General William Shafter had excluded General Calixto García from the surrender ceremony and that Spaniards remained in positions of authority in the city while Cubans were sidelined. Ignoring the important fighting García's forces had performed, Shafter responded that this was a war between Spain and the United States.[9] This disregard for García and the Cuban army that had fought with such determination for three years before the U.S. landing angered many Cubans, including Poyo.

Over the next months, Poyo's concerns and suspicions increased. In August, despite the fact that the PRC fund-raising infrastructure was crumbling, Key West Cubans sent Gómez's troops clothing and provisions in an expedition that included high-ranking military officials returning to Cuba.[10] The following month, the United States prevented revolutionaries from supplying Cuban troops in the field, revealing its intention to demobilize Cuban forces as quickly as possible.[11] Treaty negotiations in Paris that were signed in December placed Cuba under U.S. control and excluded Cubans. Poyo characterized this as a simple real estate transaction.

In August, Domingo Méndez Capote, the vice-president of the Cuban Republic in Arms, visited Key West as he was returning to Cuba after visiting

New York. Poyo introduced him at San Carlos Institute to thunderous applause, and Méndez Capote reminded his listeners that absolute independence had yet to been achieved. He urged the PRC to transform itself into a political party that would be capable of participating in a stable and democratic Cuban republic. This involved dislodging the pro-Spanish elements that U.S. authorities now seemed to favor. *El Yara* agreed and warned Cubans to remain vigilant and carefully analyze the electoral laws that were soon to be designed and implemented by U.S. authorities to ensure that Spaniards living in Cuba did not manipulate elections to their advantage.[12]

Méndez Capote's speech may have been a reaction to plans advanced by New York's leaders, with whom he had just met. They too supported a political party but for different reasons. In August, Fidel Pierra announced in an interview to the *New York Times* the PRC leadership's plans to transition into a Cuban Nationalist Party. He also said that the "original revolutionary party" expected to be joined by the "Left Autonomists" and that the new party would fully support policies of the U.S. government for the "rehabilitation of Cuba." Pierra and other like-minded New York leaders opposed the establishment of any independent Cuban political organization until the U.S. government certified that Cubans were ready for self-government. According to Pierra, Cubans first had to demonstrate their capacity for self-government, since, with the exception of just a few wartime leaders, most revolutionaries were of the lowest class, "largely Negroes."[13] Pierra and his New York colleagues must have thought better of these ideas, because at the end of the year they dissolved the PRC altogether, beginning the dismantling of the revolution's political and military institutional structures.

At a noontime ceremony on January 1, 1899, again with no Cuban representatives present, General John R. Brooke, the U.S. military governor of Cuba, received formal command of the island from Spain at the captain general's palace in Havana. A U.S. officer at the Morro fortress hauled down the Spanish flag while another raised the Stars and Stripes; Spain's rule ended and formal U.S. occupation began. The only Cuban flag to be seen that day was attached to a large kite that someone flew over the Morro all afternoon.[14]

On that day, the new authorities had planned a full day of festivities for the people of Havana, but Máximo Gómez opposed any celebration saying that Cuba was not yet free or independent.[15] The only festivities were a military parade of U.S. troops that began in El Vedado, a suburban district, and ended in Central Park, in downtown Havana, where General Brooke and his staff stood on a reviewing stand in front of the Hotel Inglaterra. Reflecting Gómez's mood, most of the people who watched the parade from sidewalks, streets, parks, and even roofs remained silent. According to a reporter, some cheered occasionally, but "there was no general expression of public rejoicing." Only one curious incident generated public excitement: "every last man" of the 161st Indiana Infantry took small Cuban flags out of their uniform pockets, which they waved as they entered Central Park. Then the crowd exploded into cheers. Flustered American commanders placed the entire unit under arrest.[16]

Poyo witnessed more U.S. affronts to Cuban nationalist sensibilities, which increased skepticism about Estrada Palma's claim that the PRC had already accomplished its goal of delivering an independent Cuba. In late December, General García died while leading a committee from the Cuban Assembly (the successor to the government in arms) in Washington, D.C., hoping to gain some measure of recognition. President McKinley refused to recognize what he referred to as the "so called Cuban government" and made it clear that he intended to rule Cuba directly until a proper Cuban authority was established.[17]

The USS *Nashville* transported García's body to Havana, where it lay in public view while careful conversations determined the protocol for the funeral procession. On February 11, 1899, various dignitaries took their places behind the horse-pulled hearse, but as the procession began, General John Brooke's cavalry escort forced its way between the general and the officials of the Cuban Assembly, violating the agreed-upon protocol. The governor, who wanted to avoid any appearance of legitimizing the Assembly, declared his escort had acted appropriately when Cubans protested. The stunned Assembly members withdrew from the procession, as did the Cuban honor guard. The crowd waiting for the procession erupted in shouts of "Long Live Cuba," "Death to the Yankees," and "Long Live Aguinaldo," the leader of the Philippine insurrection against United States occupation.[18]

Poyo, like most Cubans, felt the affront of having Calixto García, one of their most beloved military leaders, who had already suffered several humiliating rebuffs at the hands of U.S. authorities, buried by occupying forces without the presence of his comrades in arms. Brooke's action reaffirmed the adamant refusal of the United States to recognize Cuba's revolutionary government in any capacity and its intention to structure the occupation as it saw fit.

Meanwhile, political developments among Cubans also disillusioned the old nationalist. Leaders disagreed with each other and succumbed to the political manipulations of the occupation government. Despite having been shunted aside by the United States, the Assembly insisted that it was the only legitimate voice of the Cuban people. Just a few days after the funeral incident, the Assembly began negotiations with a group of U.S. bankers and financiers about a loan to pay the soldiers of the revolutionary army as they demobilized. Fearing that this would give the Assembly some measure of legitimacy, the U.S. government strongly and publicly opposed this negotiation and instead declared its own intention to provide the funds necessary to dissolve the army, though not in the amount the Assembly requested.

To sidestep the Assembly, U.S. authorities opened discussions with Gonzalo de Quesada, the Assembly's representative in Washington, D.C., to arrange direct conversations with General Gómez, who was still the official head of the insurgent army. Without consulting the Assembly, Quesada facilitated the meeting and a presidential envoy offered Gómez the funds needed to pay the troops. Gómez accepted the offer, further undermining the standing of the Assembly. During the war, Gómez had crossed swords with the government in arms on numerous occasions. He had little use for the body and believed that the Assembly's idea of a private loan threatened to cripple the new republic financially.[19]

The Assembly fired both Quesada and Gómez for acting without authorization, and some even characterized Gómez's cooperation an annexationist ploy, which particularly offended him. He complained to Poyo about these attacks, proclaiming that annexation would be a dark stain on the history of a "refined and heroic people." He associated such talk with political opportunists who took advantage of "differences among brothers" to advance their own interests. In fact, at that moment Gómez possessed a certain confidence that the United States did not intend to annex the island.[20]

Though the Assembly's decision to fire Gómez was an attempt by nationalists to preserve some Cuban authority in the island's affairs, the public repudiated the shoddy treatment of Cuba's most prestigious insurgent figure. Gómez disbanded the army at the end of May and accepted $3 million from the U.S. government to distribute among almost 34,000 soldiers, or $75 per soldier. The Assembly, which had no formal political authority and little public legitimacy even among Cubans, dissolved itself on June 30, 1899. The island was left without any claim to independent Cuban-controlled civil or military structures; the country was totally in the hands of the U.S. military.

The same day the Spanish left the island, January 1, 1899, General Brooke structured a new government. Using the classic colonialist strategy of cooptation, he appointed Cuban ministers to his cabinet. Brooke was succeeded by General Leonard Wood in December 1899. Wood expanded and consolidated the occupation. North American investors arrived in Cuba in waves and soon dominated the private sector. Many Cubans took government jobs. The U.S. governor appointed former military chiefs, officials of the insurgent government, and exiles to positions as provincial governors, Supreme Court judges, and executive department secretaries, among other jobs.

Most of these appointees were members of the island's petit bourgeoisie. Many had been educated in the United States at institutions such as Columbia University, Lehigh University, the University of Pennsylvania, Cornell University, New York School of Commerce, the School of Engineers in New York, and Fordham University. Many had protected and advanced their interests by becoming U.S. citizens, and most saw no alternative to cooperating with the occupation government. They generally supported the idea of an independent Cuba, but they accepted the protectorate arrangement the United States had created, even though the U.S. occupiers used the open-ended language of the Teller Amendment to justify remaining in Cuba as long as they felt was necessary to establish a government that they deemed acceptable.[21] Prominent Cuban annexationist José Ignacio Rodriguez thought it ironic that it was the PRC, a defiantly anti-annexationist revolutionary party, that "delivered Cuba with hands and feet tied to the United States of America."[22] Poyo must have recognized the irony with some bitterness.

Revolution had reached its limits, and when Cuba would become independent now depended on the decisions of the U.S. occupiers and the negotiating skills of an emerging Cuban political class. Insurgents became politicians, and Poyo's days as a nationalist editor ended—but not before a final run. The spectacle of U.S. occupation sharpened Poyo's determination to carry on the fight for Cuba's sovereignty, a goal that now seemed to be increasingly in doubt. Using funds from the sale of his printing press in Key West and helped by the director of the *Gaceta de la Habana* (where he had worked before going into exile thirty years earlier), Poyo launched *El Yara's* new incarnation. He published *El Yara* in Havana for three months, but the effort to transplant his beloved newspaper soon faltered.²³

Poyo's reputation as a radical exile activist and his uncompromising nationalist tone must have seemed out of place to many, especially U.S. authorities and conservative Cuban owners of the established newspapers like *Diario de la Marina*, *La Lucha*, and *La Discusión*. In addition, in Havana *El Yara* had to operate as a profit-making enterprise in a competitive market. Poyo lacked working capital and had few business connections. The complex political environment and the difficult economic situation worked together to seal the fate of *El Yara*.²⁴ As Gerardo Castellanos García, the son of Poyo's revolutionary colleague in Key West, explained, exiles had false ideas about what independence would bring. They expected some kind of utopia based on Martí's ideal of a Cuba "for all and the good of all," and *El Yara* continued its nationalist discourse with that mindset. "El Yara," he said, "was as exotic and impotent in Havana as a pitirre [a tropical bird] in the Sahara Desert." Few paid attention to the nationalist voice, which after twenty years of continuous publication fell silent.²⁵

Disappointed, Poyo sought employment, initially without much success; he could not even find a job as a *lector* in a Havana cigar factory. The 63-year-old exile leader finally found work as a watchman at the Customs House. Every night, he walked the docks not far from his residence at Calle Inquisidor no. 31 in the old section of Havana.²⁶ He thought his 30-year career as a revolutionary would have garnered a measure of recognition and respect, but his work among the radical working class in Key West did not translate into political prestige on the island. Without military experience, which was a political asset in post-Spanish Cuba, or the social standing necessary to catch the attention of Cuba's new elite power brokers, Poyo had little influence. Indeed, few leaders from Florida's working-class communities gained much political traction in Cuba.

To find a better livelihood in Cuba, Poyo relied on those closest to him. Máximo Gómez helped move him from his job as a night watchman to a modest but certainly better job as a clerk in the Customs House. His fortunes improved even more in January 1900. Fernando Figueredo, one of the few Florida Cubans to find favor in the new administration, had secured work as an under-secretary in the Secretaría de Estado y Gobernación (Department of Interior). He had opened doors in the department for some of his friends, including Manuel P. Delgado (Poyo's son-in-law) and Martín Herrera.[27] When the director of the Cuban National Archive passed away in December 1899, Figueredo and Delgado recommended Poyo as replacement. Instead, well-known historian Vidal Morales y Morales secured the post, but Poyo was appointed as one of three under-secretaries.

When Delgado rushed to the Customs House to give Poyo the news, Poyo just looked at him blankly for a time. He repeated the news to his father-in-law, and the relieved old man fell back in his seat. "Perhaps he mumbled a prayer of thanks," Delgado remembered. "I never felt more satisfied than when I complied with that debt of love and friendship." The appointment resolved Poyo's economic difficulties and allowed him to survive in his beloved Cuba.[28] He became director of the National Archive in 1904.

Disillusionment

From his vantage point at the Cuban National Archive, Poyo watched with considerable distress as Cuba attempted to establish a constitutional and sovereign republic.[29] In late 1900 and early 1901, a Constituent Assembly wrote a constitution, but as a condition for accepting the document and withdrawing military forces, the U.S. Congress required the attachment of a document known as the Platt Amendment, which assured Cuba's status as an American protectorate.

Under the terms of the amendment, the United States retained the right to intervene in Cuban affairs to protect U.S. interests. When Cubans protested, the U.S. government warned that the military would remain in Cuba until the amendment had been approved exactly as drafted. After a bitter debate the Constituent Assembly finally accepted the imposition by a margin of one vote on June 12, 1901. Cubans paid a heavy and humiliating price to achieve the withdrawal of U.S. troops. Though Poyo opposed the Platt Amendment, like all Cubans he had little choice but to adapt to the critical place of the United States in the life of the new Cuban nation. For the moment, Cubans had to make the best of the disappointing situation.[30]

The United States scheduled elections for early 1902, and Tomás Estrada Palma quickly emerged as the favorite candidate of U.S. authorities and most Cubans. The former *delegado* of the PRC met all the requirements of a friendly leader for the United States. He was a U.S. citizen, he had lived in New York for over twenty years, he was a conservative, and he supported the Platt Amendment. Estrada Palma could be expected to respect U.S. interests and bring honest governance to Cuba.

Despite these characteristics, many nationalists liked Estrada Palma. Poyo supported Estrada Palma less for what he stood for politically than for his long relationships with both Estrada Palma and his most important supporter, Máximo Gómez. Many prominent figures backed Estrada Palma's candidacy, including Emilio Núñez of the PRC, Domingo Méndez Capote and Alfredo Zayas of the former revolutionary government in arms, and military leaders José Miguel Gómez and Pedro Betancourt. Most saw him as a sober, competent, and honest politician. Even his less-than-militant attitude about complete Cuban sovereignty did not raise concerns that he would deliver the country to the United States through some annexationist ploy. They trusted him to honor the Cuban people's desire for independence and concluded that he, perhaps better than anyone else at that moment, could negotiate Cuba's difficult path to nationhood.

Bartolomé Masó, the former president of the Cuban Republic in Arms, had other ideas. He strongly opposed the Platt Amendment and gathered others who also objected to this imposition. He felt that Estrada Palma was insufficiently nationalist, and he put himself forward as a candidate. However, when Governor Wood appointed an election commission composed of men who were sympathetic to Estrada Palma and purged many officials in the occupation government who had declared for Masó, Masó withdrew in protest. The uncontested election was a low-key affair. Estrada Palma did not return to Cuba until after his election. He received a hero's welcome as he paraded across the island from Santiago to Havana to take office as Cuba's first president.[31]

Poyo received invitations from Estrada Palma and Gómez to the presidential inauguration, which was held on May 20, 1902, at the captain general's palace in Havana, but as the moment approached, he feared that he would be overcome with emotion and stayed home with his family. Poyo paced the house as he waited to hear the canons from the Morro fortress just across the bay confirm the transfer of power. When the first shots sounded, he looked at Clara, his body shook, and tears ran down his cheeks. As the canons continued to sound, his grandson Raoul Alpízar remembered, "[he] raised his hands to his head as if to grasp the thoughts that pounded in his brain on that historic occasion. 'Clarita,' he declared, 'we are free! Viva Cuba Libre!' He then sobbed like a child."[32]

If Poyo felt joy in response to the symbolism of Cuban independence, he remained disillusioned with the United States and the limitations it had placed on Cuba's independence. He also grieved at the spectacle of Cuban politics after the U.S. troops left the island. Poyo's excitement about Cuba's independence soon soured during Estrada Palma's administration.

Poyo lost confidence in the president's judgment early in his term over a poorly handled decision. As the new government formed, Poyo learned that Rafael Merchán had been nominated as Cuba's first minister to Spain. A well-known writer and poet, Merchán had a superb reputation, but in a recent meeting Poyo had found him strange, perhaps mentally troubled, and not up to the very delicate and important job of representing Cuba in Madrid. Poyo spoke to the president, who disregarded the warning. Within a short time, the embarrassing behavior of the new Cuban representative in Madrid had forced him to resign. Merchán was in fact suffering from a brain tumor, and he passed away shortly after returning to Cuba.

Poyo saw this incident as a great humiliation for the Cuban nation, though he expressed this only in private to his family as they gathered around the dinner table. Spaniards, he lamented, pointed to Merchán's actions as evidence of their long-standing contention that Cubans were incapable of managing their own affairs. This was perhaps a bit of an overreaction, but Poyo's sensitivity about this issue is attributable to the fact that for years he and other Cubans had heard from Spaniards that Cubans were incapable of self-rule. Poyo urged Estrada Palma to name a capable and honest member of the liberation army as the new minister, a man who had earned the right to represent the Cuban nation before the Spanish government.[33] In fact, Estrada had appointed such a man, General Cosme de la Torriente, as first secretary of the Cuban diplomatic delegation, and he became the new minister.[34] Poyo never forgave the president for this fiasco, although his differences with Estrada Palma also involved policy matters.[35]

From the moment he took office, Estrada Palma pursued policies that would support unrestrained U.S. investment and promote the interests of Cuba's landowning and financial elites. He accepted the Platt Amendment and accommodated North American interests, though he did defend Cuba's right to the Isle of Pines and gave the U.S. military only one of the bases it demanded. As his term unfolded, Estrada Palma joined a newly formed political party known as the Moderates that was composed of conservatives who supported close relations with the United States. One of their highest priorities was the Reciprocity Treaty of 1903, an agreement that eliminated trade restrictions and reduced tariffs, accelerating the integration of Cuba into the economic orbit of the United States.[36]

Politics during Estrada Palma's first term became very contentious as political parties formed, staked out their positions, and consolidated their constituencies. Nationalists condemned the president's unwillingness to defend Cuban interests, especially his refusal to ask the United States to reconsider the Platt Amendment. Many who initially supported Estrada Palma broke with him, including Máximo Gómez, who established the Cuban National Party (Partido Nacional Cubano) to challenge the influence and growing economic dominance of the United States. In 1905, the National Party and elements of other groups formed the Liberal Party, which nominated another prominent war veteran, General José Miguel Gómez, for president in the 1906 elections.[37]

Before the campaign began, 69-year-old Máximo Gómez suffered an infection in his hand that spread rapidly through his weakened body, and on May 17 he died, just three days before the third anniversary of the Cuban republic. Despite their recent political differences, Estrada Palma had gone to see the ailing general shortly before he died. He declared a day of national mourning and honored him as if he were a head of state. Gómez's embalmed body lay in state for three days at the presidential palace surrounded by an honor guard. The public visited continually, along with his comrades in arms and Poyo, who deeply grieved the loss of the man he had always admired as the indispensable figure of the Cuban independence struggle. On May 20, a crowd followed the funeral procession that slowly made its way from downtown to Colon Cemetery, where Gómez was laid to rest with full honors.[38]

The electoral campaign continued in earnest after Gómez's death, but in the months leading up to the elections the Moderates used the power of incumbency to purge opponents from national and local government. They also rigged the electoral rolls in many places. The Liberal candidate, José Miguel Gómez, made public accusations of fraud and withdrew in protest, ensuring that Estrada Palma was reelected in March 1906. This time the losers denounced the election and prepared an armed insurrection. The government responded by arresting many opposition leaders and mobilizing the military. Estrada Palma then invoked the Platt Amendment and appealed to the U.S. government for support, as did the opposition forces led by José Miguel Gómez, who called for new elections. Estrada Palma resigned, precipitating a formal intervention by the United States and the establishment of another occupation government. This one was in place until 1909, when new elections brought the Liberal Party to power. The Platt Amendment had created a political system whereby Cuban actors regularly looked north for resolutions to their disagreements, in effect recognizing U.S. control of the island.[39]

The Cuban National Archive

Although Poyo joined the Liberal Party in the San Francisco barrio of Havana where he lived, he maintained a low political profile to avoid losing his job.[40] He put his political career in the past and turned his attention to the job at hand. Poyo learned firsthand of the desperate condition of the national archives when Vidal Morales assigned him to visit the country's major depositories to document their scope and condition. His report alerted authorities to the problems he found and recommended that certain document collections be transferred to the National Archive for proper care and handling. He also located the archive of the Junta Superior de Sanidad, which included invaluable documents about Cuba's health and sanitation. The papers arrived at the National Archive in 1902, where Poyo's grandson, Bolívar Alpízar Poyo, inventoried them.[41] Later, Bolívar's son, Luís Alpízar Leal, also became an archivist, deepening the family's legacy at the institution.

The struggle to protect the nation's historical record, however, ran into difficulties when political instability engulfed the country in 1906. When rumors of rebellion prompted the government to strengthen its military forces in and around Havana, a contingent of the Rural Guard settled into a section of the archive building, a fortress called Castillo de la Fuerza. Poyo complained to the Interior Ministry, characterizing the situation as untenable. Not only did the presence of a military garrison with ammunition and other flammable materials threaten the nation's documentary legacy, but it took up space that was urgently needed for the rapidly growing collections. Poyo recommended the archive be moved to a vacant and larger building called the Cuartel de Artillería, also known as El Palenque, on the southern end of Calle Compostela. The building had once been a military installation and a barracks for government-owned slaves engaged in public works activities.

The government delayed the archive's move until armed rebellion seemed imminent. It reinforced the military contingent at Castillo de la Fuerza, and then on July 23, 1906, the president ordered a complete evacuation of the archive as quickly as possible to the site Poyo had suggested earlier. Planning began, but a week later, at six in the morning, before preparations were complete, Interior Department officials arrived with vehicles to begin the move. Despite the difficult conditions, Poyo began the transfer carefully and systematically, ensuring that the bundles of documents remained in their appropriate order, beginning with the judicial records. But on August 8, as the work proceeded, the Secretary of Public Works arrived and handed Poyo a presidential order demanding that the work be completed within forty-eight hours.

Poyo protested, and Estrada Palma offered him the city's sanitation workers and their vehicles to accelerate the transfer of documents. The next day, a public works official took charge of the operation from Poyo, and a contingent of men constructed wooden slides from the windows on the second floor to the ground. "And as if throwing large quantities of trash from a building in demolition," noted young archivist Joaquín Llaverías, who watched the spectacle, they threw tied bundles of archival documents down the slides. Many cords around the bundles snapped, dispersing and damaging the papers and creating terrible confusion. It left such a disaster that Llaverías prayed never to see such a thing again for the rest of his life.[42]

Over the next forty-eight hours, workers loaded the bundles and the loose papers strewn on the ground into horse-drawn garbage trucks and transported them to the new archive building, dropping documents along the way, some of which were salvaged by policemen accompanying the line of vehicles. At the destination, workers unharnessed the horses from the trucks and then raised the truck beds, dumping the documents in piles sometimes four meters high in the courtyard of the new archive. A line of workers stretching from the courtyard to the interior of the building then passed bundles from hand to hand as strong winds swirled the loose papers in the air. To make matters even worse, a torrential storm destroyed papers that were still outside as archive workers frantically tried to salvage what they could.

On August 20, 1906, authorities formerly inaugurated the new archive but Poyo could not be consoled. His official report to superiors at the Interior Department said that the transfer of the archive had "had been carried out under the worst conditions with disastrous results," despite efforts by the archive staff to mitigate the damage during the days and nights they watched the Department of Public Works ravage the nation's historical record. But even more bad news followed. Although the government promised that the new building would be for the exclusive use of the archive, a portion of it became an armory filled with military supplies, again placing the documents in grave danger of destruction.[43] Any remaining admiration Poyo may have had for Estrada Palma dissipated in the face of this tragic episode.[44]

Poyo then turned his attention to another disturbing problem. Though less dramatic than the wholesale transfer of the entire archive in forty-eight hours, it nevertheless threatened the long-term integrity of the archive's holdings. In July 1907, Poyo told a reporter for *La Discusión* that he did not have enough authority to protect the archive's holdings. Previous archive and government officials, especially historian Vidal Morales, had allowed prominent writers and scholars to take original documents from the archive for use in their personal writing projects. Poyo told the reporter that Vidal Morales had "loaned" the original of the 'Himno del Desterrado,' of the immortal [José María] Heredia" to *El Fígaro* magazine for publication. When Poyo tried to recover the document, the borrower claimed he had loaned it to a third person and that it could no longer be traced. Poyo cited another case in which the Secretary of Interior ordered him to give Manuel Sanguily—who was now a senator—important historical documents for his personal use.

The article in *La Discusión* caused a public scandal and Sanguily and others quickly returned documents to the archive, but Heredia's "Himno del Desterrado" never appeared. Poyo's denunciation forced the hand of the U.S. occupation government, which prohibited the extraction of documents from the National Archive and ordered that the almost 400 documents that were listed as "on loan" be immediately returned.[45] For Poyo, these problems in the archive were a microcosm of the challenges the nation faced in organizing itself, and he could not help be disturbed with the way Cubans conducted themselves politically after independence.

Poyo particularly wanted to ensure that documents relating to the independence movement were protected. When he became director of the National Archive, Poyo also became editor of the *Boletín del Archivo Nacional*, which his predecessor Morales had begun and Joaquín Llaverías managed. In addition to publishing indexes of archival holdings, Poyo oversaw the publication of interesting and important documents relating to the revolutionary and exile experience, hoping to spark interest in and writing about this important period.[46] When Estrada Palma left the presidency in September 1906, he turned over to the National Archive all of the documents of the Delegation of the Cuban Revolutionary Party (1895–1898), and Poyo made processing the collection a priority. The collection came to the archive in sixteen boxes, five foot lockers, and fifteen loose books, and Poyo assigned Llaverías the task of processing and inventorying the materials. This project was completed at the end of 1909.[47] For just over a decade, Poyo considered the guardianship of the new nation's historical memory and records his greatest responsibility.

Preserving the Nationalist Legacy

In addition to doing what he could to protect the nation's historical legacy, Poyo and many like-minded revolutionary colleagues promoted the legacy of José Martí, who quickly emerged as the very symbol of Cuban nationalism. Even before Gómez agreed to disarm the rebel army, Poyo understood that Cuba had for the time being reached the limits of its sovereignty. Although demanding full independence through revolutionary action was out of the question, Poyo had little stomach for participating in the politics of compromise in the new republic. No longer able to express the powerful nationalist ideology that had appeared in the pages of *El Yara* for twenty years, he simply lived the life of a republican citizen. As a practical revolutionary journalist he had written more about how to create revolution than about how to visualize the future republic, but he now recognized the importance of transmitting nationalist ideals to the next generations, especially as they were articulated in the writings of José Martí. Poyo participated in honoring Martí, believing that his historical accomplishments and prolific writings would preserve, revive, and inspire the nationalist gospel in the hearts and minds of Cubans, which they did.

Efforts to promote Martí's legacy began very quickly after the Spanish left the island. On the first official commemoration of José Martí's birth in Havana, held on January 29, 1899, 4,000 people representing eighty-two societies carried banners and flags through the streets of Havana, accompanied by several bands. The crowd gathered in the pouring rain at Paula Square, next to the house where Martí was born. After six eulogies in Martí's honor, one of which was likely given by Poyo, participants unveiled a marble plaque on the exterior wall of the house that memorialized Martí's life. Key West tobacco workers had paid for the plaque. Orators emphasized the imperative need for absolute independence.[48]

In March 1899, authorities removed a prominent statue of Spain's Queen Isabel II in Havana's Central Park, and *El Fígaro* sponsored a survey to determine what should replace it. Suggestions included a replica of the Statue of Liberty, a statue of Christopher Columbus, and statues of Maceo and Gómez, but votes for Martí won by a slight margin. The next February, a Comisión Monumento Pro-Martí (Pro-Martí Monument Commission) comprised of Poyo, Emilio Núñez, Fernando Figueredo, and José A. Malberty, began raising funds.[49]

After much persistent work, at nine o'clock on the morning of February 24, 1905, the president and his entire cabinet watched Máximo Gómez raise the Cuban flag and deliver the first speech of the day in honor of the martyred Martí. A crowd of over 10,000 people attended the event. After Estrada Palma gave a speech, a veil covering a large statue of José Martí fell away while a military band played the national anthem. Emilio Núñez, the governor of Havana Province, officially presented the statue to the city. Poyo, Ramón Rivero, Francisco M. González, Juan Gualberto Gómez, and Horatio Rubens offered remembrances of their friend. Though the event was primarily a civic affair, the conservative *Diario de la Marina* complained that it had been organized by the nationalists who did not invite important members of the Moderate Party, which the newspaper claimed gave it a political inflection before the following year's elections.[50]

The statue was the first significant step toward putting Martí at the forefront of Cuba's pantheon of national heroes, but Poyo and many of his colleagues also worked to protect Martí from those who tried to taint his image as a revolutionary. In 1906, some conservatives questioned the integrity of the revolutionaries and even accused Martí and his followers of accepting ransom money from the likes of the notorious *bandolero* Manuel García to fund the uprising. Fermín Valdés Domínguez and Juan Gualberto Gómez came to Martí's defense, arguing that he had refused to accept money from García and condemned such funds as unworthy.

As historian Rosemarie Schwartz has pointed out, in the "overheated political climate [of the early republic], reflecting the disillusionment and bitterness of the period," Manuel García became a "weapon on the political battlefield." Conservative politicians accused nationalists of being corrupt and of being connected with unsavory characters, while nationalists denied any important association with Manuel García. "To realize Martí's national ideal of self-sacrifice for the good of the whole," Schwartz noted, Cubans sought a noble and untainted revolutionary who was worthy of occupying the role of national hero.[51]

The truth of whether Martí actually accepted funds from García or others like him was less important than the need of nationalists to advance the image of idealism and revolutionary purity. Despite García's closeness to the revolutionary movement and the Key West community, of which Martí had been clearly aware, those who had known him now had to deny him and condemn his activities in order to protect Martí's purity and, perhaps equally important, to protect the nationalist leaders who were now making their way into the new Cuban political system. This may explain why Manuel Deulofeu, Gerardo Castellanos, and other historians said as little as possible about García's relations with Poyo and Key West and perhaps why Poyo never wrote about his own revolutionary experiences.

Poyo's work with the *bandeleros* was largely unknown, but it was chronicled in popular lore that transformed Manuel García from a cruel bandit, kidnapper, and assassin into a "courageous, patriotic, virile, enduring" folk hero.[52] Cipriano (Chanito) Isidrón Torres, a popular folk poet and singer who had been born in Las Villas in 1903, for example, wrote a long poem in *decimas* that was published in the 1980s. It traced Manuel García's career and life in heroic terms, highlighting his strong connections with Key West and its revolutionary leadership. As one stanza recounted, "Poyo and Patricio Delgado / in an instant, gave Manuel / a commandant's commission / with two signatures and a seal / He was the designated chief / for these operations / and with vivas and applause / the steamer headed out to sea / while the chief began to study / the conditions he would encounter."[53] Poyo's most controversial grassroots work received some acclaim among the popular classes, but otherwise it was not widely known.

Poyo also promoted nationalist consciousness generally by serving as president of the Association of Revolutionary Émigrés (Asociación de Emigrados Revolucionarios), an organization dedicated to disseminating the contributions and values of the exile communities.[54] He also remained committed to Masonic values, which for him were inseparable from those of the Cuban revolution. In 1901, with Martín Herrera and Fernando Figueredo and others, he founded Logia Cuba, which met at the Gran Logia de la Isla de Cuba, located at no. 6, Carlos III Avenue.[55]

In keeping with their Masonic beliefs and their idea of a Cuban nation dedicated to all its citizens, Poyo and Herrera served on the Board of Directors of a private shelter for unemployed and homeless people known as La Misericordia, which was founded in Havana's El Cerro neighborhood in 1886. In addition to material aid, the shelter offered spiritual guidance and training in particular skills. In September 1909, the Cuban president tasked Poyo (who was known for his work with the needy) and several government ministers to accompany him on an inspection tour of a region of Pinar del Rio that had been devastated by a hurricane. They sought ways to meet the immediate needs of those affected by the storm and advised local officials about economic recovery plans.[56]

Death

Sometime in 1911 Poyo began to experience abdominal pain that proved to be a symptom of stomach cancer. Not wanting to alarm his family, he kept the malady to himself as long as possible. He continued to arrive punctually to work until October 8, 1911, when he became too ill. The tumor had sealed the entrance to his small intestine, and he vomited everything he ate. The day before, Poyo made what he knew would be his final visit to the Masonic lodge, where he completed work related to his obligations as treasurer. During the next two weeks he grew weaker and the pain increased. He told his family that little time remained.

He was mostly bedridden in the last weeks. He moaned quietly and reminisced with Clara at his side, but, stoic as ever, he refused morphine because he wanted his mind to be clear to the end. He prepared his burial suit and instructed his grandchildren to bury him in his old flexible shoes since his new ones would not fit his bloated extremities. He asked his son Francisco to place the Orden del Sol banner that had been created in Key West in 1878 for his secret revolutionary association under his head and to cover his body with the Cuban flag that the members of the Club Hijas de la Libertad had used when they took their oaths of loyalty to Cuba. He also asked his family not to let his body out of the home except to take it directly to the cemetery—evidence of his distaste for how politicians and authorities used the passing of independence veterans to orchestrate emotional patriotic "actas" for political purposes. "You will see," he told the family around him, "[that] as soon as I have died, authorities, government officials, soldiers will come.... I am not interested in any of that," he declared, "and neither should you [be].... I complied with my duties. I was a good son, a good husband, a good father, a good grandfather, and a good Cuban."[57]

In the early hours of October 26, Poyo announced that the end had come. "Look, it has arrived. It is entering from below. My legs are already cold. Call the family." As they gathered, he spoke to each, giving his last blessings and advice. Poyo finally passed away at ten minutes to four in the morning. In his final breath, he called to "Clarita," his wife of fifty-one years. At the simple burial, which took place without priest, religious ceremony, or ritual, a few government representatives, many ordinary people, and old comrades gave him a tribute. Francisco María González, with whom Poyo had often shared the *tribuna* at the Gato factory, spoke warmly of his old friend, as did Enrique Loynaz del Castillo, the insurgent general Poyo had helped launch to Cuba with Serafín Sánchez and Carlos Roloff, both of whom were already dead. A formal memorial service at the Masonic lodge included a eulogy delivered by Fernando Figueredo, his closest friend and a colleague of many years.[58]

Francisco had little money and buried his father in a common grave (*fosa común*) at the Colón Cemetery. In 1912, in order to raise funds to acquire land for a dignified grave, Francisco published and sold the album that Máximo Gómez had ordered compiled in April 1898 under the title *Album del Estado Mayor del Cuartel General del Ejército Libertador Cubano*. Figueredo wrote the introduction to the album, in which he said that although people might not have ever heard of José Dolores Poyo or *El Yara*, they should buy the book because of the patriotism it represented. Poyo had died poor and had probably been forgotten, but he had been happy, Figueredo told his readers, and now his son had published the book to give his father a modest but appropriate tomb. "Who can deny this son?"[59]

With the proceeds Francisco purchased a private burial site in the Colón Cemetery. The next year Francisco added a marble *boveda* (sarcophagus), where he expected Poyo's remains to lie "tranquil and eternally." But on February 24, 1918, the Association of Revolutionary Émigrés honored Poyo and Martí's Tampa guardian Paulina Pedroso, with whom he always stayed whenever he visited Tampa. They transferred both their remains to a new pantheon that had been erected in memory of revolutionary exiles.[60] After that, Poyo's empty *boveda* received the remains of Francisco and his family.

Transitions

Above all, José D. Poyo was a grassroots man of action dedicated to revolutionizing Cuba. He participated in a Cuban tradition of revolution that existed before his birth and continued after his death. His colleagues especially remembered the uncompromising and impatient revolutionary advocacy he expressed in *El Yara* throughout the 1880s, when most Cubans had begun to doubt that insurrection was practical or even feasible. Whether during times of enthusiasm and economic prosperity or skepticism and few resources, he and the Key West community remained determined. Effective leadership, an enthusiastic constituency, a clear ideology, enduring institutions that included newspapers and political clubs, revolutionary traditions and myths, geographic proximity to Cuba, extraordinary economic and political influence in Key West, and an unwavering persistence made this possible. Those who challenged the community's goals and methods were usually met with a firm and determined response.

Nevertheless, revolutionary ideals are rarely implemented in practical and satisfying ways right away, and Cuba's separation from Spain was no exception. That long-sought event produced additional turmoil in the twentieth century. After his political career was behind him, Poyo secured a living outside the realm of politics, and at the time of his death he fully understood that the nationalist project had ultimately fallen short. As the United States consolidated its occupation and militant discourses faded in the wake of the compromises that were necessary to achieve the withdrawal of U.S. troops, nationalist intransigence dissipated.

The economic system fell mostly into the hands of Americans, and Cubans succumbed to political divisions that were ultimately mediated by the United States. Poyo had never envisioned a Cuban republic that was politically and economically beholden to the United States, and his expectations succumbed to the cruel realities of a nation plagued by the chaotic aftermath of war. Raoul Alpízar Poyo wrote that his grandfather did not realize "the great number of disagreeable surprises and painful obstacles that waited. He did not imagine that his entire life had been a glorious fantasy that would collide with a disconcerting reality very different from what people in exile had dreamed."[61]

When dreams of independence were replaced with disturbing political and economic realities, revolutionary nationalists reacted in different ways. Some participated in and collaborated with the new political system, concluding that the nationalist project had done what it could and turning their attention to making a living the best they could. Many, after all, had done the same under Spanish rule after the Zanjón Pact. Others grew angry and resentful when they saw Americans benefiting from their 30-year struggle and sacrifices and gave birth to an anti-American tradition that embedded itself in sectors of Cuban society. Still others blamed Cubans themselves. Francisco shared his father's disappointments but attributed many of the problems of his homeland to the inability of Cubans to transcend the challenging circumstances. Francisco recognized that Americans pursued their own interests and structured economic and political matters for their advantage, but his disappointment was about what Cubans might have accomplished but did not, even in this situation.

Cubans, Francisco thought, turned their backs on their own ideals and did as much harm to their own country and people as the Americans had. He saw Cubans struggling for economic and political advantage over each other and constantly appealing to the United States to mediate their differences. He spoke often to his children and grandchildren about the political corruption he encountered as an employee of the Havana city government and often noted that Cubans acted like Spaniards because "we carry their blood in our veins."[62]

Poyo never returned to Key West, though his children and grandchildren occasionally visited relatives. Only Raoul Alpízar Poyo, the son of América and Francisco, returned there to live. He eventually became the Cuban vice-consul and honorary consul in Key West. He was the only family member to write about his grandfather, probably precisely because he remained in Key West. For a generation or two the Key West Cuban community retained its nationalist identity. They remembered with pride and celebrated their contributions to and support for José Martí, Máximo Gómez, Antonio Maceo, and dozens of others. San Carlos Institute stood as a visible symbol of the revolutionary past, as did the monument to Cuban martyrs in the Key West cemetery. With the help of a $2,400 annual stipend approved by the Cuban government in 1904, the San Carlos school continued its role of teaching children the Spanish language and educating them about Cuban history, geography, and culture. The school's theater also served as an important cultural and entertainment center.

In 1919 when a hurricane destroyed the fragile building, the community's primary visual reminder of its past, Cuba came to the rescue. In recognition of the school's historic contributions to independence, the Cuban government provided funds to rebuild the institution and installed the Cuban consulate in one of its offices.[63] In 1937, at the initiative of a Cuban congressman, a committee raised funds to put a statue of José Martí in Bayview Park.[64] And perhaps most important, Key West gained a special place in the Cuban nation's creation story, and this was a source of great satisfaction for its Cuban residents.

But also, inevitably, Key West became a very different place. The arrival of the railroad from the mainland connected the keys, visitors from the north who had discovered a pleasant tropical and even exotic and quaint Caribbean island, and a strengthened public school system, among many other things, integrated the Cuban community into American life. The Key West revolutionary community dissolved quickly as nationalists closed their political clubs and no longer thundered their message in the factories. The city's cigar industry, which competed with the industries in Tampa and Cuba, fell on hard times after 1900, and Cuban tobacco workers no longer came to Key West to settle. Most *lectores* fell silent, and the few that remained read about labor matters; nationalist discourses quieted.[65]

The revolutionary generation passed and memories faded. "Callejón de Poyo" (officially Bahama Street), where Poyo had lived, morphed into English as "Chicken Alley," and while the names of the old local revolutionary personalities remained vaguely familiar, they disappeared from the consciousness of the community. As Raoul Alpízar Poyo wrote in the mid-1940s, "Key West has lost its cubanness." "Today," he noted, "the attractive city has all the characteristics of a southern town.... The street cars are gone, and little Spanish is spoken." The descendants of the Cuban pioneers who had built the city "prefer to feel American." But this was not surprising, he explained, since for Key West cigar workers, Cuban independence did not translate into anything of consequence; old-timers died believing that despite all they had done for their country, Cuba provided them with few opportunities to return home and make a secure living. Not surprisingly, their children looked north instead of south for educational and economic opportunities. They fought in Europe and Asia for the Allied cause and became Cuban-Americans.[66]

The common denominator for exiles, whether they remained in Key West or returned to Cuba, was a grave sense of disappointment that revolutionary nationalist aspirations failed to transform Cuba into a democratic sovereign nation with an inclusive economic and social system. It was perhaps because of this that in 1958, just three years before his death, as revolutionary forces descended from the Sierra Maestra Mountains, Francisco Poyo, like millions of Cubans, expressed the hope that another nationalist and democratic revolution might finally bring the Cuban republic his father had struggled to create. He did not live to see that happen, but the revolutionary tradition continued. Like previous efforts, it twisted and turned in unpredictable ways.

NOTES

Introduction

1. Pérez, *On Becoming Cuban*; Poyo, "With All, and for the Good of All"; Casasús, *La emigración cubana*.
2. Poyo, "With All, and for the Good of All."
3. Deulofeu, *Martí: Cayo Hueso y Tampa*, 5–6.
4. Deulofeu, *Heroes del destierro*; Castellanos, *Motivos de Cayo Hueso*.
5. Pérez, *Lords of the Mountain*; Ferrer, *Insurgent Cuba*; Casanovas, *Bread, or Bullets*; Schwartz, *Lawless Liberators*; Childs, *The 1812 Aponte Rebellion in Cuba*.
6. Casasús, *Calixto García*; Foner, *Antonio Maceo*; Franco, *Antonio Maceo: Apuntes*; Infiesta, *Máximo Gómez*; Souza, *Máximo Gómez: el generalísimo*; Cairo, *Máximo Gómez: 100 años*. Useful biographies of Martí include Lisazo, *José Martí: Martyr*; Mañach, *José Martí: Apostle*; Ibarra, *José Martí: Dirigente político*; Kirk, *José Martí: Mentor*.
7. This interpretation first appeared in the work of a young tobacco worker, Angel Peláez: *Primera jornada de José Martí en Cayo Hueso* (1896), 30.

Chapter 1. Community

1. Alpízar Poyo, *Cayo Hueso y José Dolores Poyo*, 52. Castellanos indicates that Poyo left Cuba in August 1869, but Alpízar's January date is more likely. See Castellanos, *Misión a Cuba*, 57.
2. Bravo, *Revolución cubana*; Macías, *Deportados políticos a Fernando Poo*.
3. Pérez Rolo, *Mis recuerdos*.
4. Guerra, *Guerra de los 10 Años*, 1:198–212.
5. Alpízar Poyo, *Cayo Hueso y José Dolores Poyo*, 52–53; Llaverías, *Contribución a la historia de la prensa periódica*, 1:219–221.
6. Figueredo, *José Dolores Poyo*, 6–7.
7. All secondary sources cite Poyo's year of birth as 1837. His age in the Monroe County, Florida schedules of the 1870 and 1880 U.S. federal censuses is consistent with a birth date of 1837. However, his baptismal record indicates a birth date in 1836: José de los Dolores de la Encarnación Poyo y Remiréz de Estenoz, June 30, 1836, Libro

22 de Bautismo, Folio 129, no. 696, Guadalupe Parish, Havana, Cuba. Handwritten transcriptions of birth and marriage records contained in a notebook entitled "Genealogía del apellido Pollo [sic], y demás," given to author by Luis Alpízar Leal, who was an employee of the Cuban National Archive in Havana. The Poyo surname is often rendered as Pollo in baptismal and marriage records.

8. Antonio Poyo's birthplace is included in the baptismal record of his daughter. Antonia María Ana Poyo y Méndez, September 3, 1759, Libro 11 de Bautismo, Folio 213, no. 215, Cathedral, Havana, Cuba, in "Genealogía del apellido Pollo [sic], y demás."

9. Baptismal and marriage records of Clara Leonor Camús y de la Merced Hoz, September 27, 1837, Libro de Bautismo, Folio 220, no 1297, 25 de Marzo de 1861, Libro de Matrimonios, Folio 55, no. 162, Guadalupe Parish, Havana, Cuba, in "Genealogía del apellido Pollo [sic], y demás."

10. Schedules of the U. S. federal censuses of 1870 and 1880, Monroe County, Florida; "Baptismal Index," Monroe County Public Library, Key West, Florida. Poyo's children who were born after Francisco do not appear in 1880 census.

11. "Ibrahim Poyo," *La Voz de la Patria*, September 15, 1876; "Gratitud," *El Yara*, April 11, 1885; Diddle, "The History of Civilian Medical Care in Key West," 383–389.

12. "Gacetilla," *El Yara*, July 3, 1886.

13. "Marriage Index," Monroe County Public Library, Key West, Florida.

14. "Key West," *New York Times*, January 11, 1874; "Florida: Key West Sketches," *New York Times*, January 19, 1874.

15. Browne, *Key West*, 81.

16. "Patria adoptiva," *El Yara*, May 8, 1886.

17. Browne, *Key West*, 7–20.

18. Ibid., 169–173; Poyo, "Cuban Emigré Communities," 207–208.

19. Westfall, *Key West*, 20–27.

20. Poyo, "Cuban Émigré Communities," 207–210.

21. Advertisements in *El Yara*, *La Propaganda*, *El Pueblo*, and *El Cubano*, 1885–1890.

22. "Florida: A Cuban City in the United States," *New York Herald-Tribune*, May 15, 1891.

23. Castellanos, *Motivos de Cayo Hueso*, 142–144.

24. Naturalizations, Southern District of Florida, Record Group 21, National Archives at Atlanta, Atlanta, Georgia.

25. Rodríguez, *The Case of the Arrest, Trial, and Sentence . . . of Julio Sanguily*.

26. Tinajero, *El Lector*, 15–20.

27. Gálvez, *Tampa*, 165–199.

28. Figueredo, *José Dolores Poyo*, 11.

29. Browne, *Key West*, 118.

30. "Key West," *New York Times*, January 11, 1874.

31. Tinajero, *El Lector*, 18–20.

32. "Lectura en los talleres," *El Yara*, April 11, 1885.

33. Del Rio, *Yo fuí uno de los fundadores de Ybor City*, 10.

34. Castellanos, *Motivos de Cayo Hueso*, 221.
35. Alpízar Poyo, *Cayo Hueso y la Independencia de Cuba*, 8.
36. In 1982 Luis Alpízar Leal told me the story of Orozco's flight as recounted in family tradition. See Armas, *Combate*.
37. "Nuestra suspención," *El Yara*, January 16, 1892; Pedro Solís to Encargado de Negocios, January 19, 1892, Leg. 750, Caja 54/7992, Fondo 26.1, Grupo 10, AGA.
38. Castellanos, *Motivos de Cayo Hueso*, 302.
39. "Florida: A Cuban City in the United States," *New York Herald-Tribune*, May 15, 1891.
40. Alpízar Poyo, *Cayo Hueso y José Dolores Poyo*, 66.
41. José D. Poyo to Ernesto Bavastro, March 29, 1881. See also José D. Poyo to Ernesto Bavastro, September 9, 1882, photocopies from the collection of Fred Salinero, Key West, Florida.
42. José D. Poyo to Antonio Maceo, July 12, 1881, in Llaverías, *Papeles de Maceo*, 1:268, 284, 287.
43. "Estrada," *El Yara*, March 17, 1888.
44. "Despedida," *Patria*, August 25, 1897.
45. Gómez, *Album del Estado Mayor*, 72.
46. Casasús, *La emigración cubana*, 149; Castellanos, *Motivos de Cayo Hueso*, 155–156; Deulofeu, *Héroes del destierro*, 26–27.
47. Alpízar Poyo, *Cayo Hueso y José Dolores Poyo*, 43–44; Emilia Casanova de Villaverde to José D. Poyo, December 19, 1874, in Villaverde, *Apuntes biográficos*, 205–207; Rosario Lamadriz and Ernestina Agüero to Calixto García, December 16, 1878, in Rodríguez y Colina, *Documentos para servir la historia de la Guerra Chiquita*, 1:115–116; Rosario Lamadriz and Celia Poyo to Calixto García, May 17, 1879, in Rodríguez y Colina, *Documentos para servir la historia de la Guerra Chiquita*, 2:79; Celia Poyo and Mercedes García to Calixto García, July 2, 1879, in ibid., 141.
48. Benjamín Pérez to Miguel de Aldama, February 14, 1876, Donativos y Remisiones, Leg. 161, no. 70-17, Archivo Nacional de Cuba (hereafter ANC), Havana, Cuba.
49. "Nomina de ciudadanos de color" and "Nomina de personas que asistieron a la mesa," Colección Manuscrito Ponce, 190–191, Colección Cubana, Biblioteca Nacional "José Martí," (hereafter BNJM), Havana, Cuba.
50. Morúa Delgado, *Jenios olvidados*; Serra, *Ensayos políticos*; Deschamps, *Rafael Serra y Montalvo*.
51. Morúa Delgado, *Obras completas*, vol. 3.
52. Morúa Delgado, *Jenios olvidados*, 25; Deulofeu, *Héroes del destierro*, 32.
53. "Nuestras sociedades," *El Pueblo*, April 7, 1888.
54. Castellanos, *Motivos de Cayo Hueso*, 237–242.
55. Ibid.
56. Gálvez, *Tampa*, 148–150.
57. Figueredo, *José Dolores Poyo*, 11.
58. Valdés Domínguez, *Tragedy in Havana*.

59. Castellanos, *Motivos de Cayo Hueso*, 216–220.
60. Deulofeu, *Héroes del destierro*, 29.
61. Pérez, *To Die in Cuba*, 84.
62. Deulofeu, *Martí: Cayo Hueso y Tampa*, 40–41.
63. Casasús, *La emigración cubana*, 150.
64. Castellanos, *Motivos de Cayo Hueso*, 166–167.
65. "San Carlos," *El Yara*, September 8, 1883.
66. Castellanos, *Misión a Cuba*, 59–62.
67. Deulofeu, *Héroes del destierro*, 12–13; Casasús, *La emigración cubana*, 417–418.
68. Castellanos, *Motivos de Cayo Hueso*, 112–118.
69. "San Carlos," *La Propaganda*, November 21, 1888.
70. Henríquez Ureña, *Eugenio María de Hostos*, 13–15.
71. Ibid., 471–475.
72. "Cayo Hueso," *El Yara*, March 17, 1888.

Chapter 2. Nationalism

1. Guerra, *Guerra de los 10 Años*, 2:17; Céspedes, *Quesada y Loynaz*, 101.
2. Casasús, *La emigración cubana*, 75–76.
3. Céspedes, *Quesada y Loynaz*, 73–94.
4. Morales, *Iniciadores y primeros mártires*, 381.
5. Brinton, *The Anatomy of Revolution*, 270.
6. De la Cova. "Filibusters and Freemasons," 100–120.
7. Torres-Cuevas, *Historia de la masonería cubana*, 36–127; Ponte Domínguez, *El delito de francmasonería en Cuba*, 150–187.
8. Castellanos, *Motivos de Cayo Hueso*, 159; Browne, *Key West*, 138; Figueredo, *José Dolores Poyo*, 10–11.
9. Rodríguez, *Félix Varela*.
10. "De Tallahassee," *El Yara*, May 22, 1889.
11. Payne, *A History of Spain and Portugal*, 2:422–423.
12. "Decídase Cuba," *El Yara*, April 17, 1886.
13. Benjamin, *The Atlantic World*, 589–595.
14. "Decídase Cuba," *El Yara*, April 17, 1886.
15. Ibid.
16. Payne, *A History of Spain and Portugal*, 2:424–425.
17. Rodríguez, *Félix Varela*, 195–244.
18. Guerra, *Historia de la nación cubana*, 3:139–151.
19. "Decídase Cuba," *El Yara*, April 17, 1886; Guerra, *Historia de la nación cubana*, 6:3–12.
20. "La guerra á muerte," *El Yara*, April 11, 1885; "La honra nacional," *El Yara*, February 13, 1886.
21. Pérez, *Lords of the Mountain*, 10–12.

22. "Conflicto entre dos sociedades," *El Yara*, April 18, 1885; "Oído a la caja," *El Yara*, February 6, 1886.

23. "Decídase Cuba," *El Yara*, April 17, 1886.

24. "El clericalismo en España," *El Yara*, February 6, 1886.

25. Eastman, *Preaching Spanish Nationalism*, 92–93.

26. Martínez-Fernández, *Protestantism and Political Conflicts*, 135; Castellanos, *Motivos de Cayo Hueso*, 247; Deulofeu, *Héroes del destierro*, 37, 96–103.

27. "Los partidos políticos en Cuba," *El Yara*, April 23, 1881; "La Independencia," *El Yara*, July 3, 1886.

28. "Derecho a la vida," *El Yara*, April 11, 1885.

29. "Ser patriota," *El Yara*, November 15, 1886.

30. Deulofeu, *Héroes del destierro*, 29–30.

31. "Antes y después," *El Yara*, March 29, 1890; Chaffin, *Fatal Glory*.

32. "Nuestro credo político," *La Voz de la Patria*, October 6, 1876; J.D Poyo to editor, *La Voz de la Patria*, November 1, 1876; Henríquez Ureña, *Eugenio María de Hostos*, 15–16.

33. Poyo, "With All, and for the Good of All," 1–34.

34. Lazo, *Writing to Cuba*, 94–95.

35. "La Sociedad Republicana de Cuba y Puerto Rico," *La Voz de América*, September 20, 1866; ibid., September 30 1866; Poyo, "With All, and for the Good of All," 35–51; Lazo, *Writing to Cuba*, 57–58.

36. Rodríguez, *Estudio histórico*; Poyo, "With All, and for the Good of All," 30–33; "Sociedad de Artesanos Cubanos," *El Demócrata*, September 9, 1870; "Reglamento: Sociedad de Artesanos Cubanos," *El Demócrata*, September 21, 1870; "Sociedad Artesanos," *El Demócrata*, October 26, 1870; "Elecciones: Sociedad de Artesanos Cubanos," *El Demócrata*, November 1, 1870; "La Socidedad de Artesanos Cubanos de N.Y.," *El Demócrata*, November 2, 1870; Andreu Iglesias, *Memorias de Bernardo Vega*, 92–93; Villaverde, "La revolución de Cuba vista desde New York"; Horrego Estuch, *Emilia Casanova*.

37. Céspedes, *Quesada y Loynaz*, 101; Camacho, *Aguilera, el percursor sin gloria*, 191; Antonio Rios to Hilario Cisneros, February 16, 1874, described in Plasencia, *Bibliografía de la Guerra de los Diez Años*, 199.

38. Casasús, *La emigración cubana*, 127–139.

39. Céspedes' removal from office was a complex matter that involved more than exile politics. Plasencia, "La destitución del Presidente Céspedes," 75–88; Salvador Cisneros to C. Director del Republicano de Cayo Hueso, November 1, 1873 and José D. Poyo to Sr. Carlos del Castillo, January 7, 1874, both in Alpízar Poyo, *Cayo Hueso y José Dolores Poyo*, 53–54.

40. Federico Horstman to Miguel de Aldama, January 20, 1874, Donativos y Remisiones, Leg. 157, no. 49-53, ANC.

41. "Sociedad Independencia de Cuba: Cayo Hueso," *El Republicano*, January 8, 1876; Federico de Armas to Hilario Cisneros, December 15, 1874 and Juan Henríquez to *El*

Correo de New York, March 6, 1875, both described in Plasencia, *Bibliografía de la Guerra de los Diez Años*, 190–191; Antonio Rios, Federico de Armas, and Juan de la Guardia to Hilario Cisneros, February 16, 1875 and Federico Horstman to Miguel de Aldama, May 20, 1875, both in Donativos y Remisiones, Leg. 157, no. 49-37, ANC.

42. Enrique Parodi to Miguel de Aldama, May 12, 1875, Donativos y Remisiones, Leg. 161, no. 69-27, ANC.

43. "Política y trabajo," *El Yara*, November 26, 1887.

44. Ibid.

45. "La insurreccion de Cuba," *La Voz de América*, March 10, 1866; "La revolución de Cuba. Otra faz del movimiento libertad de los negros," *La Voz de América*, April 11, 1866; "La esclavitud de los negros," *La Voz de América*, June 21, 1866; "Colaboración" and "A los cubanos," *La Voz de América*, January 20, 1867.

46. Ferrer, *Insurgent Cuba*, 76–80.

47. Portuondo, *Francisco Vicente Aguilera: Epistolario*, 142–145.

48. Poyo, "Cuban Revolutionaries," 407–422; Alvarez Estevez, *La emigración cubana en Estados Unidos*.

49. "Cayo Hueso," *La Voz de la Patria*, April 21, 1876; "Cayo Hueso," *La Voz de la Patria*, June 2, 1876; "Quedo constituida la Sociedad Constitución de Guáimaro," *La Voz de la Patria*, June 9, 1876; "Cayo Hueso," *La Voz de la Patria*, June 23, 1876; "Sociedad Independencia de Cuba de Cayo Hueso," *El Republicano*, January 8, 1876.

50. "Derecho de las minorías," *La Voz de la Patria*, August 4, 1876.

51. Scott, *Slave Emancipation in Cuba*, 63–70, 127–130.

52. "Otra vez 'El Popular,'" *El Yara*, February 6, 1886; "Hombres de color, oid," ibid., May 15, 1886.

53. Ferrer, *Insurgent Cuba*, 128–136.

54. Casanovas, *Bread, or Bullets*, 71–96.

55. Guerra, *Historia de la nación cubana*, 7:251.

56. "A los tabaqueros," *La Voz de América*, August 10, 1866.

57. "A los tabaqueros," *La Voz de América*, August 30, 1866.

58. "Revolución y obreros habaneros," *El Yara*, October 27, 1883.

59. "Los donantes de París," *El Yara*, December 18, 1886.

60. Guerra, *Historia de la nación cubana*, 6:24–44.

61. "Zambrana," *El Yara*, December 16, 1888.

62. "Conservadores y autonomistas," *El Yara*, January 7, 1888.

63. "Una lección de autonomía," *El Yara*, December 18, 1886.

64. "Otra vez 'El Popular,'" *El Yara*, February 6, 1886.

65. "Punto final," *El Yara*, February 13, 1886; "Una lección de autonomía," *El Yara*, December 18, 1886.

66. "La protesta contra el despotismo," *El Yara*, February 20, 1886.

67. "La exposición de los llorones," *El Yara*, September 8, 1883.

68. "Punto final," *El Yara*, February 13, 1886.

69. "No hay otro camino," *El Yara*, December 11, 1880.

Chapter 3. Revolution

1. J. J. de Empuranza to Capitán General de la Isla de Cuba, March 12, 1878, *Boletín del Archivo Nacional* 8, no. 3 (May–June 1909): 98; Carlos M. de Céspedes and José D. Poyo to Comité Revolucionario de New York, April 6, 1878, in Rodríguez y Colina, *Documentos para servir la historia de la Guerra Chiquita*, 1:3–4.
2. Ferrer, *Insurgent Cuba*, 54–69.
3. José D. Poyo to Antonio Maceo, April 1878, Caja 476, no. 54, Donativos y Remisiones, ANC; Carlos M. de Céspedes and José D. Poyo to Presidente del Comité Revolucionario de New York, April 6, 1878, in Rodríguez y Colina, *Documentos para servir la historia de la Guerra Chiquita*, 1:7.
4. Franco, *Antonio Maceo: Apuntes*, 1:157.
5. "En nuestro puesto," *El Yara*, September 26, 1886.
6. Castellanos, *Misión a Cuba*, 58.
7. "La Revolución se impone," *El Yara*, November 26, 1887.
8. "Despierta, pueblo," *El Yara*, October 29, 1881.
9. "Acción, no expectación," *El Yara*, September 29, 1883.
10. Poyo, "Key West and the Cuban Ten Years War," 289–307.
11. Alpízar Poyo, *Cayo Hueso y José Dolores Poyo*, 57–61.
12. García del Pino, *Leoncio Prado*, 29–48; "La captura del Moctezuma," 90–98.
13. José D. Poyo to Franciso V. Aguilera, January 8, 1877, Aguilera Rojas, *Francisco Vicente Aguilera*, 2:369–379.
14. Leoncio Prado to José D. Poyo, February 11, 1878, and José D. Poyo to Leoncio Prado, February 11, 1878, both in Alpízar Poyo, *Cayo Hueso y José Dolores Poyo*, 56–57; J. J. de Empuranza to Capitán General de la Isla de Cuba, February 26, 1878, *Boletín del Archivo Nacional* 8:3 (May–Junio 1909): 96.
15. García del Pino, *Leoncio Prado*, 50; Manuel Yrigoyen, Ministerio de Relaciones Exteriores, Peru, to Señor Ministro de Relaciones Exteriores, Estados Unidos, October 22, 1878, in *Notes from the Peruvian Legation in the United States to the Department of State, 1827–1906*, reel 4.
16. Trujillo, *Album de El Porvenir*, 1:95–97; Casusús, *La emigración cubana*, 421.
17. Casasús, *La emigración cubana*, 402.
18. "La Razón de Estado," *El Yara*, May 17, 1884.
19. Ibid.
20. "Recursos," *El Yara*, January 2, 1886.
21. Ferrer, *Insurgent Cuba*, 93–111; Pérez, *Lords of the Mountain*, 3–10.
22. Schwartz, *Lawless Liberators*, 46–49.
23. "Nuestras ventajas," *El Yara*, February 28, 1884.
24. Stebbins, *City of Intrigue*, 130, 134.
25. Ibid., 136.
26. "Al Ciudadano General Castillo," *El Ubiquitario*, November 12, 1883.
27. Ibid.
28. Stebbins, *City of Intrigue*, 130.

29. Augusto Bermúdez to Ministro de Estado, May 27, 1884, H1868, Archivo del Ministerio de Asuntos Exteriores (hereafter AMAE), Madrid, Spain; Stebbins, *City of Intrigue*, 132.

30. Anonymous letter, August 29, 1883, and Bryant to Enrique Dupuy de Lome, October 23, 1883, both in Leg. 767, Caja 54/7965, Fondo 26.1, Grupo 10, AGA.

31. Miguel Suárez to Ministro de España, March 1, 1884, Leg. 442, Caja 54/7883, Fondo 26.1, Grupo 10, AGA.

32. Stebbins, *City of Intrigue*, 131.

33. Miguel Suárez to Ministro de España, March 1, 1884, Leg. 442, Caja 54/7883, Fondo 26.1, Grupo 10, AGA.

34. Maceo, *Papeles de Maceo*, 1:336.

35. "Manifiesto del Comité Revolucionario Cubano," in Rodríguez y Colina, *Documentos para servir la historia de la Guerra Chiquita*, 1:42–44.

36. Martín Herrera and José D. Poyo to Calixto García, December 7, 1878, in Rodríguez y Colina, *Documentos para servir la historia de la Guerra Chiquita*, 1:151; José D. Poyo and Martín Herrera to Presidente del Club Central, January 31, 1878, in ibid., 155; "Nomina de socios fundadores, Club R. Cubano, No. 25," January 31, 1878, in ibid., 159–160.

37. Ferrer, *Insurgent Cuba*, 70–89; Franco, *Antonio Maceo*, 1:176–196.

38. Casasús, *Calixto García*, 166–170, 177.

39. Carlos Roloff to Serafín Sánchez, December 23, 1879, in Rodríguez y Colina, *Documentos para servir la historia de la Guerra Chiquita*, 3:124; José D. Poyo to Presidente del Comité Revolucionario Cubano, March 14, 1880, in ibid., 124.

40. Olimpo to Presidente del Comité, January 8, 1880, in ibid., 82–83; Olimpo to Presidente del Comité, February 26, 1880, in ibid., 118; Cuba and Machete to Comité Revolucionario Cubano, March 5, 1880, in ibid., 121; Franco, *Antonio Maceo*, 1:208.

41. Franco, *Antonio Maceo*, 1:207; Casasús, *Calixto García*, 166–170, 177; Guerra, *Historia de la nación cubana*, 5:356.

42. Alpízar Poyo, *Cayo Hueso y José Dolores Poyo*, 59–60.

43. Sánchez, *Héroes humildes*, 91.

44. Casasús, *La emigración cubana*, 184; José D. Poyo to Enrique Bavastro, March 19, 1883, photocopy from the collection of Consuelo E. Stebbins.

45. F. García to Miguel Suárez, February 25, 1883, Leg. 676, Caja 54/7965, Fondo 26.1, Grupo 10, AGA; Stebbins, *City of Intrigue*, 111.

46. Trujillo, *Apuntes históricos*, 7–10; Casasús, *La emigración cubana*, 184–185, 376, 392–393; Bryant to Enrique Dupuy de Lome, August 19, 1883, Leg. 676, Caja 54/7965, Fondo 26.1, Grupo 10, AGA.

47. "La Verdad," *El Yara*, September 8, 1883; Bryant to Enrique Dupuy de Lome, September 27, 1883, Leg. 676, Caja 54/7965, Fondo 26.1, Grupo 10, AGA; Casasús, *La emigración cubana*, 184–185.

48. Ramón Bonachea to Antonio Maceo, August 1 and September 13, 1883, Leg. 621, no. 12, Donativos y Remisiones, ANC; Antonio Maceo to Fernando Figueredo,

December 16, 1883, in Maceo, *Papeles de Maceo*, 1:85–87; Máximo Gómez to various recipients in Key West and New Orleans, August–September 1884, Archivo Máximo Gómez, no. 8, Leg. 81, ANC.

49. "La Verdad," *El Yara*, September 8, 1883; "Proclama," *El Yara*, August 18, 1883; José D. Poyo to Ramón L. Bonachea, August 22, 1883, in Casasús, *Ramón Leocadio Bonachea*, 250–251; Bryant to Enrique Dupuy de Lome, September 15, 1883, Leg. 676, Caja 54/7965, Fondo 26.1, Grupo 10, AGA.

50. Ballesteros, "Carlos Aguero."

51. "Noticias importantes de Cuba: Llegada del General Aguero," *El Yara*, November 17, 1883.

52. Bryant to Enrique Dupuy de Lome, December 1, 11, and 17, 1883, Leg. 676, Caja 54/7965, Fondo 26.1, Grupo 10, AGA; Stebbins, *City of Intrigue*, 132; Casasús, *Bonachea*, 194.

53. Miguel Suárez to Ministro de España, March 1, 1884, Leg. 442, Caja 54/7883, Fondo 26.1, Grupo 10, AGA; Casasús, *La emigración cubana*, 406.

54. Schwartz, *Lawless Liberators*, 105.

55. Castellanos, *Motivos de Cayo Hueso*, 229–230; Stebbins, *City of Intrigue*, 99–100, 215–216; Casasús, *La emigración cubana*, 190.

56. José D. Poyo to Ramón Bonachea, August 22, 1883 in Casasús, *Bonachea*, 250–251; ibid., 152.

57. Franco, *Antonio Maceo*, 1:262.

58. Infiesta, *Máximo Gómez*, 221–223; Franco, *Ruta de Antonio Maceo*, 93–107; Gómez, *Diario de campaña*, 177–178.

59. Infiesta, *Máximo Gómez*, 221–223.

60. "10 de Abril de 1868," *El Yara*, April 11, 1885.

61. Alpízar Poyo, *Cayo Hueso y José Dolores Poyo*, 71–72; Gómez, *Diario de campaña*, 177–181; Stebbins, *City of Intrigue*, 100–101.

62. Laura Lomas, *Translating Empire*, 86–129.

63. José Martí to Antonio Maceo July 20, 1882, in Martí, *Epistolario*, 1:234–236; José Martí to Máximo Gómez, in ibid., 236–240; Casasús, *Bonachea*, 177.

64. Anonymous letter, October 11, 1883, Leg. 676, Caja 54/7965, Fondo 26.1, Grupo 10, AGA. Martí is quoted as follows: "*Los cubanos ibamos al mismo fin, aunque por diferente camino—que unos creían que debían levantarse la casa sin tener el arma preparada y otros con mas juicio (los liberales) que no se debiera levantar la casa hasta no tener el arma y tenerla cargada y preparada. En su oportunidad y sin que sea muy largo plazo, se verá el trabajo de los ultimos.*"

65. Guerra, *Historia de la nación cubana*, 5:362–364; Gómez, *Diario de campaña*, 180–182.

66. José Francisco Lamadriz to Manuel de la Cruz Beraza, April 4, 1885, Caja 553, no. 43, Donativos y Remisiones, ANC.

67. Morúa Delgado, *Obras completas*, 3:167–168; "Se imparta la revolución," *La República*, June 13, 1885; "En nuestro puesto," *La República*, June 20, 1885.

68. Máximo Gómez to Juan Arnao, December 29, 1884, Leg. 81, no. 8, Archivo Máximo Gómez, ANC.

69. "Los Bertoldos de la revolución," *El Yara*, February 13, 1886.

70. "Funesta herencia," *El Yara*, May 15, 1886.

71. Trujillo, *Apuntes históricos*, 8–19; "Dictador o dictadura," *El Avisador Cubano*, July 1, 1885; "De donde venimos y a donde vamos," *Avisador Cubano*, July 15, 1885.

72. Martí, *Obras completas*, 4:222–223.

73. Trujillo, *Apuntes históricos*, 25.

74. Anonymous letter, October 11, 1883, Leg. 676, Caja 54/7965, Fondo 26.1, Grupo 10, AGA.

75. Lizaso, *José Martí: Martyr*, 198.

76. Martí, *Obras completas*, 4:222–223.

77. *El Avisador Cubano*, "A El Pueblo," August 1, 1888; José Martí to Director de El Pueblo, October 26, 1887, in Martí, *Epistolario*, 1:420–421.

78. Máximo Gómez to José D. Poyo, January 19, 1885, Leg. 81, no. 8, Archivo Máximo Gómez, ANC; José Francisco Lamadriz to Manuel de la Cruz Beraza, April 4, 1885, Leg. 553, no. 43, Donativos y Remisiones, ANC; "Circular a los clubs y comités revolucionarios cubanos," March 18, 1885, Leg. 81, no. 8, Archivo Máximo Gómez, ANC; "La junta magna," *La República*, June 20, 1885.

79. Carbonell, *El General Ramón Leocadio Bonachea*, 28.

80. Máximo Gómez to Director del El Yara, March 18, 1885, in Rodríguez de la O, *Máximo Gómez, una vida extraordinaria*, 22–23; *Key of the Gulf* article quoted in *The Weekly Floridian*, August 27, 1885.

81. Castellanos, *Motivos de Cayo Hueso*, 229–230; Schwartz, *Lawless Liberators*, 105.

82. Casasús, *La emigración cubana*, 190–191; "Mourning for Aguero," *New York Herald*, March 23, 1885; Máximo Gómez to José D. Poyo, April 30, 1885, C. M. Morales, T. 37, no. 4, Colección Cubana, BNJM; Guerra, *Historia de la nación cubana*, 5:360–361.

83. Cordoví, *Máximo Gómez*, 85–88.

84. Castellanos, *Motivos de Cayo Hueso*, 231–232; Hernández, *Maceo*, 154–156; Stebbins, *City of Intrigue* 114–118; "Mysterious Filibusters," *New York Herald*, August 29, 1885.

85. "Ultima hora," *El Yara*, February 6, 1886; Franco, *Antonio Maceo*, 1:291–303; Cordoví, *Máximo Gómez*, 88–91.

86. "Conflagración," *El Yara* (suplemento), March 31, 1886; "Key West in Flames," *The Macon Telegraph*, March 31, 1886; Westfall, *Key West*, 38–39;

87. Stebbins, *City of Intrigue*, 79–83.

88. "Habla El General Gómez," *El Yara*, May 8, 1896.

89. Joaquín M. Torroja to Enviado Extraordinario, April 28, 1886, Leg. 771, Caja 54/7995, Fondo 26.1, Grupo 10, AGA; Franco, *Antonio Maceo*, 1:291–320.

Chapter 4. Preservation

1. Pérez, *Lords of the Mountain*, 10–12; Ferrer, *Insurgent Cuba*, 94–98.

2. "Españolización imposible," *El Yara*, December 16, 1888.

3. "Key West," *New York Times*, January 11, 1874; "El socialismo y La Internacional" and "Alto," *El Republicano*, October 31, 1874.

4. Juan María Reyes to Hilario Cisneros, August 19, 1875, and González Mendoza to Hilario Cisneros, July 20, 1875, described in Plasencia, *Bibliografía de la Guerra de los Diez Años*, 191; "To the Americans of Key West," *El Republicano*, July 13, 1875; "La huelga de Cayo Hueso," *La Independencia*, July 29, 1875; "Corresponsal," *La Independencia*, August 26, 1876; "Strike among the Cigar Makers," *The Weekly Floridian*, August 17, 1875; "Cuban Cigar Makers," *The Weekly Floridian*, August 24, 1875; Alvarez Estevez, *La emigración cubana*, 100–106.

5. José D. Poyo to José F. Lamadriz, April 9, 1878, in Rodríguez y Colina, *Documentos para server la historia de la Guerra Chiquita*, 1:7; José F. Lamadriz to Leandro Rodríguez, May 18, 1880, in Rodríguez y Colina, *Documentos para server la historia de la Guerra Chiquita*, 3:154; "La Unión de Tabaqueros," *Tobacco Leaf*, November 8, 1879; "A Union of Tobacco Workers," *Cigar Makers' Official Journal*, December 10, 1879. Materials from *Tobacco Leaf* in this book are courtesy of L. Glenn Westfall.

6. Máximo Gómez to Carlos Recio, April 23, 1885, Leg. 81, no. 8, Archivo Maximo Gómez, ANC; "Key West News," *Tobacco Leaf*, July 11, 1885; "Key West News," *Tobacco Leaf*, September 12, 1885; Westfall, *Key West*, 35–38.

7. "Errores," *El Yara*, November 7, 1885, in Cordoví, *Máximo Gómez*, 92; Joaquín M. Torroja to Enviado Extraordinario, February 17, 1886, Leg. 771, Caja 54/7995, Fondo 26.1, Grupo 10, AGA.

8. Fink, *Workingman's Democracy*.

9. "Alerta," *El Ubiquitario*, November 12, 1883.

10. "El progreso y nosotros," *El Yara*, October 23, 1886.

11. "Alerta," *El Ubiquitario*, November 12, 1883.

12. "La sinrazón de 'La Razón,'" *El Yara*, December 11, 1880.

13. Castillo, *Autobiografía del General Rogelio Castillo*, 86-87

14. Castellanos, *Misión a Cuba*, 114–115; Stebbins, *City of Intrigue*, 155–156.

15. "El trabajo y la política," *The Equator/El Ecuador*, February 19, 1886.

16. Joaquín M. Torroja to Enviado Extraordinario, May 8, 1886, Leg. 771, Caja 54/7995, Fondo 26.1, Grupo 10, AGA.

17. Casanovas, *Bread, or Bullets*, 168–169.

18. Instituto de Historia, *Carlos Baliño*, 9–11.

19. C. B. Pendleton to Hon. T. V. Powderly, May 25, 1886, Terence Vincent Powderly Collection, Department of Archives, Manuscripts, and Museum Collections, Mullen Library, Catholic University of America, Washington, D.C.; Castellanos, *Motivos de Cayo Hueso*, 225.

20. "Manifestación," *La Propaganda*, November 21, 1886; "Avancemos," *The Equator/El Ecuador*, July 6, 1886.

21. "Todos en su puesto," *El Yara*, April 17, 1886; "Pátria adoptiva," *El Yara*, May 8, 1886.

22. "Todos en su puesto," *El Yara*, April 17, 1886.
23. "Se acerca la hora," *El Yara*, May 29, 1886.
24. "Manos a la obra," *El Yara*, May 22, 1886.
25. Issues of *El Yara*, May–December 1886.
26. Joaquín M. Torroja to Enviado Extraordinario, September 17, 1886, Leg. 802, Caja 54/8008, Fondo 26.1, Grupo 10, AGA.
27. "Ecos de Ibor City" and "En nuestro puesto," *El Yara*, September 26, 1886.
28. "La Velada," *El Yara*, December 6, 1886.
29. "Bien" and "Correspondencia," *El Yara*, May 29, 1886.
30. "En nuestro puesto," *El Yara*, September 26, 1886.
31. "El progreso y nosotros," *El Yara*, October 23, 1886.
32. "Como 30!," *El Yara*, November 15, 1886.
33. Joaquín M. Torroja to Enviado Extraordinario, November 18, 22, 1886, Leg. 802, Caja 54/8008, Fondo 26.1, Grupo 10, AGA.
34. "A Dios rogando," *El Yara*, December 6, 1886; Delgado is quoted in Ingalls, *Urban Vigilantes in the New South*, Tampa, 35–36.
35. "La cuestión patria," *La Propaganda*, December 19, 1886; "La Federación Cubana," *El Pueblo*, December 18, 1886; Morúa Delgado, *Obras completas*, 3:110–111, 134–137, 147–151.
36. "Extraordinario," *El Yara*, January 27, 1887; "Carta de Ybor City," *La Propaganda*, January 30, 1887; Ingalls, *Urban Vigilantes*, 36–37; *El Productor*, April 20, 1890; Deulofeu, *Martí: Cayo Hueso y Tampa*, 23.
37. Horrego, *Martín Morúa Delgado*, 80; Stebbins, *City of Intrigue*, 201; "Lo de Ybor City," *El Pueblo*, January 29, 1887.
38. "Los sucesos," *El Yara*, January 27, 1887; "Carta de Ybor City," *La Propaganda*, January 30, 1887; "Lo de Ybor City," *El Pueblo*, January 29, 1887; Joaquín M. Torrado to Ministro de Estado, February 8 and 11, 1887, H1868, AMAE; Stebbins, *City of Intrigue*, 199–208.
39. Fernández, *Cuban Anarchism*, 20–21; Casanovas, *Bread, or Bullets*, 146–177.
40. "El socialismo y La Internacional," *El Republicano*, October 3, 1874; Anonymous to Hilario Cisneros, November 10, 1874, described in Plasencia, *Bibliografía de la Guerra de los Diez Años*, 190; Casanovas, *Bread, or Bullets*, 112–113.
41. "To Be or Not to Be," *El Productor*, July 28, 1889; Morúa Delgado, *Obras Completas*, 3:131; Partido Comunista de Cuba, *Carlos Baliño*, 41–44.
42. "Carta de Cayo Hueso," *El Productor*, November 22, 1888; "Carta de Cayo Hueso," *El Productor*, November 28, 1888; "Carta de Cayo Hueso," *El Productor*, April 18, 1889.
43. "La patria y los obreros," *El Productor*, May 12, 1889, in Plasencia, *Enrique Roig San Martín*, 459–461.
44. "Carta de Cayo Hueso," *El Productor*, June 8, 1889.
45. "Carta de Cayo Hueso," *El Productor*, November 22, 1888; "Carta de Cayo Hueso," *El Productor*, December 12, 1888.

46. Joaquín M. Torroja to Enviado Extraordinario, March 2, 1888, Leg. 714, Caja 54/7984, Fondo 26.1, Grupo 10, AGA; Stebbins, *City of Intrigue*, 121, 125, 228.

47. "Del Pino Bros. Factory," *Tobacco Leaf*, February 27, 1889; "Key West, Florida," *Tobacco Leaf*, July 11, 1889; "Review of the Key West Strike," *Tobacco Leaf*, September 27, 1889; "Key West News," *Tobacco Leaf*, October 7, 1889; "Key West Cigar Strikers," *Tobacco Leaf*, October 23, 1889.

48. "Contesta," *El Yara*, September 13, 1889.

49. Ibid.

50. "Carta de Cayo Hueso," *El Productor*, October 20, 1889.

51. "Consideraciones," *El Yara*, November 2, 1889.

52. "Review of the Key West Strike," *Tobacco Leaf*, September 27, 1889; "Key West Cigar Strikers," *Tobacco Leaf*, October 23, 1889; ; Luis Marinas to Enviado Extraordinario, November 20, 1889, Leg. 721, Caja 54/7986, Fondo 26.1, Grupo 10, AGA; Stebbins, *City of Intrigue*, 86–88.

53. "Carta de Cayo Hueso," *El Productor*, April 18, 1889; "Carta de Cayo Hueso," *El Productor*, May 2, 1889; "Carta de Cayo Hueso," *El Productor*, June 2, 1889.

54. "Carta de Cayo Hueso," *El Español*, December 21, 1889 in newspaper clippings, January 1–14, 1890, Leg., no. 262, no. 2, Asuntos Políticos, ANC.

55. "Carta de Cayo Hueso," *El Productor*, December 19, 1889.

56. José D. Poyo to Máximo Gómez, December 28, 1889, Leg. 4, no. 123, Archivo Máximo Gómez, ANC.

57. Westfall, *Key West*, 48–49.

58. "Triunfo completo," *El Productor*, January 9, 1890; "Carta de Cayo Hueso," *El Productor*, January 12, 1890; "The Key West Strike Practically Ended," *The Tobacco Leaf*, January 8, 1890.

59. "Comité de Medios y Arbitrios de Key West," *El Productor*, January 23, 1890.

60. "Fatalidades históricas," *El Productor*, February 2, 1890.

61. "Como viene," *El Productor*, February 13, 1890; "Carta de Cayo Hueso," *El Español*, in newspaper clippings, February 4–March 6, 1890, Leg. 262, Signatura 4, Asuntos Políticos, ANC.

62. "Carta de Cayo Hueso," *El Productor*, January 30, 1890; "Obreros de Cayo Hueso," *El Productor*, March 20, 1890; Stebbins, *City of Intrigue*, 88.

63. "Aun no es tiempo," *El Yara*, March 13, 1890; Círculo de Trabajadores de Key West, "Al Pueblo Trabajador," in Joaquín M. Torroja to Enviado Extraordinario, March 20, 1890, Leg. 731, Caja 54/7988, Fondo 26.1, Grupo 10, AGA.

64. Joan Casanovas, *Bread, or Bullets*, 203–214.

Chapter 5. Persistence

1. Joaquín M. Torroja to Ministro de Estado, August 22 and September 14, 1887, H1868, AMAE; "Manifiesto," *Las Novedades*, November 8, 1888; "Key West Excited," *The Wheeling Register*, September 17, 1887; "Bravery of an Insurgent," *The New Haven Register*, October 24, 1887.

2. "Carta de Cayo Hueso," *Las Novedades*, May 17, 1888.
3. Pérez, *Lords of the Mountain*, 23, 29.
4. Schwartz, *Lawless Liberators*, 105–106; Pérez, *Lords of the Mountain*, 1–42; Ballesteros, "Carlos Aguero."
5. Joaquín M. Torroja to Enviado Extraordinario, March 6 and May 8, 1886, Leg. 771, Caja 54/7995, Fondo 26.1, Grupo 10, AGA; Schwartz, *Lawless Liberators*, 117; Deulofeu, *Héroes del destierro*, 33.
6. Joaquín M. Torroja to Ministro de Estado, July 16, 1887, H1868, AMAE.
7. Trujillo, *Album de El Porvenir*, 1:91.
8. Stebbins, *City of Intrigue*, 102; Schwartz, *Lawless Liberators*, 115; Joaquín M. Torroja to Enviado Extraordinario, [May 10, 1886], Leg. 771, Caja 54/7995, Fondo 26.1, Grupo 10, AGA.
9. Stebbins, *City of Intrigue*, 199–202.
10. "Manifiesto," *Las Novedades*, November 8, 1888.
11. "Beribén Joined by 400 Men," *New York Herald-Tribune*, September 9, 1887.
12. Castellanos, *Misión a Cuba*, 97–98.
13. "Manifiesto," *Las Novedades*, November 8, 1888; Joaquín M. Torroja to Ministro de Estado, February 25, 1887, H1968, AMAE; Joaquín M. to Enviado Extraordinario April 5, 1888, Leg. 714, Caja 54/7984, Fondo 26.1, Grupo 10, AGA.
14. "Isidro Cejas," *The Daily Equator-Democrat*, June 8, 1888, newspaper clippings, H1868, AMAE; Stebbins, *City of Intrigue*, 161–162; Schwartz, *Lawless Liberators*, 122.
15. "Manifiesto," *Las Novedades*, November 8, 1888; José Martí to Juan Ruz, October 20, 1887, in Martí, *Epistolario*, 1:415–419; Trujillo, *Apuntes históricos*, 28–29.
16. "Manifiesto," *Las Novedades*, November 8, 1888; Joaquín M. Torroja to Enviado Extraordinario, January 8, March 15, 1888, Leg. 714, Caja 54/7984, Fondo 26.1, Grupo 10, AGA.
17. Trujillo, *Album de El Porvenir*, 1:55–56.
18. Ibid.
19. Joaquín M. Torroja to Enviado Extraordinario, January 14, February 24, March 4, April 7, and August 4, 1888, Leg. 714, Caja 54/7984, Fondo 26.1, Grupo 10, AGA; "Manifiesto," *Las Novedades*, November 8, 1888.
20. Joaquín M. Torroja to Enviado Extraordinario, March 2, 1888, Leg. 714, Caja 54/7984, Fondo 26.1, Grupo 10, AGA.
21. Joaquín M. Torroja to Enviado Extraordinario, March 4, 10, and 15, 1888, Leg. 714, Caja 54/7984, Fondo 26.1, Grupo 10, AGA.
22. Joaquín M. Torroja to Enviado Extraordinario, April 12 and 13, 1888, Leg. 714, Caja 54/7984, Fondo 26.1, Grupo 10, AGA.
23. Padrón, *El General Flor*, 274–277.
24. "Nuestra actitud," *El Yara*, January 8, 1888.
25. "Manifiesto de Ruz," *El Yara*, November 18, 1888.
26. Padrón, *El General Flor*, 239.
27. Quoted in *Las Novedades*, February 16, 1888.

28. José D. Poyo to Máximo Gómez, April 1, 1888, Leg. 4, no. 56, Archivo Máximo Gómez, ANC.

29. Quoted in "Carta de Cayo Hueso," *Las Novedades*, May 17, 1888.

30. Pérez, *Lords of the Mountain*, 34–36.

31. Joaquín M. Torroja to Enviado Extraordinario, February 16, 1889, Leg. 721, Caja 54/7986, Fondo 26.1, Grupo 10, AGA; Stebbins, *City of Intrigue*, 162–163, 181–182.

32. Joaquín M. Torroja to Enviado Extraordinario, January 20 and 29, February 16, and May 31, 1889, Leg. 721, Caja 54/7986, Fondo 26.1, Grupo 10, AGA.

33. Ibid.

34. Stebbins, *City of Intrigue*, 215; Justiz, *Elogio del Sr. Néstor Leonelo Carbonell*, 22; Joaquín M. Torroja to Enviado Extraordinario, January 20 and August 13, 1889, Leg. 721, Caja 54/7986, Fondo 26.1, Grupo 10, AGA; Helg, *Our Rightful Share*, 44, 83–84.

35. Joaquín M. Torroja to Enviado Extraordinario, January 29, 1889, Leg. 721, Caja 54/7986, Fondo 26.1, Grupo 10, AGA.

36. Joaquín M. Torroja to Enviado Extraordinario, April 10, 1889, Leg. 721, Caja 54/7986, Fondo 26.1, Grupo 10, AGA; Gómez, *Album del Estado Mayor*, ix–x.

37. Tone, *War and Genocide in Cuba*, 57–68.

38. "Dilema cubano," *El Yara*, October 23, 1886.

39. "Convención Cubana," Leg. 699, no. 11, Donativos y Remisiones, ANC; Alpízar Poyo, *Cayo Hueso y José Dolores Poyo*, 71–79; Stebbins, "The Cuban Convention."

40. Lagomasino, *La Guerra de Cuba*, 10; Castellanos, *Motivos de Cayo Hueso*, 166–169; Casasús, *La emigración cubana*, 200–201; Franco, *Antonio Maceo: Apuntes*, 1:332–333.

41. Casanovas, *Bread, or Bullets*, 208.

42. Granda, *La Paz de Manganeso*; Franco, *Antonio Maceo: Apuntes*, 1:331–375; Castellanos, *Misión a Cuba*, 107–109.

43. Joaquín M. Torroja to Enviado Extraordinario, April 30, May 6, and June 6, 1890, Leg. 731, Caja 54/7988, Fondo 26.1, Grupo 10, AGA.

44. Francisco de Baguer to Enviado Extraordinario, May 6 and June 6, 1890, Leg. 731, Caja 54/7988, Fondo 26.1, Grupo 10, AGA.

45. Trujillo, *Album de El Porvenir*, 2:85–86.

46. Schwartz, *Lawless Liberators*, 207–208; Iglesia y Santos, *Manuel García, El Rey de los Campos*, 30–32; Rodríguez, *The Case of the Arrest, Trial, and Sentence . . . of Julio Sanguily*, 13–19.

47. Schwartz, *Lawless Liberators*, 132; Franco, *Antonio Maceo: Apuntes*, 1:331–372; Granda, *La Paz de Manganeso*, 23.

48. Franco, *Antonio Maceo: Apuntes*, 1:331–372; Granda, *La Paz de Manganeso*, 23; Francisco de Baguer to Enviado Extraordinario, September 18, 1890, Leg. 731, Caja 54/7988, Fondo 26.1, Grupo 10, AGA; Lagomasino, *La Guerra de Cuba*, 9–17.

49. Francisco de Baguer to Enviado Extraordinario, September 9, 10, and 12, 1890, Leg. 731, Caja 54/7988, Fondo 26.1, Grupo 10, AGA; Schwartz, *Lawless Liberators*, 137.

50. Francisco de Baguer to Enviado Extraordinario, September 30, 1890, Legajo 731, Caja 54/7988, Fondo 26.1, Grupo de Fondo 10, AGA.

51. Francisco de Baguer to Enviado Extraordinario, November 18 and 21, 1890, Leg. 731, Caja 54/7988, Fondo 26.1, Grupo 10, AGA.

52. Schwartz, *Lawless Liberators*, 139–142, 203.

53. Franco, *Antonio Maceo: Apuntes*, 2:13–14; Pérez, *Lords of the Mountain*, 46.

54. Stebbins, *City of Intrigue*, 107.

Chapter 6. Martí

1. There are many accounts of José Martí's first visits to Tampa and Key West. See Deolufeu, *Héroes del destierro*; Mañach, *José Martí: Apostle*; Lisazo, *José Martí: Martyr*; Ronning, *José Martí*.

2. José F. Lamadriz to Secretario del Comité Revolucionario Cubano, February 17, 1880, in Rodríguez y Colina, *Documentos para server la historia de la Guerra Chiquita*, 3:114.

3. Lisazo, *José Martí*, 206–207; Bellido de Luna and Trujillo, *La anexión de Cuba*.

4. Casasús, *La emigración cubana*, 200.

5. José Martí to José D. Poyo, November 29, 1887, in Martí, *Epistolario*, 1:429–431.

6. José Martí to Máximo Gómez, December 16, 1887, in ibid., 440; Franco, *Antonio Maceo: Apuntes*, 1:321–328.

7. José D. Poyo to Máximo Gómez, April 1, 1888, Leg. 4, no. 56, Archivo Máximo Gómez, ANC.

8. Rivero Muñiz, "Los cubanos en Tampa," 39–52.

9. Carbonell, *Resonancias del pasado*, 43–53.

10. Ibid., 92–93; Rivero Muñiz, "Los cubanos en Tampa," 52.

11. Poyo, "With All, and for the Good of All," 103–107.

12. Deulofeu, *Martí: Cayo Hueso y Tampa*, 147–148; Ronning, *José Martí*, 42.

13. José Martí to José D. Poyo, December 5, 1891, in Martí, *Epistolario*, 2:330.

14. Arnao, *Páginas para la historia*, 256–257.

15. José Martí to Máximo Gómez, December 16, 1887, in Martí, *Epistolario*, 1:440.

16. Deulofeu, *Heroes del destierro*, 131; Arnao, *Páginas para la historia*, 256–257; Trujillo, *Apuntes históricos*, 25–35; José Martí to Máximo Gómez, December 16, 1887, in Martí, *Epistolario*, 1:440; José Martí to Serafín Bello, October 12, 1889, in Martí, *Epistolario*, 2:129–130; José Martí to Serafín Bello, November 16, 1889, in ibid., 158–161; José Martí to Serafín Bello, February 21, 1890, in ibid., 184–187.

17. José Martí to Angel Peláez, December 16, 1891, in Martí, *Epistolario*, 2:332; Arnao, *Páginas para la historia*, 256–257.

18. "Oración de Tampa y Cayo Hueso," February 17, 1892, in Martí, *Obras completas*, 4:298–299.

19. Delgado, "Martí en Cayo Hueso," 72–80; Padilla Miyares, "El ultimo convencional martiano," 98–100.

20. "Martí," *El Yara*, December 30, 1891, newspaper clipping, and Pedro Solís to

Encargado de Negocios, January 18, 1892, both in Leg. 750, Caja 54/7992, Fondo 26.1, Grupo 10, AGA.

21. *A Martí*.

22. Ronning, *José Martí*, 48–64; Deulofeu, *Heroes del destierro*, 70–80; Peláez, *Primera jornada de José Martí en Cayo Hueso*.

23. "Bases del Partido Revolucionario Cubano," Martí, *Obras Completas*, 1:279–284.

24. Castellanos, *Motivos de Cayo Hueso*, 263.

25. "Acta de la constitución del Partido Revolucionario Cubano en Cayo Hueso, 5 de enero de 1892," Leg. fuera de caja 150, no. 7, Donativos y Remisiones, ANC; Hidalgo Paz, "Reseña de los clubes fundadores," 217.

26. Ronning, *José Martí*, 57–64.

27. Pedro Solís to Encargado de Negocios, January 7, 11 1892, Leg. 750, Caja 54/7992, Fondo 26.1, Grupo 10, AGA.

28. Pedro Solís to Encargado de Negocios, February 4, 1892, Leg. 750, Caja 54/7992, Fondo 26.1, Grupo 10, AGA.

29. Pedro Solís to Encargado de Negocios, January 18 1892, Leg. 750, Caja 54/7992, Fondo 26.1, Grupo 10, AGA.

30. "El meeting del lunes," *El Yara*, January 16, 1892.

31. Ronning, *José Martí*, 73–74.

32. José Martí to José D. Poyo, March 2, 1892, in Martí, *Epistolario*, 3:53–55.

33. Ronning, *José Martí*, 75–79.

34. José Martí to José D. Poyo, March 2, 1892, in Martí, *Epistolario*, 3:53–55.

35. "Cuba Determined to be Free from Spain," *New York Herald*, September 13, 1891.

36. "El meeting de anoche. El 10 de Abril. Proclamación del Partido Revolucionario Cubano," *El Yara*, April 11, 1892, quoted in Deulofeu, *Héroes del destierro*, 112–113.

37. Deulofeu, *Héroes del destierro*, 114.

38. "Clubs cubanos," *Patria*, April 10, 1892.

39. "Contestación a El Porvenir de El Yara," *El Porvenir*, June 8, 1892.

40. Padilla Miyares, "El ultimo convencional martiano," 98–100.

41. "Nuestra actitud," *El Porvenir*, April 13, 1892; "Continuamos," *El Porvenir*, April 20, 1892; "Continuamos," *El Porvenir*, April 27, 1892; Rodríguez, *Estudio histórico*, 278–286.

42. "Ante la opinion," *El Porvenir*, May 18, 1892; "Contestación a El Porvenir de El Yara," *El Porvenir*, June 8, 1892.

43. "José Francisco Lamadriz," *El Yara*, February 3, 1892, newspaper clipping, and Pedro Solís to Encargado de Negocios, February 4, 1892, Leg. 750, Caja 54/7992, Fondo 26.1, Grupo 10, AGA.

44. Lagomasino, *La guerra de Cuba*, 9–15.

45. Partido Comunista, *Apuntes biográficos del Mayor General Serafín Sánchez*; Casasús, *La emigración*, 444.

46. Lagomasino, *La Guerra de Cuba en 1895*, 9–17. See also Lagomasino, *Reminiscencias pátrias*; and Deulofeu, *Héroes del destierro*, 89–92.

47. José Martí to Club Presidents of the Key West Cuerpo de Consejo, May 13, 1892, in Martí, *Epistolario*, 3:91–97.

48. José Martí to Club Presidents of the Key West Cuerpo de Consejo, May 16, 1892, in ibid., 3:101–103; José Martí to Club Presidents of the Key West Cuerpo de Consejo, May 27, 1892, in ibid., 113–115; José Martí to President of the Key West Cuerpo de Consejo, June 9, 1892, in ibid., 117–118.

49. José Martí to Club Presidents of the Key West Cuerpo de Consejo, June 9, 1892, in ibid., 3:118–121; José Martí to Club Presidents of the Key West Cuerpo de Consejo, June 10, 1892, in ibid., 126–127.

50. José Martí to President of the Key West Cuerpo de Consejo, June 11, 1892, in ibid., 129–130.

51. José Martí to Serafín Sánchez, June 1892, in ibid. 133–134; José Martí to President of the Key West Cuerpo de Consejo, July 2, 1892, in ibid., 144; Pedro Solís to Encargado de Negocios, July 12, 1892, Leg. 750, Caja 54/7992, Fondo 26.1, Grupo 10, AGA.

52. Pedro Solís to Encargado de Negocios, July 2 and 5, 1892, Leg. 750, Caja 54/7992, Fondo 26.1, Grupo 10, AGA; Alvarez Estevez, *Mayor General Carlos Roloff*, 156–160.

53. Pedro Solís to Encargado de Negocios, July 16, 1892, Leg. 750, Caja 54/7992, Fondo 26.1, Grupo 10, AGA.

54. *El Yara* quoted in "Organización y disciplina," *El Porvenir*, July 27, 1892.

55. *El Yara* quoted in "Las revoluciones," *El Porvenir*, July 13, 1892.

56. José D. Poyo to Gerardo Castellanos García, April 8, 1908, in Castellanos, *Soldado y conspirador*, 92–94.

57. Castellanos, *Misión a Cuba*, 138, 176–177, 193–194.

58. José Martí to President of the Convención Cubana, August 6, 1892, in Martí, *Epistolario*, 3:165–166; José Martí to President of the Key West Cuerpo de Consejo, August 6, 1892, in ibid., 166–167.

59. Lagomasino, *La guerra de Cuba*, 17–18; Castellanos, *Misión a Cuba*, 155–219.

60. Stebbins, "The Cuban Convention," 202–203.

61. Castellanos, *Misión a Cuba*, 138, 176–177, 193–194; Lagomasino, *La guerra de Cuba*, 17–18.

62. "Desde Cayo Hueso" and "Manifestación política en Tampa," *Patria*, July 30, 1892; "Manifestación patriótica en Tampa," *Patria*, August 6, 1892; "A War Fund for Cuba," *New York Times*, July 26, 1892.

63. Poyo, "Baseball in Key West and Havana," 103; Burgos, "Entering Cuba's Other Playing Field," 15.

64. "José Martí y el juego de pelota," *Opus Habana*, 52–57; González Echeverría, *The Pride of Havana*, 83.

65. Poyo, "Baseball in Key West and Havana," 103.

66. Pedro Solis to Ministro Plenipotenciario, November 9, 11, 14, 16, 21, 24, and 28, 1892, and December 7, 1892, Leg. 750, Caja 54/7992, Fondo 26.1, Grupo 10, AGA; Stebbins, "The Cuban Convention," 202.

67. Pedro Solís to Ministro Plenipotenciario, November 28, 1892, Leg. 750, Caja 54/7992, Fondo 26.1, Grupo 10, AGA.

68. Pedro Solís to Ministro Plenipotenciario, November 28 and December 7, 1892, Leg. 750, Caja 54/7992, Fondo 26.1, Grupo 10, AGA.

69. "El conflicto de Cayo Hueso," *El Porvenir*, January 24, 1894.

70. Pedro Solís to Ministro Plenipotenciario, November 14 and December 7, 1892, Leg. 750, Caja 54/7992, Fondo 26.1, Grupo 10, AGA.

71. "Viva La Cuba," *The Daily Equator-Democrat*, October 10, 1892, newspaper clipping; and Pedro Solís to Encargado de Negocios, October 11, 1892, Leg. 750, Caja 54/7992, Fondo 26.1, Grupo 10, AGA.

72. "El Diez de Octubre," *El Yara*, October 12, 1892; "Viva La Cuba," *The Daily Equator-Democrat*, October 10, 1892, newspaper clipping, Pedro Solís to Encargado de Negocios, October 11, 1892, Leg. 750, Caja 54/7992, Fondo 26.1, Grupo 10, AGA.

73. José Martí to José D. Poyo, December 20, 1893, in Martí, *Epistolario*, 3:486–488.

74. Mañach, *Martí: Apostle*, 295–320; José Martí to President of the Key West Cuerpo de Consejo, February 17, 1893, in Martí, *Epistolario*, 3:272–275; José Martí to Eduardo Hidalgo Gato y otros, March 9, 1893, and March 17, 1893, in ibid., 302–304.

75. José Martí to Club Presidents of the Key West Cuerpo de Consejo, March 18, 1893, in ibid., 305.

76. Stebbins, "The Cuban Convention," 201; Hidalgo Paz, *José Martí: Cronología*, 83; Trujillo, *Apuntes históricos*, 86–87.

77. José D. Poyo to Máximo Gómez, July 14, 1893, Leg. 5, no. 93, Archivo Máximo Gómez, ANC.

78. Hidalgo Paz, *José Martí: Cronología*, 88–89.

79. Pedro Solís to Enviado Extraordinario, May 16, 1893, August 12 and 15, 1893, and September 12, 1893, Leg. 813, Caja, 54/8011, Fondo 26.1, Grupo 10, AGA.

80. Stebbins, "The Cuban Convention," 204.

81. Various communications from José Martí to José D. Poyo, Serafín Sánchez, Gonzalo de Quesda, Máxmo Gómez, and Fernando Figueredo, November 7–14, 1893, in Martí, *Epistolario*, 3:433–455.

82. Ronning, *José Martí*, 98–105.

83. José Martí to José D. Poyo, August 18, 1892, in Martí, *Epistolario*, 3:188–189.

84. Hidalgo Paz, *José Martí*, 84–85; Rodríguez-Silva, *Cronología Martiana*, 287–288; Alvarez Estévez, *Mayor General Carlos Roloff*, 152; Mañach, *Martí: Apostle*, 309–310.

85. José Martí to José D. Poyo, December 22, 1892, in Martí, *Epistolario*, 3:228–229.

86. Martí to Poyo, May 16, 1893, inscription on back of photo; copy of photo and inscription in author's possession.

Chapter 7. Crisis

1. Castellanos, *Motivos de Cayo Hueso*, 287–291.

2. *Key West Dispatch* quoted in *The Weekly Floridian*, August 15, 1876.

3. "Florida: A Cuban City in the United States," *New York Herald-Tribune*, May 15, 1891. Monte was a Cuban card game.

4. "A Question of Citizenship," *The Weekly Floridian*, reprinted in *Key of the Gulf*, July 1, 1876.

5. "Bahama Negroes and Cubans," *The Weekly Floridian*, November 24, 1874.

6. "Lo de Cayo Hueso," *El Español*, November 26, 1889, newspaper clippings, November 23–December 1, 1889, Leg. 260, no. 4, Asuntos Políticos, ANC.

7. "Nuestra misión en el destierro," *El Yara*, February 6, 1885.

8. Poyo, "Cuban Revolutionaries," 407–419; Browne, *Key West*, 69.

9. *Key West Democrat* quoted in *The Semi-Weekly Floridian*, September 17, 1880; *Key West Democrat* quoted in *The Semi-Weekly Floridian*, October 8, 1880; *Key West Democrat* quoted in *The Semi-Weekly Floridian*, October 12, 1880; "The First Democratic Gain," *The Semi-Weekly Floridian*, October 15, 1880; "Monroe-Official," *The Weekly Floridian*, November 23, 1880; "Democrats of Monroe County," *The Weekly Floridian*, February 7, 1882; "Elections—Monroe," *The Weekly Floridian*, November 21, 1882.

10. Browne, *Key West*, 120–121.

11. Stebbins, *City of Intrigue*, 167–169.

12. "Senator Call," *The Weekly Floridian*, February 12, 1884; "Aguero Discharged," *The Weekly Floridian*, February 26, 1884.

13. "Absolución del General Aguero," *El Yara*, February 23, 1884.

14. "Actividad," *La Voz de Hatuey*, March 1, 1884.

15. "General Carlos Aguero," *The Weekly Floridian*, April 22, 1884; "Wicker Dismissed," *The Weekly Floridian*, April 29, 1884; Browne, *Key West*, 120; Augusto Bermúdez to Ministro de Estado, March 29, 1884, H1868, AMAE.

16. U.S. v. Emilio Díaz, case no. 213 (1–8); U.S. v. Bruno Alfonso, case no. 214 (9–14); U.S. v. Clinton Shavers, case no. 221 (25–35); U.S. v. Carlos Aguero, case no. 222 (37–40), U.S. v. Federico Gil Marrero, case no. 220 (18–24), Criminal Final Record, July 1884–May 1906; United States v. José D. Poyo, July 5, 1884, Violation of Neutrality Law, General Minutes, February 1883–April 1888; Southern District of Florida, Record Group 21, National Archives at Atlanta, Atlanta, Georgia.

17. Stebbins, *City of Intrigue*, 137–139.

18. "Bethel Elected Mayor of Key West," *The Weekly Floridian*, October 28, 1884; "Elections," *The Weekly Floridian*, December 9, 1884; "Legislature," *The Weekly Floridian*, February 3, 1885.

19. Westfall, *Key West*, 53.

20. "What They Deserve," *The Daily Equator-Democrat*, June 12, 1888, newspaper clippings, H1868, AMAE.

21. *El Bandolerismo en Cuba*, 1:117–123.

22. "Florida: A Cuban City in the United States," *New York Herald-Tribune*, May 15, 1891.

23. "Estrada," *El Yara*, March 17, 1888; "El entierro," *La Propaganda*, March 15, 1888.

24. Stebbins, *City of Intrigue*, 157–158; Joaquín M. Torroja to Ministro de Estado, February 8 and February 11, 1887, H1868, AMAE.

25. "Five Gamblers Caught and Placed under Heavy Bonds," and "The Board of Trade Consider the Crime of Blackmailing," *The Daily Equator-Democrat*, May 31, 1888; "A Winning Fight," *The Daily Equator-Democrat*, June 6, 1888; in newspaper clippings, H1868, AMAE.

26. "Isidro Cejas," *The Daily Equator-Democrat*, June 8, 1888, in newspaper clippings, H1868, AMAE.

27. "What They Deserve," *The Daily Equator-Democrat*, May 31, 1888, in newspaper clippings, H1868, AMAE.

28. "Carta de Cayo Hueso," *El Productor*, November 3, 1889.

29. "El atentado del sábado," *El Yara*, October 29, 1889.

30. "Elections," *The Weekly Floridian*, January 1, 1888.

31. "Cubans return to Havana," *Tobacco Leaf*, August 9, 1893.

32. Serafín Sánchez to Gerardo Castellanos, January 17, 1894, in Castellanos, *Motivos de Cayo Hueso*, 293–294.

33. Rubens, *Libertad*, 2–10.

34. Ibid., 26–36; "Cuban Revolutionists Hope Spain and Uncle Sam Will Quarrel," *Charlotte Observer*, January 10, 1894; "Washington News: The Key West Strike," *The State* (Columbia, SC), January 12, 1894.

35. "Agitation in Key West," *Tobacco Leaf*, July 20, 1892; "Key West Reflected," *Tobacco Leaf*, July 27, 1892; "Labor Troubles in Key West," *Tobacco Leaf*, August 3, 1892.

36. José Martí to Serafín Sánchez, José D. Poyo, and Gualterio García, January 25, 1894, in Martí, *Epistolario*, 4:28–31.

37. "The Cuban Cigar Makers to Be Sent Back Home," *Charlotte Observer*, January 21, 1894; "At the National Capital," *Savannah Tribune*, January 27, 1894; "Deporting Alien Cigar Makers," *The State* (Columbia, SC), January 29, 1894; Pedro Solís to Enviado Extraordinario, February 9, 1894, Legajo 825, Caja 54/8016, Fondo 26.1, Grupo de Fondo 10, AGA.

38. "Fragmentos de una carta del Cayo," *Patria*, February 16, 1894.

39. "Arrested in Key West," *Columbus Daily Enquirer*, February 10, 1894; "Deportation of Cigar Makers," *Columbus Daily Enquirer*, February 11, 1894; Pedro Solís to Enviado Extraordinario, February 12, 1894, Leg. 825, Caja 54/8016, Fondo 26.1, Grupo 10, AGA.

40. José Martí to President of the Key West Cuerpo de Consejo, April 4, 1894, in Martí, *Epistolario*, 4:96; José Martí to Gualterio García, April 3, 1894, in ibid., 101–102.

41. "José D. Poyo," *Patria*, March 16, 1894; U.S. vs. M. P. Delgado, May 10, 1895, Box #5, nos. 318–446, Southern District of Florida, Criminal Cases, 1886–1908, Record Group 21, National Archives at Atlanta, Atlanta, Georgia. The file does not include the disposition of the case.

42. Marti, *Obras completas*, 3:61.

43. "El conflicto de Cayo Hueso," *El Porvenir*, January 24, 1894.

44. "La verdad se abre paso" and "Buen consejo de cubanos a cubanos," *El Porvenir*, February 28, 1894.

45. "Una carta razonada," *El Porvenir*, February 28, 1894.

46. "El nuevo partido," *El Yara*, February 6, 1894 quoted in *El Porvenir*, February 14, 1894; "Bases Constitutivas del Partido Independiente," published in *El Yara* and reprinted in *El Porvenir*, Feburary 21, 1894; José Martí to Antonio Maceo, February 1, 1894, in Martí, *Epistolario*, 4:37–38; Castellanos, *Motivos de Cayo Hueso*, 301.

47. "Leemos en El Yara, fecha 7 del corriente," *El Porvenir*, March 14, 1894; "Cuban Workers," *Tobacco Leaf*, March 14, 1894; *Patria*, March 16, 1894.

48. Westfall, *Key West*, 54–55.

49. "Inducements," *Tobacco Leaf*, April 11, 1894; José Martí to Ramón Rivera, [April] 1894, in Martí, *Epistolario*, 4:125; Pedro Solís to Enviado Extraordinario, February 22, 1894, Leg. 825, Caja 54/8016, Fondo 26.1, Grupo 10, AGA.

50. *El Yara* quoted in "Los sucesos del Cayo," *Patria*, April 5, 1894.

51. "El Yara en inglés," *Patria*, March 16, 1894.

52. "Rioting in Key West," *The Sun* (Baltimore), March 24, 1894; "Riot at Key West," *Tobacco Leaf*, March 28, 1894; "Seidenberg and Manufacturers Move to Tampa," *Tobacco Leaf*, April 4, 1894; Pedro Solís to Enviado Extraordinario, March 22, 1894, and April 27, 1894, Leg. 825, Caja 54/8016, Fondo 26.1, Grupo 10, AGA.

53. "Los sucesos del Cayo," *Patria*, April 5, 1894.

54. "En el Cayo, el 10 de Abril," *Patria*, April 28, 1894; Pedro Solís to Enviado Extraordinario, April 9, 1894, Leg. 825, Caja 54/8016, Fondo 26.1, Grupo 10, AGA.

55. Hidalgo Paz, *José Martí*, 96; "Mass Meeting," *El Yara*, May 19, 1894, reprinted in Martí, *Obras Completas*, 4:335.

56. José Martí to Comisión de Colectas del Comercio de Cayo Hueso, April 7, 1894, in Martí, *Epistolario*, 4:104–105.

57. José Martí to George Jackson and Salvador Herrera, May 18, 1894, in ibid., 141–142; Pedro Solís to Enviado Extraordinario, May 21, 1894, Leg. 825, Caja 54/8016, Fondo 26.1, Grupo 10, AGA.

58. José Martí to José D. Poyo, Serafín Sánchez, and Fermín V. Dominguez, May 27, 1894, in Martí, *Epistolario*, 4:149–150.

59. José Martí to Serafín Sánchez, May 30, 1894, in ibid., 168–169.

60. José Martí to José D. Poyo, July 7, 1894, in ibid., 213–214.

61. "Como ha de ser!" *El Yara*, July 7, 1894, newspaper clipping enclosed in Pedro Solís to Enviado Extraordinario, July 9, 1894, Leg. 825, Caja 54/8016, Fondo 26.1, Grupo 10, AGA.

62. José Martí to Gualterio García, April 3, 1894, in Martí, *Epistolario*, 4:96.

63. *El Yara*, July 30, 1894 quoted in *Patria*, August 18, 1894.

64. "Nuestro 'Yara,'" *Patria*, September 22, 1894.

65. "En su puesto," *Patria*, September 22, 1894.

66. José Martí to Fermín Valdés Domínguez, September 12, 1894, in Martí, *Epistolario*, 4:257.

67. Quoted in "Nuestro 'Yara,'" *Patria*, September 22, 1894.
68. Ibid.
69. Delgado, "Martí en Cayo Hueso," 72–80; José D. Poyo to Tomás Estrada Palma, August 17, 1895, in Primelles, *La Revolución del 95*, 1:218–219; Alvarez Estévez, *Mayor General Carlos Roloff*, 170; Tomás Estrada Palma to President of the Key West Cuerpo de Consejo, July 11, 1896, in Primelles, *La Revolución del 95*, 5:100–101.
70. Juan Fraga to Joaquín del Castillo, March 15, 1896, in ibid., 3:384–388.

Chapter 8. War

1. Máximo Gómez to José D. Poyo, April 27, 1895 in Alpízar Poyo, *Cayo Hueso y José Dolores Poyo*, 114.
2. José D. Poyo to Máximo Gómez, December 9, 1893, Archivo Máximo Gómez, Legajo 5, no. 93, ANC.
3. Hidalgo Paz, *José Martí*, 100.
4. José Martí to Eduardo Hidalgo Gato, October 27, 1894, in Martí, *Epistolario*, 4:296.
5. Collazo, *Cuba independiente*, 20–55; Loynaz del Castillo. *Memorias de la guerra*, 104–113.
6. Collazo, *Cuba independiente*, 46–48; Loynaz del Castillo, *Memorias de la guerra*, 104–105.
7. Collazo, *Cuba independiente*, 46–49; Ronning, *José Martí*, 125; José Martí to José D. Poyo, January 17, 1895, in Martí, *Epistolario*, 5:21.
8. José Martí to Juan Gualberto Gómez, January 17, 1895, Martí, *Epistolario*, 5:17–20; Loynaz del Castillo, *Memorias de la guerra*, 140–144; Hidalgo Paz, *José Martí*, 104.
9. José Martí to Máximo Gómez, August 29, 1893, in Martí, *Epistolario*, 3:396; José Martí to Máximo Gómez, November 10, 1893, in ibid., 3:442; Loynaz del Castillo, *Memorias de la guerra*, 118–119, 134–135.
10. Rodríguez, *The Case of the Arrest, Trial, and Sentence . . . of Julio Sanguily*, 4–17.
11. Schwartz, *Lawless Liberators*, 234–235.
12. Tone, *War and Genocide in Cuba*, 43–56.
13. Valdés Domínguez, *Diario de soldado*, 1:43–46, 62.
14. José Martí to José Dolores Poyo, February 19, 1895, in Martí, *Epistolario*, 5:72.
15. "Discurso," *Patria*, October 27, 1897.
16. "Señor Palma the Man," *New York Herald-Tribune*, July 11, 1895.
17. José Martí to Gonzalo de Quesada, April 1, 1895, in Martí, *Epistolario*, 5:138–141.
18. *El Guáimaro*, September 19, 1895; "Talk of Expeditions," *New York Herald-Tribune*, September 18, 1895; Pedro Solís to Enviado Extraordinario, September 21, 1895, Leg. 900, Caja 54/8053, Fondo 26.1, Grupo 10, AGA.
19. Loynaz del Castillo, *Memorias de la guerra*, 140–142.
20. Fermín Valdés Dominguez, *Diario de soldado*, 1:39.
21. Ibid., 1:35–62; Collazo, *Cuba independiente*, 142–146; Loynaz del Castillo, *Memorias de la guerra*, 180–187; Alvarez Estevez, *Mayor General Carlos Roloff*, 186–193; Pedro

Solís to Enviado Extraordinario, March 23, 1896, Leg. 900, Caja 54/8053, Fondo 26.1, Grupo 10, AGA.

22. Castellanos, *Motivos de Cayo Hueso*, 311–312; Alvarez Estévez, *Mayor General Carlos Roloff*, 186–191; Castellanos, *Tarja de Bronce*, 96–98; J. M. Rodríguez to Tomás Estrada Palma, July 9, 1895, in Primelles, *La Revolución del 95*, 1:13–15; José D. Poyo to Tomás Estrada Palma, July 19, 1895, in ibid., 1:21–24.

23. Castellanos, *Motivos de Cayo Hueso*, 311–312; Alvarez Estévez, *Mayor General Carlos Roloff*, 186–191; Castellanos, *Tarja de Bronce*, 96–98.

24. Pedro Solís to Enviado Extraordinario, July 31, 1894, Leg. 900, Caja 54/8053, Fondo 26.1, Grupo 10, AGA.

25. Enrique Collazo to Tomás Estrada Palma, November 14, 1895, in Primelles, *La Revolución del 95*, 2:341–343.

26. Enrique Collazo to Tomás Estrada Palma, November 20, 1895, in ibid., 2:345–347.

27. Benjamín J. Guerra to Tomás Estrada Palma, November 15, 1895, in ibid., 2:343–345; Enrique Collazo to Tomás Estrada Palma, November 20, 1895 in ibid., 2:345–347; Enrique Collazo to Tomás Estrada Palma, December 18, 1895, in ibid., 2:348–356; José D. Poyo to Tomás Estrada Palma, December, 10–28, 1895 (five letters), in ibid., 2:343–363; Collazo, *Cuba Independiente*, 142–146, 152; Casasús, *La emigración cubana*, 294–295.

28. "Carlos Céspedes in Key West," *New York Times*, June 19, 1895; "Proclamation for Cuba: Obedience to Neutrality Laws Admonished by the President," *New York Times*, July 13, 1895; "Treasury Department Has Issued Orders," *New York Times*, July 19, 1895.

29. "El derecho internacional y el derecho de los cubanos," *El Yara*, May 11, 1897, quoted in Hidalgo Paz, *Cuba*, 146–147.

30. O'Toole, *The Spanish War: An American Epic—1898*, 63–64.

31. "The Cabinet Conference," *New York Times*, July 21, 1895.

32. José D. Poyo to Tomás Estrada Palma, July 19, 1895, in Primelles, *La Revolución del 95*, 1:23.

33. Tomás Estrada Palma to Emilio Núñez, February 10, 1896, in ibid., 3:172–173; Rodríguez Altunaga, *El General Emilio Núñez*; Casasús, *La emigración cubana*, 332.

34. Tomás Estrada Palma to Francisco Chenard, January 25, 1896, in Primelles, *La Revolución del 95*, 3:121–123; Tomás Estrada Palma to Francisco Chenard, February 28–29, 1896, in ibid., 3:227; Tomás Estrada Palma to José D. Poyo, February 29, 1896, in ibid., 3:228; Carlos Roloff to Tomás Estrada Palma, March 19, 1896, in ibid., 3:166–167; Pedro Solís to Enviado Extraordinario, April 6, 1896, Leg. 900, Caja 54/8053, Fondo 26.1, Grupo 10, AGA.

35. José D. Poyo to Tomás Estrada Palma, April 1, 1896, in Primelles, *La Revolución del 95*, 4:78–79; José D. Poyo to Tomás Estrada Palma, April 8, 1896, in ibid., 4:85–86; Casasús, *La emigración cubana*, 320.

36. Fernando Figueredo to Tomás Estrada Palma, March 23, 1896, in Primelles, *La Revolución del 95*, 3:337–338; Casasús, *La emigración cubana*, 320.

37. Tomás Estrada Palma to Salvador Cisneros Betancourt, April 16, 1896, in Primelles, *La Revolución del 95*, 4:113.

38. Pérez, *Lords of the Mountain*, 211; Antonio Maceo to José D. Poyo, *Patria*, July 10, 1896.

39. José D. Poyo to Tomás Estrada Palma, April 8, 1896, in Primelles, *La Revolución del 95*, 4:95–97.

40. Alvarez Estevez, *Mayor General Carlos Roloff*, 225–233.

41. José D. Poyo to Tomás Estrada Palma, July 4, 1896, in Primelles, *La Revolución del 95*, 5:75–76; José D. Poyo to Tomás Estrada Palma, September 23, 1896, in ibid., 5:357–358; J. A. Huau to Tomás Estrada Palma, September 21, 1896, in ibid., 5:353–355; Joaquín D. Castillo to Tomás Estrada Palma, September 23, 1896, in ibid., 5:356

42. Tomás Estrada Palma to Salvador Cisneros Betancourt, May 30, 1896, in ibid., 5:11–25; to Máximo Gómez, July 29, 1896, in ibid., 5:36–42.

43. José D. Poyo to Tomás Estrada Palma, April 25, 1896, in ibid., 4:93.

44. André, *Explosiones*, 15–29.

45. José D. Poyo to Tomás Estrada Palma, July 19, 1895, in Primelles, *La Revolución del 95*, 5:21–24.

46. José D. Poyo to Tomás Estrada Palma, March 6, 1896, in ibid., 3:285–286.

47. Tomás Estrada Palma to Francisco Chenard, February 28, 1896, in ibid., 3:227; Tomás Estrada Palma to Francisco Chenard, February 29, 1896, in ibid., 3:227–228; Tomás Estrada Palma to José D. Poyo, February 29, 1896, in ibid., 3:228–229; Joaquín D. Castillo to José D. Poyo, May 9, 1896, in Alpízar Poyo, *Cayo Hueso y José Dolores Poyo*, 117.

48. Pérez, *Cuba between Empires*, 99–108.

49. Tomás Estrada Palma to Dr. R. E. Betances, July 16, 1897, in Estrada Palma, *Correspondencia diplomática de la Delegación Cubana en Nueva York*, 1:126–128; Alpízar Poyo, *Doctor Ramón O'Farrill*, 7; "Telegramas," *Patria*, June 30, 1897; "Telegramas," *Patria*, July 3, 1897; "Telegramas," *Patria*, July 7, 1897; "Partido Revolucionario Cubano. Cuerpos de Consejo," *Patria*, July 14, 1897.

50. Castellanos, *Motivos de Cayo Hueso*, 313–314.

51. Esteban Borrero E. to Tomás Estrada Palma, August 18, 1897, in Estrada Palma, *Correspondencia diplomática de la Delegación Cubana en Nueva York*, 2:202–204.

52. Ferrer, *Insurgent Cuba*, 173–178.

53. Ramón Dobarganes to Teodoro Pérez, May 16, 1896, in Primelles, *La Revolución del 95*, 4:378–379.

54. Dobarganes to Tomás Estrada Palma, September 9, 1896, in Primelles, *La Revolución del 95*, 5:299–301.

55. Ramón Dobarganes to Teodoro Pérez, May 16, 1896, in Primelles, *La Revolución del 95*, 4:378–379; "A nivel," *El Yara*, reprinted in *La Doctrina de Martí*, March 15, 1897; "Para todos y no para unos," *El Yara*, September 24, 1897, reprinted in *El Intransigente*, October 2, 1897; *El Yara* quoted in *Patria*, September 11, 1897.

56. "Nuestra labor," *La Doctrina de Martí*, July 25, 1896; "Lo que dicen los amigos,"

La Doctrina de Martí, August 22, 1896; "El Señor Varona y el periódico Patria," *La Doctrina de Martí*, January 30, 1897; "El decoro popular en acción," *La Doctrina de Martí*, February 15, 1897; "El Cayo en su puesto," *La Doctrina de Martí*, March 31, 1897; "Nuevos colegas," *La Doctrina de Martí*, August 31, 1897.

57. Pedro Solís to Ministro Plenipotenciario, November 14, 1892, and December 7, 1892, Leg. 750, Caja 54/7992, Fondo 26.1, Grupo 10, AGA.

58. "Huelga," *El Yara*, November 12, 1897.

59. "Amen," *El Yara*, November 26, 1897; "Que es eso?" *El Vigía*, November 27, 1897.

60. Cabrera, *Diego Vicente Tejeda*, xl–xli, xliv.

61. "Convocatoria," *El Vigía*, December 11, 1897; "Primera piedra," *El Vigía*, December 25, 1897.

62. Ramón Dobarganes to Teodoro Pérez, June 13, 1896, in Primelles, *La Revolución del 95*, 4:381–382; Francisco Chenard to Tomás Estrada Palma, July 4, 1896, in ibid., 5:77–78.

63. "Cubans Reject a War Tax," *New York Times*, July 2, 1897; "Habla de patriotismo," *Patria*, July 14, 1897; "Nuestro deber," *Patria*, July 28, 1897.

64. José D. Poyo to Tomás Estrada Palma, June 24, 1896, in Primelles, *La Revolución del 95*, 4:373–376; Tomás Estrada Palma to José D. Poyo, June 27, 1896, in ibid., 4:376–377.

65. Ramón Dobarganes to Teodoro Pérez, June 13, 1896, in ibid., 4:382–384.

66. Fernando Figueredo to Tomás Estrada Palma, March 23, 1896, in Primelles, *La Revolución del 95*, 3:337.

67. Tomás Estrada Palma to President of Key West Cuerpo de Consejo, July 11, 1896, in Primelles, *La Revolución del 95*, 5:100–101.

68. Alpízar Poyo, *Doctor Juan Ramón O'Farrill*, 8; Azcuy, *El Partido Revolucionario Cubano*, 118; José D. Poyo to Tomás Estrada Palma, April 1, 1896, in Primelles, *La Revolución del 95*, 4:79–80; Tomás Estrada Palma to José D. Poyo, April 11, 1896, in ibid., 86–87.

69. "Justicia y libertad," *El Intransigente*, October 2, 1897.

70. "Parece Mentira," *El Yara*, reprinted in *Guáimaro*, November 14, 1895.

71. Tone, *War and Genocide*, 184; Castellanos, *Tarja de Bronce*, 162.

72. Pérez, *Cuba between Empires*, 148.

73. Ibid., 141–148; Tone, *War and Genocide*, 232–236.

74. Pedro de Solís to Enviado Extraordinario, August 30, December 8, 1897, Leg. 900, Caja 54/8053, Fondo 26.1, Grupo 10, AGA.

75. "Telegrama," *Patria*, October 6, 1897.

76. "Dice El Yara," *Patria*, October 30, 1897.

77. "Key West. Nov. 5 de 1897," *Patria*, "Discurso de Tomás Estrada Palma," *Patria*, November 10, 1897, "Exposición que dirigen las emigraciones al Gobierno de la República de Cuba," *Patria*, November 13, 1897, "Adhesiones a la Exposición de 1 de noviembre de 1897," *Patria*, January 8, 1898.

78. Tone, *War and Genocide*, 86–87.

79. Pérez, *Cuba between Empires*, 133–135, 187–189.
80. "Calma! calma!" *El Independiente*, October 1, 1898.
81. "La intervención directa," *El Vigía*, January 22, 1898.
82. "El sentimiento cubano," *Patria*, February 23, 1898; "El viaje del Delegado," *Patria*, February 26, 1898; Casasús, *La emigración cubana*, 413.
83. "Resoluciones por los cubanos de Tampa, Fla.," *Patria*, March 19, 1898.
84. "La catastrophe del *Maine*," *Patria*, February 19, 1898.
85. "Excitement at Key West," *New York Times*, February 17, 1898.
86. "Convincing Evidence of a Submarine Mine," *St. Louis Republic*, March 4, 1898; "Why Maine Still Rests at Bottom of Havana Harbor," *Lexington Herald*, March 13, 1910; "The Cuban Opportunity," *New York Times*, February 26, 1898; "The Big Fleet at Key West," *New York Times*, March 17, 1898; "Alarm Felt at Key West," *New York Times*, March 26, 1898; "War Expected at Key West," *New York Times*, March 27, 1898.
87. "*Maine* Wreck Evidence," *New York Times*, March 29, 1898; "The Mascotte Brings Refugees," *New York Times*, April 9, 1898; "A Spanish Consul Gets Out," *New York Times*, April 14, 1898.
88. Horatio Rubens, *Libertad*, 291–293.
89. Pérez, *Cuba between Empires*, 185–186.
90. "An Exciting Day in Key West," *New York Times*, April 20, 1898; "Resoluciones del Cuerpo de Consejo de Cayo Hueso," *Patria*, May 11, 1898.
91. "Del General Gómez," *Patria*, May 18, 1898.
92. Pérez, *Cuba between Empires*, 189–190.
93. Tone, *War and Genocide*, 133, 269–271.
94. "Gen. Núñez at Key West," *New York Times*, May 2, 1898; "To Fight with the Cubans," *New York Times*, June 1, 1898; "Fighting Filibusters," *New York Times*, July 15, 1898; "De Cayo Hueso. Nomina de expedicionarios," *Patria*, May 14, 1898.
95. Tomás Estrada Palma to José D. Poyo, August 6, 1898, quoted in Casasús, *La emigración cubana*, 368.
96. Tone, *War and Genocide*, 274–282.
97. Alpízar Poyo, *Cayo Hueso y José Dolores Poyo*, 121.
98. Gómez, *Album del Estado Mayor*, 72–82.

Chapter 9. Legacy

1. Deulofeu, *Heroes del destierro*, 191–193.
2. Poyo, "Baseball in Key West and Havana," 540–564.
3. Alpízar Poyo, *Cayo Hueso y José Dolores Poyo*, 125–126.
4. Azcuy, *El Partido Revolucionario Cubano*, 125.
5. "Refugees Return to Cuba," *New York Times*, October 2, 1898.
6. Castellanos, *Misión a Cuba*, 272–275; Fernández, *Cuban Anarchism*, 41; Partido Comunista de Cuba, *Carlos Baliño*, 15–17.
7. "Situación excepcional," *Patria*, July 2, 1898.
8. Alpízar Poyo, *Cayo Hueso y José Dolores Poyo*, 123.

9. Guerra, *Historia de la nación cubana*, 6:446–448.

10. "Cuban Expedition Landed," *New York Times*, August 14, 1898.

11. "No Relief for Insurgents," *New York Times*, September 12, 1898.

12. "Correspondencia de Cayo Hueso," *Patria*, August 17, 1898; "Prudente opinión," *Patria*, August 22, 1898.

13. "Cuban Nationalist Party," *New York Times*, September 9, 1898.

14. Guerra, *Historia de la nación cubana*, 6:455–461; "Parade of American Troops," *New York Herald-Tribune*, January 2, 1899.

15. "Comments on the Address of General Máximo Gómez," *New York Herald-Tribune*, January 4, 1899.

16. "Parade of American Troops," *New York Herald-Tribune*, January 2, 1889.

17. Pérez, *Cuba between Empires*, 255–256.

18. "Los funerales de Calixto García," *Las Novedades*, February 16, 1899; Guerra, *Historia de la nación cubana*, 7:18–19; Iglesias, *A Cultural History of Cuba*, 139.

19. Guerra, *Historia de la nación cubana*, 7:21–36.

20. Máximo Gómez to José D. Poyo, March 16, 1899 in García Domínguez, *El pensamiento vivo de Máximo Gómez*, 2:290–291; Ibarra, *Máximo Gómez*, 69–106.

21. Pérez, *Cuba between Empires*, 290–292.

22. Rodríguez, *Estudio histórico*, 286.

23. Padilla Miyares, "El último convencional martiano," 98–100.

24. Alpízar Poyo, *Cayo Hueso y José Dolores Poyo*, 126; Figueredo, *José Dolores Poyo*, 26.

25. Castellanos, *Motivos de Cayo Hueso*, 224–225.

26. Alpízar Poyo, *Cayo Hueso y José Dolores Poyo*, 127; Figueredo, *José Dolores Poyo*, 26.

27. Castellanos, *Misión a Cuba*, 274.

28. Figueredo, *José Dolores Poyo*, 27.

29. Disillusionment was the most prominent feeling expressed in the Poyo and Alpízar family oral traditions about this period.

30. Pérez, *Cuba between Empires*, 316–327; Ibarra, *Máximo Gómez*, 145–163.

31. Pérez, *Cuba between Empires*, 371–373.

32. Alpízar Poyo, *Cayo Hueso y José Dolores Poyo*, 134–135.

33. Ibid., 135–136; Lavié Vera, *La personalidad de Rafael María Merchán*, 42–43; Merchán, *Patria y cultura*, 44–47.

34. Cuba Departamento de Estado, *Relación de los funcionarios diplomáticos y consulares*, 1903; Cuervo, *Libro de Homenaje al Coronel Cosme de la Torriente*, 121–126.

35. Alpízar Poyo, *Cayo Hueso y José Dolores Poyo*, 135–136.

36. Pérez, *Cuba between Empires*, 346–365.

37. Ibarra, *Máximo Gómez*, 164–186.

38. Cairo, *Máximo Gómez: 100 Años*, 266–272.

39. Pérez, *Cuba under the Platt Amendment*, 88–138.

40. Alpízar Poyo, *Cayo Hueso y José Dolores Poyo*, 133.

41. "El Archivo de la Junta Superior de Sanidad," 53.
42. Llaverías, *Historia del Archivo de Cuba*, 270.
43. Ibid., 267–275; Poyo, "Informe," 91.
44. Conversation with Luis Alpízar Leal, 1982.
45. Llaverías, *Historia del Archivo de Cuba*, 290–305.
46. *Boletín del Archivo Nacional*, 1903–1912.
47. "Nota explicativa," in Primelles, *La Revolución del 95*, 1:5–6.
48. Iglesias, *A Cultural History of Cuba*, 138–139; "Cubans Eulogize Martí," *New York Times*, January 30, 1899.
49. Alpízar Poyo, *Cayo Hueso y José Dolores Poyo*, 139–140.
50. "La estatua de Martí," *Diario de la Marina*, February 24, 1905; Iglesias, *A Cultural History of Cuba*, 25–28.
51. Schwartz, *Lawless Liberators*, 244–248.
52. Ibid., 248–249.
53. "Poyo y Patricio Delgado / dan a Manuel, al instante /, diploma de comandante / con dos firmas y acuñado / Es el jefe designado/ para las operaciones / y entre vivas y ovaciones/ el vapor se hace a la mar / y el jefe empieza a estudiar/ el pliego de condiciones," Isidrón, *Manuel García*, 57.
54. Alpízar Poyo, *Cayo Hueso y José Dolores Poyo*, 146.
55. Figueredo, *José Dolores Poyo*, 28–29.
56. "De Cuba," *El Diario de Tampa*, September 25, 1909.
57. Alpízar Poyo, *Cayo Hueso y José Dolores Poyo*, 143.
58. Ibid., 141–145; Figueredo, *José Dolores Poyo*, 28–30.
59. Gómez, *Album del Estado Mayor*, ix–xii.
60. Legajo 593, no. 50, Donativos y remisiones, ANC.
61. Alpízar Poyo, *Cayo Hueso y José Dolores Poyo*, 126.
62. Francisco Poyo's grandchildren José, Sergio, and Jorge Poyo often repeated this statement, which they found to be striking and telling.
63. "Materiales relacionados con el Instituto Patriótico Docente San Carlos, 1910–1933," in Poyo, *Records of the Cuban Consulate, Key West, Florida, 1886–1961*, Box 18, Item 1 & Folders 1-4, Reel 56.
64. "Fiestas pátrias, el busto de Martí, y otros documentos," *Records of the Cuban Consulate, Key West, Florida, 1886–1961*, Box 120, Folders 1-3, Reel 56.
65. Sosa, *Cuba y Cayo Hueso*, 130–142, 183–190.
66. Alpízar Poyo, *Cayo Hueso y José Dolores Poyo*, 34–36; Castellanos, *Motivos de Cayo Hueso*, 333–359; Pérez Rolo, *Mis recuerdos*, 48–56.

BIBLIOGRAPHY

Primary Sources

Archives and Libraries
Archivo del Ministerio de Asuntos Exteriores (AMAE), Madrid, Spain
Archivo General de Administración (AGA), Alcalá de Henares, Spain
Archivo Nacional de Cuba (ANC), Havana, Cuba
Biblioteca Nacional "José Martí" (BNJM), Havana, Cuba
Instituto de Literatura y Lingüística, Havana, Cuba
Mullen Library, Catholic University of America, Washington, DC
National Archives at Atlanta, Atlanta, Georgia
Microfilm
Notes from the Peruvian Legation in the United States to the Department of State, 1827–1906. Microfilm. 6 reels. Washington, D.C.: National Archives and Records Service, 1962.
Poyo, Gerald E., and Jane Garner, eds. *Records of the Cuban Consulate, Key West, Florida, 1881–1961.* Microfilm. 64 reels. Austin, TX: General Libraries, University of Texas at Austin, 1983.

Secondary Sources

Aguilera Rojas, Eladio. *Francisco Vicente Aguilera y la Revolución de Cuba de 1868.* 2 vols. Havana: El Avisador Comercial, 1909.
Alpízar Leal, Luis. *Documentos inéditos de José Martí a José D. Poyo.* Havana: Editorial Ciencias Sociales, 1992.
Alpízar Poyo, Raoul. *Cayo Hueso y José Dolores Poyo: Dos símbolos pátrios.* Havana: Imp. P. Fernández y Cia, 1947.
———. *Cayo Hueso y la independencia de Cuba.* Key West, FL: Imprenta Florida, 1921.
———. *Doctor Juan Ramón O'Farrill (Apuntes biográficos de su vida y sus servicios a la patria).* Havana: Imprenta Rambla, Bouza y Cia., 1926.

Alvarez Estévez, Rolando. *La emigración cubana en Estados Unidos, 1868–1878*. Havana: Editorial de Ciencias Sociales, 1986.

———. *Mayor General Carlos Roloff Mialofsky: Ensayo biográfico*. Havana: Editorial Ciencias Sociales, 1981.

A Martí. Havana: Editorial Ciencias Sociales, n.d.

André, Armando. *Explosiones en la ciudad de La Habana en 1896*. Havana: Avisador Comercial, 1901.

Andreu Iglesias, César. *Memorias de Bernardo Vega: Contribuciones a la historia de la comunidad puertoriqueña en Nueva York*. Puerto Rico: Ediciones Huracán, Inc., 1977.

Armas Céspedes, Ignacio. *Combate de Russell House: Cayo Hueso, 1870. Muerte de Castañón*. Havana: Editorial Alfa, 1938.

Arnao, Juan. *Páginas para la historia de la Isla de Cuba*. Havana: Impr. La Nueva, 1900.

Azcuy Alón, Fanny. *El Partido Revolucionario Cubano y la independencia de la pátria*. Havana: Molina y Compañía, 1930.

Ballesteros Rodríguez, Humberto. "Carlos Aguero, un general mambí." *Anuario del Archivo Histórico Insular de Fuerteventura* 11 (1998): 171–194.

Bellido de Luna, Juan, and Enrique Trujillo. *La anexión de Cuba a los Estados Unidos*. New York: Imprenta El Porvenir, 1892.

Benjamin, Thomas. *The Atlantic World: Europeans, Africans, Indians, and Their Shared History, 1400–1900*. Cambridge, UK: Cambridge University Press, 2008.

Bravo Sentéis, Miguel. *Revolución Cubana: Deportación a Fernando Poo: Relación de uno de los deportados*. New York: Hallet and Breen, 1869.

Brinton, Crane. *The Anatomy of Revolution*. New York: Vintage Books, 1965.

Browne, Jefferson B. *Key West: The Old and the New*. Gainesville: University Press of Florida, 1977.

Burgos, Adrian, Jr. "Entering Cuba's Other Playing Field: Cuban Baseball and the Choice between Race and Nation, 1887–1912." *Journal of Sport and Social Issues* 29 (February 2005): 9–40.

Cabrera García, Olga. *Diego Vicente Tejeda: Textos escogidos*. Havana: Editorial Ciencias Sociales, 1981.

Cairo Ballester, Ana, ed. *Máximo Gómez: 100 años*. Havana: Editorial Ciencias Sociales, 2006.

Camacho, Pánfilo D. *Aguilera, el precursor sin gloria*. Havana: Ministerio de Educación, 1951.

Carbonell, Néstor Leonelo. *Resonancias del pasado*. Havana: La Prueba, 1916.

Carbonell Rivero, Néstor. *El General Ramón Leocadio Bonachea*. Havana: Academia de la Historia de Cuba, 1947.

———. *Tampa, cuna del Partido Revolucionario Cubano*. Havana: Impr. El Siglo XX, 1957.

Casanovas, Joan. *Bread, or Bullets! Urban Labor and Spanish Colonialism in Cuba, 1850–1898*. Pittsburgh, PA: University of Pittsburgh Press, 1998.

Casasús, Juan J. E. *Calixto García, el estratega*. Havana: Oficina del Historiador de la Ciudad de la Habana, 1962.
——. *La emigración cubana y la independencia de la patria*. Havana: Editorial Lex, 1953.
——. *Ramón Leocadio Bonachea, el jefe de la vanguardia*. Havana: Editorial Librería Martí, 1955.
Castellanos García, Gerardo. *Misión a Cuba: Cayo Hueso y Martí*. Havana: Imprenta Alfa, 1944.
——. *Motivos de Cayo Hueso*. Havana: UCAR, García y cia, 1935.
——. *Soldado y conspirador*. Havana: Editorial Hermes, 1923.
——. *Tarja de bronce: Serafín Sánchez a través de su siglo*. Havana: Impr. El Siglo XX, 1946.
Castillo Zúñiga, José Rogelio. *Autobiografía del general José Rogelio Castillo*. Havana: Instituto Cubano del Libro, 1973.
Céspedes Quesada, Carlos Manuel. *Manuel de Quesada y Loynaz*. Havana: Impr. El Siglo XX, 1925.
Chaffin, Tom. *Fatal Glory: Narciso López and the First Clandestine U.S. War against Cuba*. Charlottesville: University of Virginia Press, 1996.
Childs, Matt D. *The 1812 Aponte Rebellion in Cuba*. Chapel Hill: University of North Carolina Press, 2006.
Collazo, Enrique. *Cuba independiente*. Santiago de Cuba: Editorial Oriente, 1981.
Cordoví Núñez, Yoel, ed. *Máximo Gómez en perspectivas*. Santiago de Cuba: Editorial Oriente, 2007.
Cuba. Departamento de Estado. *Relación de los funcionarios diplomáticos y consulares de la república y de los agentes diplomáticos y consulares extranjeros acreditados en Cuba*. 1903; repr., Havana: Imprenta y Papelería de Rambla y Bouza, 1905.
Cuervo Rubio, Gustavo. *Libro de Homenaje al Coronel Cosme de la Torriente en reconocimiento de sus grandes servicios a Cuba*. Havana: UCAR, García, SA, 1951.
De la Cova, Antonio Rafael. "Filibusters and Freemasons: The Sworn Obligation." *Journal of the Early Republic* 17 (Spring 1996): 95–120.
Delgado, Manuel Patricio. "Martí en Cayo Hueso." *Revista Cubana* 29 (July 1951–December 1952): 72–80.
Del Rio, Emilio. *Yo fui uno de los fundadores de Ybor City*. Tampa, 1950.
Deschamps Chapeaux, Pedro. *Rafael Serra y Montalvo, obrero incansable de nuestra independencia*. Havana: Unión de Escritores y Artistas de Cuba, 1975.
Deulofeu Lleonart, Manuel. *Héroes del destierro. La emigración. Notas históricas*. Cienfuegos, Cuba: Imp. de M. Mestre, 1904.
——. *Martí. Cayo Hueso y Tampa*. Cienfuegos: Antonio Cuevas y Hermano, 1905.
Diddle, A. W. "The History of Civilian Medical Care in Key West up to 1945." *The Journal of the Florida Medical Association* 33 (January 1947): 383–389.
Eastman, Scott. *Preaching Spanish Nationalism across the Hispanic Atlantic, 1759–1823*. Baton Rouge: Louisiana State University Press, 2012.

"El Archivo de la Junta Superior de Sanidad." *Boletín del Archivo Nacional* 4 (March–April 1905): 53–60.

El Bandolerismo en Cuba. 3 vols. Havana: Establecimiento Tipográfica, 1890.

Estrada Palma, Tomás. *Correspondencia diplomática de la Delegación Cubana en Nueva York durante la Guerra de Independencia, 1895–1898*. 5 vols. Havana: Impr. El Siglo XX, 1943–1946.

Fernández, Frank. *Cuban Anarchism. The History of a Movement*. Tucson, AZ: Sharpe Press, 2001.

Ferrer, Ada. *Insurgent Cuba: Race, Nation, and Revolution, 1868–1898*. Chapel Hill: University of North Carolina Press, 1999.

Figueredo Socarrás, Fernando. *José Dolores Poyo: Conferencia*. Havana: Imprenta P. Fernández y Comp., 1912.

Fink, Leon. *Workingman's Democracy: The Knights of Labor and American Politics*. Champaign: University of Illinois Press, 1985.

Foner, Philip. *Antonio Maceo*. New York: Monthly Review Press, 1977.

Franco, José L. *Antonio Maceo: Apuntes para una historia de su vida*. 3 vols. Havana: Editorial de Ciencias Sociales, 1975.

———. *Ruta de Antonio Maceo en el Caribe*. Havana: Oficina del Historiador de la Ciudad de la Habana, 1961.

Gálvez, Wen. *Tampa: Impresiones de emigrado*. Tampa, FL: Establecimiento Tipográfico Cuba, 1897.

García del Pino, César. *Leoncio Prado y la revolución cubana*. Havana: Editorial ORBE, 1980.

García Domínguez, Bernardo. *El pensamiento vivo de Máximo Gómez*. 2 vols. Santiago de Cuba: Ediciones CEDEE/Casa del Caribe, 1991–1992.

Goldstone, Jack A., ed. *The Encyclopedia of Political Revolutions*. Washington, D.C.: Congressional Quarterly, 1998.

Gómez, Máximo. *Album del Estado Mayor del Cuartel General del Ejército Libertador Cubano*. Havana: El Score, 1912.

———. *Diario de campaña, 1868–1898*. Havana: Instituto Cubano del Libro, 1968.

González Echeverría, Roberto. *The Pride of Havana: A History of Cuban Baseball*. New York: Oxford University Press, 1988.

Granda, Manuel J. de. *La paz de manganeso*. Havana: Impr. El Siglo XX, 1939.

Guerra y Sánchez, Ramiro. *Guerra de los 10 Años*. 2 vols. Havana: Editorial Ciencias Sociales, 1972.

Guerra y Sánchez, Ramiro, José M. Pérez Cabrera, Juan J. Remos, and Emeterio S. Santovenia, eds. *Historia de la nación cubana*. 10 vols. Havana: Editorial Historia de la Nación Cubana, 1952.

Helg, Aline. *Our Rightful Share: The Afro-Cuban Struggle for Equality, 1886–1912*. Chapel Hill: University of North Carolina Press, 1995.

Henríquez Ureña, Camila. *Eugenio María de Hostos: Obras*. Havana: Casa de las Américas, 1976.

Hernández, Eusebio. *Maceo: Dos conferencias históricas*. Havana: Instituto Cubano del Libro, 1968.

Hidalgo Paz, Ibrahím. *Cuba, 1895–1898: Contradicciones y disoluciones*. Havana: Centro de Estudios Martianos, 1999.

———. *José Martí: Cronología, 1853–1895*. Havana: Editorial Ciencias Sociales, 1992.

———. "Reseña de los clubes fundadores del Partido Revolucionario Cubano." *Anuario del Centro de Estudios Martianos* 4 (1981): 208-230

Horrego Estuch, Leopoldo. *Emilia Casanova: La vehemencia del separatismo*. Havana: Academia de la Historia de Cuba, 1951.

———. *Martín Morúa Delgado: Vida y mensaje*. Havana: Editorial Sánchez, 1957.

Ibarra Cuesta. Jorge. *José Martí: Dirigente político e ideólogo revolucionario*. Havana: Editorial Ciencias Sociales, 1980.

———. *Máximo Gómez frente al imperio, 1898–1905*. Havana: Editorial Ciencias Sociales, 2000.

Iglesias, César Andreu. *Memorias de Bernardo Vega: Contribuciones a la historia de la comunidad puertorriqueña en Nueva York*. Puerto Rico: Ediciones Huracán Inc., 1977.

Iglesia Santos, Álvaro de la. *Manuel García, El Rey de los Campos: Su vida y sus hechos*. Havana: La Comercial, 1895.

Iglesias Utset, Marial. *A Cultural History of Cuba during the U.S. Occupation, 1898–1902*. Chapel Hill: University of North Carolina Press, 2011.

Infiesta, Ramón. *Máximo Gómez*. Havana: Academia de la Historia de Cuba, 1937.

Ingalls, Robert P. *Urban Vigilantes in the New South, Tampa, 1882–1936*. Knoxville: University of Tennessee Press, 1988.

Isidrón Torres, Cipriano. *Manuel García: Rey de los campos de Cuba. Camilo y Estrella*. Havana: Editorial Letras Cubanas, 1989.

"José Martí y el juego de pelota en los Estados Unidos." *Opus Habana* 9, no. 1 (2005): 52–57.

Jústiz y del Valle, Tomás. *Elogio del Sr. Néstor Leonelo Carbonell*. Havana: Academia de la Historia de Cuba, 1946.

Kirk, John. *José Martí: Mentor of the Cuban Nation*. Gainesville: University Press of Florida, 1983.

"La captura del Moctezuma." *Boletín del Archivo Nacional* 7 (September–October 1908): 90-98.

Lagomasino, Luís. *La Guerra de Cuba*. Veracruz, México: Imprenta de Las Selvas, 1897.

———. *Reminiscencias pátrias*. Manzanillo: Tip. "El Reporter," 1902.

Lavie Vera, Nemesio. *La personalidad de Rafael María Merchán*. Havana: Academia de la Histórica de Cuba, 1951.

Lazo, Rodrigo. *Writing to Cuba: Filibustering and Cuban Exiles in the United States*. Chapel Hill: University of North Carolina Press, 2005.

Lisazo, Félix. *José Martí: Martyr of Cuban Independence*. Translated by Esther Elise Shuler. Albuquerque: University of New México Press, 1953.

Llaverías, Joaquín. *Historia de Archivo de Cuba*. Havana: Impr. La Universal de Ruiz y Cia, 1912.

———. *Contribución a la historia de la prensa periódica*. 2 vols. Havana: Archivo Nacional de Cuba, 1957.

Llerena, María Cristina. *Sobre la Guerra de los 10 Años, 1868–1878*. Havana: Instituto Cubano del Libro, 1971.

Lomas, Laura. *Translating Empire: José Martí, Migrant Latino Subjects, and American Modernities*. Durham, NC: Duke University Press, 2008.

Loynaz del Castillo, Enrique. *Memorias de la guerra*. Havana: Editorial de Ciencias Sociales, 1989.

Maceo, Antonio. *Papeles de Maceo*. 2 vols. Havana: Editorial de Ciencias Sociales, 1998.

Macías, José Miguel. *Deportados políticos a Fernando Poo: Expresión de profesiones, edad, naturalidad y fecha de prisión, fuga y fallecimiento*. New York, 1882.

Mañach, Jorge. *José Marti: Apostle of Freedom*. Translated by Colet Taylor. New York: The Devin-Adair Co., 1950.

Márquez Sterling, Manuel. *Martí: Ciudadano de América*. New York: Las Américas, 1965.

Martí, José. *Epistolario*. Edited by Luis García Pascual and Enrique H. Moreno Pla. 5 vols. Havana: Editorial Ciencias Sociales, 1993.

———. *Obras completas*. 28 vols. Havana: Editorial Nacional de Cuba, 1963.

Martínez-Fernández, Luís. *Protestantism and Political Conflicts in the Nineteenth-Century Hispanic Caribbean*. New Brunswick, NJ: Rutgers University Press, 2003.

Merchan, Rafael M. *Patria y cultura*. Havana: Ministerio de Educación, 1948.

Morales y Morales, Vidal. *Iniciadores y primeros mártires de la revolución cubana*. Havana: Imprenta Avisador Comercial, 1901.

Morúa Delgado, Martín. *Jenios olvidados: Noticias biográficas por Francisco Segura y Pereyra*. Havana: El Comercio Tipográfico, 1895.

———. *Obras completas*. 4 vols. Havana: Comisión Nacional del Centenario de Don Martín Morúa Delgado, 1957.

Muñiz, José Rivero. "Los Cubanos en Tampa." *Revista Bimestre Cubana* 74 (January–June 1958): 5–140.

O'Toole, G.J.A. *The Spanish War: An American Epic 1898*. New York: W. W. Norton, 1984.

Padilla Miyares, Oscar. "El ultimo convencional martiano." *Carteles* 34 no. 21 (1953): 98–100.

Padrón Valdés, Abelardo. *El General Flor: Apuntes históricos de una vida*. Havana: Editorial Arte y Literatura, 1976.

Partido Comunista de Cuba. *Carlos Baliño: Documentos y artículos* Havana: Instituto de Historia del Movimiento Comunista, 1976.

Partido Comunista de la Provincia de Sancti Spíritus. *Apuntes biográficos del Mayor General Serafín Sánchez*. Havana: Unión de Escritores y Artistas de Cuba, 1986.

Payne, Stanley G. *A History of Spain and Portugal*. 2 vols. Madison: University of Wisconsin Press, 1973.
Peláez, Ángel. *Primera jornada de José Martí en Cayo Hueso*. New York: Imprenta América, 1896.
Pérez, Louis A., Jr. *Cuba between Empires, 1878–1902*. Pittsburgh, PA: University of Pittsburgh, 1983.
———. *Cuba under the Platt Amendment, 1902–1934*. Pittsburgh, PA: University of Pittsburgh Press, 1986.
———. *Lords of the Mountain: Social Banditry and Peasant Protest in Cuba, 1878–1918*. Pittsburgh, PA: University of Pittsburgh Press, 1989.
———. *On Becoming Cuban: Identity, Nationality & Culture*. Chapel Hill: University of North Carolina Press, 1999.
———. *To Die in Cuba: Suicide and Society*. Chapel Hill: University of North Carolina Press, 2005.
Pérez Rolo, Juan. *Mis recuerdos*. Key West, 1928.
Plasencia, Aleida. "La destitución del Presidente Céspedes." *Universidad de la Habana* 32 (October–December 1968): 75–88.
———. *Bibliografía de la Guerra de los Diez Años*. Havana: Instituto del Libro, 1968.
Ponte Domínguez, Francisco J. *El delito de francomasonería en Cuba*. México: Editorial Humanidad, 1951.
Portuondo, Fernando. *Francisco Vicente Aguilera: Epistolario*. Havana: Editorial de Ciencias Sociales, 1974.
Poyo, Gerald E. "The Anarchist Challenge to the Cuban Independence Movement, 1885–1890." *Cuban Studies/Estudios Cubanos* 15 (Winter 1985): 29–42.
———. "Baseball in Key West and Havana, 1885–1910: The Career of Francisco A. Poyo." *Florida Historical Quarterly* 87 (Spring 2009): 540–564.
———. "Cuban Émigré Communities in the United States and the Independence of their Homeland, 1852–1895." PhD diss., University of Florida, 1983.
———. "The Cuban Experience in the United States, 1865–1940: Migration, Community and Identity." *Cuban Studies* 21 (1991): 19–36.
———. "Cuban Patriots in Key West, 1878–1886: Guardians of the Separatist Ideal." *Florida Historical Quarterly* 61 (July 1982): 20–36.
———. "Cuban Revolutionaries and Monroe County Reconstruction Politics, 1868–1876." *Florida Historical Quarterly* 55 (April 1977): 407–422.
———. "The Impact of Cuban and Spanish Workers on Labor Organizing in Florida, 1870–1900." *Journal of American Ethnic History* 5 (Spring 1986): 46–63.
———. "Key West and the Cuban Ten Years War." *Florida Historical Quarterly* 57 (January 1979): 289–307.
———. *"With All, and the Good of All": The Emergence of Popular Nationalism in the Cuban Communities of the United States, 1848–1898*. Durham, NC: Duke University Press, 1989.

Poyo, José Dolores. "Informe elevado al Sr. Secretario de Gobernación." *Boletín del Archivo Nacional* 8 (September–October 1909): 91–94.
Primelles, León. *La Revolución del 95, según la correspondencia de la Delegación Cubana en Nueva York*. 5 vols. Havana: Editorial Habanera, 1932.
Rejai, Mostafa, with Kay Philips. *Leaders of Revolution*. London: Sage Publications, 1979.
Rodríguez, José Ignacio. *Estudio histórico sobre el origen, desenvolvimiento y manifestaciones prácticas de a idea de la anexión de la isla de Cuba a los Estados Unidos de América*. Havana: La Propaganda Literaria, 1900.
———. *The Case of the Arrest, Trial, and Sentence in the City of Havana, Island of Cuba of Julio Sanguily, a Citizen of the United States of America*. Washington, D.C.: W.F. Roberts, 1897.
———. *Vida del Presbítero Don Félix Varela*. New York: Imprenta de O Novo Mundo, 1878.
Rodríguez Altunaga, Rafael. *El general Emilio Núñez*. Havana: Sociedad Colombista Panamericana, 1958.
Rodríguez Colina, Leandro. *Documentos para servir la historia de la Guerra Chiquita*. 3 vols. Havana: Archivo Nacional de Cuba, 1949–1950.
Rodríguez de la O, Raúl. *Máximo Gómez, una vida extraordinaria*. Havana: Editora Política, 1986.
Rodríguez-Silva, Delfín. *Cronología Martiana: La ruta apostólica de José Martí, 1853–1895*. Miami, FL: Ediciones Universal, 1996.
Ronning, C. Neal. *José Martí and the Émigré Colony in Key West: Leadership and State Formation*. New York: Praeger, 1990.
Rubens, Horatio. *Libertad: Cuba y su apóstol*. Translated by Adolfo G. Castellanos. Havana: La Rosa Blanca, 1956.
Sánchez, Serafín. *Héroes humildes y los poetas de la guerra* Havana: Editorial Ciencias Sociales, 1981.
Schwartz, Rosalie. *Lawless Liberators: Political Banditry and Cuban Independence*. Durham, NC: Duke University Press, 1989.
Scott, Rebecca J. *Slave Emancipation in Cuba: The Transition to Free Labor, 1860–1899*. Princeton, NJ: Princeton University Press, 1985.
Serra y Montalvo, Rafael. *Ensayos Políticos*. Havana: El Reporter, 1899.
Sosa Rodríguez, Enrique, Francisco López Civeria, Antonio Aja Díaz, and Miriam Rodríguez Martínez. *Cuba y Cayo Hueso. Una historia compartida*. Havana: Editorial Ciencias Sociales, 2006.
Souza, Benigno. *Maximo Gómez: el generalísimo*. Havana: Editorial Ciencias Sociales, 1972.
Stebbins, Consuelo E. *City of Intrigue, Nest of Revolution: A Documentary History of Key West in the Nineteenth Century*. Gainesville: University Press of Florida, 2007.
———. "The Cuban Convention and Its Role in the Cuban Revolutionary Party." *Florida Historical Quarterly* 86 (Fall 2007): 186–215.

Tinajero, Araceli. *El Lector: A History of the Cigar Factory Reader*. Austin: University of Texas Press, 2010.
Tone, John Lawrence. *War and Genocide in Cuba, 1895–1898*. Chapel Hill: University of North Carolina Press, 2006.
Torres-Cuevas, Eduardo. *Historia de la masonería cubana*. Havana: Imagen Contemporánea, 2004.
Trujillo, Enrique. *Album de El Porvenir*. 4 vols. New York: Imprenta El Porvenir, 1890–1894.
———. *Apuntes históricos: Propaganda y movimientos revolucionarios cubanos en los Estados Unidos desde enero de 1880 hasta febrero de 1895*. New York: Tipografía El Porvenir, 1896.
Valdés Domínguez, Fermín. *Diario de soldado*. 2 vols. Havana: Universidad de la Habana, 1972.
———. *Tragedy in Havana: November 27, 1871*. Edited and translated by Consuelo E. Stebbins. Gainesville: University Press of Florida, 2000.
Villaverde, Cirilo. *Apuntes biográficos de Emilia Casanova de Villaverde*. New York, 1874.
———. "La revolución de Cuba vista desde New York," *Cuba en la UNESCO: Homenaje a Cirilo Villaverde*. Havana: Comisión Nacional Cubana de la UNESCO, 1964.
Westfall, Loy Glenn. *Key West: Cigar City, USA*. Key West, FL: Willis & Co., 1997.

INDEX

Aguero, Carlos, 171–72; death of, 90; expedition, 172; fund-raising, 171; guerrilla activities, 80–81; Martí and, 86; support for, 82
Aguilera, Francisco Vicente, 10, 56; visit to Key West, 69
Aldama, Manuel de, 51–54, 65
Alien Contract Labor Law of 1888, 179
Alpízar, Francisco, 24
Alpízar Leal, Luís, xii–xiii
Alpízar Poyo, Raoul, 12, 25, 247–48
La América (newspaper), 85
Anarchism, 108–11; in Cuba, 116; worker solidarity and, 108–9
André, Armando, 207
Anglo-Americans (*concos*): *conco taons* (Anglo-American neighborhoods), 17; Cubans' conflict with, 178–84, 188; in Key West, 168–69, 177, 205; Poyo and, 189–90; Roloff and, 205
Annexation, 49–50, 64, 228; Cuban independence compared with, 50–51
Antillean confederation, 49
Aponte, José Antonio, 4
Arms and ammunition, 75, 160, 192, 204
Arnao, Juan, 79, 87, 138, 143, 147, 184, 227
Asociación Patriótica de Cayo Hueso (Patriotic Association of Key West), 27
Association of Revolutionary Émigrés (Asociación de Emigrados Revolucionarios), 244, 246

La Aurora (newspaper), 59
Autonomist Liberal Party. *See* Partido Liberal Autonomista
Autonomists, 60–64, 89, 217–18; Left Autonomists, 229; Partido Liberal Autonomista, 61–62
El Avisador Cubano (newspaper), 88, 89

Baliño, Carlos, 100–101, 104, 109, 125; return to Cuba, 227
Baluarte cubano (Cuban bulwark), 68; in Ybor City, 103
Banderas, Quintín, 210
Bandoleros (bandits): expeditions, 128; politicized, 119–22
Barranco, Manuel, 15–16
Baseball, 158–59
Battlefield oratory. *See Oratoria manigüera*
Bavastro, Ernesto, 25
Bellido de Luna, Juan, 139, 149
Belligerency status for Cubans, 202, 216
Bello, Serafín, 143, 147, 148
Benítez, Santos, 104–7
Beribén, Manuel, 118; expedition, 121–22
Bethel, Livingston W., 171–73
Board of Trade: Key West, 175–76; Tampa, 108
Boletín del Archivo Nacional, 241
Bonachea, Ramón, 79–80, 82; execution of, 89–90
Borrego, Carlos, 27, 57

Borrero, Esteban, 210
Brooke, John R., 229–30; government structured by, 232
Browne, Jefferson B., 20
El Buñuelo (newspaper), 115

Camús y de la Merced Hoz, Clara Leonor, 12, 25; Club Hijas de la Libertad, 27
Cánovas del Castillo, Antonio, 217
Carbonell, Eligio, 140
Carbonell, Néstor Leonelo, 128, 140–41, 187; return to Cuba, 227
Caribbean, Cuban exiles in, 78
Carrero, Enrique, 57
Casanova, Emilia, 50
Casanova de Villaverde, Emilia, 27
Castañon, Gonzalo, 23
Castellanos, Gerardo, 16; leaves Key West, 184; and PRC, 145, 148; return to Cuba, 227; revolutionary activity of, 155; trip to Cuba, 155–56
Castellanos García, Gerardo, 233
Castillo, José Rogelio, 100
Catholic Church, 46–48
Cayo Hueso (Isle of Bones). *See* Key West, FL
Céspedes, Carlos Manuel de, 10, 37, 52–53, 61
Céspedes y Céspedes, Carlos Manuel, 53, 65, 169–70
Chenard, Francisco, 203, 208; Poyo and, 209; as president of Cuerpo de Consejo in New York, 209
Cigar industry, 2–3; cigar worker solidarity *versus* nationalism in, 98–103; class and, 59–60; entrepreneurs, 15–16; in Key West, 7, 14–16; *lectura* in, 19–21; manufacturing process, 20–21; Spaniards in, 99–101, 111–12, 115; stresses in management and labor relations within, 97; in Tampa, 174; in Ybor City, 103. *See also* Labor issues, cigar industry; Strikes, cigar industry; Workers' unions, cigar industry

Círculo de Trabajadores (labor organization), 115
Cisneros Betancourt, Salvador, 52–53, 79, 87; Consejo de Gobierno de la República and, 208
Class: in cigar industry, 59–60; in Cuba, 55; fund-raising and working, 212; Gómez, M., and, 87; Key West immigrants, 210–11; middle- and upper-, 210–11; Poyo and, 59; *El Yara* and, 59–60
Cleveland, Grover, 201–3
Club Democrático Cubano (Cuban Democratic Club), 57
Club Hijas de la Libertad (Daughters of Liberty), 27
Club Independiente, 79–80
Coast Guard, U.S., 202–3
Collazo, Enrique, 147, 193; Vuelta Abajo expedition, 200–201
Colonialism: in Cuba, 47–48; Spanish, 6
Concos. See Anglo-Americans
Conco taons (Anglo-American neighborhoods), 17
Consejo de Gobierno de la República (Government Council of the Republic in Arms), 208
Conservatives, 61–62
Constitución de Guáimaro, 56
Constituent Assembly, Cuban, 234
Constitutional Union Party. *See* Partido Unión Constitucional
Convención Cubana, 129–36, *130*; committees, 129; expeditions organized by, 132, 163; Poyo and, 129, 151
Cosmopolitan Order of the Sun. *See* Orden Cosmopolita del Sol
Creci, Enrique, 115
Crombet, Flor, 123; death of, 195; fund-raising efforts, 124–26; Poyo and, 125–26; Ruz and, 123–24
Cuba: abolition in, 72–73; activists returning to, 227; anarchism in, 109, 116; anti-American tradition, 247; *bandoleros* in, 119–22; belligerency status and, 202,

216; Castellanos, Gerardo in, 155–56; Catholic Church in, 46–47; class divisions in, 55; colonial experience, 47–48; Constituent Assembly, 234; economy, 46, 227; elections, 234–35; Estrada Palma as first president of, 235; exiles returning to, 227; Fernando Poo island, 10; Figueredo and, 227, 233–34; Gómez, M., and, 233; governmental structure in, 209, 232; House of Representatives, 37–39, 52, 56; insurrection, 193–98; Isle of Pines, 237; Key West's proximity to, 35–36; kidnappings in, 119–20; labor issues in, 95; legislature, proposed, 62; martial law in, 126–27; military occupation in, 222; national identity, 54; nationalism, 40; Oriente Province revolt, 76–78; political autonomy promised for, 60–64; politics in, 230–32, 238; post-revolutionary challenges, 8; Poyo's employment in, 233–34; Poyo's return to, 226–27; press limits in, 62; racial stresses in, 55–56, 210; Reformist Club, 45; revolutionary attempts in, 76–78, 131–33, 162–63; sabotage campaigns in, 207; slavery and, 49–50, 55–56, 72–73; Spaniards emigrating to, 95–96; Spanish negotiations in, 217–18; Spanish reforms in, 217; Spanish rule of, 45–46; U.S. authority in, 222; U.S. control of, 228; U.S. trade with, 2; Las Villas region of, 151–53, 155, 198–200; Vuelta Abajo (Pinar del Rio), 69, 200–201, 204, 216, 244; weapons and ammunition sent to, 52, 69, 160, 192, 204; *El Yara* in, 233
Cuba (newspaper), 26
Cuba, annexation of, 64, 228; Cuban independence compared with, 50–51; U.S. and, 49–50, 228
Cuban-Americans, 249
Cuban Assembly, 230; dissolution of, 232; Gómez, M., fired by, 231; U.S. and, 231
Cuban bulwark. *See Baluarte cubano*

Cuban Democratic Club. *See* Club Democrático Cubano
Cuban exile communities, 5, 34–35; *baluarte cubano*, 68; black and mulatto members of, 27–28; comparing, 87, 93–94; cultural and ethnic identity in, 7; generals, support for, 209–10; in Key West, 4, 10, 78; nationalism in, 7, 32, 40; oratory in, 28–29; politics in, 56–57, 168–71; race and, 56–57; relocation within, 18; representatives from, 209–10; revolutionary activism, 35; in U.S., 2; U.S. intervention accepted by, 218–19; war efforts by, 222–23; war supplies sent from, 52. *See also specific communities*
Cuban exiles, 2; in Caribbean, 78; education, 32–33; identity of, 3, 32; middle- and upper-class, 210–11; nationalism, 32; press, 22–26, 67; returning to Cuba, 227; Ten Years' War support by, 35, 51–52, 68
Cuban Federation of Tobacco Workers. *See* Federación Cubana de Tabaqueros
Cuban identity, 17–18; in Cuban communities, 7; of exiles, 3, 32; national, 54
Cuban immigrants, 95; Anglo-American conflicts with, 178–84, 188; local politics and, 183; middle- and upper-class, 210–11; political parties and, 183; politics and, 169–71, 177; repatriation of, 178; voting rights, 169, 171
Cuban independence, 1, 3–5; annexation compared with, 50–51; elections and, 234–35; first president and, 236; insurgent cells, 73–74; Key West and, 5, 6; leaders in, 66–67; McKinley and, 228; military leaders in, 5; Poyo and, 221–22; Poyo's disillusionment with, 234–38; PRC and, 226; race and, 213; realities of, 246–47; struggle for, 4–5; Ten Years' War and, 66; warfare tactics, 73. *See also* Ten Years' War
Cuban liberation army, 8

294 · Index

Cuban National Archive, 238–41; *Boletín del Archivo Nacional* and, 241; Delegation of the Cuban Revolutionary Party documents, 241; documents extracted from, 240–41; "Donativo José Dolores Poyo," xi; Poyo and, 238–41; transfer of, 239–40
Cuban National Party (Partido Nacional Cubano), 237
El Cubano (newspaper), 23, 109, 128
Cuban occupation, 3, 229, 232; Platt Amendment and, 234; U.S. troop withdrawal and, 234
Cuban Republic in Arms, 51, 228
Cuban revolutionary nationalist tradition, 4, 6–7
Cuban Revolutionary Party. *See* Partido Revolucionario Cubano
Cuban War of Independence, 192–225; exile communities' efforts and, 222–23; guerrilla tactics, 223; Spain's surrender ceremony, 228; tragedy of, 218; U.S. congressional action and, 221; U.S. control of Cuba after, 228; U.S. intervention in, 216–25; USS Maine's sinking and, 220–21
Cuban Workers' Society of New York. *See* Sociedad de Artesanos Cubanos de New York
Cuerpo de Consejo: creation in Key West, 149; final meeting of, 226; funds controlled by, 160; oppose exile election for representatives, 209; Poyo and, 151. *See also* Partido Revolucionario Cubano

Daughters of Liberty. *See* Club Hijas de la Libertad
Delegation of the Cuban Revolutionary Party, 241
Delgado, Manuel P., 24–25, 234; elected to Florida legislature, 177; Marti, J., and, 144, 149–50; Partido Independiente and, 183; PRC crisis committee, 167; as union president, 105–6; *La Voz de Hatuey* (newspaper), and, 172
Del Pino, Antonio, 15–16
Democratic Party, 170; Club Democrático Cubano, 57; Cuban immigrants and, 183
Deulofeu, Manuel, 47
Deulofeu Lleonart, Manuel, 4
Díaz, Emilio, 176
Dobarganes, Ramón, 210; Poyo and, 211
La Doctrina de Marti (newspaper), 211–12
Dr. Félix Varela Lodge No. 64, 42–43
Dulce, Domingo, 9; Grito de Yara and, 10–11
Dynamite and explosives, 73–76

Echeverría, José Antonio, 51
Equator-Democrat (newspaper), 174, 182, 183, 185
Equator/El Ecuador (newspaper), 26, 101, 103, 104, 107
Estrada, Don Juan de, 14
Estrada, José Rafael, 26, 175
Estrada, Rafael, 28
Estrada Palma, Tomás, *130*; Consejo de Gobierno de la República and, 208; Cuban elections and, 234–35; as Cuba's first president, 235; as diplomatic representative to U.S., 208; fund-raising by, 206; in Key West, 219–20; Platt Amendment and, 236–37; policies pursued by, 236–37; Poyo and, 198, 236–37; PRC and, 196–98, 208–9; public relations campaign against Spain, 213; reelection of, 237–38; resignation of, 238
Exiles. *See* Cuban exiles
Expeditions, 205; Aguero, C., and, 81, 172; *bandoleros*,' 128; Beribén and, 121–22; Bonachea, R., and, 79–80; Castro, P., and, 205; Collazo, E., and, 200–201; Convención Cubana-approved, 163; Figueredo and planning, 206; García, C., and, 77, 201; García, M., and, 121–22, 133–35; Gómez, M., and, 91; González, C., and, 77; Huau and planning, 206;

Maceo's, 90–91, 133; Núñez and planning, 209, 224; Poyo and planning, 119–20, 204, 206, 224; PRC's Department of, 203; Roloff, C., and, 198–200, 205–6; Ruz and planning, 119–24; Sánchez, L., and P. Varona, 82; Sánchez, S., and, 198–200; Sanguily, J., and, 163; U.S. and revolutionary, 201–2; to Las Villas region of Cuba, 198–200; Vuelta Abajo, 200–201

Federación Cubana de Tabaqueros (Cuban Federation of Tobacco Workers), 105–6; Knights of Labor and, 106
Fernandina Plan, 193–94
Fernando Poo (island), 10
Figueredo, Fernando, 12, 83, 187, 245; Consejo de Gobierno de la República and, 208; Convención Cubana, 129; in Cuba, 233–34; expeditions planned by, 206; Partido Independiente and, 183; PRC and, 145–46; PRC crisis committee, 167; return to Cuba, 227
Figueredo Socarrás, Fernando, 71
Figueroa, Sotero, 211–12
Franco, José Luciano, 6
Freemasonry, 41; Dr. Félix Varela Lodge No. 64, 42–43; in Key West, 42–43; Poyo's affiliation with, 42–43
Fund-raising: Aguero's, 171; challenge of, 206; Crombet's, 125–26; Cuban exiles returning to Cuba and, 227; Estrada Palma's, 206; in Key West, 161; kidnapping and, 135–36; Martí's, 161–62, 188–89; nationalism and, 7, 97–98, 136; police action against coercive, 176; Poyo's, 214–15; PRC's, 156–60; PRC wage deductions and, 213; strikes and, 212; after U.S. intervention, 224; among working class, 212

Gaceta de la Habana (newspaper), 9, 232
García, Calixto, 5; death of, 230; Oriente Province revolt and, 76–77; U.S. intervention and, 223–24; visit to New York, 76
García, Emilio, 127, 175–76
García, Manuel, 118; expedition, 121–22, 133–35; folk lore regarding, 243–44; Maceo and, 132; murder of, 195; Poyo and, 126–27; revolutionaries' disassociation with, 243
García, Rosendo, 81, 90, 120–21, 132, 168, 172, 179–80
Gato, Eduardo Hidalgo, 15, 183
Gil Marrero, Federico, 74, 92, 124, 134, 173
GOCA. See Gran Oriente de Cuba y las Antillas
Gómez, José Miguel, 237
Gómez, Juan Gualberto, 194–95, 242
Gómez, Máximo, 5, 80; in Cuba, 233; Cuban Assembly and, 231; Cuban National Party established by, 237; death of, 237; expedition, 91; Key West community's support of, 93–94; Maceo's project with, 83–84; Martí and, 86, 159; military campaigns, 83; in New York, 84–89; Poyo and, 83–84, 192, 224–25, 231; radicalization opposed by, 75; trip to Key West, 83–84; U.S. payment of troops and, 231–32; Weyler and, 216
Gómez Toro, Panchito, 186, 216
González, Cecilio, 77
González, Francisco María, 140–41, 245; defends Martí, 147–49; return to Cuba, 227
González Lanuza, José Antonio, in Key West, 219–20
Government Council of the Republic in Arms. See Consejo de Gobierno de la República
Govín, Antonio, 63
Gran Oriente de Cuba y las Antillas (GOCA), 41–42
Grito de Yara: Dulce and, 10–11; *voluntarios* and, 9

Guáimaro Constitution, 83
Guerra, Benjamín, 148, 197, 198, 218
La Guerra Chiquita. *See* The Little War

Hernández, Eusebio, 93
Herrera, Martín, 33, 161, 234; Partido Independiente and, 183; return to Cuba, 227; Zanjón Pact protested by, 65
Hostos, Eugenio María, 34–35, 49
Huau, Alejandro, 203, 205; expeditions planned by, 206

La Igualdad (newspaper), 23, 57–58
La Independencia (newspaper), 67
Independentistas, 54
Independent Party, 170–71
Insurgent cells: attacks launched by, 74–75; explosives used by, 75; Martí's meetings with, 161; Nihilistas Ubiquitarios Cubanos de Key West, 73–75
Insurgent republic, 37–38
Insurrectionists, underground, 9
Insurrections: in Cuba, 193–98; *Laborantes*, 9; Lagomasino and planning, 152
El Intransigente (newspaper), 215
Isle of Bones. *See* Key West, FL
Isle of Pines, 237

José de los Dolores de la Encarnación Poyo y Remírez de Estenóz. *See* Poyo, José Dolores
J. S. Navarro & Co., 15
La Justicia (newspaper), 109

Key West (Cayo Hueso), FL, 13–19; Aguilera's visit to, 69; Anglo-Americans in, 168–69, 177, 205; Asociación Patriótica de Cayo Hueso, 27; bad press regarding, 174–75; changes in, 248–49; cigar industry in, 7, 14–16; "company town" model in, 109–10; crime in, 175–76; Cuban businesses in, 16–17; Cuban Catholic congregation in, 47–48; Cuban exile community, 4, 10, 78; Cuban independence and, 5, 6; Cuban revolutionary nationalist tradition in, 4; Cuba's proximity to, 35–36; economic crisis, 188; Estrada Palma in, 219–20; ethnic conflict in, 177–84, 188; exile community, 4, 10; exodus from, 183–84; fire, 92, 102; Freemasonry in, 42–43; fund-raising in, 161; Gómez, M., and, 83–84, 93–94; González Lanuza in, 219–20; growth and development, 14; local politicians, 171–73; Maceo and, 83–84, 93–94; Martí and, 4, 137–38, 144–46, 151, 165; middle- and upper-class immigrants to, 210–11; nationalism in, 116, 248; New York exile community compared with, 87, 93–94; orators, 29; political divisions in, 110–11; politics and, 169–70, 171–78, 177; race in, 27–28, 56–58, 177; racism in, 169; reconstruction, 102; revolution and, 72; revolutionaries in, 76–84; revolutionaries supported by, 93–94; revolutionaries visiting, 83; revolutionary activism, 93; as revolutionary community, 7, 34–35, 68, 116–17; revolutionary community rebuilding in, 191; slavery in, 14; Spaniards emigrating to, 96, 99–100; Spanish government's diplomatic presence in, 202; visiting revolutionaries to, 68–69
Kidnappings, 135–36
King Fernando VII of Spain, 43–44
Knight, Peter, 176–77
Knights of Labor, 98–99, 101; Federación Cubana de Tabaqueros and, 106

Laborantes (underground insurrectionists), 9
Labor issues, cigar industry: Alien Contract Labor Law of 1888 and, 179; anarchism and, 108–9; in Cuba, 95; hiring and, 99–100; nationalism and, 98–108; Poyo and, 212–13; PRC wage deductions and, 213; Seidenberg & Co. cigar factory, 185; Spanish workers and, 99–101,

111–12, 115; stresses in management and labor relations as, 97; worker solidarity *versus* nationalism and, 98–103. *See also* Strikes, cigar industry
Lagomasino, Luis, 151; insurrection planned by, 152
Lamadriz, José Francisco, 70–71, 83, 87; Convención Cubana, 129; death, 151; grave, 161; PRC and, 145–46
Latin America, independence in, 40, 50–51, 54
The League of Cuban Daughters. *See* La Liga de las Hijas de Cuba
Lectores (readers): moral authority, 22; Poyo as, 19–22, 114
Lectura (reading aloud), 19–22
Left Autonomists, 229
Leijas, Isidoro, 107–8, 121, 175–76
Lemus, Morales, 51
Liberalism: governance and, 43–48; Spanish, 43–45
Liberal Party, 237–38; Partido Liberal Autonomista, 61–63
La Liga de las Hijas de Cuba (The League of Cuban Daughters), 27
The Little War (La Guerra Chiquita), 76–78
Llaverías, Joaquín, 239, 241
López, Narciso, 10, 51
Loynaz del Castillo, Enrique, 193, 245

Maceo, Antonio, 5, 25–26, 65–66, 80, 131; death of, 216; expedition, 90–91, 133; García, M., and, 132; Gómez, M., and, 83–84; Key West and, 83–84, 93–94; Martí and, 86; in New York, 84–89; Oriente Province revolt and, 76–77; radicalization opposed by, 75; trip to Key West, 83–84
Macfarlane, Hugh, 183–84
Maloney, N., 176–77
Marinas, Luis, 113
Marrero, Francisco, 15
Martí, José, xi, 85–86, 130, 137–66, 157, 186, *187*; Aguero and, 86; armed action opposed by, 88; assassination attempt, 165; as autonomist, 89; commemoration of birth of, 242; correspondence with revolutionaries, 152–53; critics of, 143, 147–48; death of, 195–96; Fernandina Plan, 193–94; fund-raising efforts, 161–62, 188–89; Gómez, M., and, 86, 159; insurgents and meetings with, 161; Key West and, 4, 137–38, 144–46, 151, 165; legacy of, 241–42; Maceo and, 86; nationalism, 139; *Obras Completas*, xi; as orator, 141–42; organizing efforts, 161; Poyo and, xi, 138, 190–91, 196, 241–42; Poyo's correspondence with, xii, 139–40, 164; Poyo's friendship with, 164–66; PRC and, 142–51; press's attack on, 182; as revolutionary, 143; revolutionary politics, 154–55; Roloff and, 153–54; Sánchez's correspondence with, 153; statue, 242–43; in Tampa, 138–42; Trujillo, E., and, 149–50
Martínez, Saturnino, 59
Martínez Campos, Arsenio, 60, 65
Martínez Ybor, Vicente, 15, 22; in Ybor City, 103
Martínez Ybor (cigar) factory, 15, 103, 106–7, 157, 158
Martyrs, 31, 90; monument to, 161, 196
Masó, Bartolomé, 235
Masonic secret societies, 41
McKinley, William, 202; Cuban independence and, 228; U.S. intervention and, 219
Méndez Capote, Domingo, 228–29
Menéndez, Alejandro, 32
Merchán, Rafael, 236
Messonier, Enrique, 110, 176–77; return to Cuba, 227
Militias. *See Voluntarios*
La Misericordia, 244
Moderates, 237
Montoro, Rafael, 63
Monzón, Juan, 16, 203–4

Morales y Morales, Vidal, 234, 238, 240
Moreno, Manuel, 127, 128, 134, 183
Moret Law, 58
Morúa Delgado, Martín, 28, 107; radicalization opposed by, 75–76

Nationalism, 37–64, 246–47; challenges to, 95–96; cigar worker solidarity *versus*, 98–103; Cuban, 40; in Cuban communities, 7, 17–18, 32; fund-raising, 7, 97–98, 136; in Key West, 116, 248; Key West fire and, 102; labor activism and, 98–108; Martí's, 139; newspapers, 26; Poyo and, 40, 70–71, 96; preserving legacy of, 241–44; *El Yara* and, 102–3
Newspapers: in Cuba, 62; Cuban exiles and, 22–26, 67; Martí in, 182; nationalism, 26; Poyo and, 22–26; socialism in, 109. *See also specific newspapers*
New York exile community, 84–89; Cuban political thinkers in, 85; Cuerpo de Consejo in, 209; García, C., in, 76; Key West community compared with, 87, 93–94; Poyo and, 198; PRC in, 211–12; Sociedad de Artesanos Cubanos de New York, 51; *El Yara* and, 87–88
Nihilism, 74
Nihilistas Ubiquitarios Cubanos de Key West (Ubiquitous Cuban Nihilists of Key West), 73–75
November 27, 1871 executions, 29–31, *30*
Núñez, Emilio, 201, 203; expeditions planned by, 209; Poyo and, 209

Obras completas (Complete Works) (Martí), xi
O'Farrill, Juan Ramón, 215
Oratoria manigüera (battlefield oratory), 29
Oratory, 28–29; Martí's, 141–42; *oratoria manigüera*, 29
Orden Cosmopolita del Sol (Cosmopolitan Order of the Sun), 69–70, 78
Oriente Province revolt, 76–78
Orozco, Mateo, 23

Panic of 1873, 96
Partida la Tranca, 92, 100, 167–68
Partido Independiente, 183
Partido Liberal Autonomista (Autonomist Liberal Party), 61–63
Partido Nacional Cubano. *See* Cuban National Party
Partido Revolucionario Cubano (PRC; Cuban Revolutionary Party), 8, 142–51; arms provided by, 204; authority in, 207–8; chain of command, 208–9; charter document, 145; clubs affiliated with, 191; crisis committee, 167; critics of, 147–48; Cuban independence and, 226; *delegado*, 208; Delegation of, 241; Department of Expeditions, 203; disagreements and divisions within, 210; dissolution of, 226; Estrada Palma and, 196–98, 208–9; Figueredo and, 145–46, 167; funding controversies and, 214; fund-raising efforts, 156–60, 213; hierarchy in, 207–8; Lamadriz and, 145–46; local authorities' disruption of, 181–82; lottery, 191, 214–15; Martí and, 142–51; in New York, 211–12; Poyo and, 142–51; Poyo's hierarchy of authority in, 207–8; Poyo's support of, 211–12; resistance to, 149–50; revolutionary government and, 208; setback, 184; stipends provided by, 214; support of, 148–49; third anniversary celebration, 186; transition to Cuban Nationalist Party, 229; Trujillo, E., and, 149–51; wage deductions for, 213; weakening of, 213–14; welfare fund, 214–15; *El Yara's* support of, 150, 211–12
Partido Unión Constitucional (Constitutional Union Party), 61
Patria (newspaper), 149, 182, 185, 190, 211
El Patriota (newspaper), 23, 66
Patriotic Association of Key West. *See* Asociación Patriótica de Cayo Hueso
Patterson, George B., 171–73
Pedroso, Paulina, 246
Pedroso, Ruperto, 28

Pendleton, Charles, 174–77, 181, 183, 185
Pequeño, Pedro, 128
Pérez, Teodoro, 16; Partido Independiente and, 183; PRC crisis committee, 167; return to Cuba, 227
Philbrick, John J., 176–77
Pierra, Adolfo, 218
Pierra, Fidel, 218, 229
Pine Key, 198–99
Platt Amendment, 234; Estrada Palma and, 236–37
Pómpez, José G., 28
El Porvenir (newspaper), 149, 150, 182
Pouble, Cirilo, 18
Poyo, America, 12, 25, 27, 33
Poyo, Blanca, 12, 27, 33
Poyo, Celia, 12, 25, 27, 31, 33
Poyo, Francisco, 12, 33, 144, 152, 158, 165, 217, 245–49
Poyo, José Dolores, xi, *38*, *130*, *157*, *187*; Anglo-American community and, 189–90; anti-Spanish attitudes, 40–41; appearance, 19; arrest warrant, 173; Asociación Patriótica de Cayo Hueso, 26; Association of Revolutionary Émigrés and, 244; authority of, 207–8; *Boletín del Archivo Nacional* and, 241; Chenard and, 209; cigar industry strike and, 111–12; class and, 59; Consejo de Gobierno de la República and, 208–9; as consul for Peru, 70; Convención Cubana and, 129, 151; critics of, 128; Crombet and, 125–26; as Cuban exile community leader, 5–6; Cuban independence and, 221–22; Cuban independence and disillusionment of, 234–38; Cuban National Archive and, 238–41; Cuban National Archive document extraction and, 240–41; Cuban National Archive transfer and, 239–40; as Cuban Revolutionary Party president, 8; Cuerpo de Consejo and, 151; death of, 244–46; Dobarganes and, 211; "Donativo José Dolores Poyo," xi; employment in Cuba, 233–34; Estrada Palma and, 198, 236–37; exile of, 1–2, 9; in exile press, 22–26; expeditions planned by, 119–20, 204, 206; family, 11–13, 24–25; Freemasonry affiliation, 42–43; frustration, 189–91; fundraising by, 214–15; García, M., and, 126–27; Gómez, M., and, 83–84, 192, 224–25, 231; in hiding, 9–10; in Key West, 1, 6; labor issues and, 212–13; as *lector*, 19–22, 114; liberalism and, 43–48; Martí and, xi, 138, 190–91, 196; Martí's correspondence with, xii, 139–40, 164; Martí's friendship with, 164–66; Martí's legacy and, 241–42; middle- and upper-class immigrants to Key West and, 211; La Misericordia and, 244; nationalism and, 40, 70–71, 96; nationalist activism, 6; as nationalist leader, 70–71; in New York, 198; Núñez and, 209; as orator, 29; Orden Cosmopolita del Sol, 69–70; as patriarch, 11–12; personal attacks on, 113–14; personal papers of, xi–xii; politics in Cuba and, 230–31, 238; PRC and, 142–51; PRC and hierarchy of authority of, 207–8; PRC crisis committee, 167; PRC's support from, 211–12; preserving nationalist legacy of, 241–44; radicalization, 71–72, 127–28; return to Cuba, 226–27; as revolutionary, 1, 6–7, 21–22, 39–43, 67–68, 125–26; in revolutionary community, 26–36; Ruz and, 122–23, 125–26; separatism, 48–54; social questions, 54–60; Sociedad de Instrucción y Recreo San Carlos, 32–33; U.S. intervention and, 223–24; Valdés Domínguez and, 190, 224–25; values, 48–49; Villaverde and, 52; work and politics, 19–22; *El Yara*, xi, 5–6, 23–24; *El Yara* in Cuba, 233; in Ybor City, 103–8; Zanjón Pact protested by, 65
Prado, Leoncio, 70
PRC. *See* Partido Revolucionario Cubano

Press. *See* Newspapers
El Productor (newspaper), 109–10; *El Yara* and, 112–13
La Propaganda (newspaper), 26, 87, 107, 175–76
Propaganda campaigns, 80, 85
Protesta de Baraguá, 65
El Pueblo (newspaper), 28, 89, 106, 107, 109

Quesada, Gonzalo de, 194, 197, 219, 228, 231
Quesada, Manuel de, 37–39, 51

Race: in Cuba, 210; in Cuban exile communities, 56; Cuban independence and, 213; of Cubans, 27–28; in Key West, 27–28, 56–58, 177; revolutionaries and, 57; Ten Years' War and, 56. *See also* Slavery
Racism in Key West, 169
Radicalization, 66–76; opponents of, 75–76; Poyo's, 71–72, 127–28
Readers. *See Lectores*
Reciprocity Treaty of 1903, 237
Reformist Club, 45
Reformists, 54
Refugees, 210
La República (newspaper), 87, 106
El Republicano (newspaper), 23, 96; socialism and, 109
Republican Party, 169–70; Cuban immigrants and, 183
La Revista de Florida (newspaper), 26, 109, 114, 115
Revolution, 65–94; in Cuba, 131–32; discipline and, 207–15; financial support of, 92; government structure and, 209; Key West and, 72; limits of, 227–34; setbacks to, 90; structure of, 209; unity, 207–15
Revolutionaries, 6–7; in Cuba, 131; female, 27; ideology of, 7; in Key West, 68–69, 76–84; Key West's support of, 93–94; Martí as, 143; Martí's correspondence with, 143; military veterans as, 153–54; news for, 25–26; political participation of, 7; Poyo as, 1, 6–7, 21–22, 39–43, 67–68, 125–26; race and, 57
Revolutionary activism, 35; in Key West, 93
Revolutionary communities, 26–36; Key West as, 7, 34–35, 68, 116–17; rebuilding in Key West of, 191
Revolutionary infrastructure, 69–70
Revolutionary martyrs, 31, 90
Reyes, Juan María "Nito," 22–23
Rios, Antonio, 57
Rivero, Ramón, 26, 100–101; return to Cuba, 227
Rodríguez, Carolina "La Patriota," 29, 165, 179
Rodriguez, José Ignacio, 139, 149, 232
Rodríguez, Mayía, 76, 193
Rodríguez, Tuerto, 76, 82, 91, 93, 120, 203; PRC's fund-raising campaign, 156–58
Roig de San Martín, Enrique, 109
Roloff, Carlos, 82, *130*, 199; expedition, 205–6; Martí and, 153–54; PRC's fund-raising campaign, 156–58
La Rosa Española cigar factory, 167–68
Rubens, Horatio, 179–80, 221; contract labor case, 180–81
Ruz, Juan Fernández, 118, 121–22, 203; Crombet and, 123–24; expedition planned by, 119–24; Poyo and, 122–23, 125–26

Saladrigas, Carlos, 63
Salas, Juan Pablo, 14
San Carlos Educational and Recreation Society (Sociedad de Instrucción y Recreo San Carlos). *See* San Carlos Institute
San Carlos Institute, 32–34; activities and challenges, 33–34; destroyed by fire, 102; new building inaugurated, 127; symbol of revolutionary past, 248
Sánchez, Serafín, 151–52, 157, 188; death of, 216; Martí's correspondence with, 153; at Pine Key, 198–99; PRC's fund-raising campaign, 156–58

Sánchez-Haya cigar factory, 106
Sanguily, Julio, 18, 132, 195; expedition, 163
Sanguily, Manuel, 240
Sartorio, Manuel, 162
Sartorio, Ricardo, 162
Segura, Francisco, 100–101
Seidenberg & Co. cigar factory, 178–79; first opened, 15; labor dispute, 185; Poyo reader at, 19
Separatism, 48–54, 62–63
El Separatista (newspaper), 106, 109, 187
Serra, Rafael, 28; *La Doctrina de Martí*, 211–12
Seven Years' War, 2
Shafter, William, 228
El Siglo (newspaper), 45
Simonton, John W., 14
Slavery, 49–50; abolition of, 58, 72–73; in Cuba, 49–50, 55–56, 72–73; in Key West, 14; Moret Law, 58; in Spain, 58
Socialism, 109
Socialist Club, 213
Sociedad de Artesanos Cubanos de New York (Cuban Workers' Society of New York), 51
Soria, Cayetano, 15
Sorondo, Guillermo, 27–28, 100–101
Spain: Cuban rule by, 45–46; Cuban War of Independence, xi, 3–4, 5; diplomatic presence in Florida and, 202; Estrada Palma's public relations campaign against, 213; immigrants to Cuba from, 95–96; immigrants to Key West from, 96, 99–100; King Fernando VII of, 43–44; liberalism in, 43–45; negotiations in Cuba by, 217–18; policies of self-interest, 72; reforms in Cuba, 217; slavery and, 58; surrender ceremony, 228; U.S. relations with, 201–3, 219–20
Spaniards: in cigar industry, 99–101, 111–12, 115; emigrating to Cuba, 95–96; strikebreakers, 167–68; in unions, 106–7
Spanish Abolitionist Society, 58

Spanish Constitution, 43–44
Spanish language, 17; education, 32; institutions, 7
Strikes, cigar industry, 96–98, 111–17; fundraising and, 212; leaders, 176–77; Poyo and, 111–12; Spanish strikebreakers, 167–68; *El Yara* and, 212
Sugar plantations, 72

Tacón, Miguel, 44–45
Tampa, FL, 103; cigar industry in, 174; Cubans relocating to, 183; Martí in, 138–42. *See also* Ybor City, FL
Tejera, Diego Vicente, 212–13
Teller, Henry M., 221
Teller Amendment, 221, 223; Cuban occupation and, 232
Ten Years' War, 10; consequences of, 54; Cuban independence and, 66; exile support of, 68; nationalist thought and, 7; race and, 56; revolutionary martyrs of, 31
Torres, Perico, 81, 90, 119–21, 172, 203
Torriente, Cosme de la, 236
La Tribuna del Trabajo (newspaper), 109
Trujillo, Bernardino, 127, 176
Trujillo, Enrique, 88, 139, 182; Martí and, 149–50; PRC and, 149–51
Trujillo, Ricardo, 203

El Ubiquitario (newspaper), 74, 99
Ubiquitous Cuban Nihilists of Key West. *See* Nihilistas Ubiquitarios Cubanos de Key West
Unión de Tabaqueros, 99
United States (U.S.): authority in Cuba of, 222; belligerency status for Cubans and, 202, 216; Coast Guard, 202–3; congressional action by, 221; Cuba and troop withdrawal by, 234; Cuba controlled by, 228; Cuban annexation and, 49–50, 228; Cuban anti-American tradition, 247; Cuban Assembly and, 231; Cuban communities in, 2–3; Cuban exile

United States—*continued*
communities in, 2; Cuban immigrants in, 95, 169; Cuban independence and occupation by, 232; Cuban occupation by, 3, 229, 232; Cuban trade with, 2; Cuban troops paid by, 231–32; Estrada Palma as diplomatic representative to, 208; exiles returning to Cuba from, 227; obstructionist policies of, 201–2; Platt Amendment and, 234; revolutionary expeditions and government of, 201–2; Spain's relations with, 201–3, 219–20

U.S. intervention in Cuban War of Independence, 216–25; Cuban exile communities' acceptance of, 218–19; Estrada Palma and, 221–22; fund-raising after, 224; García, C., and, 223–24; McKinley and, 219; Poyo and, 223–24; USS *Maine* and, 220–21

USS *Maine*, sinking of, 220–21

Valdés Domínguez, Fermín, 31, 185, 188; defends Martí's reputation, 243; *Patria* and, 190; Poyo and, 190, 224–25
Valiente, Ambrosio, 69
Varela, Félix, 42–43, 44
Varona, José Enrique de, 211–12
El Vigía (newspaper), 212, 219
Las Villas region of Cuba, 151–53, 155; expedition to, 198–200
Villaverde, Cirilo, 50–51; Poyo and, 52; Sociedad de Artesanos Cubanos de New York, 51
Voluntarios (militias): Grito de Yara and, 9; violence, 11
La Voz de America (newspaper), 59
La Voz de Cuba (newspaper), 11, 23

La Voz de Patria (newspaper), 49–50
Vuelta Abajo, Cuba, 200–201

Weyler, Valeriano, 216–17; counteroffensive, 223; Gómez, M., and, 216; Spanish recall of, 217
Wood, Leonard, 232
Workers' unions, cigar industry, 96–97; Federación Cubana de Tabaqueros, 105–6; hiring and, 99–100; Sociedad de Artesanos Cubanos de New York, 51; Spaniards in, 106–7; worker solidarity *versus* nationalism and, 98–103; in Ybor City, 105–6

El Yara (newspaper), xi, 5–6, 23–24; class issues in, 59–60; contributors, 25–26; in Cuba, 233; nationalism and, 102–3; New York exile community and, 87–88; Partido Liberal Autonomista and, 61–63; Poyo and, xi, 5–6, 23–24; Poyo family and, 24–25; PRC supported by, 150, 211–12; *El Productor* and, 112–13; revolutionary news, 25–26; social issues in, 54–55; strikes and, 212; in Ybor City, 104–5
Ybor City, FL: cigar industry in, 103; Poyo in, 103–8; as revolutionary center, 104, 108; workers' unions in, 105–6; *El Yara* in, 104–5

Zaldívar, Miguel A., 183; PRC crisis committee, 167
Zambrana, Antonio, 61
Zanjón Pact, 60–61, 65; protests of, 76
Zola, Émile, 22

GERALD E. POYO is professor of history and O'Connor Chair for the History of Hispanic Texas and the Southwest at St. Mary's University in San Antonio. He grew up in Latin America and has a special interest in the history of Cuba, his father's land of origin. He is the author of *"With All, and for the Good of All": The Emergence of Popular Nationalism in the Cuban Communities of the United States* and *Cuban Catholics in the United States*. He is also an editor of books on U.S. Latino Catholicism and Mexican American history and literature.

The University Press of Florida is the scholarly publishing agency for the State University System of Florida, comprising Florida A&M University, Florida Atlantic University, Florida Gulf Coast University, Florida International University, Florida State University, New College of Florida, University of Central Florida, University of Florida, University of North Florida, University of South Florida, and University of West Florida.

www.ingramcontent.com/pod-product-compliance
Lightning Source LLC
Chambersburg PA
CBHW031429160426
43195CB00010BB/662